A CULTURAL HISTORY OF DISABILITY

VOLUME 5

A Cultural History of Disability
General Editors: David Bolt and Robert McRuer

Volume 1
A Cultural History of Disability in Antiquity
Edited by Christian Laes

Volume 2
A Cultural History of Disability in the Middle Ages
Edited by Jonathan Hsy, Tory V. Pearman, and Joshua R. Eyler

Volume 3
A Cultural History of Disability in the Renaissance
Edited by Susan Anderson and Liam Haydon

Volume 4
A Cultural History of Disability in the Long Eighteenth Century
Edited by D. Christopher Gabbard and Susannah B. Mintz

Volume 5
A Cultural History of Disability in the Long Nineteenth Century
Edited by Joyce L. Huff and Martha Stoddard Holmes

Volume 6
A Cultural History of Disability in the Modern Age
Edited by David T. Mitchell and Sharon L. Snyder

A CULTURAL HISTORY
OF DISABILITY

IN THE LONG NINETEENTH CENTURY

VOLUME 5

*Edited by Joyce L. Huff
and Martha Stoddard Holmes*

BLOOMSBURY ACADEMIC
LONDON • NEW YORK • OXFORD • NEW DELHI • SYDNEY

BLOOMSBURY ACADEMIC
Bloomsbury Publishing Plc
50 Bedford Square, London, WC1B 3DP, UK
1385 Broadway, New York, NY 10018, USA
29 Earlsfort Terrace, Dublin 2, Ireland

BLOOMSBURY, BLOOMSBURY ACADEMIC and the Diana logo are trademarks
of Bloomsbury Publishing Plc

First published in hardback in Great Britain 2020
This paperback edition 2024

Copyright © Joyce L. Huff and Martha Stoddard Holmes and contributors, 2020

Joyce L. Huff and Martha Stoddard Holmes and contributors have asserted their right under the
Copyright, Designs and Patents Act, 1988, to be identified as the Authors of this work.

Series design: Raven Design
Cover image: The Art of Talking with the Fingers © Institut National
des Jeunes Sourds/FranceArchives Charmet/Bridgeman Images

All rights reserved. No part of this publication may be reproduced or transmitted
in any form or by any means, electronic or mechanical, including photocopying,
recording, or any information storage or retrieval system, without prior
permission in writing from the publishers.

Bloomsbury Publishing Plc does not have any control over, or responsibility for,
any third-party websites referred to or in this book. All internet addresses given
in this book were correct at the time of going to press. The author and publisher
regret any inconvenience caused if addresses have changed or sites have ceased
to exist, but can accept no responsibility for any such changes.

A catalogue record for this book is available from the British Library.

A catalog record for this book is available from the Library of Congress.

ISBN: HB: 978-1-3500-2907-1
HB Set: 978-1-3500-2953-8
PB: 978-1-3504-3672-5
PB Set: 978-1-3504-3676-3

Series: A Cultural History of Disability

Typeset by Integra Software Services Pvt. Ltd.
Printed and bound in Great Britain

To find out more about our authors and books visit www.bloomsbury.com
and sign up for our newsletters.

CONTENTS

LIST OF FIGURES	vi
NOTES ON CONTRIBUTORS	x
SERIES PREFACE	xii
Introduction: Negotiating Normalcy in the Long Nineteenth Century *Joyce L. Huff and Martha Stoddard Holmes*	1
1 Atypical Bodies: The Cultural Work of the Nineteenth-century Freak Show *Nadja Durbach*	23
2 Mobility Impairment: From the Bath Chair to the Wheelchair *Karen Bourrier*	43
3 Chronic Pain and Illness: "The Wounded Soldiery of Mankind" *Maria Frawley*	61
4 Blindness: Creating and Consuming a Nonvisual Culture *Vanessa Warne*	79
5 Deafness: Representation, Sign Language, and Community, ca. 1800–1920 *Esme Cleall*	95
6 Speech: Dysfluent Temporalities in the Long Nineteenth Century *Daniel Martin*	113
7 Learning Difficulties: The Transformation of "Idiocy" in the Nineteenth Century *Patrick McDonagh*	129
8 Mental Health Issues: Alienists, Asylums, and the Mad *Elizabeth J. Donaldson*	149
NOTES	169
REFERENCES	174
INDEX	200

LIST OF FIGURES

0.1 "The Crippled Street-Seller of Nutmeg-graters," from *London Labour and the London Poor*, vol. 1 (1861–62). Photo courtesy of Dartmouth Medical School Photography and Illustration — 4

0.2 Prosthetic hands with spoon attachments. Credit: Wellcome Collection. https://wellcomecollection.org/works/xafwb7ea; https://creativecommons.org/licenses/by/4.0 — 7

0.3 Boys at a woodwork class with their teachers, in London. Photograph by Walter C. Tyler, ca. 1895. Credit: Wellcome Collection. https://wellcomecollection.org/works/hed63tjg; https://creativecommons.org/licenses/by/4.0 — 9

0.4 "The cow-pock - or - the wonderful effects of the new inoculation!" Edward Jenner among patients in the Smallpox and Inoculation, Coloured etching after James Gillray, 1802. Credit: Wellcome Collection. https://wellcomecollection.org/works/dgbwm835; https://creativecommons.org/licenses/by/4.0 — 13

0.5 Frankenstein observing the first stirrings of his creature. London: H. Colburn and R. Bentley. Engraving by W. Chevalier after Theodor von Holst, 1831. Credit: Wellcome Collection. https://wellcomecollection.org/works/tepefezv; https://creativecommons.org/licenses/by/4.0 — 19

1.1 The Barnum and Bailey Greatest Show on Earth. The Peerless Prodigies of Physical Phenomena. with Smallest Man Alive and the Congo Giant. 1898. New York and Cincinnati: Strobridge & Co. Lith. Photograph. https://www.loc.gov/item/2002719038/ — 24

1.2 Charles B. Tripp, Photograph by Charles Eisenmann, c. 1890. Credit: Wikimedia Commons, PD-US-expired. https://commons.wikimedia.org/wiki/File:Charles_B_Tripp_by_Eisenmann_c1890.png — 27

1.3 The Wonderful Spotted Indian, John Boby. Reproduction of an etching, 1803. Credit: Wellcome Collection. https://wellcomecollection.org/works/c8cbrhse; https://creativecommons.org/licenses/by/4.0/ — 32

1.4 Maximo and Bartola, supposed to be Aztecs, advertised for exhibition. Colour lithograph. Credit: Wellcome Collection. https://wellcomecollection.org/works/nrwb3n58; https://creativecommons.org/licenses/by/4.0/ — 34

1.5 Laloo, "the Double-Bodied Hindoo Boy," Figure 57, from Gould and Pyle, 1901. Credit: Wellcome Collection. https://wellcomecollection.org/works/ec6zfkpc; https://creativecommons.org/licenses/by/4.0/ — 37

LIST OF FIGURES   vii

1.6 Joseph Merrick, "the Elephant Man," medical illustration, Plate XX
     in Treves (1885), Credit: Wellcome Collection. https://wellcomecollection.org/
     works/ndkxc9af; https://creativecommons.org/licenses/by/4.0   39

2.1 "Comfort For Invalids" advice page. The Lancet General Advertiser, 1856.
     Credit: Wellcome Collection. https://wellcomecollection.org/works/rj7sj97f;
     https://creativecommons.org/licenses/by/4.0/   48

2.2 Eadweard Muybridge "Animal locomotion"; deformed child. 1887.
     Credit: Wellcome Collection. https://wellcomecollection.org/works/czn9qhxq;
     https://creativecommons.org/licenses/by/4.0/   50

3.1 "The Life and Sufferings of Leonard Trask, the wonderful invalid." Published
     by Tucker in Portland, Maine, 1858. General Research Division, The New York
     Public Library. "The life and sufferings of Leonard Trask, the wonderful invalid."
     The New York Public Library Digital Collections. 1858. http://digitalcollections.
     nypl.org/items/efa4d5d0-6ce8-0131-5d94-58d385a7bbd0   62

3.2 "Granite State Water-cure, Franklin, N.H." Art and Picture Collection,
     The New York Public Library. "Granite State Water-cure, Franklin, N.H."
     The New York Public Library Digital Collections. 1855–07. http://digitalcollections.
     nypl.org/items/510d47e1-38cd-a3d9-e040-e00a18064a99   66

3.3 "The Packing." This cartoon mocks the treatments available at fashionable
     water spas during the hey-day of hydropathy. Image reference DCHQ003153.
     Location: A Hydropathic Institution. Town: Matlock. Image available via
     Picture the Past   67

3.4 "Robert Louis Stevenson, seated in bed playing a woodwind instrument."
     The Miriam and Ira D. Wallach Division of Art, Prints and Photographs:
     Print Collection, The New York Public Library. "[Robert Louis Stevenson seated
     in bed playing a woodwind instrument.]" *The New York Public Library Digital
     Collections.* http://digitalcollections.nypl.org/items/c5831e4d-c426-1ecb-e040-
     e00a18067b87   73

4.1 "Work-School for the Blind, Euston Road." Reproduced with permission
     of University of Manitoba, Archives & Special Collections   86

4.2 John Everett Millais, "The Blind Girl." 1856. Courtesy of Birmingham
     Museums Trust   87

4.3 Ford Madox Brown, "Henry Fawcett; Dame Millicent Fawcett." 1872.
     Courtesy of the National Portrait Gallery, Britain   88

5.1 The French sign language alphabet with ornate border, above it,
     the Abbé C.M. de l'Épée and the Abbé Sicard. Lithograph.
     Credit: Wellcome Collection. https://wellcomecollection.org/works/nx975xa2;
     https://creativecommons.org/licenses/by/4.0/   103

5.2 A vicar using sign language to the congregation at a service at a deaf and
     dumb church. Wood engraving after A.S. Hartick (?). A. S. Hartick, 1882.

Credit: Wellcome Collection. https://wellcomecollection.org/works/jmmbhc8d; https://creativecommons.org/licenses/by/4.0/ 107

5.3 A Christmas entertainment, presented in sign language for the deaf and dumb, at the Hanover Square rooms, London, 1865. Wood engraving. Credit: Wellcome Collection. https://wellcomecollection.org/works/shgczhp2; https://creativecommons.org/licenses/by/4.0/ 108

6.1 "A Sense of Proportion" (1888), *Punch*, 94, 28 Jan.: 40. Credit: Punch Cartoon Library/TopFoto 123

7.1 "Title page with frontispiece illustration," from *An historical account of the discovery and education of a savage man: or, Of the first developments, physical and moral, of the young savage caught in the woods near Aveyron in the year 1798* (1802). Credit: Chronicle/Alamy Stock Photo 132

7.2 "Barnaby in Newgate," by Hablot Knight Browne ("Phiz"), in *Barnaby Rudge* (1841) 138

7.3 "The Royal Earlswood Asylum (The National Asylum for Idiots)," *London Illustrated News* 11 March 1854, #672, page 213. Artokoloro Quint Lox Limited/Alamy Stock Photo 139

7.4 "Little Mother," by Hablot Knight Browne ("Phiz") in *Little Dorrit* (1857) 145

8.1 "Pinel à la Salpêtrière." By Tony Robert-Fleury, 1876. Wikimedia Commons, (PD-US-expired). https://commons.wikimedia.org/wiki/File:Philippe_Pinel_%C3%A0_la_Salp%C3%AAtri%C3%A8re_.jpg 151

8.2 "Une leçon clinique à la Salpêtrière." By André Brouillet, Painting, 1887. Brouillet, André. "Une leçon clinique à la Salpêtrière." Painting. 1887. Collection: Paris Descartes University, Paris. Wikimedia Commons, (PD-US-expired). https://commons.wikimedia.org/wiki/File:Une_le%C3%A7on_clinique_%C3%A0_la_Salp%C3%AAtri%C3%A8re.jpg 151

8.3 "Attitudes Passionelles: Extase," from *Iconographie Photographique de la Salpêtrière*, plate 23. By Paul-Marie-Léon Regnard, 1878. Planche XXII. Attitudes Passionelles. Extase. Credit: Wellcome Collection. https://wellcomecollection.org/works/wd3d9kv7; https://creativecommons.org/licenses/by/4.0/ 152

8.4 William Norris restrained by chains at the neck and ankles in Bethlem hospital, London. Coloured etching by G. Arnald, 1815, after himself, 1814. Credit: Wellcome Collection. https://wellcomecollection.org/works/rfxu9rvd; https://creativecommons.org/licenses/by/4.0/ 154

8.5 "Popular Mode of Curing Insanity!," in Packard (1873), *Modern Persecution*, between pages 288–289. Credit: Cushing Center, Harvey Cushing/John Hay Whitney Medical Library, Yale University 164

8.6 "Nellie Practices Insanity at Home." Illustration. Nelly Bly, *Ten Days in a Mad-House*, 1887. Wikimedia Commons. https://en.wikisource.org/wiki/Ten_Days_in_a_Mad-House/Chapter_I   167

The third-party copyrighted material displayed in the pages of this book are done so on the basis of "fair dealing for the purposes of criticism and review" or "fair use for the purposes of teaching, criticism, scholarship or research" only in accordance with international copyright laws, and is not intended to infringe upon the ownership rights of the original owners.

NOTES ON CONTRIBUTORS

Karen Bourrier is Associate Professor in the Department of English at the University of Calgary, Canada. She is the author of *The Measure of Manliness: Disability and Masculinity in the Mid-Nineteenth-Century Novel* (University of Michigan Press, 2015) and *Victorian Bestseller: The Life of Dinah Craik* (University of Michigan Press, 2019). She is also project director of the online resource, *Nineteenth-Century Disability: Cultures and Contexts* (peer reviewed by NINES, 2014).

Esme Cleall is a senior lecturer in the History of the British Empire at the University of Sheffield, UK. Her first book was *Missionary Discourses of Difference: Negotiating Otherness in the British Empire, c. 1840–1900* (Palgrave Macmillan, 2012). She is now working on a monograph on the history of disability in the British Empire, a topic on which she has published several articles.

Elizabeth J. Donaldson is Associate Professor of English at New York Institute of Technology, where she directs the Medical Humanities minor program. She has published essays on LSD-inspired disability-immersion experiences of schizophrenia, mental illness in graphic medicine, antipsychiatry in Lauren Slater's memoirs, and physiognomy and madness in *Jane Eyre*. She coedited *The Madwoman and the Blindman: Jane Eyre, Discourse, Disability* (Ohio State University Press, 2012) and coedits the book series *Literary Disability Studies*. She recently edited the collection *Literatures of Madness: Disability Studies and Mental Health* (Palgrave Macmillan, 2018), and her current book project is titled *Writing Madness: Psychiatry and American Literature*.

Nadja Durbach was born in the UK. She grew up in Canada and attended the University of British Columbia, earning a BA (Hons.) in 1993. In 2000, she completed her PhD at the Johns Hopkins University and joined the faculty of the University of Utah's History Department, where she is currently a professor. She is the author of *Bodily Matters: The Anti-Vaccination Movement in England, 1853–1907* (Duke University Press, 2005) and *Spectacle of Deformity: Freak Shows and Modern British Culture* (University of California Press, 2009). She is currently finishing a book entitled *Many Mouths: The Politics of Food in Britain from the Workhouse to the Welfare State*.

Maria Frawley is a professor of English at George Washington University, where she teaches courses in nineteenth-century literature. She is the author of *Invalidism and Identity in Nineteenth-Century Britain* (University of Chicago Press, 2005) and edited for Broadview Press an edition of Harriet Martineau's *Life in the Sick-Room* (2004). In addition to these projects, she has written widely on nineteenth-century women writers and has written books on Anne Brontë and on Victorian women travel writers. She is currently coediting the *Routledge Companion to Jane Austen* and working on projects related to nineteenth-century disability history.

Martha Stoddard Holmes teaches British literature, creative writing, health humanities, and film at California State University, San Marcos, where she is Professor of Literature and Writing Studies. She is the author of *Fictions of Affliction: Physical Disability in Victorian Culture* (University of Michigan Press, 2004), and is coeditor of *The Teacher's Body: Embodiment, Authority, and Identity in the Academy* (State University of New York Press, 2003) and special issues of *Nineteenth-Century Gender Studies*, *Journal of Bioethical Inquiry*, *Journal of Medical Humanities*, and *Literature and Medicine*. A Pushcart Prize nominee for creative nonfiction, she is writing and drawing a graphic narrative (comic) about ovarian cancer.

Joyce L. Huff is an associate professor of English at Ball State University. Her research focuses on fat and disability in Victorian British literature. Her work on these subjects has appeared in collections such as *The Fat Studies Reader* (New York University Press, 2009), *Bodies Out of Bounds* (University of California Press, 2001), *Historicizing Fat in Anglo-American Culture* (Ohio State University Press, 2010), and *Victorian Freaks* (Ohio State University Press, 2008). She is currently working on a book manuscript on fat in Victorian Britain.

Daniel Martin is an associate professor of English literature at MacEwan University in Edmonton, Alberta, Canada. He has published essays and book chapters in *Journal of Victorian Culture*, *Canadian Journal of Disability Studies*, *Victorian Literature and Culture*, Blackwell's *A Companion to Sensation Fiction* (edited by Pamela K. Gilbert), *Victorian Review*, and *Studies in Canadian Literature*. His current book manuscript, entitled *The Stammerer's Complaint: An Archaeology of Victorian Dysfluency*, is in progress.

Patrick McDonagh is the author of *Idiocy: A Cultural History* (Liverpool University Press, 2008) and coeditor (with C. F. Goodey and Tim Stainton) of *Intellectual Disability: A Conceptual History 1200–1900* (Manchester University Press, 2018). He is a part-time professor in the Department of English at Concordia University, Montreal, Canada, and is also a cofounder (and current member of the board of directors) of the Spectrum Society for Community Living in Vancouver, Canada.

Vanessa Warne teaches in the Department of English, Film, Theatre and Media at the University of Manitoba in Winnipeg, Canada. Her research explores the experiences of the first generations of blind people who read and wrote using raised-print scripts, including braille. In 2018, she coedited, with Hannah Thompson, "Blindness Arts," a special issue of *Disability Studies Quarterly*.

SERIES PREFACE

As general editors of *A Cultural History of Disability*, we are based on either side of the Atlantic—in the Department of Disability and Education at Liverpool Hope University, United Kingdom and in the School of Social Sciences at Liverpool Hope University, United Kingdom, and in the Department of English at George Washington University, USA—but we are unified by our work and interests in disability studies, with a particular emphasis on culture and cultural production. This being so, the genesis of the project was in cultural disability studies, from which grew discussions about history that led us in many fruitful directions (e.g., Longmore 1985; Davis 1995; Garland-Thomson 1997; Mitchell and Snyder 2000; Kudlick 2003; Snyder and Mitchell 2006; Burdett 2014a; Coogan 2014; Doat 2014; Tankard 2014; Rembis 2017). The name mentioned more than any other was that of Henri-Jacques Stiker, whose work was prominent in our thoughts at the proposal stage, and as such resonates here. The method in his most famous book, *A History of Disability*, "ranges from close readings of literary texts as exemplary of dominant myths to discussions of the etymology of disability terminology to medical taxonomies of specific conditions and test cases to an examination of current legislative initiatives" (Mitchell 1999: vii). The real interest, as Stiker states in an interview published more than thirty years after the first edition of his book, is not "History with a capital H like trained historians do," but "grand representations, systems of thought, the structures beyond history" (Kudlick 2016: 140). The spirit if not the letter of this method is adopted in *A Cultural History of Disability*, our focus being how disability has been portrayed in various aspects of culture and what these representations reveal about lingering and changing social attitudes and understandings.

A Cultural History of Disability is indebted to contemporary disability activism and to other movements for social justice. As David Serlin writes in the introduction to an important anthology on the intersections of disability and masculinity,

> Within academic culture, tectonic disciplinary and intellectual shifts of the 1960s and 1970s gave rise to the fields of ethnic studies and critical race theory, women's and gender studies and men's studies, LGBT studies and queer studies, and disability studies, and crip theory. Scholars in these fields have not always been in alignment, of course, but they do increasingly recognize each other as workers and activists in adjacent and overlapping fields of critical inquiry, cultural production, and social justice. (Serlin 2017: 8)

Many chapters in *A Cultural History of Disability* are thus deeply and necessarily intersectional, attending to gender, race, sexuality, nation, and other axes of human difference. In the process, the project attends to multiple modalities of disability experience, past and present. In presenting such an interdisciplinary and theoretical project, we therefore depart from the kind of history of disability that, for example, focuses on the story of so-called special schools from the perspective of their governors

(Burdett 2014b), or the history of major medical advances (Oshinsky 2005), in favour of one that delves into the underpinning social attitudes faced by disabled people beyond and long before such institutions or advances.

We are keenly attuned as well to the many ways in which disability has been *represented*. A *"system* of representation," according to Stuart Hall, "consists, not of individual concepts, but of different ways of organizing, clustering, arranging, and classifying concepts, and of establishing complex relations between them" (Hall 1997: 17). From this cultural studies perspective, a cultural history of disability is attuned to how disabled people have been caught up in systems of representation that, over the centuries (and with real, material effects), have variously contained, disciplined, marginalized, or normalized them. A cultural history of disability also, however, traces the ways in which disabled people themselves have authored or contested representations, shifting or altering the complex relations of power that determine the meanings of disability experience.

In formal terms, *A Cultural History of Disability* is a six-volume work on renderings of disability from Antiquity to the twenty-first century. The set of volumes is interdisciplinary insofar as it engages scholars with interests in disability studies, education, history, literature, cultural studies, drama, art, and several other related fields and disciplines. Each volume covers one of six historical periods: Antiquity (500 BCE–800 CE); the Middle Ages (800–1450); the Renaissance (1450–1650); the long eighteenth century (1650–1789); the long nineteenth century (1789–1914); and the modern age (1914–2000+). These individual volumes are edited by accomplished scholars who provide an outline of the major ideas and themes concerning disability in their given historical period.

The internal structure of the six volumes is notable. Following the period-specific introduction, each volume comprises eight chapters whose principal titles correspond throughout the set. This means that many themes can be traced across all six volumes—and thus across all six historical periods. The overarching themes of the eight chapters in each volume are tentatively listed as atypical bodies; mobility impairment; chronic pain and illness; blindness; deafness; speech; learning difficulties; and mental health issues. All of these themes are manifestly problematic, on account of the terminology and apparent focus on impairment rather than disablement or disability, not to mention categorization that swerves from the fact that many disabled people have multiple impairments. Accordingly, many of the volume editors and chapter contributors have creatively and critically worked with and beyond these problematics. The eight-part categorization across time is ultimately extended not in a positivistic but in an analytical mode, offering not sameness but a critical difference across the historical periods under review. "Learning difficulties," for example, materialize quite differently under modes of industrial or neoliberal capitalism (with their demands for a particular kind of productivity and speed) than they do in Antiquity or the Middle Ages, when "learning" and education were stratified more obviously according to caste or gender. Deaf people have not always conceptualized themselves as having a distinct language or inhabiting a "minority" identity; such a conceptualization clearly requires particular historical conditions that have only begun to germinate in the past three or four centuries. These two examples illustrate that, if somewhat simplistic, the overarching themes of the project assist readers who are keen to understand more about how disabled people are represented in culture and how ideas and attitudes have both resonated and changed down the centuries.

Historical changes in ideas and attitudes have been at times merely adaptations of a more general pattern; they have, however, at other times been more akin to what are often understood as "paradigm shifts," which fundamentally alter or reinvent the conditions in which human beings are located or rescript the underlying assumptions that give rise to how we apprehend the world. The concept of a paradigm shift comes—perhaps paradoxically for a cultural history of disability—from the history of science; Thomas S. Kuhn famously used the term to describe what happens when advocates for new scientific approaches or models (those Kuhn termed "young Turks") overturn what they perceive as the outdated views of those who came before them (Hamilton 1997: 78). As Peter Hamilton explains, however, where other systems of representation or "aesthetic domains of painting, literature or photography differ from sciences is their essentially multi-paradigmatic as opposed to uni-paradigmatic nature" (Hamilton 1997: 80). Paradigm shifts in the history of disability have thus been about *pluralizing* the ways in which disabled experiences might be apprehended or have been apprehended over the centuries.

For example, the activist invention of "disability identity" itself, in the twentieth century, could arguably be understood as an example of a paradigm shift that generated completely new vocabularies, multiplying the ways in which we might understand the embodied experience of disability. From this multi-paradigmatic perspective on embodiment, we can recognize that disablement on an attitudinal level involves a historical and changeable metanarrative to which people who have impairments are keyed in social encounters (Bolt 2014). Tracing these multiple paradigms across and through the cultural patterns of history, as well as noting the discontinuities between periods, can greatly enhance our critical understandings of the present. In turn, the new vocabularies of contemporary activism can enhance our critical understandings of the past. Indeed, only *with* the activist vocabularies of the present have we been able to conceive of disability as something that might have a cultural history worthy of being studied and debated.

A Cultural History of Disability demonstrates particular interest in the etymology of disability terminology (in keeping with the method exemplified by Stiker). In English, "disability" as a term appears to date from at least the sixteenth century, according to the *Oxford English Dictionary* (Adams, Reiss, and Serlin 2015: 6). The political scientist Deborah A. Stone linked the term to the needs of an emergent capitalist order, which newly demanded "able-bodied" workers, but which also needed to differentiate between those who would be sorted into what she identified as a "work-based" system and those who would be placed in a "needs-based" system. For its own consolidation, the emergent capitalist order needed to prioritize the former and stigmatize the latter, and Stone argues that "the disabled state" was charged (from the time "disability" circulated widely as a term) with the sorting, prioritizing, and stigmatizing (Stone 1984). Of course, various other examples of disability terminology have circulated both before and after the period Stone surveys. Often those other terms—*freak, retard, idiot*, and even *handicapped*, which until recently in English was dominant in many locations—have served to reinforce deep stigmas against disabled people and to valorize able-bodiedness and able-mindedness. At other times, various terms for what might now be understood through a disability analytic have functioned quite differently, and the early volumes of this series provide thorough considerations of the languages of disability that were available, say, in Antiquity or the Middle Ages. Contemporary activists have put forward disability as an identity and as the preferred term in many locations, as against "handicap" and so many other discarded terms, both the negative and the *seemingly* positive terms Simi Linton calls "nice words" (terms activists generally perceive as patronizing, like *differently abled* or *physically challenged*) (Linton 1998: 14). For decades, in ways similar to the world-transformative reclamations in the queer movement, activists have also played with the ways in which formerly derogative words such as *crip* might be resignified in culturally generative ways

(McRuer 2006; Bolt 2014). Disability terminology, although sometimes overlooked, thus reveals much about changing ideas and attitudes.

Languages besides English have of course similarly been the staging grounds for vibrant conversations about disability terminology. Many Spanish speakers roundly reject *minusválido* (literally, less valid) or *discapacitado/a*; some activists and artists, particularly in Spain, have put forward the preferred term *persona con diversidad funcional* (person with functional diversity). Although the revision of these terms has had a more uneven reception across Latin America, the very existence of such debates testifies to ongoing and vibrant conversations about language—critical debates that resonate in Japan (Valentine 2002) and India (Rao 2001). The anthropologist Julie Livingston uses "debility" for her important work on Botswana, since no word in the languages spoken there translates easily into "disability," even though a concept is needed for encompassing a range of "experiences of chronic illness and senescence, as well as disability per se" (Livingston 2006: 113). The international and historical scope of these debates is immense.

What we begin to explain here is that *A Cultural History of Disability* is not meant to provide readers with the history of disability. *The history of disability* is in fact, from one perspective, the history of humanity, and as such too vast for any collection, no matter how extensive, illustrative, or indicative of key periods and moments. From another perspective, what we think we understand in our own moment as "disability" varies immensely across time and space, which is why this set of volumes ultimately presents multiple and variegated *histories* of disability. *The* cultural history of disability thus is not something we could or would endeavor to document, not even with the esteemed editors and authors we have gathered to conduct this research. Rather, what we offer here is *a* cultural history that leads readers down various and sometimes intersecting paths. The cultural history this set of volumes presents is an interdisciplinary one that is driven by an appreciation of disability studies and thus disability theory, recognizing that disability as an *analytic*—like a feminist or queer analytic—can be brought to bear on many different topics and cultural contexts, even if other time periods have conceptualized bodies and minds using very different language from our own.

David Bolt and Robert McRuer, General Editors

REFERENCES

Adams, Rachel, Benjamin Reiss, and David Serlin (2015), "Disability," in Rachel Adams, Benjamin Reiss, and David Serlin (eds.), *Keywords in Disability Studies*, 5–11, New York: New York University Press.

Bolt, David (2014), *The Metanarrative of Blindness: A Re-Reading of Twentieth-Century Anglophone Writing*, Ann Arbor: University of Michigan Press.

Burdett, Emmeline (2014a), "'Beings in Another Galaxy': Historians, the Nazi 'Euthanasia' Programme, and the Question of Opposition," in David Bolt (ed.), *Changing Social Attitudes Toward Disability: Perspectives from Historical, Cultural, and Educational Studies*, 38–49, Abingdon and New York: Routledge.

Burdett, Emmeline (2014b), "Disability History: Voices and Sources, London Metropolitan Archives," *Journal of Literary and Cultural Disability Studies*, 8 (1): 97–103.

Coogan, Tom (2014), "The 'Hunchback': Across Cultures and Time," in David Bolt (ed.), *Changing Social Attitudes Toward Disability: Perspectives from Historical, Cultural, and Educational Studies*, 71–9, Abingdon and New York: Routledge.

Davis, Lennard J. (1995), *Enforcing Normalcy: Disability, Deafness, and the Body*, New York and London: Verso.
Doat, David (2014), "Evolution and Human Uniqueness: Prehistory, Disability, and the Unexpected Anthropology of Charles Darwin," in David Bolt (ed.), *Changing Social Attitudes Toward Disability: Perspectives from Historical, Cultural, and Educational Studies*, 15–25, Abingdon and New York: Routledge.
Garland-Thomson, Rosemarie (1997), *Extraordinary Bodies: Figuring Physical Disability in American Literature and Culture*, New York: Columbia University Press.
Hall, Stuart (1997), "The Work of Representation," in Stuart Hall (ed.), *Representation: Cultural Representation and Signifying Practices*, 13–74, London: Sage Publications.
Hamilton, Peter (1997), "Representing the Social: France and Frenchness in Post-War Humanist Photography," in Stuart Hall (ed.), *Representation: Cultural Representation and Signifying Practices*, 75–150, London: Sage Publications.
Kudlick, Catherine (2003), "Disability History: Why We Need Another 'Other'," *American Historical Review*, 108 (3): 763–93.
Kudlick, Catherine (2016), "An Interview with Henri-Jacques Stiker, *Doyen* of French Disability Studies," *Journal of Literary and Cultural Disability Studies*, 10 (2): 139–54.
Linton, Simi (1998), *Claiming Disability: Knowledge and Identity*, New York: New York University Press.
Livingston, Julie (2006), "Insights from an African History of Disability," *Radical History Review*, 94: 111–26.
Longmore, Paul (1985), "The Life of Randolph Bourne and the Need for a History of Disabled People," *Reviews in American History*, 13 (4): 581–7.
McRuer, Robert (2006), *Crip Theory: Cultural Signs of Queerness and Disability*, New York: New York University Press.
Mitchell, David T. (1999), "Foreword," in Henri-Jacques Stiker (ed.), *A History of Disability*, vii–xiv, Ann Arbor: University of Michigan Press.
Mitchell, David T. and Sharon L. Snyder (2000), *Narrative Prosthesis: Disability and the Dependencies of Discourse*, Ann Arbor: University of Michigan Press.
Oshinsky, David M. (2005), *Polio: An American Story. The Crusade That Mobilized the Nation against the 20th Century's Most Feared Disease*, Oxford: Oxford University Press.
Rao, Shridevi (2001), "'A Little Inconvenience': Perspectives of Bengali Families of Children with Disabilities on Labelling and Inclusion," *Disability and Society*, 16 (4): 531–48.
Rembis, Mike (2017), "A Secret Worth Knowing: Living Mad Lives in the Shadow of the Asylum," *Centre for Culture and Disability Studies YouTube Channel*, May 10, https://www.youtube.com/watch?v=Ls5BgJ2x8U0 (accessed May 17, 2017).
Serlin, David (2017), "Introduction," in Kathleen M. Brian and James W. Trent, Jr. (eds.), *Phallacies: Historical Intersections of Disability and Masculinity*, 1–21, Oxford: Oxford University Press.
Snyder, Sharon L. and David T. Mitchell (2006), *Cultural Locations of Disability*, Chicago: University of Chicago Press.
Stone, Deborah A. (1984), *The Disabled State*, Philadelphia: Temple University Press.
Tankard, A. (2014), "Killer Consumptive in the Wild West: the Posthumous Decline of Doc Holliday" in David Bolt (ed.), *Changing Social Attitudes Toward Disability: Perspectives from Historical, Cultural, and Educational Studies*, 26–37, Abingdon and New York: Routledge.
Valentine, James (2002), "Naming and Narrating Disability in Japan," in Mairian Corker and Tom Shakespeare (eds.), *Disability/Postmodernity: Embodying Disability Theory*, 213–27, London and New York: Continuum.

Introduction

Negotiating Normalcy in the Long Nineteenth Century

JOYCE L. HUFF AND MARTHA STODDARD HOLMES

> I had admired the perfect forms of my cottagers—their grace, beauty, and delicate complexions: but how was I terrified, when I viewed myself in a transparent pool! At first I started back, unable to believe that it was indeed I who was reflected in the mirror; and when I became fully convinced that I was in reality the monster that I am, I was filled with the bitterest sensations of despondence and mortification. Alas! I did not yet entirely know the fatal effects of this miserable deformity.
>
> Mary Shelley, *Frankenstein,* 1818, vol. 2, ch. 4

As we completed this volume, a series of events around the world commemorated the 200th anniversary of Mary Wollstonecraft Shelley's *Frankenstein,* many of them bringing together professionals in STEM fields as well as those in the humanities and arts. A recurrent message across these commemorations was the need for responsible and ethical scientific innovation. The message has become a familiar one, as bioethicists habitually invoke *Frankenstein* as a cautionary tale about a scientist playing god.

Disability was not a prominent thread in most of these conversations. For some scholars, however, the novel's engagements with disability are meaningful and many. For example, Victor's shock at the gap between the imagined perfection of his creation and its living, moving reality mirrors some parents' responses to their children's unexpected disabilities.[1] When the Creature develops his first and only friendship, with a blind man, the novel poses a commentary on the tyranny of the visual in social relationships—but also juxtaposes a disability experience of isolation, stigma, and peril with one in which a disabled person is an integral part of a familial or social network. The Creature's narrative of development evocatively unfolds an experience of learning to be disabled in an environment that stigmatizes those with radically unfamiliar embodiment and/or appearance; the fact that the physically robust Creature's only disabilities are aesthetic resonates forward to the "ugly laws," discussed below. Finally, reading the Creature with disability invites an intersectional analysis with the text's much-explored layers of racism, particularly Orientalism. While insufficiently recognized as such, *Frankenstein* is one of many examples of the long nineteenth century's continued attempts to come to terms with disability. As this volume demonstrates, a broad spectrum of literary texts intermingled with scientific, sociopolitical, religious, and aesthetic discourses to frame representations of people with disabilities in the nineteenth century. Issues such as the place of disabled people within the industrial workforce and the educational system– or the rights of disabled people in relation to care, independence, and agency– laid the foundation for many of the current debates surrounding disability.

One of the challenges of understanding historical viewpoints on disability is resisting the convenience of treating past perspectives as more unified or more limited than those we might encounter in our own time. Assuming a rigid nineteenth-century concept of disability is comparable to summing up complex and contradictory Victorian views of sexuality through the notion of horror at an exposed ankle. During the long nineteenth century, which stretched from the American Revolution (1776) to end of World War I (1918), constructions of disability varied both within and across cultures, and these changed over the course of the period in relation to evolving social and scientific discourses and practices. It is misleading even to imagine nineteenth-century disability as a discrete category with firm boundaries. Instead, individuals with a variety of impairments formed alliances or were grouped together by others in ways that served specific interests at the time. For example, Europe, Canada, and the USA saw the opening of schools for the joint education of deaf and blind students; workers with long-term injuries and illnesses banded together to protest unsafe factory conditions; and eugenic rhetoric lumped together and stigmatized people with intellectual disabilities, mental health issues, and neurological disabilities, along with criminals, sexual "deviants," and paupers.

Historical terminology presents an additional challenge. In the nineteenth century, "disability" was used infrequently to reference mental and bodily differences. Instead, the terminology used to denote disability in the Anglophone world included words like afflicted, infirm, defective, deformed, crippled, and invalid. The negative connotations of these terms point to the stigma attached to disability at the time. Simply substituting contemporary rhetoric for period terms, however, can be problematic. For example, as discussed in Chapter 5, the term "Deaf" with an uppercase "D" is often used today to denote members of signing communities who reject the pathologization of deafness and may also refuse the label of "disability." But, as Jennifer Esmail explains, it is difficult to categorize people as "either deaf or Deaf" if they lived before the concept of Deafness emerged in its present form (2013: 11). While we use current terms such as "disability" throughout this volume, we do so with an awareness that we are imposing our categories on the people of the past in order to frame their experiences in a manner that is meaningful to scholars in the present.

Our aim in this introductory chapter is not to provide an overarching definition of disability in the period, but rather to explore some of the relevant contexts through which to read the chapters that follow. Reflecting the current state of scholarship available to English speakers, our focus throughout this volume is primarily on Western cultures, specifically the USA and Great Britain (whose empire dominated a quarter of the globe by the end of the century).

0.1. MEDICINE AND THE PURSUIT OF HEALTH

One factor that drew together a variety of people whom we now refer to as disabled was their exclusion from emerging standards that defined the healthy body. Bruce Haley has pointed out that Western notions of health were based upon three principles that precluded much of what we think of as disability today: "wholeness"; utility; and "vitality" or "activity, growth, and responsiveness to environment" (1978: 20). The healthy individual was not simply free from disease and impairment but, rather, actively pursued "health." Those with the means to do so traveled throughout Europe and North America, questing after health; they visited spas, underwent water and rest cures, engaged in dietary and exercise regimens, took patent medicines, and devoured articles on health in popular periodicals.

For surgeon James Hinton, as for many, the pursuit of health required knowledge and a proactive approach including "air, exercise, plenty of good food, but not too much, sufficient sleep, but without sloth, temperance, cleanliness, [and] freedom from anxiety" (1861: 333). As this description demonstrates, definitions of health were intimately intertwined with middle-class morality. Pamela K. Gilbert sums up nineteenth-century views on health as "a set of hygienic practices that created a bodily habitus appropriate to the development of middle-class tastes" (2007: 8).[2] In a climate in which health was imagined to be attainable through hard work and the correct attitude, disability could be perceived as a "moral failure" (Holmes 2004: 101).

The ideal of health in the nineteenth-century West was often summed up by the concept of *mens sana in corpore sano*, or a healthy mind in a healthy body. Mind and body were viewed as interdependent, with the body often taking the predominant role. Because of this, physical disability could be easily conflated with mental disability in nineteenth-century writings; in 1848, for example, the American educator of the blind Samuel Gridley Howe argued, "To suppose there can be a full and harmonious development of character without sight is to suppose that God gave us that noble sense quite superfluously" (quoted in Klages 1999: 48). Here, Howe assumes that unimpaired senses are necessary to the development of mental and moral "character." Pseudosciences such as phrenology (the reading of character traits from the shape of the head) and physiognomy (the linking of character traits to facial features) endorsed this understanding of the relationship of mind to body. Erin O'Connor has noted that nineteenth-century theories that imagined biology as the grounds for the formation of the self naturalized the individual's position within the predominant social order (Figure 0.1):

> in works as diverse as Acton and Greg's studies of prostitution, Chadwick's sanitary reports, Galton's eugenics, Lombroso's criminal anthropology, Maudsley's psychology, Mayhew's urban profiles, and Spencer's sociology we see the same sorts of ideas at work again and again: that social roles were scripted by biology. (2000: 14)

This view of mind and body laid the groundwork for the science of eugenics, discussed below. The end of the period saw the emergence of psychoanalysis, pioneered by figures like Sigmund Freud, and, with it, new theories of the mind that lay the foundations for contemporary understandings of psychology.

As notions of the self grew increasingly medicalized, disability became pathologized. Thus, issues of access were personalized as individual health concerns, the solution for which was increasingly treatment and/or institutionalization rather than legislation and social change aimed at making the public sphere more accommodating. While more disabled people were being given the label of "patient," patients were losing agency in their encounters with the medical profession. Michel Foucault associates the long nineteenth century with the ascendency of the "clinical gaze," a way of producing knowledge based on doctors' observations rather than patients' accounts of their experiences ([1963] 1994: 108). This weakened disabled people's power to describe and define their own lives in the face of medical authority. Paradoxically, it was also at this time that, among the middle and upper classes, a new subjectivity—that of the invalid—emerged (see Chapter 3).

A major impetus for the rise of medical authority in the nineteenth century was fear of infectious disease, and, as in the case of individual health, Western medicine took a proactive and managerial stance toward the problem. In Britain, thinking on public health was dominated by the philosophies of Utilitarians like Jeremy Bentham and Edwin

FIGURE 0.1 "The Crippled Street-Seller of Nutmeg-graters."

Chadwick. As discussed in Chapter 3, inquiries into the living conditions of the poor, such as Chadwick's *Report on the Sanitary Conditions of the Labouring Population of Great Britain* (1842), resulted in a series of legislative acts that sought to ensure that homes had adequate drainage, water supplies, and waste disposal. However, such improvements were accompanied by increased surveillance as well as more invasive interventions by medical authorities. Peter Stallybrass and Allon White note a "discursive elision of disease and crime" in Victorian Britain, which implied that "disease could be policed" (1986: 133). In the 1860s, for example, Britain's Contagious Diseases Acts enabled the detention and enforced internal examination of women suspected of prostitution, in the name of protecting military men from venereal diseases. Similar legislation was enacted throughout the empire, including in Canada, Australia, and India.

0.2. THE AVERAGE MAN

Central to nineteenth-century Western definitions of disability was the emergent concept of the norm. In the 1830s, the Belgian statistician Adolphe Quetelet began to represent the distribution of human characteristics within populations using a normal distribution curve (commonly known as a "bell curve" due to its shape). Quetelet's distribution curve positioned those whose bodies and minds fell within the statistical majority as representative humans, while singling out deviations as errors. The result was the ideal of *l'homme moyen* ("the average man"), a concept that was not merely descriptive but also prescriptive (Davis 1995b: 36–7). Over the course of the nineteenth century, the new standard of the normal displaced that of the natural as the grounding for assumptions about what human beings should be and do (Baynton 2016: 65).

It is a small step from the perception of human traits as errors to the desire for their elimination. Lennard J. Davis notes that "all the early statisticians had one thing in common: they were eugenicists" (1995b: 30). In the 1880s, Sir Francis Galton, cousin of Charles Darwin, coined the term "eugenics," which he defined as "the improvement of the race" (in Levine and Bashford 2012: 5). Galton employed the bell curve to express evolutionary ideas of human perfectibility; he weighted the curve to privilege those traits he saw as most desirable—traits that were statistically abnormal but culturally valued, such as "tallness, high intelligence, ambitiousness, strength, [and] fertility" (Davis 1995b: 32–3). By the close of the nineteenth century, social norms had become detached from statistical averages and, instead, fixed upon cultural ideals.

Galton believed eugenics to be an improvement on natural selection: "Natural selection rests upon excessive production and wholesale destruction; eugenics on bringing no more individuals into the world than can be properly cared for, and only those of the best stock" (quoted in Levine and Bashford 2012: 5). At its most extreme, eugenics could involve the enforced sterilization and even "euthanasia" of disabled individuals. In eugenic thinking, the sexualities of people with disabilities were pathologized or denied expression because of the common belief that some impairments were hereditary. Samuel Gridley Howe, mentioned above, at one point described blind people as "a separate race of beings" (quoted in Klages 1999: 48), while, as further discussed in Chapter 5, inventor Alexander Graham Bell feared that marriage between deaf men and women would result in "a deaf variety of the human race" (1884: 3). When Henry Clay Sharp proposed a sterilization program in 1899 at the Indiana Reformatory, he included in the long list of those he felt would be good candidates for sterilization "the insane, the epileptic, the imbecile, the idiotic, the sexual perverts," as well as "inebriates, prostitutes, tramps, and criminals" and "the habitual pauper" (quoted in Nielsen 2012: 102). Beginning with Indiana in 1907, more than thirty states legalized forced sterilization (Nielsen 2012: 113).

The conflation of health and normalcy is vividly demonstrated by the so-called "ugly laws," the earliest of which appeared in San Francisco in 1867. A portion of this law read, "Any person who is diseased, maimed, mutilated, or in any way deformed so as to be an unsightly or disgusting object, shall not therein or thereon expose himself or herself to public view" (quoted in Schweik 2009: 291). Similar regulations existed throughout the USA in the late nineteenth and early twentieth centuries, but many remained on the books long afterward; the last recorded arrest occurred in 1974 (Schweik 2009: viii). Susan Schweik describes the agenda undergirding these laws as "the use of the law to repress the visibility of human diversity in social contexts associated with disability and poverty" (2009: 3). Pseudoscientific theories about the dangers of visual contact with disability included the theory of maternal impressions, which posited the effects of unusual (often visual) emotional stimuli on the fetus. In a passage exemplifying the ethos of ugly laws, Andrew Halliday (Mayhew's collaborator in *London Labour and the London Poor*) critiques the police for "permitting certain of the more hideous beggars to infest the streets":

Instances are on record of nervous females having been seriously frightened, and even injured, by seeing men without legs or arms crawling at their feet. A case is within my own knowledge, where the sight of a man without legs or arms had such an effect upon a lady in the family way that her child was born in all respects the very counterpart of the object that alarmed her. (4: 433)

But ugly laws only codified a more pervasive cultural stigma. For instance, an 1829 newspaper ad for artificial eyes makes it clear that even small deviations from the norm could be deemed unacceptable: "Nothing is more offensive to look upon than a sightless closed eye, and the loss ... renders the patient unfit to mingle in society" (quoted in Ott 2002: 153, ellipsis in Ott, not in original). The characterization of speech dysfluencies as "ugly speech," discussed in Chapter 6, demonstrates the pervasiveness of the association between disability and ugliness, even in relation to invisible disabilities.

0.3. INDUSTRIALIZATION AND TECHNOLOGY

Prosthetics, such as artificial eyes, were part of the changing technological landscape of the period. Coinciding with the Industrial Revolution and the Age of Steam, the long nineteenth century saw rapid advances in technology, which affected perceptions and experiences of disability. New technologies provided greater access and accommodation for a larger number of people (Figure 0.2); for instance, enhanced prosthetic limbs made possible greater freedom of movement for people with mobility impairments, as discussed in Chapter 2, while advances in printing increased the availability of books with raised type, such as the braille system, discussed in Chapter 4. Inventions like X-ray technology (discovered in 1895) and the stethoscope extended medical perception, allowing for increased knowledge of the inner workings of the human body and insight into some of the physical aspects of impairment and disease.

While some technologies could make life easier for people with disabilities, the shift from a system of primarily agricultural labor to the industrial workplace, and the accompanying mass migration from rural to urban environments, meant exposure to a variety of new causes of impairment. In addition to industrial accidents, nineteenth-century laborers faced issues such as cramped work spaces, poor lighting, contact with toxic chemicals and carcinogens, adulterated food and malnutrition, and conditions—both at work and at home—conducive to the spread of disease. O'Connor notes that diseases endemic to particular professions came to be known by names such as "grinder's asthma," "potter's rot," and "brassfounder's ague"; it was as if "industrial disease remade the worker's body in the image of his trade" (2000: 6–7). Epidemics of cholera, typhoid, and smallpox, among others, occurred around the globe, fostered by increased urbanization and spread through the processes of trade and colonization. In an industrial economy, rural communities had fewer resources to stave off poverty and its associated outcomes. Ironically, improved medical treatments also contributed to the prevalence of disability, as they transformed formerly fatal conditions into disabling ones. For example, the high mortality rates for surgical amputations due to shock and postoperative sepsis in the mid-century were significantly improved by the late century with the use of anesthesia and antiseptic principles.

New technologies also affected the ways in which war impacted both the frequency and types of impairment encountered in the long nineteenth century. Physician and

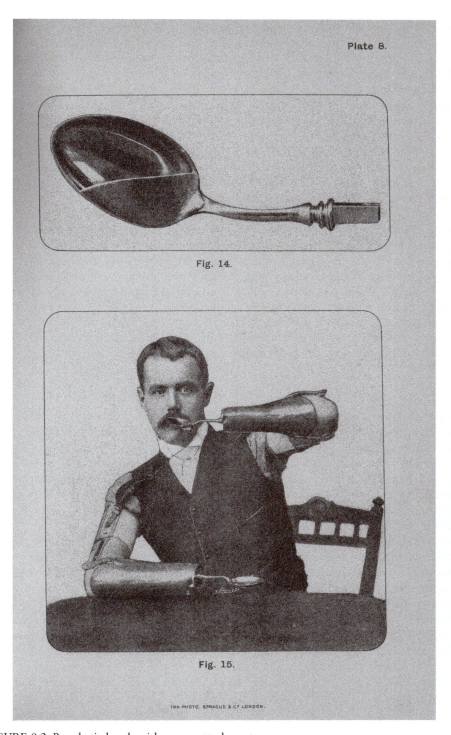

FIGURE 0.2 Prosthetic hands with spoon attachments.

author Oliver Wendell Holmes wrote that, as a result of the American Civil War, "there are few of us who have not a cripple among our friends, if not in our families" (quoted in Mihm 2002: 283). While the wounded benefitted from advances in battlefield medicine and the contributions made to nursing by women like Florence Nightingale and Clara Barton, new types of weaponry, such as the poison gas associated with World War I, resulted in additional forms of mental and physical injury. Shell shock, for example, was first identified during the American Civil War and, during World War I, became associated with the stresses of trench warfare. But wars also played a part in expanding social roles for disabled people; for instance, during the Civil War, the "invalid corps" entered the workforce to free non-disabled workers for active duty (Nielsen 2012: 82).

In addition to creating sources of impairment, industrialization contributed to making the public sphere a more hostile environment for people with disabilities. An environment constructed through mass production promoted uniformity among both consumers and workers, leaving less room for the accommodation of non-normative bodies and minds. The shift from tailor-made to off-the-rack clothing epitomized the change from a system of production that centered the individual consumer's body to one that required bodies to fit into standardized spaces (Huff 2008: 45–6). Furthermore, the factory environment did not welcome disabled workers. Sarah F. Rose argues, "employers in nearly all sectors began to demand workers who … had intact, interchangeable bodies," bodies that could easily be replaced by others (2017: 2). As Davis puts it, "the human body came to be seen as an extension of the factory machinery" (1995b: 87). Nonconforming bodies were thus disadvantaged in the industrial marketplace.

0.4. EDUCATION

While most disabilities were acquired in the course of life and work, discourses of education and charity focused on disabled children more often than disabled adults. The child/adult binary significantly underpinned the negotiation of disability and its consequent questions of who could or should have opportunities to learn and work. Nineteenth-century writers across many disciplines articulated "childhood" as a state of innocent vulnerability antithetical to participation in the workforce.[3] Supported by the passage of laws restricting the labor of children under the age of nine, working was increasingly inscribed as a characteristic of adults that distinguished them from children. Adults whose disabilities precluded activities seen as "work" disrupted the child/adult binary. Representations of disabled adults that infantilize them—often tenderly, as Wordsworth's "Idiot Boy" or the character Mr. Dick in Charles Dickens's *David Copperfield*—resolve the disruption by classifying disabled adults as children, moving them across the dividing line to a socially acceptable situation of economic dependence.

Multiple cultural influences overdetermined the growth of educational provisions for children with disabilities. Enlightenment theories of education provoked persistent philosophical and experimental interest in the educability of children seen as inhabiting a state of "nature" (like the so-called "Wild Boy of Aveyron," discussed in Chapter 7) or a state of sensory "deprivation" (like American Laura Bridgman, who became blind and deaf during a childhood illness, discussed in Chapter 4).[4] Another influence on "special" education was population growth and public concern (often a mix of benevolence and suspicion) regarding those who might not be expected to thrive economically (Figure 0.3). In Britain, educational legislation for disabled children came relatively soon after compulsory education laws for non-disabled ones (discussed in Chapters 4 and 7), even if the laws did not encompass all disabilities (Hampton 2016: 34).

FIGURE 0.3 Boys at a woodwork class with their teachers, in London.

In Britain, evangelical-led educational reforms—catalyzed by a global mission to create biblical literacy—increased access to education for some children with disabilities. Through missionary work, religion also played a role in extending education for people with disabilities globally. According to M. Miles, educational work with blind people in India and China is documented from the 1830s onward, with foundational work done by female colonial subjects who were blind themselves (2011). In Australia, "idiot" asylums modeled themselves on British institutions like Earlswood (discussed in Chapter 7), seeking "to train idiot children in simple manual work, enabling them to contribute to their upkeep, and, ideally, return to the community" (Earl 2017: 311).

As with many provisions for people with disabilities, the development of education of disabled people served to empower other groups and further other goals. The goal of biblical literacy propelled many educational initiatives, and the development of special education was bolstered by its cultivation of professional and clinical expertise. As Annemieke van Drenth argues, "theory and practice contributed to the emergence of a professional identity among physicians and teachers involved in the educational activities within asylums and institutions and in schools for disabled individuals" (2008: 445). With such examples, van Drenth and Francisca DeHaan reframe Foucault's notion of "pastoral power" (a secularization of ecclesiastical power) as "caring power" (exercising power as self-sacrifice on behalf of needy others) (1999: 18–19).

Ironically, even advocacy for independent lives for disabled people was often bankrolled by the emotional capital of disabled people's supposed abjection and gratitude rather than their capacity and rights. One educator observes that the industrial training and employment of adult blind people should be a higher priority than the education of blind children or the care for aged blind people, but addressing this need was difficult in part because "it has little of the *attractions* of the former, and not so much of the *touching* as the latter!" (Martin 1880: 44). Educational writing purposefully uses a melodramatic structure of dramatic reversals to argue the benefits of education for disabled people, a narrative pattern that relies on imagining disability as a condition of miserable deficiency. As discussed later in this introduction, the melodramatic stage featured numerous disability tropes, such as traumatic mutism and sight regained; charitable, educational, and sometimes medical discourses drew on these familiar genres to articulate disability, one of many examples in this volume of discursive threads in various social locations mutually inflecting and reinforcing each other.

0.5. THE SOCIAL BODY

Education was one of many realms in which the perceived problem of incorporating disabled individuals into the social body was played out. In nineteenth-century Europe and America, culturally determined ideals of health became central to the construction of the productive—and thus valuable—citizen. Physically and mentally "fit" citizens were seen to contribute to a well-functioning state, while disability was thought to detract from the general welfare. For social Darwinist Herbert Spencer, the "preservation of health" was thus more than an individual concern, it was "a *duty*" (quoted in Haley 1978: 17). The individual citizen's body bore a complex metaphorical relationship to the social body as a whole. As Lennard Davis points out, it was "as if a hunchbacked citizenry would make a hunchbacked nation" (1995b: 36). However, the health of the poor was often bracketed off from that of the rest of the population. Mary Poovey states that in Britain the poor were viewed as inherently "'diseased' (unproductive, criminal, plague-ridden)," and their thriving was thus "considered inimical to the health of the body politic" (1995: 7). This was due to Malthusian fears that a healthy pauper population would rapidly reproduce, placing a strain on the national economy.[5]

In Britain, disability was shored up as a category by the Poor Law Amendment Act of 1834 (the "New Poor Law"), which brought about the reduction of "outdoor relief" (outside of the workhouse) and the warehousing of poor and disabled people in workhouses, prisons, asylums, and other institutions. In terms of the Poor Law, those needing economic assistance ("paupers") included five categories of "others" that, as Deborah Stone notes, "defin[ed] who was able bodied" (1984: 40). Anyone not classified as a child, sick, insane, "defective," or "aged and infirm" was able (1984: 40). Further, one might belong to one of these categories but, through earning capacity, be classified as able, as Durbach argues in Chapter 1. The able-bodied were ineligible for relief except in the harsh and punishing context of the workhouse, which would ascertain if they were truly incapable of sustaining themselves without assistance. The operations of the New Poor Law, in conjunction with the patterns of industrialization, thus created not only economic and physical locations for people with disabilities, but also discursive and imaginative ones that shaped disabled social identities: "as benevolent paternalism yielded to self-help, disabled people were forced to take on especially supplicant behaviours" (Hampton 2016: 28).

Americans also raised questions about who was competent to participate in the political process. According to Kim Nielsen, the US government "deemed the disabled body unable to meet the individual and personal demands of a body politic that depended on self-government, self-determination, and individual autonomy" (2012: 269). This is demonstrated by the passing of "disability-based voting exclusions" in many states (2012: 50). Immigration policies formulated in the late nineteenth and early twentieth centuries epitomized the abjection of people with disabilities from the American social body. As Douglas Baynton notes, such policies were concerned not only with maintaining a vision of America as racially pure, but also with policing the admittance of "defectives," an amorphous category that included conditions as diverse as "the deaf, blind, epileptic, and mobility impaired"; those with "flat or clubbed feet"; "those who were unusually short or tall"; "people with intellectual or psychiatric disabilities"; and "hermaphrodites" (2016: 1). Additionally, a range of conditions were seen as symptoms of disability: "Immorality, criminality, deviant sexuality, poverty, and political radicalism were all described as manifestations of various kinds of mental defect" (2016: 2).

Concerns about both individual and national identity were played out on the freak show stage. The "freak" was never simply an individual with an atypical body; rather, as Robert Bogdan puts it, "'freak' is a frame of mind, a set of practices, a way of thinking about and presenting people" (1988: 3). Freak shows presented a spectacle of difference objectified and commodified. Yet, as discussed in Chapter 1, for the performers, these shows could be a way of enacting an economic and personal agency otherwise denied them. According to Rosemarie Garland-Thomson, the body of the freak functioned as a site onto which spectators "projected cultural characteristics they themselves disavowed" (1997: 55–6), providing spectators with "an opportunity to formulate the self in terms of what it was not" (1997: 59). Freak shows positioned spectators as belonging within the social body by comparison: "those whose social rank was most tenuous—immigrants, the urban working class, and less prosperous rural people—frequented the shows" (1997: 65).

Yet freaks were presented as more than simply other; they were liminal, between self and other, and thus paradoxically encouraged spectators to rethink the limits that defined "the human." The paradox of the freak as both "us" and "them" is illuminated in a much-quoted passage from the *Prelude*, in which William Wordsworth describes the human exhibits of London's Bartholomew Fair as simultaneously a "Parliament of Monsters" and a metonym for the diversity of human life within of the city of London, a "true epitome / Of what the mighty City is herself" (1805: VII, 718; 722–3). The aims and effects of scientific museums in the period often overlapped those of freak shows. According to Samuel J. M. M. Alberti, human remains deemed unhealthy or abnormal "formed the major proportion of medical collections" in the nineteenth century (2011: 3–4), and many of these are still on display. Indeed, the preserved corpses of two famous nineteenth-century human exhibits, Saartje Baartman and Julia Pastrana, were only returned to their home countries for burial in 2002 and 2013, respectively.

0.6. EMPIRE AND RACE

From the stage of the freak show to the pages of eugenicist writings, nineteenth-century disability was read through issues of race. Freak shows, as Garland-Thomson notes, "framed and choreographed bodily differences that we now call 'race,' 'ethnicity,' and 'disability' in a ritual that enacted the social process of making cultural otherness from the raw materials of human variation" (1997: 60). Typical exhibits were thus "'normal' non-Westerners and 'abnormal' Westerners" (1997: 63). Barnum's first human exhibit, Joice Heth, was a disabled African-American woman. With nothing particularly unusual in her appearance, Barnum was nonetheless able to convince audiences that she was George Washington's 161-year-old nurse, because, as Garland-Thomson points out, she embodied "the direct antithesis of the able-bodied, white, male figure upon which the developing notion of the American normate was predicated" (1997: 59). Douglas Baynton points to an 1873 geography textbook that characterized "the White Race" as "the Normal, or Typical Race" (quoted in Baynton 2016: 67).

By the end of the century, both disabled people and racial minorities were "described as evolutionary laggards or throwbacks" (Baynton 2016: 67). The physician Frederick Treves, for example, articulates his first impression of Joseph Merrick, known as the "Elephant Man" (discussed in Chapter 1), as that of a "degraded and perverted version of a human being" (quoted in Smith 2004: 45): "This fact—that it was still human—was the most repellent attribute of the creature" (quoted in Smith 2004: 48–9). Theories of evolutionary degeneration originated in Bénédict Auguste Morel's studies on intellectual disability in 1850s France and were developed in the criminal anthropology of Cesare Lombroso and sexology of Richard Von Krafft-Ebing. Max Nordau's *Degeneration* (1892) popularized these theories for a mass audience; he "refashioned a quasi-Darwinian notion that the human species could, under certain circumstances, *devolve*" (Smith 2004: 15). The stigmatization of disability was deployed to fuel racist fears of miscegenation, as "race-mixing" was said to result in "deformity." For instance, the doctor John Van Evrie wrote that the "abnormal," "blotched, deformed" children of interracial unions could be compared to "tumors, cancers, or other abnormal growths" (quoted in Baynton 2001: 37).

The rhetoric around African-American slaves and disability rearticulated the British problem of the able-bodied pauper within a racialized, American context. Slavery provided an extreme example of the body valued for its capacity to labor. According to Dea Boster, the figure of the disabled slave brought nineteenth-century American constructions of race and disability into conflict: "Slaves with disabilities could be a significant challenge to white authorities, who were often torn between the desire to categorize them as different or defective and the practical need to incorporate their disorderly bodies into daily life, labor schemes, and the strictures of the slave market" (2013: 3). Disability was also appropriated as a metaphor within the slavery debate itself; according to Boster, "proslavery advocates claimed that African Americans were inherently disabled from participating in a free society and required enslavement to thrive, whereas abolitionists argued that bondage itself was crippling to African Americans" (2013: 4).

In the context of European empire-building, fear of disease and disability could be used as a justification for imperial control. Colonial subjects were presumed by Westerners to be less civilized and therefore less likely to cultivate the practices that they deemed necessary to maintain a healthy body. Along with their notions of health, colonizers brought the medical model of disability and the pathologization of non-normative bodies and minds, which destabilized and sometimes supplanted indigenous ways of understanding disability. According to Raewyn Connell,

> colonial conquest, bringing crisis to the social orders in which embodiment had been organised, and creating new hierarchies of bodies (such as the racial hierarchy of late 19th-century imperialism), changed the ways in which bodily difference, impairment

and ability were socially constructed. Religious and cultural meanings of disability, village-and kin-based solidarities, livelihoods, and local customs of support, were all at stake and liable to disruption. (2014: 6)

However, Western ways of knowing "were never simply defused from 'center' to 'periphery' or imposed upon colonies in any straightforward way" (Peckham 2013: 3). Instead, contact between cultures produced new ways of knowing and understanding disability.

The management of colonial borders in response to fear of epidemics echoed on a macrocosmic level the management of the personal boundaries that defined the individual middle-class Western body. Health and hygiene, it was thought, depended on the ability to maintain bodily and mental integrity. The susceptibility of mind and body to harmful outside influences was a constant source of anxiety. Disease, as Athena Vrettos asserts, was a reminder of the body's vulnerability: "The permeability of [body] boundaries (implicit in actions such as eating, copulating, or giving birth) were made explicit in the presence of disease, for disease constituted a breakdown in corporeal integrity, wholeness or control" (1995: 5). Disability was similarly perceived. The fear of introducing foreign matter into the body, even in the name of health, is vividly demonstrated in James Gillray's satirical cartoon, "The Cow Pock—or—the Wonderful Effects of the New Innoculation!" (1802), which depicted humans transforming into cattle after receiving injections of cowpox as a vaccine to prevent smallpox (Figure 0.4).[6]

FIGURE 0.4 "The cow-pock - or - the wonderful effects of the new inoculation!"

0.7. MUSCULAR CHRISTIANS AND DOMESTIC ANGELS

The healthy mind and body that stood conceptually at the center of nineteenth-century Western culture were not only raced but also gendered. Victorian medicine divided bodies along gender lines, assigning to men and women anatomical and physiological differences that echoed their economic roles as producers and consumers, respectively. The ideological divisions between the masculinized public sphere and the feminized domestic one are examples of the ways in which gender and disability intersected to undergird notions of health in the period: "the disabled woman's difference is often imaginatively marked by her working (or roaming the streets for alms), by the difficulty of having her own home, and by the 'impossibility' of her marrying and having children," while the figure of the disabled man is portrayed as trapped within the domestic sphere or otherwise barred from legitimate labor (Holmes 2004: 94). Sally Shuttleworth has noted the conflation of men's traditional economic roles with their sexual health: "the primary categories of male sexual disfunction in the Victorian era, masturbation and spermatorrhoea, focused on the male need to retain vital force and to expend capital only in a productive fashion" (1989: 56). By contrast, women's health "depended on her very *inability* to control her body": "Any exertion of the mind, whether of intellectual effort, or fierce emotion, might prove fatal, it was suggested, in creating a stoppage of menstrual flow" (1989: 57). Bodies that did not fit neatly within gendered categories tended to be pathologized.

While masculinity was a multifaceted concept in the nineteenth century, many of the popular masculine ideals specifically linked manliness to physical and mental ability. One instance is the "muscular Christian," who, in 1857, was described as "a man who fears God and can walk a thousand miles in a thousand hours—who, in the language which [novelist Charles Kingsley] has made popular, breathes God's free air on God's rich earth, and at the same time can hit a woodcock, doctor a horse, and twist a poker around his finger" (quoted in Hall 1994: 7). The restrictions on who could access this particular version of masculinity are overt in this description in terms of mobility, visual acuity, intellectual ability, physical strength, and even lung capacity.

Health was so strongly linked with masculinity in the prevailing ideology that disabled men were sometimes portrayed as emasculated or feminized. Karen Bourrier suggests that this may explain, in part, the proliferation of disabled male characters in literature. Disabled men were able to play a stereotypically feminine role, expressing the emotional subtext of a story, while they could also accompany the hero into places where female characters would be prohibited (2015a: 2). By the late century, the purported emotional excesses of disabled men were perceived as symptomatic of cultural degeneracy. For Kingsley, the muscular Christian's cultivation of physical and mental fitness combated a supposed "tendency to sink into effeminate barbarism" (quoted in Smith 2004: 21).

If the normal state of the male body was "healthy," many believed that that of the female body—at least, the menstruating female body—was not; physician W. C. Taylor went so far as to proclaim that "every woman should look upon herself as an invalid once a month" (quoted in Ehrenreich and English 1973: 55). Because of the importance placed on the female reproductive system, women, like non-white and disabled people of both sexes, were sometimes perceived as less evolved than normate men; for instance, Herbert Spencer believed that "the conservation of her energies for reproduction necessarily arrested a woman's development in other areas" (Levine 2012: 54). Indeed, Edward Clarke, author of *Sex in Education* (1873), argued that girls who were educated in the same manner as men became "pale, weak, neuralgic, dyspeptic, hysterical, menorraghic, dysmenorrhoeic girls and women" (quoted in Baynton 2001: 42). Dr. William Lee Howard expressed the fear that nonconformity with prescribed gender roles would impair the health of a woman's children as well; the masculine woman "is then a menace to civilization ... the mother of physical and mental monstrosities who exist as a class of true degenerates" (Nielsen 2012: 116, ellipsis in Neilsen, not in original).

The female mind was likewise thought to be more vulnerable to impairment than the male, as discussed in Chapter 8. Elaine Showalter describes a common belief that "women were more vulnerable to insanity than men because the instability of their reproductive system interfered with their sexual, emotional, and rational control" (1985: 55). Practically any stage in a woman's sexual development could potentially presage danger to her mental health; in 1866, Dr. Isaac Ray wrote, "In the sexual evolution, in pregnancy, in the parturient period, in lactation, strange thoughts, extraordinary feelings, unreasonable appetites, criminal impulses, may haunt a mind at other times innocent and pure" (quoted in Poovey 1988: 37). For much of the century, hysteria (or the "wandering womb") was thought to be related to female anatomy; it was not until the 1890s that psychoanalysts like Sigmund Freud and Josef Breuer looked for psychological causes. Because mental health was so deeply entangled with gendered ideals of normalcy, the line between madness and unfeminine behavior was a blurry one. According to Anna Shepherd, "madness was often seen to manifest itself in inappropriate female behavior, such as bad language, lack of interest in their children or household matters, and overt sexual conduct" (2016: 9).

Of course, both the ideological constructions and the lived experiences of women in the nineteenth-century West were far more complex than these examples suggest. For instance, female factory workers, a population particularly vulnerable to industry-related impairment, were nonetheless perceived as more robust and more able to withstand disease, disability, and pain than women of higher social rank, an assumption that was used to justify their exploitation. As Helena Michie notes, "conduct books could recommend 'confining' middle-class women to their beds for weeks before and after childbirth, while working-class women would be expected by the same texts to return to work at a factory the day following delivery" (1999: 410). In America, these class divisions were racialized; in 1874, physician Lucien Warner wrote, "The African negress, who toils beside her husband in the fields of the south, and Bridget, who washes and scrubs and toils in our homes at the north, enjoy for the most part good health, with comparative immunity from uterine disease" (quoted in Ehrenreich and English 1973: 43).

0.8. RELIGION AND CARING

In opposition to ideological constructions of people with disabilities as socially extraneous beings dependent on the labor of others, disabled people's identities and relationships with the abled were varied and complex. Religion has been a particular focal point for critiques of nineteenth-century views of disability. For example, the scriptural allusion in Tiny Tim's hope that "people saw him in the church, because he was a cripple, and it might be pleasant to them to remember upon Christmas Day, who made lame beggars walk, and blind men see," articulates Tim as a specular object whose purpose is to catalyze a guilty and grateful memory of Christ (Dickens, ed. Kelly 2003: 87). With this Christian blueprint guiding the tiny representational box Dickens builds for Tim, it is easy to consider Victorian Christianity as the source of our least imaginative ideas about disability.

In fact, Judeo-Christian frameworks made people with disabilities legible in multiple, often conflicting ways, albeit mostly in terms of damage or deficiency: as signs of a vengeful god's power to afflict and punish one's own or one's parents' sins (a discourse readily imported into eugenics); as reminders of the weak and vulnerable, cherished and sometimes healed by a loving god; as spiritual agents whose role is to uplift others morally; and as spiritually and morally vulnerable beings who, neglected, sink to depravity. Like all nineteenth-century discourses of disability, religion either implicitly or directly comments on how disabled people should relate to and interact with non-disabled people; these prescriptions, however, are frequently ambiguous. For example, remembering Christ's miracles while seeing Tiny Tim, whose disability persists, may generate doubt or anxiety as much as gladness.

Those seeking support for disabled people, including disabled people themselves, drew strategically on religious discourses. Articulating disability as part of a Providential plan or as the occasion for spiritual compensation was a way to make disability legible in nineteenth-century culture. Auto/biographical texts are particularly worth examining as sites of negotiation with cultural paradigms. For example, a blind needle-seller describes his situation to Henry Mayhew as follows: "God help me! I know I am a sinner, and believe I'm so afflicted on account of my sins" (1861–2, 1: 343–4). The framework of sin may be a rhetorical stance calculated to predispose others to view him as a member of the "deserving poor" rather than as a begging impostor. The upper-class blind activist Elizabeth Gilbert uses a more nuanced religious framework to articulate her goals for the welfare of the blind; while she aims to "to reduce the dependence of the Blind as far as possible," she also asserts that, within a Christian framework, embracing what dependency cannot be avoided will foster "a spirit of humility and thankfulness" that will prove "one of their greatest blessings, as it will be the means of uniting them more closely to their fellow-creatures" (1874: 321).

Gilbert's notion of dependency as a fellowship clarifies the inherent flaw in assuming that care was unidirectional. Historicist scholarship reminds us that then, as now, people negotiate caring relationships locally. Daniel Blackie's study of disabled Revolutionary War veterans notes multiple interdependencies in families; for example, "disabled veterans undoubtedly occupied central positions in their families and in the networks of care that sustained them," directing care or giving care as well as heading households (2014: 30).

Nineteenth-century fiction, including the domestic novel and sensation fiction, has also proven generative for critical conversations about care and disability. In novels like Charlotte Mary Yonge's *The Clever Woman of the Family*, for example, characters help each other manage disabilities from domestic accidents, war injuries, stress, and old age. Here, care is mutual and dispersed across an ensemble cast rather than focused on saintly, capable givers and afflicted, dependent recipients.[7] Kristin Starkowski's critical analysis of "reciprocal" and "selfish" care in nineteenth-century domestic fiction offers another perspective, upending the assumption that self-serving care is inherently a failure (2017). Most provocatively, as Rachel Hertzl-Betz argues through Wilkie Collins's *The Law and the Lady* (1875), non-normative relationships (then and now) "complicate assumptions about acts of care in scholarship on disability and interdependence." Notions of care as "gentle and generous" are in keeping with, and possibly limited by, unexamined conventional values (2015: 35). Hertzl-Betz's work highlights the larger work within queer nineteenth-century studies to explore tensions between evolving concepts of normalcy and the variability of nineteenth-century bodies, lives, and caring relationships.

Even before we consider disability's intersectional engagement with other aspects of human variability, disability *in itself* had the effect of "queering" any number of institutions, from gender roles to the structure of the family. For example, Clare Walker Gore discusses the representations of disability-inflected "queer Victorian families" in the domestic novels of Charlotte Yonge. Marriage plans that are altered by unexpected disability offer "the possibility that disability might enable resistance to marriage, rather than disable a desired marriage plot" (Gore 2015: 128). What is produced in the abeyance of marriage is a different ideal of romantic love that, although heterosexual, is "antithetical to reproductive heterosexuality and … thrives off disability" (Gore 2015: 127). Talia Schaffer's concept of "familiar marriage" notes the alternative models of marriage that persisted in literary representations and presumably outside them; she includes those relationships freed by disability to be something more rewarding than existing models. Further, while the 1851 census defines the family in somewhat predictable ways as "composed of husband, wife, children, and, ideally, servants," it also noted the presence of families "'variously constituted'" (quoted in Dau and Preston 2015: 6). As Gore notes, "While disabled characters are generally excluded from the marriage plot because of the authors' unwillingness to write disability into reproductive heterosexual unions, they are not necessarily excluded from the families" (2015: 117). Mia Chen (2008) argues, similarly, that in Yonge's fiction, disabled characters are responsible for "social reproduction and ideological inculcation, for a form of reproduction which supplements and even corrects the biological reproduction of the non-disabled women" of the novel.[8]

0.9. LITERARY REPRESENTATIONS

In their introduction to the collection *The Madwoman and the Blindman: Jane Eyre, Discourse, Disability*, Julia Miele Rodas, Elizabeth J. Donaldson, and David Bolt note that, until recently, discussions of disability in nineteenth-century literature have focused narrowly on the metaphorical meanings that have been ascribed to disability. They cite, for example, Sandra Gilbert and Susan Gubar's interpretation of Bertha's madness as repressed feminist rage and Richard Chase's reading of Rochester's blindness as "symbolic castration" (Bolt, Rodas, and Donaldson 2012a: 2–3). Recent work by disability studies scholars, on the other hand, demonstrates the value of examining disability as a phenomenon in its own right. Several nineteenth-century genres seem particularly relevant to examine for their reliance on disability as a device: Romantic poetry, melodrama and sentimental novels, gothic and sensation novels, and children's literature. In addition, the budding interest in nonfiction prose meant the proliferation of disability memoirs, as well as secondhand accounts such as those presented in Henry Mayhew's *London Labour and the London Poor* (1851).[9]

The British Romantic period (from the late eighteenth century through the 1830s) featured recurrent engagements with representations of disability that were echoed throughout the Anglophone world. The corpus of Wordsworth, including the *Prelude*'s sections on Bartholomew Fair, "The Idiot Boy" (discussed in Chapter 7), and "The Thorn," often posits encounters with disabled people as catalysts for the speaker's development and awareness. Disabled people are set up in this dynamic as stand-ins for "nature," or as having a privileged relationship to nature, though not the self-aware relationship "the Poet" is imagined having in Wordsworth's "Preface" to *Lyrical Ballads* (1802). As the important critical collection *Disabling Romanticism* (Bradshaw 2016) demonstrates, the poetry of Samuel Taylor Coleridge, Charlotte Smith, and Mary Darby Robinson engages mental and physical disability in realistic and fantastic modes, as well as those that cross the boundaries. The speaker in Coleridge's "Dejection" (1802) articulates an experience of depression anchored in daily sensory detail; when the Lady Geraldine of his long poem "Christabel" (1816) disrobes to reveal something mysterious in "her bosom and half her side," the trope is both woven into a narrative of a shape-shifting serpent-woman and evocative of bodily differences that the reader can imagine as surgical, such as mastectomy. Across the Atlantic, Nathaniel Hawthorne's "The Birthmark" (1843) critiques the use of science to "fix" human variability, while Herman Melville's *Moby Dick* (1851) presents a reversal of the relationship between disability and "nature" that Wordsworth established, as Ahab positions himself against a nature that he views as responsible for his disability. Beginning with the Romantics, engagements with disability are central to aesthetics and aesthetic theories of the long nineteenth century. Essaka Joshua's (2016, 2018) brilliant work on "deformity aesthetics" is an exemplar of the richness of a disability studies analysis of the fragmentation that is an acknowledged feature of many Romantic texts and theories. Shelley's *Frankenstein* (1818) evokes Edmund Burke's sublime not only in its alpine and arctic landscapes, but also in the Creature of tremendous scale who reminds us of our proximity to death; Denise Gigante (2000) elaborates on Burke's concept of "ugliness" as informational to *Frankenstein*. Formally, the Creature's fragmented and sutured body mirrors the nested narratives of the text Shelley famously called her "hideous progeny" (Figure 0.5).

Nineteenth-century literary criticism and aesthetic theory, furthermore, engage disability in terms of the bodies of readers, writers, characters, and texts. The writerly disabled body, particularly the gendered body, presents a significant thread in the aesthetic theory of the period. Coleridge's laudanum addiction is famously connected to his poetic expressions. The public's and Lord Byron's own engagements with his atypical leg and foot were part of the fabric of his literary and cultural persona, as Christine Kenyon Jones (2016) and others have noted. W. D. Brewer (2016) argues that treatment of Mary Darby Robinson's disabilities (which occurred after her affairs with the Prince of Wales and Edward Fox and before her most productive period as a writer) illuminates shifts in public perceptions: "As a celebrity, Robinson became a focal point in the Romantic-era debate about disability. She was vilified by moralists who regarded her disability as a just punishment for a scandalous life, and yet respected by contemporaries who sympathised with her sufferings and admired her literary accomplishments" (122).

Melodrama, the gothic, and sensation draw characters and readers together in a fabric of tears over Tiny Tim, horror at Frankenstein's Creature, disgust in the presence of Edward Hyde (from Robert Louis Stevenson's *The Strange Case of Dr. Jekyll and Mr. Hyde*, 1886), and heightened nerves at the touch of the Woman in White from Wilkie Collins's novel of the same name (1860). Peter Brooks' influential theories of nineteenth-century melodrama suggest connections between its broad thematic concerns (the retrieval of a lost connection to the sacred) and practical/administrative ones (restrictions on the spoken word in unlicensed theatres), with situations of bodily intensity providing a productive nexus of the two (1995). It follows that disabled characters in melodrama serve as visually eloquent "speaking bodies" (Holmes 2004: 24). The Providential structure of melodrama both capitalizes on and reinforces an idea of disability as a symbolic condition with resonant ties to the sacred (not only the suffering body of Christ, but also the disabled bodies Christ heals or fails to heal). Within an overarching aesthetic in which gesture,

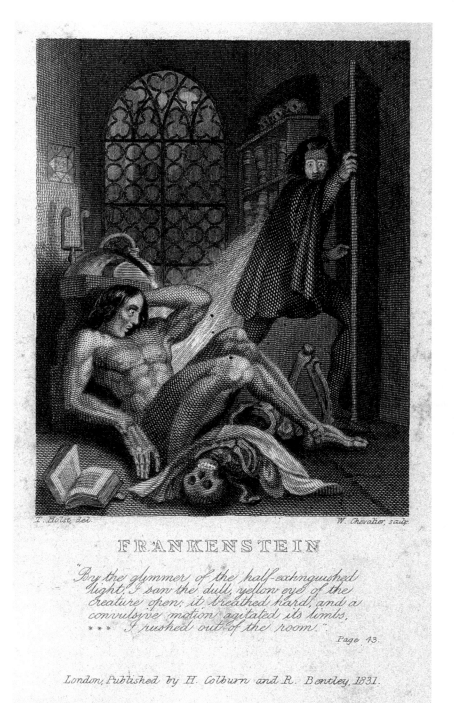

FIGURE 0.5 Frankenstein observing the first stirrings of his creature.

tableau, and music are at least as important as dialogue, bodies easily coded as different are efficient communicators.

The ghosts and monsters that haunt the gothic and its Victorian iterations provide apt vehicles for thinking through emerging norms. As Jacques Derrida writes, "faced with a monster, one may become aware of what the norm is and when the norm has a history" (quoted in Botting 2008: 9). In opposition to nineteenth-century bodily norms, the gothic offered "a body metamorphic and undifferentiated" (Hurley 1996: 3). The same themes that emerged on the freak show stage in relation to people with disabilities appeared in grotesque distortion in the gothic novel; the atypical bodies and minds of fictional monsters pointed to the limits of human ability to standardize and control both bodies and minds. The late Victorian gothic focused on fears of degeneration. As Kelly Hurley argues, works such as H. G. Wells' *The Island of Doctor Moreau* (1896) and Stevenson's *The Strange Case of Dr. Jekyll and Mr. Hyde* suggest that "the evolutionary process might be reversible: the human race might ultimately retrogress into a sordid animalism rather than progress towards a telos of intellectual and moral perfection" (Hurley 1996: 56). The title character from Bram Stoker's *Dracula* (1897), for example, has been read as the embodiment of sexual degeneration, atavistic regression, and fears of foreign invaders bringing disease.[10]

The body and disability are central to the sensation novel of the 1860s, a genre grounded in "the reader's 'nervous' reactions to dramatic, surprising, and/or scandalous plotting that often involves characters' parallel bodily crises or transformations" (Mossman and Holmes 2011: 493). Disability is frequently used both to "call[] stories into being" (Mitchell and Snyder 2000: 53) and also to call forth reader responses such as nervous thrills, tears, and terror before being excised from the plot.[11] For example, in Collins' *The Woman in White*, a young woman touches a young man's shoulder on a dark road in the early hours of the morning and both character and reader thrill at her surprising touch. The woman, Anne Catherick, is variously articulated as mentally disabled, traumatized, or mad. She serves the twists and turns of the plot, as well as its growing suspense, in significant ways—and then is written out, her work having been done on behalf of other characters.

Two other subsets of nineteenth-century literary disability are worth noting. The evolution of children's literature in British and American literature corresponded to the development of the idea of childhood as a distinct and privileged state; its first "golden age" engages disability regularly, notably as a plot pivot, as Lois Keith (2001) observes in *Take Up Thy Bed and Walk: Death, Disability, and Cure in Classic Fiction for Girls*. In protagonists, disablement is frequently used as a temporary chastener of rebellious or unladylike girls, followed by a reclamation to normalcy; in minor characters, it more often ends in death once the character has served the plot.[12] Other works thematizing disability that have intermittently been classified as "children's literature" include *A Christmas Carol* (1843), *Jane Eyre* (1847), *David Copperfield* (1850), Alcott's *Little Women* (1868–9), and Rossetti's "Goblin Market" (1862).[13] Finally, life writing figures centrally in the discourse of disability. As multiple chapters in this volume illustrate, first-person writing about disabled experiences provides crucial information about disability discourses in the long nineteenth century. First-person narratives, such as those discussed throughout this volume, reflect sophisticated negotiations with the cultural scripts that defined and often diminished people with disabilities, but were ignored at a high cost (Holmes 2001). Biographies carry a particular tension between the narrator of a disabled life and the instances in which the object of biography resists a sentimental or sacralized frame.

0.10. FUTURE DIRECTIONS

This volume's collection of important recent work in the field of nineteenth-century disability studies invites additional exploration in a number of directions. Its Western and Anglo-American emphasis points out the need for the extension of historicist cultural studies to a broader global focus, with more global connections to contextualize national narratives. Further historical studies of care relationships might explore human–animal relationality, engaging the historical development of service animals, the deployment of the category "animal" in the constructions of both intellectual disability and "race," the nexuses between anti-vivisectionism and discourses of disability, and the notion of the "natural" in relation to disabled people (from the Romantics to Darwin). Jennifer Esmail's essay on service animals is an exemplar, noting that "representations of the close connection between blind humans and sighted dogs are fruitful sites for tracing the complexities of Victorian attitudes towards poverty, disability, and animality" (2014: 22). Further, a productive return to the nineteenth-century historicist scholarship that has characterized the field of environmental cultural studies might build on the synergies between disability studies and environmental humanities exemplified by Ray and Sibarra's edited collection *Disability Studies and the Environmental Humanities* (2017). The exciting realm of disability aesthetics has yet to emerge fully in nineteenth-century studies, where we have looked more at the representation of disability than at disability as a mode of artistic and literary production and representation. Beyond ableist assumptions about the relationship between disabled embodiment and artistic production, such as John Ruskin's argument in "Fiction Fair and Foul" (1880) that authors' illnesses lead them to create disabled characters, a fuller cultural history of disability *aesthetics* in the nineteenth century might surely encompass a deeper exploration of how disability informs all aspects of the creation and production of literature and art and how disability and aesthetics are linked in the works of the period. Finally, we might further explore the naming and articulating of disability in the long nineteenth century in terms of its production of the "unmarked" categories of ability, normalcy, and health. We should continue to interrogate the relationships between illness and disability in nineteenth-century culture *and* nineteenth-century studies. Alex Tankard argues, for example, that "the vast majority of disabled Victorians owed their impairment not to the blindness, deafness, and 'deformity' that dominate existing scholarship in the field [of nineteenth-century disability studies] but to 'consumption'" (2018: 5). The chapters in this volume (and the structure of each volume in this series) represent a fuller portfolio of locations for disability as both a "made" category and a maker of identities, communities, culture, and change. We look forward to more of this important and generative work.

CHAPTER ONE

Atypical Bodies

The Cultural Work of the Nineteenth-century Freak Show

NADJA DURBACH

On January 6, 1899, performers with the Barnum and Bailey show (Figure 1.1), which was appearing in London, held an "indignation meeting" to protest the use of the term "freak" as applied to the "human abnormalities and specialty artistes" on display. They resolved that merely because they were "fortunately, or otherwise" possessed of "more or less limbs, more or less hair, more or less bodies, more or less physical or mental attributes than other people," and as such differed from "the ordinary or regulation human being," there was no reason that they should be called "freaks." This term had been widely used throughout the nineteenth century to refer to those who displayed their atypical bodies for profit, but these performers maintained that it was "opprobrious" and "without any specific meaning in an anatomical sense." They further argued that their physical distinctions might in fact be assets and intimated that "some of us are really the development of a higher type, and are superior persons, inasmuch as some of us are gifted with extraordinary attributes not apparent in ordinary beings." Their resolution underscored that although they had been "created differently from the human family as the latter exist to-day," these bodily variations might have been expressly "for their benefit," intimating that in the future all persons might be blessed with nonstandard forms ("Freaks in Council" 1899: 19). This meeting was most likely a publicity stunt. Newspaper coverage of the event used it primarily to highlight the acts that would be on display at the show, which included a bearded lady, armless and legless performers, a giant and a dwarf, a man with a parasitic conjoined twin, an elastic-skinned man, and the so-called Wild Men of Borneo. But whether it was an authentic expression of discontent over appropriate terminology, as some scholars have argued (Chemers 2008: 97–101), or an instance of the humbug inherent in all of Barnum's promotional materials (Lentz 1977; Cook 2001), what historians have called the "revolt of the freaks" sheds light on the complexities of the freak show, the primary cultural site for public and professional encounters with atypical bodies in the nineteenth century.

This chapter focuses on the cultural work that the freak show performed in the long nineteenth century. This is because if we wish to find where atypical bodies were most visible to the public, then we must look to their commercial display. By exposing these bodies for all to see, rather than segregating and silencing them through the practices of institutionalization, freak shows demanded that society engage with the fact of corporeal variation. Throughout the nineteenth century, human oddities from around

FIGURE 1.1 The Barnum and Bailey Greatest Show on Earth.

the world crisscrossed the oceans, appearing in North American and Western European cities, towns, and rural communities. Some continued on to Eastern Europe and into the Middle East, tracing and retracing what soon became an established freak show route. By the middle of the century, the freak show had thus become firmly embedded within an increasingly cosmopolitan entertainment industry. In fact, these exhibitions were one of few nineteenth-century leisure activities that attracted an extremely broad audience, which transcended national borders and cut across lines of class, gender, and age. Curious members of both the public and the medical and scientific professions eagerly flocked to see bodies that defied the norms of corporeality and challenged the divide between human and animal, male and female, black and white, civilized and savage, slave and free, self and other, as well as a range of other binaries that increasingly structured modern Western societies.

This chapter argues that it is to the popular and professional debates these spectacles generated over how to interpret extraordinary bodies that we must turn if we are to understand the various ways that the nineteenth century framed the atypical body. Section 1.1 seeks to complicate how we use the term "disability" when writing about atypical bodies in the past. It suggests that rather than seeing freak performers as people with disabilities, it is more historically accurate to locate them in relation to a range of attitudes toward and anxieties about the body that were relevant in the nineteenth century. These discourses deliberately resisted essentializing the meanings of physical difference and kept the ambiguous nature of these bodies alive. Section 1.2 explores the issue of agency, challenging the widespread assumption that freak shows were merely voyeuristic and exploitative. Instead, it demonstrates that the relationship between performers and spectators was more interactive and complex than we might imagine and that freak shows often provided financial stability and thus independence to those who were economically vulnerable. In the case of ethnographic acts, however, this issue was more complex, as the racial systems of colonialism and slavery further limited these performers' range of life choices. Section 1.3 seeks to locate these ethnographic shows within the wider history of the display of atypical bodies, arguing that these exhibitions were crucial sites for the scientific study of "the races of mankind." By displaying non-Western peoples alongside bearded ladies and legless men, these shows produced racial and ethnic difference in dynamic relationship to other forms of corporeal "deviance." This section then moves to a discussion of scientific medicine's use of the freak show for its raw material. It posits that the medicalization of the anomalous body emerged in the nineteenth century not in contrast to freakery, but directly out of negotiations between scientific professionals and freak performers. This chapter suggests, therefore, that the freak show should not be dismissed as merely prurient, exploitative, and thus degrading to those who inhabited nonstandard bodies. Rather, it was a critical site for negotiations around the meanings attached to physical diversity and thus central to understanding the place of the atypical body within nineteenth-century culture.

1.1. HISTORICIZING THE ATYPICAL BODY: ATTITUDES, ABILITY, ABNORMALITY, ANXIETY, AND AMBIGUITY

The language deployed by the performers involved in the "revolt of the freaks" resisted a reading of their atypical bodies as inherently less able. Although they acknowledged that they had been "created differently," those who attended this purported meeting suggested that their physical peculiarities could be interpreted "as additional charms of person or aids to movement" rather than in terms of disability, a term in limited circulation at this time ("Freaks in Council" 1899). During the nineteenth century, there was no omnibus term for those with atypical bodies, no category to which all, regardless of the specificity of their physical differences, could belong. Instead, a variety of labels, including "the defective," "the deformed," "the infirm," "the impotent," or "the crippled," were deployed to categorize particular forms of impairment in specific contexts (Stone 1984: 55). The use of these different terms distinguished bodily variations from each other; more significantly, it signaled appropriate social attitudes and cultural responses to these bodily states that included identifying those deserving of financial assistance. Charles Dickens's Tiny Tim, for example, is an archetypal "crippled" child, meant to evoke pity, empathy, and thus charity in the reader. This had particular resonance at Christmas, "a kind, forgiving, charitable time," *A Christmas Carol* articulates, "when men and women seem by one consent to open their shut-up hearts freely, and to think of people below them as if they really were fellow passengers to the grave, and not another race of creatures bound on other journeys" ([1843] 2003: 42). Dickens' Silas Wegg, however, the one-legged blackmailer in *Our Mutual Friend*, while similarly impaired, is never constructed as a "fellow passenger." Dickens does not describe the wooden-legged Wegg as a "cripple" precisely because, as a villainous character, Wegg was meant, as Martha Stoddard Holmes has argued, to elicit "righteous outrage" in readers, not pity (2004: 94–132). Wegg's impairment thus signals that he, unlike Tiny Tim, has in fact been consigned to that race of creatures bound on other journeys.

The term "disabled" did circulate in the Victorian period and was sometimes used to signal bodily states wrought by illness, injury, or old age. But it was rarely used at this time to describe those born with congenital anomalies. Instead, "the disabled" emerged as a category primarily in relation to wounded soldiers and sailors, particularly the limbless, who, having sacrificed their bodily integrity for the safety of the nation, had the right to make demands upon the state.[1] The American Civil War began to shape this new body–state relationship, and the concomitant rights that accrued from it, in the second half of the nineteenth century. For Europeans and their colonial subjects, it was not until the First World War that this particular meaning of "disability" took root. "Disability" thus evokes an understanding of bodily difference that expresses a specific relationship among the self, the state, and society that was largely shaped by the experience of modern mass warfare's impact on the body. The problem with using "disability" to interrogate the nineteenth-century freak show, then, is that scholars have often collapsed the project of analyzing the ways in which societies have dealt with atypical bodies over time and space and the specific meanings and connotations of this word. In an otherwise theoretically rich study of the American freak show, Rosemarie Garland-Thomson has argued that the "wondrous monsters of antiquity, who became the fascinating freaks of the nineteenth century, transformed into the disabled people of the later twentieth century" (1997: 58). This suggests that these terms and the meanings attached to them were interchangeable or evolutionary understandings of physical difference.

I deliberately employ the term "freak" when discussing those who displayed their atypical bodies for profit because it was the most common term in use for these performers throughout the nineteenth century. But using it also highlights that the practice of enfreakment was a culturally and historically specific approach to manufacturing and managing the divide between the "normal" and the "abnormal" body. In fact, freaks did not necessarily think of themselves as physically less able than those with standard bodies. As the resolutions that emerged from the "revolt of the freaks" suggested, freak performers often had bodily anomalies—abundant hair, unusual pigmentation, extra appendages—that in no way interfered with their cognitive or physical abilities. Those whose physical differences were assumed to be compromising invariably incorporated into their acts demonstrations of their capacities. Eli Bowen, a "legless wonder," could perform a wide range of skilled acrobatic tricks; his promotional materials underscored that he moved "swiftly and gracefully" and that all of his movements were "dexterous" (Bogdan 1988: 215). Oguri Kiba, who participated in the "revolt of the freaks," was armless. Her publicity materials nevertheless stressed that this did not interfere with her ability to undertake skilled labor, explaining that, "with her highly educated feet she does more things and does them better than most people fully endowed by nature with hands." Using only her toes, "she sews, threading even the finest cambric needles, spins, uses hammer, saw, and plane, makes toy ships, builds water-tight tubs and firkins, cuts delicately traced lace out of paper, makes artificial flowers, and shoots with bow and arrow with wonderful accuracy" (Dean 1899: 8–9). The armless Charles Tripp sold a souvenir photograph that depicted himself surrounded by the tools he could skillfully manipulate with his feet (Figure 1.2). Freaks of all varieties thus tended to construct themselves as skilled and adaptable. That performing in the freak show allowed them to lead independent lives further underscored their able-bodied status. For if the term "disability" was rarely used in the nineteenth century to refer to those with nonstandard bodies, the term "able-bodied" was a crucial cultural reference point. In the United Kingdom, those who could work and were able to support themselves financially without

FIGURE 1.2 Charles B. Tripp, Photograph by Charles Eisenmann, c. 1890.

relying on the state or charity were by definition able-bodied. The fact that they were being paid to exhibit their bodies and could earn their own keep thus allowed freak performers to identify not as disabled, but rather as able-bodied.

Freaks often stressed, therefore, that despite their unusual forms, when not onstage they led rather unremarkable, and in fact typical, lives. An 1898 article entitled "'EVEN AS YOU AND I' At Home with the Barnum Freaks" argued that "in public they are 'freaks,'" but when they were "off their platforms and their pedestals it is pleasant to find that, with the one particular reservation in each case, they are just men and women, normal and healthy, 'even as you and I'" (Goddard 1898). Although those who participated in the "revolt of the freaks" themselves celebrated their distance from the "regulation human being," they likely would have welcomed this kind of publicity that situated them as healthy members of the human family when not explicitly performing their otherness. Miss Annie Jones, the bearded lady who purportedly instigated the "revolt of the freaks," "would never be taken for a 'freak'" when not onstage, her promotional material stressed, "as she dresses in fine taste, and conceals her features by a cunning combination of black silk handkerchief and deep veil" (Dean 1899: 12). When Tom Norman exhibited Joseph Merrick as "the Elephant Man" in 1884, he similarly stressed in Shakespearean fashion that "were you to cut or prick Joseph he would bleed, and that bleed or blood would be red, the same as yours or mine," explicitly drawing a commonality between Merrick's body and those of his spectators (Norman and Norman 1985: 104).

But freak shows also obviously depended on drawing a distinction between the "normal" bodies of spectators and the "abnormal" bodies on display. They attracted audiences not only by using atypical bodies as others against which the self could be measured, but also by stimulating curiosity about the instability of race, gender, sexuality, class, civilization, colonialism, immigration, slavery, individualism, and, in fact, the very boundaries of humanity. "Spotted boys," whose skin was neither black nor white, challenged racial typing and, by extension, the existence of race-based slavery; conjoined twins raised troubling questions about individuality and the nature of the self; extremely hairy persons complicated the divide between human and animal, contesting the theory and nature of evolutionary processes. Freaks thus attempted to draw the spectator's eye to certain aspects of their bodies and performed roles that were intended to structure how their specific corporeal anomalies should be read.

This is why those who performed as freaks often enhanced their acts by adopting what Robert Bogdan has identified as aggrandized or exoticized modes of presentation (1988: 94–116), or by promoting themselves as liminal beings. It was the "techniques of exhibition in which corporeal difference is literally staged," including costumes, choreography, and supporting materials such as souvenir photographs and pamphlets, which in the end constructed the anomalous body as freakish (Stephens 2005: 7). For as Garland-Thomson has argued, the freak was "fabricated from the raw material of bodily variations" for entirely social purposes; the "freak of nature," she insists, was always in fact a "freak of culture" (1996: xviii, 7). The "freak" was both an occupation—like "actor," "dancer," or "acrobat"—and a role that was produced in collaboration with the audience whose spectatorship itself shaped the construction of the performer's body as aberrant (Stephens 2006: 487). Freaks thus always attempted to have it both ways: they profited off their bodies' otherness by using them to generate a range of titillating anxieties while at the same time asserting that they were not only "normal" but "able-bodied."

The freak show thus traded in ambiguity. If it directed the eye to see certain bodily traits, it nevertheless sought "to expand the possibilities of interpretation" of the atypical body, rather than containing its definition "through classification and mastery" (Garland-Thomson 1999: 95). These spectacles perpetuated the multiple potential meanings attached to corporeal anomalies, a discourse that had clear cultural reverberations. In his 1841 novel *The Old Curiosity Shop*, Dickens featured two diminutive people: "Little" Nell and Daniel Quilp. In realizing these characters, Dickens borrowed heavily from the freak show's exhibition of a range of "miniature" peoples. But, despite their shared physical resemblance to sideshow "midgets" and "dwarves," Nell and Quilp were not intended to elicit identical affective responses in readers. Nell's "small and delicate frame" was part of Dickens' positioning of her as a suffering, self-sacrificing, and ergo sentimental character who serves as the novel's heroine and thus emotional core. Quilp, in contrast, who was "so low in stature as to be quite a dwarf," is figured as grotesque, ugly, and lecherous because he was meant to be read as a melodramatic villain (Craton 2009: 41–85). That Dickens used remarkable smallness within the same text to elicit diametrically opposed reader responses to his characters suggests that what he imbibed from the freak show and then widely perpetuated was a refusal to essentialize the atypical body. Rather than trafficking in the degradation of difference—a facile and narrow understanding of freakery—throughout the nineteenth century these exhibitions succeeded in keeping the wondrous nature of corporeal variation alive by cultivating ambiguity and thus allowing for myriad interpretations of the possible meanings of physical difference.

1.2. AGENCY AND THE ATYPICAL BODY

The revolt of the freaks encouraged potential spectators to reject the idea that these human curiosities found the commercial display of their wondrous bodies shameful, as they disparaged only the negative connotations of the language of freakery, imposed on them "without our consent," but not their exhibition itself ("Freaks in Council" 1899). This raises critical questions about the agency of freak show performers. Some scholars have rightly problematized the meaning of choice and consent in the case of individuals who inhabited anomalous bodies, arguing that the freak show was an inherently exploitative institution (Gerber 1990, 1996; Mitchell and Snyder 2005). This reading, however, diminishes the agency of performers and ignores the realities of the nineteenth-century economy and the lack of social services available to those born with bodily anomalies, both of which may have limited their ability to support themselves in other ways. Although it would be misleading to celebrate the freak show as the only real sanctuary for those with atypical bodies, it is equally historically inaccurate to position nineteenth-century freakery as always already an unscrupulous practice whereby greedy managers held the most vulnerable members of society hostage. While it is important not to romanticize the show world—especially given the paucity of reliable sources produced by freaks themselves—it is nevertheless critical to attend to the agency of those who inhabited atypical bodies, especially if we are to allow for the fact that economics also shapes culture.

Most freaks were, like other types of performers, active agents in the marketplace for commercialized leisure and chose to perform in order to earn their own keep (Chemers 2005). Critics of the freak show during the nineteenth century, as now, often assumed that freaks earned little money for their performances, "live[d] in a deplorable manner," and were regarded by their drunken managers as merely "valuable cattle" (FitzGerald 1897: 410). But this is merely one reading of a much more complex relationship.

Merrick's manager, Tom Norman, asserted that, "95% of the freaks, novelties, etc. are very content" (Norman 1928: 108). While the testimonials of showmen who profited off the exhibition of the bodies of others are not sufficient evidence that freaks were not exploited, neither should this position be categorically dismissed. Some acts clearly did not elect to become freaks and in fact appear to have been sold by their parents for the purposes of exhibition. But many people born with congenital anomalies clearly chose to perform as freaks rather than seek out charitable or government support or submit to institutionalization, and they stressed this in their promotional materials (McHold 2008: 27–8). According to his promotional autobiography, it was Joseph Merrick who discharged himself from the Leicester workhouse after five years of enduring its privations, and he himself who sought out the local variety theater in order to offer up his body for display (*Life and Adventures* 1885). Norman's son, likely thinking of Merrick's case, claimed that many "novelties" were "unwanted and cast out by their own families." They were, he insisted, "grateful for the opportunity to achieve some degree of independence—their only alternative being starvation or the workhouse" (Norman and Norman 1985: ii). Those who were born with or acquired atypical bodies thus often used the freak show as a route to financial independence, which itself instilled a sense of self-worth and allowed for a life of relative freedom (Durbach 2010: 46–50). Working as a freak appears in fact to have been a fairly lucrative business, representing much better paid and easier work than other forms of labor available to those with anomalous bodies (Dennett 1997: 68).

If the relationship between freak and manager was less exploitative than many have assumed (Adams 1997: 13), the presence of performers from colonial spaces and from slave regimes does raise additional and even more complex issues of exploitation and informed consent that should not be ignored or downplayed. It is difficult to know whether or not Sara Baartman, a Khoikhoi woman exhibited as "the Hottentot Venus" in the early years of the century, consented to her public display. She was not always an enthusiastic performer. However, when she wound up in the English courts as a case of suspected slavery just a few years after the British had abolished the slave trade, Baartman maintained that she had consented to her exhibition on condition that she be paid half the profits for a period of six years (Qureshi 2004; Crais and Scully 2009: 54–7, 99–101). Baartman may well have been coached and threatened to provide this testimony. But, as Roslyn Poignant has argued, indigenous peoples whose lifeways had been destroyed by colonialism sometimes agreed to join traveling shows because this was often the best of a very limited range of options. Poignant's chronicle of the "Australian Cannibal Boomerang Throwers" reveals that while this group of indigenous Australians was essentially "abducted" and always underpaid for their labor, they were not merely victims of an avaricious showman. Instead, she reveals the troop's own investment in their identities as performers, suggesting that while not complicit in their own exploitation, they were not entirely without agency (2004). Similarly, a group of Zulus exhibited in 1899 apparently chose to perform traditional dances for English audiences rather than work in the dangerous mines of South Africa. According to *The Era*, the men seemed to relish their performance and refused to take direction from their manager, extending their songs and dances as long as they saw fit and thus exerting a degree of control over the manner of their exhibition. That showmen sometimes preferred to employ fake "savages" precisely because they were easier to control and to manage further indicates that colonial performers often asserted their own agency both on- and offstage (Durbach 2010: 12, 147–70).

The problem with fake "savages," however, was that they were liable to be recognized as locals by members of the audience, who did not hesitate to intervene in the performance if they felt that they were being duped. Indeed, these shows were highly interactive. Few freaks mutely and passively displayed their abnormalities on a stage removed from the spectators. While freaks were performing a role, they were also interacting with audience members as talented, unique individuals who were clearly proud of their many accomplishments. Exhibitions were often called "levees," a type of social reception usually held in the daytime, suggesting that freaks were receiving guests rather than merely showing their bodies to strangers. They conversed with the audience (often in several European languages), moved among their visitors, allowed people to touch them, and invited a variety of forms of interaction. Freaks often performed songs, dances, and feats of strength or agility, and sometimes they encouraged audience participation. When Field Marshall Tom Thumb performed in the 1840s, his promotional material stressed that he "excels in polite and manly accomplishments" and would demonstrate that he was an "intelligent, lively, witty, and conversant man." This suggested that he was not there merely to be looked at ("England's Native Wonder" 1846). Henry Moss, a "white negro" who exhibited himself on the eastern seaboard of the United States in the last years of the 1790s, even allowed spectators to touch him and probe his skin in the areas where the pigment seemed to be fading away. As Charles Martin has argued, in peeling back his clothes to invite spectators to have intimate access to his body, Moss (and performers like him, such as John Boby, "the Spotted Indian"; Figure 1.3) performed a type of "dual striptease": "the slow revelation of his unruly body, the even slower revelation of white skin" (2002: 36–7). The ability to actually touch the freaks (especially those of the opposite sex) in a respectable setting may have been deeply arousing to the audience and part of the lure of these types of shows (Dennett 1997: 83). Thus, while freaks may have inspired spectators to feel disgust or pity, they also stimulated a range of more complex emotions that included awe, admiration, and even sexual attraction.

In fact, while primarily the objects of the gaze, in these types of interactions, freaks sometimes returned the gaze, thus challenging the power dynamic between the spectator and the spectacle implicit in the act of staring. Chang and Eng, the original "Siamese Twins," treated their audiences as spectacles, acutely observing them and then commentating on the remarks that they had overhead during a performance (Wallace and Wallace 1978: 91; Mitchell 2003: 151). When a diminutive brother–sister act marketed as the last of the Aztec race first appeared in London, they were immediately taken to the Royal College of Surgeons' Hunterian Museum to look at the anatomical anomalies on display. They were, apparently, "much struck" by the skeletons of the giant Charles Byrne and the dwarf Caroline Crachami, who had also toured as freaks in an earlier period, and "peered with great curiosity" at the mummies in their cases (Durbach 2010: 10–11). That they were allowed—in fact, invited—to look at other freaks, rather than merely being looked at, suggests that "staring at the Other" sometimes went both ways (Garland-Thomson 2005). The mere fact of looking, even staring, need not necessarily be degrading, as seeing and acknowledging difference remain prerequisites for incorporating diversity. Indeed, if nineteenth-century freak shows reified the normal/abnormal binary, they nevertheless encouraged engagement across this divide, and in the process made space for those with atypical bodies within society. However, as we shall see, this was less true in relation to ethnographic acts, as the freak show tended to essentialize these performers through the discourses of scientific racism, producing these bodies as inferior specimens of mankind both on- and offstage.

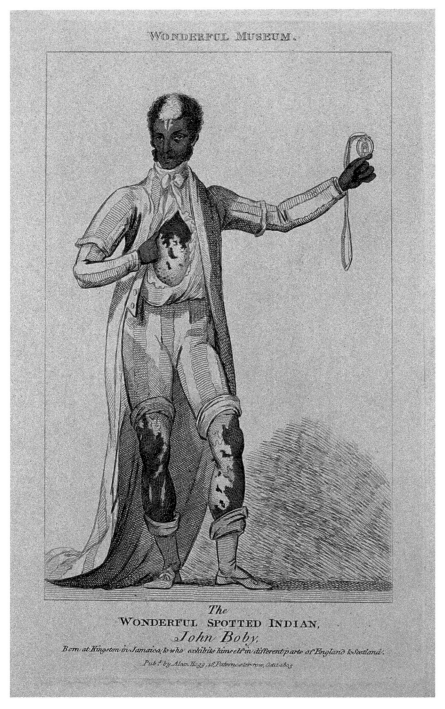

FIGURE 1.3 The Wonderful Spotted Indian, John Boby.

1.3. SCIENCE AND THE SIDESHOW

The freaks who purportedly took part in the "revolt" in 1899 did not articulate any discomfort with being objectified. However, they clearly constructed themselves not as objects of pity or disgust, but rather as "the development of a higher type" who were in fact "superior persons." They were, coverage of their revolt reported, "gifted with extraordinary attributes not apparent in ordinary beings" rather than lacking in any significant way ("Freaks in Council" 1899). Barnum and Bailey's freaks nevertheless expressed a complicated relationship toward medical science, which increasingly sought to explain and to make meaning out of their corporeal anomalies and thus to classify them accordingly. They refused to see their physical forms as wanting or inferior and thus implicitly rejected attempts to position all atypical bodies, regardless of the nature of their deviation from the norm, as pathological. They nevertheless chastised those who lumped them all together without distinguishing the "anatomical" differences among their nonstandard bodies. This tension was typical of nineteenth-century freak show performers, who resisted an exclusively medical reading of their physical difference while simultaneously fostering the symbiotic relationship between science and the sideshow in order to exploit it for their own advantage.

Scientists interested in human variation flocked to freak shows. These commercial displays of extraordinary bodies thus informed two fields of study that emerged in the nineteenth century: the sciences of anthropology and ethnology that attempted to account for differences among "the races of mankind," and those of teratology and teratogeny, the pathologization of congenital anomalies. As I have already noted, among the most popular kinds of performers were those from far-flung corners of the globe who were exhibited either explicitly as "savages" or as curious ethnographic "specimens." Historians have tended to treat these ethnographic exhibitions as a separate category of entertainment (Lindfors 1999; Ames 2004; Bancel et al. 2009; Qureshi 2011). However, it was common for shows to feature a range of acts; little distinction was made at the time among performers who were non-Western peoples, had congenital anomalies, or were "specialty artistes" whose freakishness was self-made. For, as Rachel Adams has argued, these shows "offered a panoramic view of the most sensational forms of alterity at any given historical moment" (2001: 11). In 1854, "the Aztecs" (Figure 1.4) and "the Earthmen" appeared onstage together. "The Aztecs" were exhibited as the last members of their civilization, while the latter were two San children from Southern Africa who danced and sang minstrel songs clothed in animal hides. Both acts were framed by the discourses of dying races and the inevitable extinction of primitive peoples whose civilizations had not kept pace with modernity ("Aztecs and Earthmen" 1854). Pairing "the Aztecs" with "the Earthmen" suggested that both sets of performers should be read as ethnographic types, the last of their respective races. But it was the combination of "the Aztecs'" racial otherness (which proved difficult in the end to categorize), their inevitable extinction, and their anomalous "Lilliputian" stature and tiny heads that made them so appealing to audiences. When "the Aztecs" were later exhibited in Barnum's 1889 show, no distinction was made between them (or indeed the Zulus on display) and the fat boy, Circassian beauties, tattooed people, twin giant Texas ranchmen, a legless man, "midgets," albinos, or a wooly child ("P.T. Barnum's Greatest Show on Earth" 1889). By exhibiting people of color alongside bearded ladies, armless men, and conjoined twins, sideshow performances explicitly configured racial otherness as freakish bodily difference and thus normalized the white Anglo-Saxon body.

FIGURE 1.4 Maximo and Bartola, supposed to be Aztecs.

This message was reinforced not merely by the fact that non-Western peoples shared the stage with so-called freaks of nature, but also because many acts were simultaneously congenitally anomalous and racially other. This conflation of "freak" and "type" had been commonplace since at least the early years of the nineteenth century when Baartman toured Europe as "the Hottentot Venus" (Crais and Scully 2009). Baartman was a novelty because she appeared to European audiences to possess unusually large buttocks and was rumored to have elongated outer labia, sometimes referred to as a "Hottentot apron." Some interpreted these aspects of her person as freakish physical mutations, while others argued they were merely typical of "Hottentot" women. According to contemporary reports, Baartman's form-fitting, flesh-colored costume, which was designed to draw attention to her buttocks, was "intended to give the appearance of being undressed" (Strother 1999: 43). She also wore a small cloth or hide suspended from a beaded belt to cover her pubic region. Its dangling tassels that reached almost to her toes gestured to what might be hidden underneath: the famed "Hottentot apron" that she persistently refused to show to anyone, not even George Cuvier, one of the fathers of comparative anatomy, who seems to have badgered her endlessly for access. As Bernth Lindfors has argued, Baartman thus offered the public "at least three kinds of sideshow stimulation: she was part freak, part savage, part cooch dancer" (Lindfors 1996: 3). These categories were not easily distinguishable from each other, as the colonial narratives that framed the show were dependent on widespread understandings of racialized sexual inferiority (Magubane 2001). These were embodied in the oxymoronic moniker of the "Hottentot Venus": her persona was itself a joke, as it was widely understood that a "Hottentot," a degraded racial group, could never be a "Venus," the Roman goddess of love depicted in statuary as the ideal white, civilized female form. Baartman was one of many acts that purportedly revealed to predominantly white audiences the ways in which savagery and primitiveness were inscribed onto the bodies of non-white peoples. The "science" of human variation cannot, therefore, be severed from its cultural context, for in constructing non-white peoples as inherently aberrant, the freak show helped to justify the political, social, and economic policies and practices of colonialism and slavery (Adams 1997: 184–5; Martin 2002; Poignant 2004; Qureshi 2011).

If freak shows provided those who attempted to study racial difference from a scientific perspective with raw material, so, too, did they furnish medical researchers with examples of monstrosity. Scholars have tended broadly to agree that by the eighteenth century, at the very latest, gazing at "monsters"—the medical term for those born with significant anomalies—became not only a popular pleasure, but also a scientific pursuit that was incorporated into the study of anatomy and natural history (Park and Daston 1981; Huet 1993; Wilson 1993; Moscoso 1998; Hagner 1999). With the emergence of teratology and teratogeny in the nineteenth century, it evolved into a medical specialty in its own right. Since the 1830s, Isidore Geoffroy Saint-Hilaire—who, with his father, Etienne, developed the field of teratology—had argued that congenital anomalies were not random, but rather fell into clear categories that could in fact be scientifically classified. Anomalous bodies were thus not symptomatic of a chaotic universe or a sign of divine wrath, but rather offered an opportunity for modern men "to understand the natural order more fully and to define it with greater precision" (Ritvo 1997: 137). Saint-Hilaire's 1832 book on the subject theorized that even monstrous bodies conformed to natural laws, and if correctly examined revealed their principles of organization. Despite this and other attempts to catalogue scientifically all forms of bodily difference and subsume them within knowable categories, the medicalization of the anomalous body was far from complete by the nineteenth century, as the persistence of freak shows suggests. The eventual incorporation of those with these types of bodily anomalies into the category of "the disabled" was thus never a given. It was the product of fraught negotiations between the public, scientists, and sideshow performers that took place over the course of the nineteenth century. Indeed, the scientific study of bodily anomalies, even when conducted within the confines of medical schools and professional societies, continued to rely heavily on their display as wonders.

Many medical professionals eagerly patronized freak shows, where they could see and sometimes examine firsthand the anomalous bodies on display. The British surgeon John Bland Sutton made a habit of scouting exhibitions for cases that he could exhibit to colleagues and then write up for professional journals (Bland Sutton 1930: 139). The comparative anatomist Richard Owen was so fascinated with "the Aztecs" that he not only examined them and published a scientific report of their case, but also collected souvenir photographs of them throughout their career.[2] An 1898 article in the *Guyoscope*, a comic magazine for medical practitioners, satirized this scientific obsession with sideshow acts by describing the efforts of "a senior physician on the staff of the leading London Hospital" who attended Barnum's show in order to "inspect the freaks in the scientific interest" ("Shows We Have Sampled" 1898: 42–5).

Medical researchers used the freaks they found at these exhibitions as experimental material. When Baartman died in Paris in 1815, Cuvier secured her body from the police in order to dissect her corpse and finally see her "apron" for himself. He then pickled her genitalia to preserve them for posterity, placed her skeleton alongside others in his collection, and made a full-body cast that remained on public display in the Jardin des Plantes, one of the world's most elaborate collections of natural history specimens, until 1982 (Crais and Scully 2009: 138–41, 148). Saint-Hilaire had been similarly eager to bring Chang and Eng to Paris for scientific examination, but had been refused by the government, a ban that remained in place for almost five years (Wallace and Wallace 1978: 97, 145). George Buckley Bolton was more fortunate. A member of the Royal College of Surgeons and the Medical and Chirurgical Society of London, he became the sole medical attendant for the twins on their arrival in London. Bolton used this access to their conjoined bodies to perform a series of experiments on Chang and Eng, none of which he claimed were "unjustifiable," to isolate which of their bodily systems were and were not connected (Bolton 1830: 178–85).

These researchers then published their medical case studies in professional journals and textbooks, which often included scientific descriptions of freak performers. George M. Gould and Walter L. Pyle's *Anomalies and Curiosities of Medicine*, an "encyclopedia" of the "most striking instances of abnormality" derived from the "medical literature," drew its "rare and extraordinary cases" extensively from freak show performers and maintained that "hardly any medical journal is without its rare or 'unique' case" (1898: 2; Crockford 2012). In his manual on antenatal pathology, the well-known obstetrician J. W. Ballantyne repeatedly drew on examples from the show world, describing "Porcupine Men," "Elastic Skinned Men," and "Living Skeletons." Ballantyne even reproduced the full text of freak show handbills in his *The Diseases and Deformities of the Foetus* (1892: 80–9). By the end of the nineteenth century, these medical texts not only described freak show acts, but regularly used images of freaks as illustrations of particular congenital conditions. Gould and Pyle included the souvenir photographs of many well-known freak acts, often erasing their frames and thus effacing the commercial origins of these illustrations. The freak exhibition thus provided scientists and medical professionals access to what they increasingly perceived and constructed as medical specimens. This enabled them to assert their authority over bodies they classified as pathological despite the fact that scientific medicine could often do very little to treat either the symptoms associated with or the underlying causes of these types of anomalies.

Fig. 57.—Laloo.

FIGURE 1.5 Laloo, "The Double-Bodied Hindoo Boy."

However much scientific medicine, which was only beginning to professionalize over the course of the second half of the nineteenth century, sought to control how the public interpreted "congenital deformities," its practitioners were only marginally successful in this endeavor until late in the century. Showmen repeatedly asserted that the extraordinary bodies they displayed were wondrous precisely because they defied scientific classification. Their exhibits were not examples of known medical conditions, they argued, but rather were "unique," "singular," and "rare." Terms like "nondescript" were frequently applied to such acts to emphasize their inability to be adequately categorized ("Miss Julia Pastrana" 1857). In 1846, "the Wild Man of the Prairies; or, What is It?" capitalized on the inability of anyone to pin down how his anomalous body might fit into the Linnaean classificatory system ("The Wild Man of the Prairies" 1846). In 1860, Barnum seized on this intrigue, producing a "What is It?" nondescript act of his own whose exhibition in various iterations lasted well into the twentieth century, with the 1899 London show featuring a "What is She?" (Cook 1996). This was of course a marketing strategy: to insist that your act was one of a kind ensured a larger audience. At the same time, exhibitors challenged the medical profession's attempt to classify these bodies as medical cases and thus to close down other interpretations of their deviations from the norm (Tromp 2008: 8). Thus, "American Jack the Frog Man" advertised in 1888 that, because "he sets at defiance the laws of nature," he continues to be "a puzzle to the American medical fraternity." His promotional material positioned him as a "marvel" and underscored the inability of science adequately to account for and thus label his body as a "monstrosity" in either the medical or the moral sense of this term ("American Jack" 1888).

This did not mean that freaks shunned the medical profession. Instead, they increasingly used the language of medicine and often appealed to its expertise for their own ends. Lalloo (sometimes spelled Laloo), "the Double-Bodied Hindoo Boy," whose souvenir photograph was reproduced in Gould and Pyle (Figure 1.5), constructed his show pamphlet as a medical case report and used scientific Latinate language throughout to describe the irregular anatomy of his conjoined parasitic twin (Fracis 1886). Freaks also called upon doctors and surgeons, whether real or fake, to verify the authenticity of their bodies (McHold 2002: 67, 75, 159). Miss Alice Bounds, "the Bear Lady," noted in her souvenir autobiography that, before appearing at Castan's Panopticum in Paris, she was legally required to be presented "to the principal Professors and most distinguished doctors to be carefully examined." This was because only these authorities were trusted by the government to certify that the acts were authentic and thus to protect the public from being duped by fraudulent freaks (*Life of Miss Alice Bounds* 1911). While the medical establishment policed her body, Bounds turned this to her advantage by using their authority to promote the authenticity of her act. Mrs. Elizabeth Armitage, who weighed 445 pounds, also claimed to have "been visited by the most eminent of the medical profession of Edinburgh and other places," presumably to verify that it was her flesh rather than artificial padding that contributed to her girth ("Mrs. Elizabeth Armitage" 1846). Freak shows thus used the language and growing authority of professional medicine to attract spectators. Having the certification of the medical faculty thus became an asset in the show world: an 1899 classified advertisement for "High-Class Prodigies" declared that it "will always pay a fair price for all who have testimonials from Schools of Medicine" ("Wanted, High-Class Prodigies" 1899).

The symbiotic relationship between science and the sideshow is especially apparent in the case of the "Elephant Man" (Figure 1.6). The surgeon Frederick Treves first encountered Joseph Merrick on display as "the Elephant Man" in a rented storefront

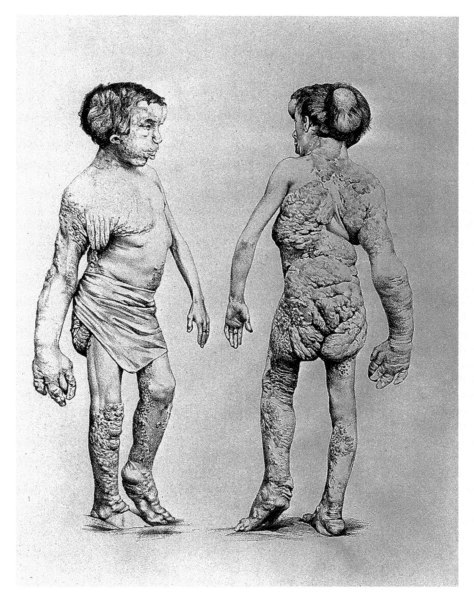

FIGURE 1.6 Joseph Merrick, "the Elephant Man."

directly across the road from the London Hospital where he worked. Its location was clearly strategic as Norman, Merrick's manager at the time, was hoping to draw in a curious professional medical community that he knew relied on the freak show for its specimens. Indeed, it was Treves' house surgeon who ultimately alerted him to the exhibition. After inducing Merrick to allow himself to be examined within the confines of the hospital, Treves then seized on the opportunity to display Merrick's unique body to his colleagues at the Pathological Society of London as a case of "congenital deformity" and to prepare a written report with illustrations for their journal (Treves 1885). In displaying "the Elephant Man" in front of learned professionals, Treves was thus enhancing his reputation for "discovering" more unusual cases than anyone else, despite the fact that he could not identify this pathological condition, nor treat its effects in any meaningful manner (Trombley 1989: 22, 34–6).

Conversely, when Norman introduced "the Elephant Man" to audiences, he declared that he intended "not to frighten you but to enlighten you," suggesting that this was an educational exhibit that could contribute to the production of knowledge, effectively turning this commercial display into a scientific space (Norman and Norman 1985: 103). More significantly, in 1885, an engraving of Merrick's partly naked body was added to the cover of his souvenir pamphlet. The illustration had been made from one of the photographs that Treves had taken to accompany his report in the Pathological Society's journal. Merrick and one of his later managers manipulated the image to exaggerate Merrick's "trunk," a thick piece of skin that grew from his upper lip, and thus to enhance his persona as "the Elephant Man" (Howell and Ford 1983: 104). "The Elephant Man's" promoters thus appropriated a scientific illustration for the purposes of showmanship. They challenged the scientific positioning of Merrick as a medical case by using a medical illustration to support their fantastic and popular interpretation of Merrick as a "monster half-man half-elephant" (Norman and Norman 1985: 103).

It should come as no surprise, then, that Barnum's prodigies desired that their conditions be properly labeled in an "anatomical sense" and thus that the "specific meanings" attached to their corporeal anomalies be explained to the audience by medical men. For, even if they refused to narrow the possible interpretations of their atypical bodies to purely medical explanations, they clearly understood that medicine had become a marketing tool. By the end of the nineteenth century, spectators were eager to understand how to interpret these anomalous bodies in ways that would safely contain them within the realm of the medical while simultaneously being reassured that their interest was educational rather than prurient. *The Lancet*—one of the leading British medical journals—claimed in 1898 on the occasion of Barnum and Bailey's annual exhibition that they had received a range of letters from the public "asking for explanations of the various physical phenomena manifested" in the bodies of these freaks ("Physical Curiosities" 1898). Freaks thus willingly participated in their medicalization once it became clear that this might make their acts more profitable. Ironically, the medical profession's growing authority to pathologize these bodies ultimately contributed to the freak show's demise.

The long process of acquiring both the scientific knowledge and the cultural authority to define what made one body normal and another abnormal was thus intimately bound up in the institution of the freak show (Kochanek 1997; McHold 2002). According to Matthew Sweet, far from being "a throwback to some barbaric past," the nineteenth-century freak show should, therefore, be understood as "an adjunct to the culture of scientific rationalism" (2001: 245). But it was precisely this scientific rationalism that led to the recasting of corporeal deviations as pathologies, rather than "wondrous" deviations from the norm that could be variously interpreted, and that eventually made the propriety of the freak show questionable. This new paradigm that began to emerge in the late nineteenth century implied that freaks were in fact afflicted with medical conditions and intimated that it was inappropriate to stare at those who were sick or diseased and thus presumed to be suffering. This positioning in turn enhanced the medical profession's ability to gain greater access to atypical bodies. A showman interviewed in 1910 maintained that since the public demand for freaks had waned in the early twentieth century, the only way for freaks to support themselves financially was "with the doctors." In an article sensationally titled "Doctors Buy Freaks," he maintained that "nowadays people don't seem to care about looking at monstrosities," and thus "it seems to me that the only way for a freak to earn a living now is ... by selling yourself to the medical profession, in order that they may study your deformity" (1910: 7).

The turn of the century, with its increasing emphasis on medicalization, thus marked the end of the heyday of the freak show; the "revolt of the freaks" in 1899 was a symptom of this decline. But it was the First World War that seems finally to have rendered displays of deformity unseemly and inappropriate (Fahy 2000: 529). Although the public did not immediately reject armless and legless entertainers, these types of exhibitions became less common as communities across the world struggled to incorporate large numbers of war-wounded back into families, workplaces, and society more generally. Indeed, by the end of the First World War, those with disfigured bodies could no longer be comfortably "othered," for they were undeniably sons, fathers, husbands, brothers, fellow citizens, and national heroes.

It is precisely because the emergence of a visible community of disabled men restructured social attitudes to the atypical body for the generations that followed that it is easy today to dismiss freak shows as prurient, exploitative, and degrading. That some displays did inspire pity, disgust, and contempt and served to enhance a range of social and racial hierarchies is indisputable. It is equally true that some performers did not—or were unable to—give informed consent to their exhibition. They may thus have been exploited for profit, though so too were a range of other nineteenth-century workers with little social capital—the poor, women, children, immigrants, racial and ethnic minorities—who were also economically vulnerable. But in their heyday, freak shows' audiences were often encouraged to admire, not abjure, these marvelous bodies, and to be educated, edified, and amazed by their interactive performances, rather than merely to gawk at or denigrate their physical difference. There is ample evidence that spectators respected freak performers and in doing so made the acts respectable entertainment. Throughout the nineteenth century, many freaks were treated as celebrities: the public purchased and collected their photographs, invited them into their homes, wrote them love letters, sought to interact with and engage them in surprisingly intimate ways, and eagerly consumed press coverage of their private lives and public appearances. Thus, if we can set our own moral framework aside, the freak show can be properly historicized as an institution that served a social purpose for those with atypical bodies and, in the process, did profound cultural work.

On a practical level, it provided many who did not wish to become dependent on charity or the state, and did not have families that could afford to support them, a respectable and often lucrative form of employment that was not necessarily always experienced as degrading. Of equal importance, in an age that witnessed the growth of institutions for "defectives," the freak show ensured that those who were clearly not "the ordinary or regulation human being" nevertheless remained socially visible and culturally relevant at a time when scientific medicine increasingly sought to pathologize and to segregate the "abnormal." Nineteenth-century freak shows, as spaces of resistance to what Leslie Fiedler has called "the tyranny of the normal" (1996), are thus part of a longer, though decidedly uneven, history of the making of diverse societies.

CHAPTER TWO

Mobility Impairment

From the Bath Chair to the Wheelchair

KAREN BOURRIER

One of Anthony Trollope's most memorable characters in *Barchester Towers* is Signora Madeline Neroni, a seductress with a mysterious mobility impairment. Madeline is a woman of "surpassing beauty," who is rumored to have been a victim of domestic abuse at the hands of her cruel husband, Signor Neroni, from whom she is separated ([1857] 1996: 74). She claims to have fallen in ascending a ruin and to have "injured the sinews of her knee" so fatally that she has lost "eight inches of her height"; when she tries to move, she can "only drag herself painfully along, with protruded hip and extended foot in a manner less graceful than that of a hunchback" ([1857] 1996: 75). But the reader never witnesses Madeline walking. Following her accident, she makes up her mind, "once and for ever, that she would never stand and never attempt to move herself" ([1857] 1996: 79). When her family returns from Italy to the sleepy cathedral town of Barchester, she is determined to amuse herself by making a conquest of all the neighboring clergymen without ever leaving her sofa.

Madeline Neroni is a striking and unusual example of mobility impairment in the nineteenth-century novel. For twenty-first-century readers, Trollope's representation of her disability weaves together issues of gender and sexuality, assistive technology, and even race. Indeed, the reception of Madeline's disability in Barchester society almost seems more important than the exact nature of the impairment itself. Although Trollope attributes her mobility impairment to an injury to the sinews of her knee, for most of Barchester's inhabitants, the cause and nature of her impairment is never quite clear. The bishop's daughters discuss the new arrival with much anticipation. The youngest daughter claims that she "has got no legs," only to be quickly corrected by her older sister, who claims, "She has got legs, but she can't use them" ([1857] 1996: 89). Far from being above this type of speculation about Madeline's body, the bishop himself is "dying with curiosity about the mysterious lady and her legs" ([1857] 1996: 89). The curiosity aroused by Madeline's disability is never quite satisfied.

Much more important to the townsfolk of Barchester than the medical nature of Madeline Neroni's impairment is the social nature of her disability. The hidden mobility impairment that marks the lower half of her body seems in some ways indicative of her aberrant sexuality: no modest daughter of a clergyman should be eloping with strange Italian men or carrying on flirtations with half of the men in town. Madeline manages and stages her disability quite carefully: she dresses herself with special care, even going so far as to find out whether she will be seated on a right- or left-hand sofa so as to wear her bracelets on the correct arm ([1857] 1996: 92). We are clearly to understand that she means to make a spectacular entrance into the bishop's palace by being carried "head foremost" by her brother, "an Italian man-servant," as well as a "lady's maid and the lady's Italian page" ([1857] 1996: 91). Her disability is also a marker of her foreignness and the foreign sexual relationship that resulted in her impairment. Indeed, her self-presentation draws on the exoticism of her time in Italy. Madeline Neroni (née Stanhope) is English, and her employment of "three Italian servants" to assist her movement is meant to attract notice; though the servants might not be "peculiar" in Italy, they are "very much so" in Barchester ([1857] 1996: 92). Seated on a sofa at the bishop's palace, "in white velvet" and "rich white lace," with her body and feet concealed underneath "a crimson silk mantle or shawl," Madeline's disabled body, as Suzanne Rintoul points out, is at once "highly visible yet obfuscated"; she is both on display and concealed (2011). The inhabitants of Barchester interpret Madeline Neroni's mysterious disability through a number of lenses: for them, her sexuality, foreignness, and femininity are intertwined with her disability from the first. None of these interpretations follows inherently from the mobility impairment itself; instead, they are part of the complex interaction between disability and society.

In this chapter, I consider the social construction of mobility and immobility in the long nineteenth century, a time in which people with mobility impairments became increasingly visible. I begin by looking at the development of assistive technology. In the second half of the nineteenth century, the device that was to become a visual symbol of all disabilities (the wheelchair) was developed in its modern form, alongside increasingly sophisticated prostheses, crutches, and canes, and the last of which were used by the disabled and the able-bodied alike. Indeed, the use of assistive technology by both able-bodied and disabled people leads me to explore the way that ideas about walking and deportment depended on immobility and disability in the nineteenth century. Male amputees, who appeared in greater numbers due to industrial accidents and the US Civil War, and who had a greater chance of surviving due to the development of antisepsis, were a particularly visible social group. Their visible presence called for new developments in prosthetics. While disabilities that were the result of work or war seemed to be a collective, social issue in the nineteenth century, congenital disabilities, such as a clubfoot, were understood as a source of individual pain and sorrow. Yet some writers who experienced mobility impairment, including Walter Scott and Harriet Martineau, lauded the benefits of the enforced immobility of invalidism, which could allow time for observation and reflection. Paradoxically, immobility could also allow for greater opportunities to travel. Technologies such as train travel increased everyone's mobility in the nineteenth century, including that of some people with disabilities; I end this chapter with a consideration of invalids who traveled in search of health.

Throughout this chapter, I tend to use modern terms such as "mobility impairment" and "assistive technology"; these terms were not used in the nineteenth century. Instead, people referred to those with mobility impairments as "crippled" or "lame." Some disability studies scholars, including Nancy Mairs and Robert McRuer, have attempted to reclaim the term "cripple" in particular (Mairs 1986, McRuer 2006), but, as will become apparent in the course of this chapter, these terms can retain pejorative connotations from the nineteenth century: a person who was crippled was perceived to be damaged or less than whole in some sense. There was also a gendered dimension to terminology. For example, a female "cripple" might be associated with damaged and deviant sexuality, as we see in the case of Signora Neroni, and there was a greater imperative for female amputees to disguise their physical difference (Sweet 2017). Yet a mobility impairment might be seen as more congruent with nineteenth-century ideals of femininity than with those of masculinity: all women, on the whole, had less mobility than their male counterparts. By contrast, a mobility impairment, such as an amputated leg, was in tension with a hearty, hale, and–above all–mobile masculinity. I argue, however, that as the century progressed, developments in assistive technology gradually shifted the understanding of these impairments to one of increased mobility, particularly for men with the wealth and leisure to travel.

2.1. ASSISTIVE TECHNOLOGY

One of the most important facets of the lived experience of mobility impairment in the nineteenth century was the rise of assistive technology. When the actress, author, and former royal mistress Mary Robinson began to lose the use of her lower limbs in the 1780s, she had to rely on servants to lift and carry her from place to place (Brewer 2016: 108). Robinson provides us with a case study of the lived experience of paralysis of the lower limbs at the turn of the century. Some of her contemporaries readily made a connection between her former life as a courtesan and her progressive paralysis, speculating variously that the cause of her disability was a venereal disease, a miscarriage, or an abortion followed by an infection. There was no medical evidence to back up any of these claims; for these observers, the cause of Robinson's impairment was "moral rather than medical" (Brewer 2016: 110). In contrast to these readings of Robinson's paralysis as divine punishment, Robinson's memoirs present her progressive paralysis as the motivation for her "astoundingly productive literary career" (Brewer 2016: 108). William D. Brewer argues that Robinson herself understood "disability as a social construction"; as long as her financial resources permitted her to hire the caregivers who would facilitate her social life, her writing, and her travel around London, she considered herself able bodied (2016: 107).

By the mid-nineteenth century, though the fictional Madeline Neroni refuses to avail herself of them, additional technologies of mobility had developed, including the bath chair, a precursor to the modern wheelchair. Madeline's insistence upon being carried by three Italian servants harkens back to an older technology of mobility, the sedan chair. A sedan was a covered chair with room for one passenger; it was carried on poles by two chairmen. Such chairs were used to cover relatively short distances in urban locations, allowing the well-to-do to hire a sedan chair to avoid London's dirty streets and inclement weather. Indeed, since sedan chairs were narrow enough to fit through most doors, the passenger could be carried straight from one house to another without ever setting foot outside (Garry 2016: 47). Sedan chairs were imported to England beginning in the 1630s from Italy. They were used by able-bodied and disabled people alike, and there was some public outcry by those who considered it "shockingly offensive to employ [one's] fellow countrymen as beasts of burden" (Garry 2016: 46). The public overcame their shock, and sedan chairs reached their heyday in the mid-eighteenth century; by the late eighteenth century, however, London's urban sprawl (which now included Chelsea, Islington, and Paddington) made transport via sedan chair impracticable (Garry 2016: 60). It is not entirely clear whether Madeline Neroni is in a type of sedan chair or litter when she enters the bishop's house, but it does seem much more likely that this is the case than that the Italian manservant is carrying her directly. In either scenario, Madeline's insistence upon being carried aligns her with the well-to-do sedan chair users of the eighteenth century.

In contrast to the sedan chair, the bath chair had three wheels and required only one man to push it. Named for the spa town to which invalids flocked, bath chairs were seen as "purely invalid vehicles"; they were appropriate for those for whom illness, age, or physical impairments made walking difficult, but not for the able-bodied (Fawcett 1998: 126). The first wheelchairs began to appear in Bath at the end of the eighteenth century (Fawcett 1998: 126). In fact, the credit for the first modern wheelchair generally goes to John Dawson of Bath, who styled himself a "Wheel-chair maker" as early as 1798. Bath chairs were outdoor vehicles with two wheels in the back and a smaller wheel in front. They were pushed by one attendant rather than two, and the passenger could direct the chair with a steering handle. In a nod to the invalid status of the passengers, there was a canvas hood to protect one from the weather and a "hinged flap" to protect the passenger's legs (Kamenetz 1969: 209).

Indoor vehicles that could be self-propelled quickly followed the outdoor bath chair. As Kamenetz notes, the increased use of a midline swiveling wheel "led to the construction of chairs with wheels large enough to be turned directly by the seated person, without any intervening chains, cranks, or other devices" (1969: 209). While such self-propelling chairs were pictured as early as 1766, they came into greater use throughout the nineteenth century (Kamenetz 1969: 209–10). In 1791, Fanny Burney was amazed to see her friend, Lady Ducannon, who was partially paralyzed, use a self-propelling chair to move herself across the room (Fawcett 1988: 126). While outdoor bath chairs were made of iron, throughout the early nineteenth century, self-propelling wheelchairs were made of lighter wood or wicker, including the wheels. In the last twenty-five years of the nineteenth century, wheelchair manufacturers replaced these wooden wheels with the wire-spoked rubber wheels used on the new bicycles (Kamenetz 1969: 209–10). In fact, these wheelchair makers bought their tires directly from bicycle manufacturers. According to Kamenetz, the bicycle craze actually coincided with an increased use of wheelchairs (1969: 210).

Although bath chairs used one man instead of two to propel the passenger and self-propelling wheelchairs used the strength of the chair user him or herself, some of the more negative connotations of employing one's fellow men to aid in transportation remained in nineteenth-century depictions of wheelchair users. Jennifer Janechek alerts us to Dickens' negative portrayal of Mrs. Skewton, Edith Dombey's mother, in *Dombey and Son*. While most bath-chair users had some physical impairment, Dickens tells us that there is "nothing whatever, except the attitude" to prevent Mrs. Skewton from walking (Dickens 2001: 306). A page aptly called Withers pushes Mrs. Skewton in her chair. Dickens repeatedly compares Withers to a beast of burden, recalling the sedan chairman; he is a battering ram or an elephant (Janechek 2015: 153). The connotation seems to be that both characters become withered through their association with the chair. As Janechek argues, "Withers is engulfed by the chair, and Mrs. Skewton decays within the chair, eroding into the various objects that comprise her mostly artificial self" (2015: 154). In *Bleak House*, Grandfather Smallweed, who has lost the use of his lower limbs, travels with the aid of an anachronistic sedan chair. Despite his need for assisted transportation, Dickens characterizes him as a "broken puppet" or "a mere clothes-bag with a black skull-cap on the top of it" (Dickens 1998a: 309). Janechek argues that the fact that the "lame but quite mobile" Phil Squod "manages to carry Mr. Smallweed despite his impediments" might lead us to stigmatize Grandfather Smallweed, who uses other people both economically, as he cheats them out of their money, and as a mode of transport around town (Janechek 2015: 157). By contrast, for Dickens, Phil's insistence on walking, even if it means "hobbling with a couple of sticks!" (Dickens 1998a: 388), renders him "morally superior to those like Mr. Smallweed, who cast their burden on others to carry him" (Janechek 2015: 157).

The sight of wheelchair users could also make the able-bodied feel uncomfortable. Margaret Oliphant recollects what it was like to meet fellow novelist, Frank Smedley (1818–64), who had suffered an illness in infancy that restricted his growth, left his spine malformed, and made him unable to walk. He wore a steel undercoat and used a self-propelled wheelchair (Mitchell 2011). In her memoir, which was not intended for publication, Oliphant wrote that Smedley was "a terrible cripple, supposed to be kept together by some framework of springs and supports" (2002: 80). Oliphant calls Smedley "an extraordinary being" with "an imperfect face (as if it had somehow been left unfinished in the making)" (80). Her comments portray Smedley as an incompletely manufactured industrial product. He, rather than his wheelchair, is "kept together" by mechanical "springs and supports." She admits that "the appearance of this poor man somewhat frightened me," and she finds an incongruity between his physical appearance and his chosen subject as a novelist, sporting novels "full of feats of athletic strength and horsemanship" (80). We do not have Smedley's side of this encounter.[1]

A more positive representation of a wheelchair user might be Mr. Omer in *David Copperfield*. Unlike Grandfather Smallweed, Omer reframes his invalidism as a contemplative state and does not rely on those below him in the class scale for his mobility. Omer has lost the use of his limbs, and he now lives on the ground-level floor of his house with the parlor turned into a bedroom for him. He spends his days smoking and reading in his wheelchair, which, he says, "runs as light as a feather, and tracks as true as a mail-coach." The wheelchair seems to bring opportunities for his family and friends to care for him; in a humorous repetition of the animal tropes that characterize working-class labor in pushing wheelchairs, Omer's granddaughter, Minnie, is his "little elephant" who pushes her grandfather's chair with "marvellous" dexterity (Dickens 1998b: 676). As Omer describes his chair, it is so light that Minnie "puts her little strength against the back, gives it a shove, and away we go, as clever and merry as ever you see anything! And I tell you what—it's a most uncommon chair to smoke a pipe in" (Dickens 1998b: 674). Omer is "as radiant, as if his chair, his asthma, and the failure of his limbs, were the various branches of a great invention for enhancing the luxury of a pipe" (Dickens 1998b: 674). Omer proclaims that his lot would have been much more difficult if his sight or hearing had deteriorated rather than his limbs; he declares that "there's twice as much in the newspaper, since I've taken to this chair," and that he has become a great one for general reading (Dickens 1998b: 674). David seems surprised that a wheelchair user can be so content. He proclaims that Omer's "supreme contempt for his own limbs, as he sat smoking, was one of the pleasantest oddities I have ever encountered" (Dickens 1998b: 674).

The oddity of the sight of Omer in his wheeled chair—and Omer's pride in it—is enhanced by the fact that his wheelchair is a technical marvel. Indeed, commercial purveyors developed wheelchair technology throughout the nineteenth century. An 1856 advertisement in the prestigious London medical journal *The Lancet*, "Comfort for Invalids" (see Figure 2.1), demonstrates the extent to which stationary and wheeled chairs became commodities in the mid-nineteenth century. The manufacturer, J. Alderman

FIGURE 2.1 "Comfort For Invalids" advice page. The Lancet General Advertiser, 1856.

of Soho, London, was pleased to announce that, "after many years' experience in the manufacture of all kinds of Invalid Beds, Couches, Chairs, Carriages, &c," he had received Her Majesty's Letter Patent for "imperceptibly Graduating, Mechanical, and Elastic Adjustments, which he has invented for the comfort and convenience of Invalids; he has also made them applicable to all kinds of Operating Couches and Chairs, for surgical and dental purposes" (1856: 330). The fact that Alderman obtained a patent for his graduating couches and chairs suggests that there was a lucrative market in these articles. The advertisement shows a dizzying array of chairs and couches for use at home or in hospital. There are chairs that can be "self-adjusted" by the invalid, chairs that can be carried up and down the stairs without disturbing the occupant or straining the muscles of those carrying the chair, and a self-propelling chair that makes the invalid "quite independent, being able to go from room to room without any assistance" (1856: 330). Nor is there a shortage of ailments that Alderman imagines might require the use of this "invalid furniture." He recommends it for "Spinal Affections [sic], Hip Complaints, Paralysis, Fractures, and in all cases where perfect rest is required" (1856: 330). He also specifically recommends it to heavily pregnant and postpartum women, who, requiring "complete rest before and after their Confinements, will find this Couch a great luxury" (1856: 330). The number of people with both temporary and long-term mobility impairments that Alderman imagines might benefit from the use of his invalid furniture is a testament to the insight in contemporary disability studies that we are all temporarily able-bodied, and may find ourselves in need of assistance with mobility through a variety of circumstances.[2]

Not all mobility aids in the nineteenth century were associated with disability. The case of the cane is similar to that of the sedan chair in this respect. While today we are likely to see a cane, along with a walker or a wheelchair, as a universal sign of a mobility impairment, in the nineteenth century, walking sticks and canes were widely used by the able-bodied and the disabled alike. Stylized walking sticks or canes made of luxurious materials such as ivory with decorative and sometimes even jeweled knob handles were the descendants of the sturdier staff; these canes were meant for urban perambulations, and, according to Joseph Amato, were as much a fashion accessory as a mobility aid, though those with gout or arthritis still used them as well (2004: 89). There was a gendered dimension to the use of walking sticks and canes in the city, as women may have been more likely to use their umbrella or parasol (or a gentleman's arm) to lean on in their peregrinations (Amato 2004: 89).

2.2. WALKING

The fluidity of assistive technology, wherein some aids, like the wheelchair, came to be associated with disability in the nineteenth century, while some, like the cane, did not gain an association with disability until the twentieth century, leads us to reconsider the socially constructed nature of walking itself. Walking and mobility are central themes of Romantic poetry. Yet the speakers of Romantic poems are often confronted with immobility and stasis. In William Wordsworth's poem "Resolution and Independence," the speaker comes upon a leech-gatherer on the moor, "his body bent double feet and head / Coming together in life's pilgrimage" as if in immense pain (1807: 66–7). The leech-gatherer props himself "limbs, body, and pale face, / Upon a long grey staff of shaven wood" (1807: 71–2). His difficulty with mobility as he roams from "pond to pond" and "moor to moor" (1807: 103) making a precarious living gathering leeches

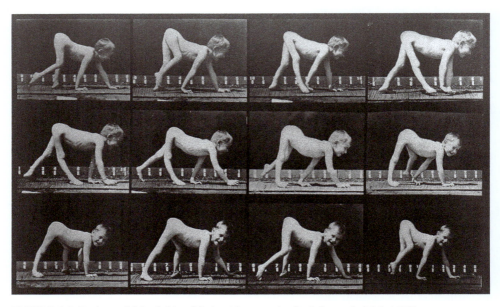

FIGURE 2.2 Eadweard Muybridge "Animal locomotion"; deformed child. 1887.

stands in contrast with the easy mobility of the speaker, who announces, "I was a Traveller then upon the moor" (1807: 15). In Samuel Taylor Coleridge's conversation poem "This Lime Tree-Bower my Prison," the speaker contrasts his immobility with the freedom of mobility of his friends, who "Wander in gladness" on "springy heath" and "along the hill-top edge," while he nurses his injured foot (1800: 8, 7). The speaker laments his temporary immobility at the beginning of the poem: "Well, they are gone, and here must I remain, / This lime-tree bower my prison," imagining that he has lost "Beauties and feelings, such as would have been / Most sweet to my remembrance even when age / Had dimm'd mine eyes to blindness!" (1800: 1–4). In these lines, the speaker imagines that the remembered pleasures of mobility would have compensated him in future times for the impairment of his vision in old age. Mobility is central to the poets' identities in these poems, yet it is constantly coming under threat.

Mobility itself became an object of scientific and artistic study in the nineteenth century. Toward the end of the century, the American photographer Eadweard Muybridge photographed several people with mobility impairments in his eleven-volume collection, *Animal Locomotion: An Electro-Photographic Investigation of Consecutive Phases of Animal Movement*. Muybridge had been commissioned to undertake a scientific study of the movements of animals through photography, and he began his work at the University of Pennsylvania in 1884 (Braun 2012: 182). The images in the final collection followed a strict hierarchy: the first subjects to appear in the volume are men, followed by women and children. Those with mobility impairments appear after children and before domestic and wild animals. The implication is clear; as Keren Hammerschlag (n.d.) notes, those with disabilities rank lower than those with "healthy" bodies, regardless of gender or age, and just above animals. Hammerschlag notes that "Figures were photographed without clothes, allowing for the unobstructed scrutiny of their bodies, and in front of grids, which invited viewers to treat the pictures as scientific studies." Two of Muybridge's photographs feature amputees. Plate 537, "An Amputee on Crutches," shows a man with an amputation at the ankle walking from the front, side, and back. The next plate, 538, shows a double amputee who has lost both of his legs walking on his hands and climbing on and off a chair. Interestingly, a young woman with cerebrospinal sclerosis is shown walking with the aid of a nurse rather than assistive technology. Plate 539, "Deformed Child Walking on Arms and Legs" (see Figure 2.2), shows a young boy in profile. Perhaps in contrast to the serious scientific mood of Muybridge's study, the boy appears quite pleased with himself, as he turns to smile at the camera in the last five frames. All of the figures are shown nude, with the exception of the nurse who helps the young woman move, a factor that contributes to their portrayal as objects of scientific study.

2.3. AMPUTEES AND PROSTHETICS

Amputees who had lost one or both legs, typically through war or industrial accident, were a striking reminder of the fragility of the body. A combination of factors increased the visibility of amputees—and the demand for prosthetics—in the second half of the nineteenth century. As Erin O'Connor notes, the mortality rate for amputations was high throughout the period, from 75 percent of amputations at the hip to around 25 percent of those done at the ankle (2000: 106). Nonetheless, the development of anesthesia and antisepsis at mid-century improved the outcomes of amputation. Veterans of the American Civil War were particularly visible amputees, with an estimated 15,000 American men who had lost a limb still living in 1871 (O'Connor 2000: 106). Increasing numbers of people also survived industrial accidents, meaning that "amputation became an increasingly visible phenomenon as the century progressed" (O'Connor 2000: 106).

The loss of limbs in the Civil War and, on the other side of the Atlantic, in the Crimea, as well as the prevalence of industrial accidents, meant that amputees were predominantly male. As O'Connor notes, the vast majority of amputations done in Britain and America were performed on injured soldiers and industrial workers (2000: 104). This was problematic since, as O'Connor reminds us, "Victorian ideals of health, particularly male health, centered on the concept of physical wholeness," which meant that amputation could be seen as unmanning or feminizing male amputees (2000: 104). At the same time, technologically sophisticated prosthetics seemed to offer a solution to the problems created by war and industrial accident: "Fixed up nearly as good as new by the same system that crippled him, the prosthetic man became a symbol of all that was possible in the modern world of manufacture, a walking advertisement for the personal and social benefits to be had from a full-scale embrace of machine culture" (O'Connor 2000: 134). Given this demand, prosthetics became increasingly sophisticated throughout the nineteenth century. The first modern artificial limbs were displayed in London at the Crystal Palace in the Great Exhibition of 1851 (O'Connor 2000: 105). While previous bearers of prosthetic limbs were limited to legs made of wood or cork, the limbs made in the latter half of the nineteenth century used "custom-fitted wood-and-wax sockets, ball-bearing joints, and self-correcting suspenders" (O'Connor 2000: 134–5). Above all, the manufacture of rubber feet on prosthetic legs, patented by A. A. Marks, "silenced the tell-tale squeaking of the wooden leg" (O'Connor 2000: 136).

Although state-of-the-art prosthetics were increasingly available, perhaps the most common prosthetic available in the nineteenth century was the peg leg. As Ryan Sweet notes, these were the "cheapest and most basic devices" on the market, and had been available for several centuries (Sweet 2015). The amputee's stump was fitted into a wooden bucket, which was fixed to a peg leg that would reach the ground. Slightly more expensive models might include a knee joint that would allow the peg to bend while the user was sitting down, or a leather sheath that would make the bucket more comfortable (Sweet 2015). Sweet notes that peg legs were commonly used by the working class and street beggars, so that Dickens' Silas Wegg, the owner of a street stall, would have been a typical user. Wegg's peg leg is associated with negative stereotypes and marks him as a villain for Dickens. Sweet argues that Wegg's peg leg speaks to cultural anxieties that artificial parts would make the whole man artificial, or in Wegg's case, wooden (2015). Dickens' Silas Wegg's use of a rudimentary wooden leg seems to have made him a wooden man himself:

> Wegg was a knotty man, and a close-grained, with a face carved out of very hard material, that had just as much play of expression as a watchman's rattle. When he laughed, certain jerks occurred in it, and the rattle sprung. Sooth to say, he was so wooden a man that he seemed to have taken his wooden leg naturally, and rather suggested to the fanciful observer, that he might be expected—if his development received no untimely check—to be completely set up with a pair of wooden legs in about six months. (Dickens 1998b: 45–6)

Dickens' portrayal of Wegg's wooden leg testifies to the nineteenth-century anxiety over whether artificial parts might dehumanize men. Herbert Sussman and Gerhard Joseph suggest that Dickens' portrayals of prosthetics usually insist "upon a humanist primacy of the natural over the artificial" (2004: 619).

The journalist Henry Mayhew gives us several portraits of the lives of those with mobility impairments, including amputees, in *London Labour and the London Poor*. First published as a series of articles in *The Morning Chronicle* and later collected and published in three volumes in 1851, *London Labour and the London Poor* gives an account of the lives of people working in the streets in mid-nineteenth-century London. Many of the men and women that Mayhew interviewed for these articles were on the streets because they were disabled. Martha Stoddard Holmes argues that part of Mayhew's aim in his journalism is to distinguish between the "deserving poor" and the figure she calls the "begging impostor," the "disabled person whose economic resilience was the product of corruption and whose bodily condition did not signify complete and utter incapacity" (2004: 100). In other words, Mayhew took it as his job to distinguish between those people with disabilities that were severe enough to merit sympathy (and alms) and those who were exaggerating their incapacities. Mayhew, according to Holmes, is "fiercely concerned with distinguishing the innocent from the guilty, a distinction he often characterizes as that between those who are forced to take to the streets or even to beg, and those who by disposition or breeding simply hate to work and love to rove" (2004: 124).

Mayhew gives several striking examples of mobility impairment in his sketches of street life in London. One example of a man whom Mayhew thinks deserving of our compassion is the "Crippled Street Seller of Nutmeg Graters." Significantly, the Seller of Nutmeg Graters has a congenital disability, which, for Mayhew and his readers, may remove all culpability from him. Mayhew gives him as an example of someone who is "driven to the streets by utter inability to labour," yet who still attempts to earn his living by selling his wares. Mayhew assures his readers that he has "every title to our assistance" and is a "noble example" of a man driven to the streets (2009: 110). Mayhew frames his interview with this worthy man in melodramatic terms to gain the reader's sympathy: "The poor creature's legs and arms are completely withered; indeed he is scarcely more than head and trunk. His thigh is hardly thicker than a child's wrist" (2009: 111). Mayhew's comparison of the proportions of the street-seller of nutmeg graters to that of a child is certainly telling, as is his assertion that his "countenance is rather handsome than otherwise" (2009: 111). Mayhew gives the reader specific details of the man's domestic life and his need for assistance. He cannot dress and undress himself, and so is obliged to pay someone to do it for him out of his meager wages. When it rains, he is truly immobilized, as he tells Mayhew, "it *is* very miserable indeed lying in bed all day" (2009: 111, emphasis in original). The street-seller's misery at being incapacitated, as well as his willingness to go without dinner if he does not earn it, can be taken as signs of his deserving nature. The street-seller of nutmeg graters gives a graphic description of the immense pain it costs him to go even a short distance to sell his wares. As he tells Mayhew:

> I can't walk no distance. I suffer a great deal of pains in my back and knees. Sometimes I go in a barrow, when I'm travelling any great way. When I go only a short way I crawl along on my knees and toes. The most I've ever crawled is two miles. When I get home afterwards, I'm in great pain. My knees swell dreadfully, and they're all covered with blisters, and my toes ache awful … Often after I've been walking, my limbs and back ache so badly that I can get no sleep … When I go up-stairs I have to crawl upon the back of my hands and knees. (2009: 112)

The street-seller is immobilized to the extent that he cannot feed himself well, but is "obliged to have things held to my lips for me to drink, like a child" (2009: 112). The pain that movement costs the street-seller seems, for Mayhew, to be an indication of his earnestness and his need. Surely a person who would go to such extreme lengths to move and try to earn an honest living is deserving of our sympathy and our alms, Mayhew's portraits seems to say.

Mayhew does not hold everyone up as such an exemplar. In fact, it seems that the more the disabled person has to say on his own behalf, the less likely he is to be held up as an example of the deserving poor. Race may also play a part in this distrust, as becomes apparent in Mayhew's interview with a Jamaican man who is a double amputee. Edward Albert, whom Mayhew titles "The Negro Crossing-Sweeper, who had lost both his Legs," does not consider himself as foreign since he was born in Kingston, Jamaica, which was a British colony until 1962. The crossing-sweeper is a strong advocate for his own rights, but Mayhew is unsure of the entire truth of his story (although he does believe that there is some truth in it) (2009: 210). Albert tells his own story in a leaflet that he has had printed and a placard that hangs around his neck; he was a cook on board a ship crossing from Glasgow to California and on to China. He gives a graphic description of the circumstances that led to his amputation. When his legs became frostbitten as the vessel "rounded Cape Horne," he became unfit for duty. To try and cure his frostbite, the master of the vessel took him to the ship's oven, which was very hot, and took out a fowl to make room to warm his feet. As Albert explains, "in consequence of the treatment, my feet burst through the intense swelling, and mortification ensued" (2009: 211). He was hospitalized at Valpariso for five and a half months, and both legs were amputated three inches below the knee. The captain told him he was a dead man and denied him his wages. Albert made his way back to London, where he began work as a crossing-sweeper. He describes the staggering pain it costs him to get to his crossing in pragmatic terms. He only sweeps when "the weather is cold enough to let him walk; the colder the better, as he says, as it 'numbs his stumps like'" (2009: 209). Although this is hard, as he tells Mayhew, "The loss of my limbs is bad enough, but it's still worse when you can't get what is your rights, nor anything for the sweat that they worked out of me" (2009: 212). Albert's insistence on his rights is unusual in the Victorian discourse around disability. The Victorians were much more likely to view a mobility impairment in the melodramatic terms of sympathy and pity rather than the framework of inherent rights that Albert discusses.

Perhaps one of the most extraordinary street performers that Mayhew interviews is an Italian soldier who lost his leg in the first Italian War of Independence. He is now on the streets of London, where he works as a street exhibitor, performing an entire military charge for curious passersby. He plays all of the parts on one leg, from the drummers and the soldiers to the captains and the general, with great enthusiasm and vigor. He uses a crutch rather than a prosthetic leg, and this mobility aid becomes part of the performance as a pretend gun. He calls out, "PORTEZ AR-R-RMES!" then, "I hold the gun—my crutch, you know—in front of me, straight up. The next is 'Repose AR-R-RMES!' and I put it to my hip, with the barrel leaning forwards. When I say, barrel, it's only my crutch, you understand" (Mayhew 2009: 270). The street exhibitor performs his masculinity with great vigor. Although he concedes that it hurts his voice to call out the commands, and that he has developed a tumor under his arm from using his crutch, he proudly proclaims, "It does not fatigue me to hop about on one leg. It is strong as iron. It is never fatigued. I have walked miles on it with my crutch" (Mayhew 2009: 272). The Italian soldier proudly demonstrates his strength, agility, and balance in his daily performance of a military charge. Far from making an effort to conceal his disability or pass as able-bodied, for him, his crutch and his one strong leg are all part of the performance of his injured but vigorous masculinity.

Others made an effort to conceal their disabilities, aided by the new prosthetics on the market in the second half of the nineteenth century. Recent research suggests that the ability to pass as able-bodied may have been especially important for female amputees. Sweet argues that, throughout the nineteenth century, "incomplete" women, were "pressured into and provided advice [on] how to 'pass' by commercially resonant literary texts" (2017: 116). These stories provided women with "specific guidance on devices to avoid—noisy and showy devices—buttressing the necessity for female prostheses to be unnoticeable" (Sweet 2017: 117). This perceived need for invisibility may have been driven by the hope that a missing limb would not hamper a woman on the marriage market. Indeed, many of the stories and poems published about female users of prosthetic devices involve a marriage plot. As Sweet demonstrates, though "the historical figures we associate with artificial body parts" are for the most part men, including "pirates, veterans and maimed industrial workers," women made up an important segment of the market and may have made different aesthetic demands of their prosthetic limbs (2017: 115).

Vanessa Warne and Ryan Sweet complicate the association of prosthetics with working-class men in their work on female amputees. Although working-class men injured in war or industrial accident formed the largest market for prosthetic legs, in her reading of Thomas Hood's comic poem, "Miss Kilmansegg and her Golden Leg," Warne shifts the critical focus "away from working class men and toward wealthy female amputees" (2009: 83). When the wealthy heiress, Miss Kilmansegg, loses her leg in a riding accident, she begs her parents to buy her a golden prosthesis, which she proceeds to flaunt in society. She gets her comeuppance when she marries an adventurer, an Italian count, who kills her using her own golden leg, leading to what Warne terms the rather heavy-handed moral of Hood's poem, "the love of gold costs Miss Kilmansegg both life and limb" (2009: 89). Although the poem is far from a positive presentation of a woman with a mobility impairment, as Warne points out, Hood does at least complicate "the conventional association of disability with dependency, challenging images of amputees as street beggars and identifying disability with financial power" (2009: 94).

Amputee George Craik, husband of the novelist Dinah Craik, lost one of his legs in a railway accident in 1861. His story, and his future wife's reaction to it, gives us some idea of the lived experience of amputation for those with greater financial resources. After one of the wheels broke on an unoccupied first-class carriage, Craik's carriage was dragged for quite some time on the tracks before the engine driver could stop it. He sustained a compound fracture so serious that his leg had to be amputated. The novelist framed her future husband's convalescence as a kind of overcoming narrative for friends and family; with a stalwart character and optimism combining to help him through this time of adversity. She wrote to her brother that she was impressed with his cheerfulness under difficulties. Describing a visit they paid to an art exhibit, she wrote:

> George managed to get in & out with his crutches & enjoyed it as much as any of us.—It is strange what a wonderful fund of happiness lies at the bottom of the saddest trouble—George keeps us all merry with his unfailing brightness & cheerfulness.—helpless as he still is.—& suffer as he must in many ways for the rest of his life. (1861)

As time wore on, she became more and more impressed with George's character. She wrote to Ben several months later, "his leg is still unhealed & he goes upon crutches & the railway have refused him all compensation, but he bears all as brave & firm as a rock" (n.d.). George Craik used, at a various points, a wheelchair, crutches, and a prosthetic leg, but the most important aspect of his disability for his future wife seemed to be the opportunity it gave him to showcase the strength of his character, and perhaps also for the pair to get to know one another in the sacred space of the sickroom.[3] In her recent work on marriage in the Victorian novel, Talia Schaffer has suggested that, in the nineteenth-century novel, a marriage to a man with a disability could provide the heroine with an opportunity to become familiar with her suitor (and even his body) before marriage, as she joined an enriching circle of caregivers (2016: 170). For Dinah and George Craik, this was true in real life as well.

Indeed, mobility impairments could sometimes give welcome opportunities for greater physical contact between friends and lovers. Dinah Craik portrays one such relationship in her bestselling novel, *John Halifax, Gentleman* ([1856] 2005). The narrator of the novel, Phineas Fletcher, is a chronic invalid whose unspecified illness makes it difficult at times for him to walk. At various points in the novel, Phineas uses what he describes as an easy chair with wheels ([1856] 2005: 136), crutches, and a "little hand-carriage," which he can propel himself with "a little external aid" ([1856] 2005: 31, 32). But he seems happiest when his strong friend, John, carries him. Phineas describes this intimate contact at one of their first meetings:

> "Suppose you let me carry you. I could—and—and it would be great fun, you know."
>
>   He tried to turn it into a jest, so as not to hurt me; but the tremble in his voice was as tender as any woman's—tenderer than any woman's I ever was used to hear. I put my arms round his neck; he lifted me safely and carefully, and set me at my own door. ([1856] 2005: 43)

John carries his friend throughout the first third of the novel, culminating in a scene where the two have been out to the theater (which is against Phineas' father's religion as a Quaker) and been pickpocketed, and John carries him back the whole ten miles home on his back in consequence ([1856] 2005: 37–8).[4] This scene gives us an idea of the opportunities for intimacy afforded by mobility impairment, which could require not only assistive technologies, but also the aid of friends and family.

2.4. CONGENITAL MOBILITY IMPAIRMENTS

In contrast to mobility impairments caused by accidents or temporary invalidism, congenital mobility impairments may have been particularly associated with emotional susceptibility. This was not a natural association, but rather one that was built through cultural associations with orthopedic deformities. Indeed, in an earlier article, I note that, throughout the nineteenth century, it came to seem natural that "a physical deformity was a deeply individual mark that could cause as much psychological suffering as it did physical" (Bourrier 2014: 1). Two famous authors, Byron and Walter Scott, were born with clubfeet, and it was popularly supposed that this experience led them to be particularly emotionally susceptible. Walter Scott credited his lameness with his ability to observe and to write to some extent. Scott claimed, "My lameness and my solitary habits had made me a tolerable reader," and noted that he spent his weekdays reading aloud to his mother (Lockhart 1845: 8). Byron's reputation was not as positive. The orthopedic surgeon, William Adams, noted that it "has generally been supposed that the existence of congenital talipes varus exerted an unfavourable influence on the highly susceptible mind of Lord Byron" (quoted in Bourrier 2014: 7). In *Daniel Deronda*, George Eliot similarly compares her hero's illegitimate birth to Byron's "susceptibility about his deformed foot":

> The sense of an entailed disadvantage—the deformed foot doubtfully hidden by the shoe, makes a restlessly active spiritual yeast, and easily turns a self-centered, unloving nature into an Ishmaelite. But in the rarer sort, who presently see their own frustrated claim as one among a myriad, the inexorable sorrow takes the form of fellowship and makes the imagination tender. (Deronda 1998: 148–9)

Throughout the nineteenth century, then, orthopedic disabilities like clubfoot came to be seen as problems in need of a "cure," for the sake of both the physical and the mental health of the patient. That cure increasingly became a surgical one. In the nineteenth century, orthopedic medicine became a specialized branch of surgery. Early in the century, orthopedic disabilities such as a clubfoot would have been treated mechanically, without recourse to surgery. For example, Byron's clubfoot was treated mechanically, through massage, machines, and bandages; one doctor took to "rubbing the foot over, for a considerable time, with handfuls of oil, and then twisting the limb forcibly round, and screwing it up in a wooden machine" (quoted in Bourrier 2014: 5–6). By the middle of the century, however, a surgeon called R. W. Tamplin proclaimed that the treatment of "deformed patients" had been taken out of "the hands of the mechanists" and put into the hands of surgeons who promoted "the scientific treatment of deformities" (quoted in Bourrier 2014: 6). The Royal Orthopaedic Hospital of London, established in 1838 in Bloomsbury Square, had moved to Oxford Street by 1865 and treated more than 1,600 patients annually (Bourrier 2014: 6). Surgeons generally treated clubfoot through tenotomy, or the subcutaneous splitting of the affected muscles. Today, treatment for clubfoot in infants has shifted back to the mechanical method of stretching and casting (called the Ponseti method); tenotomy is reserved only for severe cases. Congenital impairments came to be associated with increased emotional susceptibility throughout the nineteenth century.

2.5. INVALIDISM AND MOBILITY

The forced immobility of invalidism could be seen as providing an opportunity for introspection and observation; when this immobility lead to moral improvement, it was associated with women. Nineteenth-century novels are filled with invalid characters who lay claim to greater powers of observation because their own lives are so quiet. Henry James' Ralph Touchett, who is dying from tuberculosis, asks his cousin, "What's the use of being ill and disabled and restricted to mere spectatorship at the game of life if I really can't see the show when I've paid so much for my ticket?" (James 2009: 157). For Ralph, the pleasures of observation serve as a fantasy of compensation for the pain of his invalidism. In Charlotte Mary Yonge's bestselling novel *The Daisy Chain*, the eldest sister of a family of eleven siblings is confined to the invalid's couch after a carriage accident. Margaret is left in a "helpless state," yet "her patience, and capabilities" are immense, and everyone in the family comes "to her with all their cares" (1977: 146). For those who observe her, Margaret serves as a lesson in moral courage and self-denial, qualities expected in Victorian women. As one character, who has been in danger of being spoiled by a wealthy father, remarks, "To see that church making Margaret happy as she lies smiling on her couch, is a lesson of lessons" (1977: 610). This type of character became so common in the mid-nineteenth century that one literary critic lamented the loss of "an angelic being with a weak spine, who, from her sofa, directed with mild wisdom the affairs of this family or the parish" when racier sensation fiction by the likes of Mary Elizabeth Braddon became more common (1866: 438). Sometimes, nineteenth-century authors used an accident or bout of illness resulting in a period of immobility and rest as a plot device to reform headstrong characters. The eponymous heroine of the American children's novel *What Katy Did* (1872) injures her spine from a fall off a swing. She spends four years in her room as an invalid, during which time she reforms her tomboy ways and runs the household from her bed. At the end of the novel, she learns to walk again, as if in reward for conforming to nineteenth-century ideals of femininity.

Women could also enter the intellectual sphere through the time and space that invalidism sometimes afforded. Harriet Martineau, an intellectual best known for her work on political economy, was deaf from childhood and spent six years as an invalid. Perhaps surprisingly, she found her time confined in the sickroom to be a reprieve from the stresses of daily life. Yet this was not unusual for the Victorians. As Miriam Bailin notes, in Victorian fiction, the sickroom is a "haven of comfort, order, and natural affection" (1994: 6). Martineau addresses her book, *Life in the Sickroom*, to her fellow invalids, writing, "You and I, and our fellow-sufferers, see differently, whether or not we see further. We know and feel, to the very centre of our souls, that there is no hurry, no crushing, no devastation attending Divine processes" (2003: 41). The invalid so edified by this newfound spiritual connection can only view the rush and hurry of daily life with amusement. For Martineau, it is a transcendent experience: "Nothing is more impossible to represent in words, even to one's self in meditative moments, than what it is to lie on the verge of life and watch, with nothing to do but think, and learn from what we behold" (2003: 78). The invalid who spends her days on her bed or couch becomes, for Martineau, a privileged figure who transcends the worries of daily existence with a greater knowledge of her soul and a greater connection to the divine.

While Martineau praised the spiritual benefits of immobility for invalids, as Maria Frawley notes, there was also a thriving tourist industry that mobilized invalids to travel in search of health. In fact, a new and popular genre emerged, that of travel literature written by invalids (Frawley 2004: 116). It seemed in some ways contradictory that invalids, who were popularly supposed to be confined to their couch or bath chair, should undertake strenuous travel in search of health. As Frawley writes, "emphasis placed on the revivifying power of sensation and the medicinal value of motion provides a fascinating counterpoint to the association of invalidism with stasis" (2004: 114). These traveling invalids—whose destinations included the more bracing atmospheres of places like the Swiss Alps, as well as warmer climes along the Mediterranean—took advantage of the opportunities for travel that opened up for the middle classes through the development of the steam-powered boats and railways that connected Europe from the mid-nineteenth century onwards (Frawley 2004: 121). Most of the invalids who wrote travel narratives were men, perhaps because they were linked with agency, while women who wrote travel narratives were "associated with physical fortitude" (Frawley 2004: 118).

One such travel narrative, *San Remo as a Winter Residence* by W. B. Aspinall, showcases the invalid's agency in determining his treatment. San Remo, a city on the Italian Mediterranean, was a popular destination for invalids; Henry James' Ralph Touchett also whiles away "a dull, bright winter beneath a slow-moving white umbrella" there (James 1998: 242). Aspinall, whose authority comes from his experience as an invalid rather than medical training, confidently asserts that San Remo combines "the invigorating qualities of Nice with the warmth of Mentone," making it an ideal recuperative environment for "diseases of the chest" (tuberculosis, or possibly bronchitis or emphysema), "especially if the digestive organs are involved" (1865: 10). Aspinall gives authoritative recommendations on modes of travel and hotels, and he hopes that invalids following his journey will make it far enough outside their doors to step "into the lemon and olive groves without risk of exposure to wind and dust" (1865: 11).

2.6. CONCLUSION

The experience of mobility impairment in the nineteenth century was one of contradictions. Invalids might be confined to their couch in the sickroom, or that couch, like those advertised by J. Alderman of Soho, might have wheels. They might, like Harriet Martineau, write about the spiritual enlightenment they gained through the stillness of the sickroom, or they might, like W. B. Aspinall, board steam-powered ships and railways to undertake strenuous journeys in search of health. Amputees gained new visibility and new opportunities for mobility as they survived in greater numbers due to medical advances and reentered the workplace with the aid of sophisticated prosthetics. These same prosthetics, however, could also make amputees invisible, with hinged joints and rubber feet so sophisticated that they might allow amputees, especially women, to pass as able-bodied. A person with a congenital mobility impairment might be supposed to be especially sensitive and moody about it, like Lord Byron, or he might claim to develop a special capacity for observation and writing because of his lameness, like Walter Scott. The able-bodied might be encouraged to view those with mobility impairments with sympathy, as in the case of Mayhew's seller of nutmeg graters, or with suspicion, as with Edward Albert, the crossing-sweeper and double amputee. It is important that we attend to these complexities and contradictions in the nineteenth-century construction of mobility impairment. As Lennard Davis notes, our contemporary concept of disability as a medicalized, personal problem has its roots in "late eighteenth- and nineteenth-century notions of nationality, race, gender, criminality, sexual orientation" (1995b: 24). If we are to understand the roots of our own concepts of disability, we need to understand how they emerged in the nineteenth century.

CHAPTER THREE

Chronic Pain and Illness

"The Wounded Soldiery of Mankind"

MARIA FRAWLEY

In 1855, Harriet Martineau—journalist, essayist, fiction writer, and cultural commentator—wryly wrote in her autobiography of the "tracts and religious books" that "swarm among us, and are thrust into the hands of every body by every body else, which describe the sufferings of illness, and generate vanity and egotism about bodily pain and early death" (1877: vol. 1, 439–40). Author of "A Letter to the Deaf" in 1843 and *Life in the Sick-Room* in 1844, Martineau was no stranger to suffering or to its representation; she arguably stood at mid-century as her period's most well-known invalid.[1] Martineau's observation points not simply to the ubiquity of ill health in the nineteenth century, but also to the role that a burgeoning print culture played in circulating narratives of affliction and in helping to foster a culture of suffering. Although in this particular passage of her autobiography Martineau alludes to materials generated by Evangelical organizations such as the Religious Tract Society, which tended to valorize suffering as "improving" and a God-given instrument of conversion, she might have referred to any number of books and pamphlets intended for an audience of the "afflicted." The very titles of works such as *Cheering Texts for Days of Trial: A Companion for Invalids*, *Wanderings in Search of Health*, and *The Invalid's Friend* imply a wide-ranging community of sufferers compelled to share their stories and solutions with others. Works such as the American Leonard Trask's *A Brief Historical Sketch of the Life and Sufferings of Leonard Trask, the Wonderful Invalid* (1858) (Figure 3.1) and the British William Dodd's *Narrative of the Experience and Suffering of William Dodd, a Factory Cripple* (1841) provided rich and moving accounts of disability resulting from severe injuries. Within the pages of the nineteenth-century periodical press (quarterly, monthly, and weekly magazines in particular) can be found hundreds of articles, essays, and poems documenting the experience of being ill. Travel books and medical guides written by medical authorities (e.g. James Clark's *The Sanative Influence of Climate: With an Account of the Best Places of Resort for Invalids in England, The South of Europe, &C* or Jonah Horner's *Instructions to the Invalid on the Nature of the Water Cure*) as well as case histories published in medical journals such as *The Lancet* added to the wide-ranging and diffuse cultural conversation around protracted illness and disability. Experiences of chronic pain and illness were not confined, in other words, to the sickrooms in which so many nineteenth-century men and women were sequestered during protracted periods of illness; rather, the proliferation of print itself facilitated an expansion of understanding that percolated through many layers of nineteenth-century society, helping to make disease, illness, pain, and kindred conditions of disability something of a shared experience.

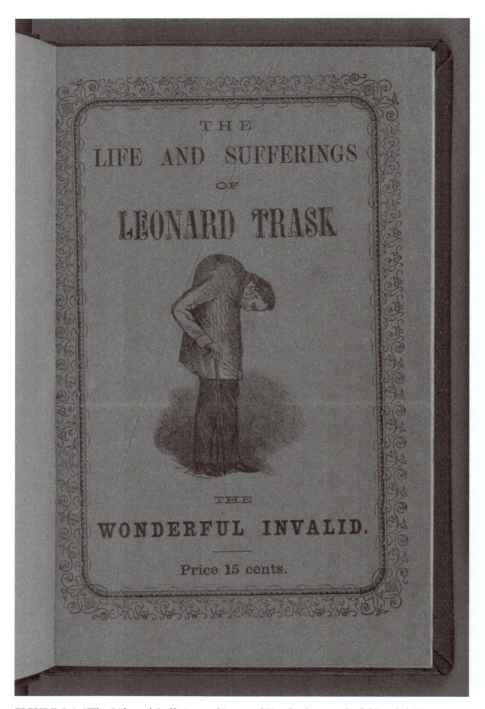

FIGURE 3.1 "The Life and Sufferings of Leonard Trask, the wonderful invalid."

The small mountain of print that the nineteenth-century sick left behind provides crucial material with which to construct a medical history that foregrounds the experiences of the men and women who may or may not have been under medical care, but who identified as chronically ill or disabled. The print history suggests an even larger population of people whose experiences with ill health or pain were not recorded. In an 1845 review of Martineau's *Life in the Sick-Room*, published in the *Christian Examiner*, the author suggests just such a wider world of affliction, writing, "What small community cannot array a host of invalids? What family is without one or more?" (Review of *Life in the Sick-Room* 1845: 165).

In a 1985 article titled "The Patient's View," Roy Porter influentially advocated for "medical history from below," history based on the experiences and reports of sufferers. Calling instead for "history from the middle," Andrew Wear revised Roy Porter's paradigm to emphasize the "diaries, letters, autobiographies, travelers' accounts, doctors' case books, religious tracts, cookery and medicine books, etc." produced by the middling classes (1985: 231). Whether advocating history from "below" or "the middle," Porter, Wear, and other medical historians were responding to the fact that medical history had so long been constructed around physician biographies, institutional records, or studies of specific diseases and epidemics. N. D. Jewson and others have shown the range of ways that the emergence of scientific medicine resulted in the "disappearance" of the patient from nineteenth-century medical cosmology.

While individual accounts of experiences with affliction enhance immeasurably our understanding of the culture of chronic illness and pain, comprehending that culture nevertheless requires recognizing myriad related histories that converge, overlap, and inform one another. Medical history, in other words, is inflected with an array of narratives: histories of science and pseudoscience; of class relations and attendant notions of labor and able-bodiedness; of gender ideology, with its assumptions about the purportedly natural differences between the sexes and the different relations of men and women to work within the private and public spheres; of Evangelicalism and other religious understandings of the reasons behind or value of suffering; and even of conceptions of national health and imperial identity. Evangelicalism in particular legitimized affliction as God-given and found in protracted illness opportunity for spiritual transformation. The industrialization that propelled so much growth in the early and middle decades of the nineteenth century spawned new categories of work that relied on assumptions about physical and mental performance, capacity, and ability; these in turn influenced medical terminology and diagnosis. Moreover, the keywords in this chapter's title—*chronic*, *illness*, and *pain*—each requires scrutiny attentive to its multivalent meanings in the context of nineteenth-century medical history.

This chapter will explore how these terms inform several representative works of the period that detail the physical and mental experiences of ailment or disability, arguing that these case histories, while based on British authors, showcase well the intersectional nature of nineteenth-century medical history more broadly and, in doing so, shed light on an array of the period's social and cultural preoccupations. Before turning to these case studies, it is worth emphasizing an important assumption about the medical history of illness and pain undergirding the foundational distinction between the chronic and the acute. To an extent, the very notion that some illness and pain might be experienced as extended or even permanent—as *chronic*—implies commentary on the profession of medicine and its ability both to diagnose and to treat underlying pathologies and conditions. That is, successful medicine typically advances along an expected trajectory from symptom recognition to diagnosis through treatment to cure. To be chronically ill or in pain is to recognize and embody the inadequacy of medicine. While the nineteenth century is generally regarded as witnessing the emergence of modern medicine (i.e. medicine more firmly rooted in sound science and more professionalized), the consensus among medical historians is that diagnostic tools and understanding outpaced an ability to treat diseases or offer cures. Still, by the end of the century, scientific understanding of disease etiology had advanced significantly from the century's beginning, and even its midpoints. Using an 1848 edition of William Buchan's widely regarded compendium *Domestic Medicine* as an illustration, Jan Marsh notes that the general causes of illness associated with smallpox, scarlet fever, and measles included "'diseased parents', night air, sedentary habits, anger, wet feet and abrupt changes of temperature." She continues: "Cholera, shortly to be epidemic in many British cities, was said to be caused by rancid or putrid food, by 'cold fruits' such as cucumbers and melons, and by passionate fear or rage" (Marsh 2017).

While such examples of the inadequate scientific knowledge underpinning attitudes about health and illness in the nineteenth century abound, they are overshadowed by key breakthroughs in understanding that dramatically improved both the experiences of many individuals suffering from acute illnesses and public health more generally. In Britain, with his commissioned *Report on the Sanitary Conditions of the Labouring Classes* in 1843, Edwin Chadwick established the link between poor living conditions and contagion, and included trenchant recommendations for clean water and improved drainage. Roughly a decade later, Dr. John Snow intervened during the disastrous cholera outbreak of 1854 to prove that infection was spread via contaminated water from a public pump in a crowded city neighborhood. This crucial discovery led to a variety of public health projects, some designed to provide clean water, safe sewage systems, and less crowded housing conditions, and all advancing the idea and ideals of sanitary medicine. The 1850s also witnessed significant advances in physiology, chemistry, and biology, perhaps most notably with Louis Pasteur's identification of micro-bacterial organisms and the concomitant emergence of a germ theory of disease. Equally groundbreaking was the invention of anesthesia in the USA in the late 1840s and the emergence of antiseptic protocols for surgery. These and other major discoveries would not have been possible without the development or improvement of scientific instruments designed to aid in the understanding of illness and health—the stethoscope (invented in France early in the century), the kymograph (used to measure blood pressure), and microscopes powerful enough to detect microorganisms.

Not surprisingly, the "rise" of scientific medicine and increased attention to public health needs had an inevitable influence on medicine's methods and its social standing, as well as on the understanding of the role of the doctor, which in turn altered the role of the patient. Before the nineteenth century, quacks or "sham doctors" with little or no medical training competed with more orthodox practitioners—the learned gentleman doctors—to treat those in need of care. While the creation of a Medical Registry to recognize qualified medical practitioners in Britain, via The Medical Act of 1858, is often seen as a watershed moment in the history of medicine, in fact the struggle to professionalize began much earlier in the century. George Eliot's masterpiece novel *Middlemarch*, published in 1871–2 but set in 1830, represents well the struggle. Eliot narrates the ultimately unsuccessful endeavors of the generally admirable and ambitious— but overly idealistic—physician Tertius Lydgate. Lydgate is eager to bring more modern medical practices to the provincial town of Middlemarch, to share the benefits of his impressive scientific education and strong understanding of disease, newly acquired via schooling in Edinburgh and Paris. He greatly underestimates the habits and preferences of the townspeople, who prefer an older, familiar model of doctoring—the family friend whose bedside manner compensates for a lack of scientific understanding and expertise. Lydgate, despite his training and ambitious desire to do good, ultimately fails in his mission of medical progress.

It is against this backdrop of steady but inconsistently experienced progress in medical understanding and the emergence of professionalized medicine over the course of the century that we must situate a study of chronic illness and pain—first and foremost as experienced by men and women, but also as processed (or understood) by them, and as treated (or not) by a medical community. The epidemics for which the nineteenth century is best known—smallpox, typhus, cholera, and scarlet fever—tended to be fast moving and produced patients aplenty. But so, too, did "lingering" or "wasting" diseases, such as tuberculosis. Additionally, there were the numerous instances of illness and pathologies for which there was no definitive diagnosis, no medical consensus on what exactly was wrong or how consequently to treat the patient. As A. D. Hodgkiss notes, "Chronic pain without lesion was recognized throughout the century, initially by surgeons and physicians and later by psychiatrists … Terminology and taxonomy were complex, including Hypochondria, Spinal Irritation and Neuralgia" (1991: 27). The longer-lasting or even permanent conditions of incapacity evidence the ways that a history of medicine cannot fully account for the experiences of chronic illness and pain, as the then-popular term "incurables" signifies. To be chronically ill, then as now, was to experience something understood as a medical condition, but recognized as impervious to medical intervention. To be chronically ill was also therefore to adopt what medical sociologists such as Talcott Parsons refer to as the "sick role" in response to that condition. The basic idea of the sick role is that individuals who have become ill not only experience the physical or psychological symptoms associated with their illness, but they also adhere to social expectations of being sick, expectations that their society and culture have shaped. For example, some societies assume the sick are obligated to try to get well. Examining the ways that those who experienced chronic illnesses adopted and adapted that "sick role" helps to expose the intricate interplay of the various forces that shaped their experiences. The case histories that follow do just that, with each case highlighting a convergence of discourses around issues of gender, class and occupation, religious belief, and nationality, among other things, which shaped an individual's understanding of his or her experience of protracted ill health and disability.

3.1. EXHIBIT A: "CONFESSIONS AND OBSERVATIONS OF A WATER-PATIENT," IN A LETTER TO THE EDITOR OF *THE NEW MONTHLY MAGAZINE*

"Confessions and Observations of a Water-Patient" originally appeared as the lead essay in the September 1845 edition of the popular *New Monthly Magazine*.[2] Masquerading as a "Letter to the Editor" (despite being sixteen pages in print), the piece by British writer and politician Edward Bulwer-Lytton frames his detailed and lengthy exposition of his experiences in seeking a cure for a range of chronic complaints with explicit attention to the changing terrain of magazine culture. Having once served as the magazine's editor, he characterizes his decision to put his experiences into print as a "momentary return to [his] ancient haunts" (Bulwer-Lytton 1845). Stressing the changed landscape of print culture, he describes himself as addressing a "new assembly," writing further that "the reading public is a creature of rapid growth—every five years a fresh generation pours forth from our institutes, our colleges, our schools, demanding, and filled with fresh ideas, fresh principles, and hopes" (1845). In an intriguing adaptation of the sick role, Bulwer-Lytton uses the rhetorical device of a ghost returning to his haunts to upend the expectations of his readership; rather than augur death, as a ghost would seem to do, his purpose is, he writes, to "promise healing." He beckons his readers "not to graves and charnels, but to the Hygeian spring."[3] Bulwer-Lytton goes on to tout the "intimacy with water" he experienced as a hydropathy patient as nearly analogous to sexual experience; he compares water to the mythical water spirit Undine, describing it as "sportive and bewitching," yet "tender and faithful." The anxiety that Bulwer-Lytton brought to his experience of being chronically ill, as well as to the task of writing about the relief he found via hydropathy, was clearly not simply a manifestation of professional stress or a product of the changing terrain of magazine culture. He wanted also to link his experience to a perceived crisis in masculinity, one loosely associated in his mind with the nature of work and to cultural condemnation of "incapacity" in men. Other men apparently shared his views; author of *Life at the Water Cure, Or, A Month a Malvern*, Richard Lane claimed that advocacy of hydropathy "may well prepare the way for other workmen in the same field" (1846: ix).

By the 1840s, Bulwer-Lytton was far from alone in touting the benefits of "the water cure" (Figure 3.2). Indeed, "patient testimonies" as a genre proliferated around a variety of treatments throughout the nineteenth century. Although initially regarded as a kind of

FIGURE 3.2 "Granite State Water-cure, Franklin, N.H."

"fringe medicine," hydropathic spas—water-cure establishments, as they were sometimes known—dotted the countryside in the UK and had hundreds—even thousands—of visitors, among them well-known figures like Alfred Lord Tennyson, Charles Darwin, and John Ruskin. Nor was the popularity of the treatment and of the institution of a water-cure spa limited to the UK; men and women sought treatment and relief in Budapest, Hungary; Baden-Baden, Germany; Saratoga Springs, New York; and many other places in the USA, Africa, and Australasia. By the early decades of the nineteenth century, hydropathy had become a popular treatment for illnesses ranging from depression to rheumatic arthritis, skin diseases, and digestive disorders, but was especially appealing to "nervous system diseases" and therefore to hypochondriacs. Janet Oppenheim writes that its efficacy was understood to be greatest in "disorders over which it is allowed that medicine possesses scarcely any control" or "for which no specific cause can be assigned" (1991: 134). Patients who could afford it—these places were decidedly not destinations for the working classes—went to healing spas to try the water cure, a treatment that included drinking large quantities of mineral water, wrapping oneself in wet sheets to induce sweating (Figure 3.3), and taking various forms of baths and showers.

While readers could learn much about the regimen of the water cure from Bulwer-Lytton's essay, it is most revealing in the way it addressed the causes of chronic illness and, indeed, what it means to have a "chronic" complaint. He explains that while he was not experiencing a life-threatening condition, he "was in that prolonged and chronic state of ill health, which made life at best extremely precarious" (1845). He goes on, "I do not say that I had any malady which the faculty could pronounce incurable—I

FIGURE 3.3 "The Packing."

say only that the most eminent men of the faculty had failed to cure me." To a real extent, Bulwer-Lytton diagnoses himself in a way the medical community evidently failed to do, identifying the source of his "malady" as overwork and linking his work ethic to ideologies of masculinity. "I began to write and to toil, and to win some kind of a name, which I had the ambition to improve, while yet little more than a boy," he explains. "To a constitution naturally far from strong, I allowed no pause or respite. The wear and tear went on without intermission—the whirl of the wheels never cease." His allusion here is to a disorder commonly known as "the wear and tear complaint," one associated in the Victorian era with nervous disorders and written about in works like C. H. F. Routh's *On Overwork and Premature Mental Decay: Its Treatment* and Robson Roose's *Fortnightly Review* essay on "The Wear and Tear in London Life." Some in the medical community may have understood men and women to be equally susceptible to overwork, but Bulwer-Lytton clearly believed it to be nearly unique to men of his station and profession. In his emphasis on work, overwork, and their consequences for physical and mental health, Bulwer-Lytton reflects well the pervasive anxiety manifest in early Victorian society surrounding idleness. To be considered idle was to risk association with the shiftlessness and helplessness that left the working classes especially vulnerable to the New Poor Law of 1834, which linked "able-bodiedness" to the ability to support oneself through employment. Reflecting on his own shattered nerves and those of his fellow overworked journalists, Bulwer-Lytton describes a band of brothers as a "restless, striving brotherhood," professional men whose labor is intellectual, not physical, but who are no less susceptible to debilitation. He writes, "We ... forget our ailments in our excitements, and when we pause at last, thoroughly shattered, with complaints grown chronic, diseases fastening to the organs, send for the doctors in good earnest" (1845). He ends his essay with an address to his fellow community of male journalists, imagined as fellow sufferers: "O brothers, O afflicted ones, I bid you farewell," he writes in a closing rhetorical flourish (Bulwer-Lytton 1845).

Confessions and Observations of a Water-Patient instantiates nearly as well as any text in the nineteenth century the variety of beliefs that might converge to shape an individual's experience and understanding of illness. Diagnosing himself as a victim of "shattered nerves," Bulwer-Lytton, like many others in his day, understood the physical and emotional or psychological dimensions of his disorder as inextricably bound to one another. Moreover, he located the source of his distress in "overwork," and, in doing so, sought to understand his medical condition and his experience as a patient through the twin lenses of gender and professional class. Economic metaphors pervade his narrative, particularly in his description of the etiology of his affliction: "Worn out and wasted, the constitution seemed wholly inadequate to meet the demand," he writes (Bulwer-Lytton 1845). The tropes of supply and demand are economic, yet arguably have sexual correlates as well, illustrating what Ben Barker-Benfield (1978) called a "spermatic economy" to capture the anxieties surrounding male sexuality and the loss entailed in the ejaculation of sperm. Herbert Sussman, too, in his study, *Victorian Masculinities*, observes that the "interior energy" that early Victorians like Bulwer-Lytton used to understand maleness was "consistently imagined or fantasized in a metaphorics of fluid" (1995: 10). Writing of his physical and emotional state after completing the regimen, he waxes rhapsodic on the "pure taste, the iron muscles, the exuberant spirits, the overflowing sense of life" that are to be found at Malvern.

Framing his essay through the rhetoric of the private and personal—a "confession"—while at the same time marshaling the circulation and readership of a widely read monthly magazine, Bulwer-Lytton adapted the familiar genre of the patient testimonial to his own purposes, constructing an imaginary audience of fellow (male) sufferers along the way. Highlighting in his conclusion the retrospective nature of his reflections on the water cure, he implies that his restoration to health was not, in fact, permanent. He looks back, in other words, on the period as offering a temporary experience of health. "I can recall no periods of enjoyment at once more hilarious and serene than the hours spent on the lonely hills of Malvern," he writes, "none in which nature was so thoroughly possessed and appreciated" (Bulwer-Lytton 1845). Perhaps most crucially, then, Bulwer-Lytton's essay locates chronic illness in a particular rhetorical space, anchored at one end by decidedly "incurable" diseases and at the other by illnesses more permanently amenable to medical intervention.

3.2. EXHIBIT B: HARRIET MARTINEAU'S *LIFE IN THE SICK-ROOM* (1844)

Life in the Sick-Room, Harriet Martineau's book-length study of protracted illness, shares with Bulwer-Lytton's confessional essay an investment in the idea of what constitutes a chronic condition. Writing at one point in a three-volume autobiography (drafted in 1855, but not published until 1877) of her reaction to a physician's diagnosis of a heart "too feeble for work," she comments, "a momentary thrill of something like painful emotion passed through me,—not at all because I was going to die, but at the thought that I should never feel health again" (1877: vol. 2, 102). Martineau implies here that she would exist in a state of limbo, "not dying, yet hardly living either," as Robert Louis Stevenson would later write (see below). *Life in the Sick-Room* goes a step further, essentially associating the experience of chronic illness not only with the ill person's own perceptions of his or her likelihood of recovery, but also with the response that prolonged illness manifests in others; "in a sharp sickness of a few days or weeks," she explains, "all good and kind people act and speak much alike; are busy and ingenious in hastening the recovery, and providing relief meantime. It is when death is not to be looked for, nor yet health, that the test is applied" (Martineau 1844: 49).

Martineau's autobiography documents a life replete with experiences of suffering both physical and emotional, only a small portion of it caused by her partial deafness. Like so many of the accounts of chronic illness published in the nineteenth century, Martineau's narrative might well strike readers today as vague, referring to a "beggarly nervous system" that left her "infirm and ill-developed" (1877: vol. 1, 8–9). Medical historians and biographers now associate many of Martineau's symptoms with an ovarian cyst, but the overarching sense of infirmity that she linked to her nervous system better explains her sense of herself as chronically ill. *Life in the Sick-Room* does not attempt to compass Martineau's lifetime of affliction, but rather situates itself within a period of roughly five years beginning in 1839, when she experienced a long illness that she believed, at least at its onset, would be fatal. Although she had established a robust public reputation as a journalist and author with her *Illustrations of Political Economy* series, she opted to publish *Life in the Sick-Room* anonymously. It was to be understood as written "By an Invalid," a common device of the period and one that enabled Martineau to suggest its broad applicability. Throughout the volume, she addresses "fellow sufferers" and "unknown comrades in suffering," rhetorically constructing a readership of the suffering and positing a widespread culture of affliction. She cannot be blamed for imagining this community; the pages of popular British and American middle-class magazines were filled with essays by invalids situated in sick-rooms, but not so incapacitated they could not write about it. Lives "lived on one's back / in long hours of repose," as W. H. Henley wrote in the long poem "In Hospital," were lives worth better understanding. "The Invalid's World," as A. B. Ward called it in his essay on the topic, was worthy of writing about.

Like other documents featured in this chapter, *Life in the Sick-Room* reveals in myriad ways the intersectional nature of medical history. Most prominently, religious sensibility inflects the work as written—and as later reflected on and written about—in fascinating ways. Although Martineau was born into a Unitarian family, by the time she took to her sick-room in Tynemouth, she had ceased to identify as such. Whatever her religious heritage or the precise evolution of her religious beliefs, one gleans from her prose a latent Evangelical understanding of illness that percolated through many layers of nineteenth-century society, particularly in the first half of the century. "I was patient in illness and pain because I was proud of the distinction, and of being taken into such special pupilage by God," she wrote in the *Autobiography*, reflecting back on her years in Tynemouth (1877: vol. 1, 440). At the same time, Martineau took pains to critique the culture that shaped her thinking about protracted illness at the time. When Martineau later took stock of *Life in the Sick-Room* while writing her autobiography, she defended the "facts" and "practical doctrine" that had informed it. Instead, she took issue with the way she had "magnified" her experience, conveying (to her chagrin) "the desperate concern as to my own ease and happiness, the moaning undertone running through what many people have called the stoicism" (1877: vol. 1, 458). Still, at the time she was drafting *Life in the Sick-Room*, Martineau felt compelled to process her experiences with a language of Christian education. She closes chapter 9, "On the Perils of Pains of Invalidism," with this revealing pronouncement:

> The most fitting sick-room aspiration is to attain to a trusting carelessness as to what becomes our poor dear selves, while we become more and more engrossed by the vast interests which our Father is conducting within our view, from the birdie which builds under our eaves, to the gradual gathering of the nations towards the fold of Christ, on the everlasting hills. (1844: 146)

At the same time that *Life in the Sick-Room* reflects the influence of Evangelical understandings of suffering on Martineau's mind-set, so too does it comment, if obliquely, on doctor–patient relations and the nature of medical authority. Martineau had been under traditional medical care just prior to her extended sick-room stint, and treatment for her ailments included gynecological surgical (i.e. the removal of polypous tumors) and various kinds of drug therapy, including morphine dosing. When she took to the sick-room and became what she would describe as a "prisoner to the couch," she had excised herself from the routine care of her physician. Like so many others who felt themselves to be beset with a "chronic" condition, Martineau distrusted the ability of traditional medicine to offer a satisfactory cure. As I note in an introduction to a contemporary edition of *Life in the Sick-Room*, "most critics sensibly agree that felt emotional burdens and exhaustion from work combined with the prolapsed uterus and ovarian cyst to incapacitate Martineau" (2003: 20). Martineau's autobiography describes an "anxious period" that preceded her sick-room stint; as I write in *Invalidism and Identity in Nineteenth-Century Britain*, Martineau's references to being "overworked" and needing more "domestic peace and ease" than she found with her mother "remind us of [her] status as one of the relatively rare middle-class women working in the public sphere who could creditably claim 'overwork'—a diagnosis far more likely to be applied to men—as a rationale for her distress" (2004: 222).

Yet, *Life in the Sick-Room* is anything but a diatribe against overwork; still less is it a document representing the perils of life without medical oversight. Even still less is it a straightforward paean to Christian submission in the manner, for example, of Ellen Chadwick's *Echoes from a Sick Room*, which equated chronic illness with Christian education and was replete with references to the benefits of studying "in the school of long affliction" (1903: 112). Martineau's was not a body or a mind rendered prostrate by her affliction. While the gendered ideology of separate spheres may have naturalized the association of women with domestic interiors, Martineau did not construct the sick-room as a site of submission. As Alison Winter observes, she transformed her sick-room into a space of comfort and utility, overturning the expectation that the invalid was a figure of utter dependency (1995: 603). Moreover, through the mere act of writing her book, Martineau sought to make her experience of prolonged affliction useful. The maneuver might be read, at least partially, as a reflection of Martineau's particular inclination to identify herself through work (and specifically writing), and also as a nod to her society's embrace of Utilitarian beliefs about the value of usefulness. Even those who were not "able-bodied," *Life in the Sick-Room* implied, could function as useful members of society.

The structure of *Life in the Sick-Room*, with chapters devoted to such topics as "The Transient and the Permanent in the Sick-Room," "Sympathy to the Invalid," "Nature to the Invalid," "Becoming Inured," and "Some Perils and Pains of Invalidism," suggests that while Martineau overtly reached out to a community of fellow men and women who experienced chronic ill health or pain, she wanted a readership of the healthy as well, one that she could educate by offering up a kind of proto-social psychology of invalidism. In the volume's opening chapter, she paints the sick-room as a space of "intense convictions," and claims for "long sickness" the value of teaching "the permanent nature of good and the transient nature of evil" (1844: 43). At times, Martineau is positively ebullient in her claims for the powers of mind available to one rendered bedridden: "To what soaring heights of speculation are we not borne up! What is there of joy or sorrow, of mystery and marvel, in human experience that is not communicated to us," she writes near her volume's end (1844: 154–5). Still, *Life in the Sick-Room* functions more as treatise than as memoir, each chapter finding ways to make suggestions that other sufferers or their caregivers might adopt to make the experience of sustained illness profitable. Indeed, in a letter to a friend written just after she completed her book, Martineau expressed her sense of obligation "to suffer for other people's information,—to be a sort of pioneer in the regions of pain, to make the way somewhat easier,—or at least more direct to those who come after" (quoted in Frawley 2004: 200). Such a remark helps to elucidate the spirit behind so many pronouncements in *Life in the Sick-Room*, such as when she begins chapter 3 (on "Nature to the Invalid") by stating, "When an invalid is under sentence of disease for life, it becomes a duty of first-rate importance to select a proper place of abode" (66). Writing appreciatively of the sea views she enjoyed in Tynemouth, she declares, "We should have a wide expanse of land or water, for the sake of a sense of liberty, yet more than for variety" (1844: 67). Later in the volume, she describes herself as "wide awake in [her] watch," observing the goings-on of the society that surrounded her and learning, she believed, "life in its entireness" (1844: 88). Throughout *Life in the Sick-Room*, Martineau constructs a division between those experienced with protracted illness and those inexperienced with the bodily distress and mind-set of sufferers. Her aim is not simply to teach the inexperienced, but to lend to the experiences of the chronically ill a kind of moral and intellectual authority. In her chapter on the "Gains and Sweets of Invalidism," she claims as "a strange and great blessing" the "abolition of the future" (1844: 147). Here, as elsewhere in Martineau's book, she attempts to represent the distinctive ways invalids experience temporality.

As when, in 1855, she prepared an obituary several decades in advance of her actual dying, Harriet Martineau earnestly believed herself to have no future when she wrote *Life in the Sick-Room*. She was wrong, of course, and she lived to leave Tynemouth and relocate to a new home in Ambleside. She traveled again as well, adding works like *Eastern Life, Present and Past* (1848) to her long list of publications and enjoying a rebirth of her journalistic career in writing leaders for the *Daily News*. Just as her retreat to the sick-room was a product of both bodily and mental ailments, so too her return to health has no single explanation. Significantly, Martineau attributed it to her experiment with mesmerism, which she documents in a series of *Letters on Mesmerism* published by Edward Moxon in 1845.[4] The experience provided her with another opportunity to confront male-dominated medical authority and to make her recovery from protracted illness every bit as controversial as had been her entry into it. After Martineau's death in 1877, many of the obituaries and tributes struggled to make sense of her protracted illness and seemingly sudden recovery. The indomitably cheerful Samuel Smiles put it this way: "whether from the potency of the remedy or the force of the patient's imagination, certain it was that she was shortly after restored to health" (1883: 509). Hers was indeed a kind of personal "restoration drama," and while the publicity surrounding *Letters on Mesmerism* helped to catapult her back to a very active public life, Martineau never abandoned her sense of the sick-room as a useful sanctuary, or protracted ill health as an experience in which resignation need not compete with the urge to be useful.

3.3. EXHIBIT C: ROBERT LOUIS STEVENSON'S HEALTH ESSAYS (1881)

Robert Louis Stevenson explored his experiences with chronic ill health through the conventions of travel writing, a form he adopted in the earliest stages of authorship in *An Inland Voyage* and *Travels with a Donkey in the Cevennes*. Essays such as "The Amateur Emigrant," "An Autumn Effect," and "Cockermouth and Keswick" are hybrid pieces that recount journeys that took him to new places both literally (i.e. physically) and imaginatively or psychologically. As he summed up in "The Amateur Emigrant," "'Out of my country and myself I go,' sings the old poet, and I was not only travelling out of my country in latitude and longitude, but out of myself in diet, associates, and consideration" (2005: 33). Many of the essays that have come collectively to be thought of as Stevenson's "health essays"—"Ordered South," "Davos in Winter," "Health and Mountains," and "The Stimulation of the Alps"—were written in tandem with his other travel writing, a popular genre in the period, and one especially conducive to the kind of introspective and meditative exploration that appealed to Stevenson (Figure 3.4). The "search for health" was a common motif in Victorian-era travel, in part because so many men and women were advised to travel for medical reasons. The phrase captures well the spirit of the pilgrimage that inflects much of the writing of the period, including that produced by Robert Louis Stevenson. "Ordered South," published in the popular middle-class monthly *Macmillan's Magazine* in 1874, captures especially well Stevenson's investment in representing the interaction of mind and body in the experiences of the invalid traveling for health:

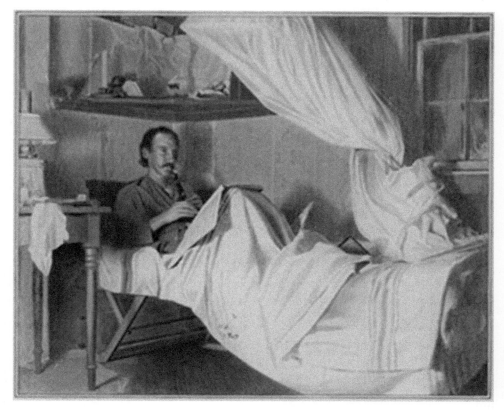

FIGURE 3.4 "Robert Louis Stevenson, seated in bed playing a woodwind instrument."

The world is disenchanted for him. He seems to himself to touch things with muffled hands, and to see them through a veil. His life becomes a palsied fumbling after notes that are silent when he has found and struck them. He cannot recognize that this phlegmatic and unimpressionable body with which he now goes burthened, is the same that he knew heretofore so quick and delicate and alive. (1874: 69)

Stevenson experienced respiratory problems for much of his adult life; in the early 1870s, he had (like many Victorians with tuberculosis) spent time in the Riviera, where physicians sent their patients to benefit from the warm Mediterranean air. Hence the title of the *Macmillan's* essay, "Ordered South," implying as it does a directive from his physician. Like many men and women of the period, Stevenson's "search for health" was essentially a form of medical treatment, an indication of the hold that climatotherapy—an approach to treatment that laid stress on fresh air, exercise, and removal from sources of stress and fatigue—were the components most key to recovery. As John Pemble shows in *The Mediterranean Passion*, invalids aplenty pursued the therapeutic benefits of the Italian and French Rivieras, as well as Malta, Malaga, and Algiers, at various points in the nineteenth century (1987). In "Ordered South," Stevenson begins by noting the "curious irony of fate" that "the places to which we are sent when health deserts us are often singularly beautiful" (1874: 68). By the time Stevenson published his essays on winter climates in *The Pall Mall Gazette* in 1881, respiratory patients were more often sent to cold-air climates than the warm environments previously recommended. Davos, Switzerland, had garnered a special reputation as a health resort extremely well suited to consumptives, thanks in part to the efforts of a German physician who sought to connect the effects of the bracing high mountain climate to the relative paucity of tuberculosis in Davos natives. In "Health and Mountains," Stevenson seems mildly dubious of the scientific claims for cold-air healing, initially presenting it as just another trend in medical treatment. "There has come a change in medical opinion, and a change has followed in the lives of sick folk," the essay blithely begins. He continues:

> A year or two ago and the wounded soldiery of mankind were all shut up together in some basking angle of the Riviera, walking a dusty promenade or sitting in dusty olive-yards within earshot of the interminable and unchanging surf—idle among spiritless idlers, not perhaps dying, yet hardly living either, and aspiring, sometimes fiercely, after livelier weather and some vivifying change. (1881c: 102)

Condensed in this introductory prose one detects several overlapping strands of thought. While Stevenson clearly hoped to physically benefit from time spent in an alpine climate, if not embracing the "medical opinion" as the last word on proper treatment for consumptives or idealizing the experience as likely to produce a cure, he was willing to give it a go if it meant a more comfortable existence. By generalizing the specifics of the cold-air cure to "medical opinion" broadly and consumptives to "sick folk," however, he rhetorically extends the reach of his essay, implying that many in his imagined community of sufferers shared an experience of medical knowledge as little more than "opinion," a belief as susceptible to change as fashion. The "wounded soldiery of mankind" functions similarly to collapse into a single category a host of sufferers rhetorically likened to soldiers doing battle with or for their health. Stevenson constructs an idea of the chronic differently than did Bulwer-Lytton in "Confessions and Observations of a Water-Patient." Whereas Bulwer-Lytton flagged the failure of medical professionals to remedy his ailments, rendering him "incurable" even if some kind of cure might have existed, Stevenson implicitly locates the idea of the chronic in the psychological experience of protracted ill health—"not perhaps dying, yet hardly living either" (1881c: 102).

Reminiscing about the experience of basking idle in the Southern sun, Stevenson reveals an anxiety about masculinity not unlike that which percolated through Bulwer-Lytton's confessional essay. The anxiety makes Stevenson's placement of the essays in *The Pall Mall Gazette* more resonant, given the association of that magazine—or at least the street after which it was named—with gentleman's clubs. "There was a lack of a manly element; the air was not reactive," Stevenson writes in "Health and Mountains." "You might write bits of poetry and practice resignation, but you did not feel that here was a good spot to repair your tissue or regain your nerve" (1881c: 457). The inertia and inactivity that he associated with protracted ill health—in "Health and Mountains" he derides himself as "an idler among idlers"—were anathema to Stevenson; throughout "Health and Mountains" and the other health essays focused on the Davos experience, he bemoans the "miasma of the sick-room" so often associated with invalidism. Elaborating on his condemnation of "resignation," the posture so idealized by Evangelical invalids in the Victorian period, he writes:

Resignation, the cowardice that apes a kind of courage and that lives in the very air of health resorts, is cast aside at a breath of such a prospect. The man can open the door; he can be up and doing; he can be a kind of a man after all and not merely an invalid. (1881c: 458–9)

One senses here and elsewhere in these essays Stevenson's genuine struggle with what he perceived as the "sick role" accorded to those who identified themselves or were identified by others as "invalids." He does not limit the implied readership of his essays to his fellow afflicted, but interspersed throughout his essays are moments of mocking address, as when, in "Davos in Winter," he writes, "You may perhaps be an invalid who likes to make bad verses as he walks about. Alas!" (1881b: 465). In a variety of ways, Stevenson probes the idea of the "invalid mind," which he most often constructs as weak and vulnerable and sets himself up against. He opens "Davos in Winter," for example, with the claim that mountain valleys and Alpine winters combine with "an invalid's weakness" to make "a prison of the most effective kind" (1881b: 463). Stevenson touts the benefits of the open air and active methods of healing evidently practiced in Colorado, writing that there one experiences "instead of the bath-chair, the spade; instead of the regular walk, rough journeys in the forest." He then concludes, "what a revolution in all his hopes and terrors, none but an invalid can know" (1881b: 102). Stevenson identifies sympathetically with, but also resists, his fellow invalids.

Stevenson's embrace of the vigor available in cold-air climes is intriguing. To an extent, he expresses a kind of gendered fantasy of able-bodied vitality, a belief that manhood and even selfhood is rendered possible only through robust physical activity. At the same time, Stevenson's essays reflect skepticism about those very claims. In "Ordered South," he writes of being "homesick for the hale rough weather," but concedes that "the stuff of which these yearnings are made, is of the flimsiest" (1874: 69). What engages Stevenson as much as the stakes for masculine vitality in the experience of chronic ill health is the opportunity to ponder and experience a heightened awareness of temporality. In this preoccupation he seems almost the direct heir of Harriet Martineau, writing about the invalid's experience of time's passage in the sick-room. When Stevenson writes in "Ordered South" that "it is not altogether ill with the invalid, after all," he explains that "If it is only rarely that anything penetrates vividly into his numbed spirit, yet, when anything does, it brings with it a joy that is all the more poignant for its very rarity" (1874: 70). Expressing this idea in another way in "The Stimulation of the Alps," he writes, "The dream of health is perfect while it lasts, and if, in trying to realise it, you speedily wear out the dear hallucination, still every day, and many times a day, you are conscious of a strength you scarce possess, and a delight in living as merry as it proves to be transient" (1881d: 476).

One more of Stevenson's essays for *The Pall Mall Gazette* series on health deserves study for what it can reveal about Stevenson's own experiences and his take on the culture of chronic ill health. Published in March of 1881, "The Misgivings of Convalescence" strikes a philosophical note from the get-go, when Stevenson writes that "there is no problem more difficult for modern thought, than to make a decent and human-hearted convalescence." He immediately associates the problem with the nature of the chronic, explaining, "It may be open to doubt whether the man will or will not make an ultimate recovery, or whether it might or might not be better for humanity that he should die" (1881e: 160). The comment seems to link his and others' experiences of chronic ill health to the project of eugenics, although the term would not be coined by Francis Galton until 1883. Galton, influenced by Darwin's theories of natural selection, propounded a system that would allow for the natural selection of "more suitable races" more likely to come out on top in a so-called survival of the fittest. In "The Misgivings of Convalescence," Stevenson contends:

> A question, perhaps essentially impertinent, but yet continually recurring and almost as old as the art of logical speech—it is hardly imperative to state it: *cui bono*? [who stands to gain?]—haunts any phthisical young man like his own shadow, and in many instances, steps between him and the beginning of recovery. (1881e, 160)

Stevenson raises the specter of the question only to banish it. The essay swiftly moves to strike a familiar tone when he writes that "there are few fights more worthy to be fought and few victories more to be lauded, than in what are fought and won against disease" (1881e: 161). The rest of the essay rehearses many of the basic claims made in the other *Pall Mall Gazette* essays—the faults of the "emasculated air" and "effeminate loveliness in nature" to be found in now out-of-medical-fashion health resorts; the comparative value of the bracing air of the Alps. "In a word if pluck, vigour, and the desire of living at all help or speed the invalid in his recovery, it is here upon the Alps, and not among the perfumed valleys of Liguria, that he will find the stimulus required," Stevenson opined (1881e: 161). At some level, Stevenson's fretful consideration of nations, their climates, and their likelihood to promote health bespeaks a deep-seated admiration of, even yearning for, purportedly robust national agendas—imperialism in Britain and manifest destiny in the USA, for example. While the argumentative trajectory of the essay is toward the embrace of possible recovery, Stevenson consistently injects cautionary comments that work against the optimism of recuperation. The invalid he posits in the closing line of the essay (he does not use "I" or identify himself as narrator) "will work briskly at his own recovery like a piece of business; and, even if he shall not succeed, he makes a better figure in defeat and is a shorter time a-dying" (1881e: 162).

3.4. CONCLUSIONS

Each of the documents exhibited here as representative of how chronic illness was experienced and understood in the nineteenth century was written by a man or woman who had already established a professional identity as an author and was well known to the reading public. Edward Bulwer-Lytton, Harriet Martineau, and Robert Louis Stevenson each experienced extended illness both personally and professionally—that is, as influencing their careers. As authors with identities already known to the reading public, they brought to their narratives a heightened sense of the relationship between public and private dimensions of identity. While they were chosen because their narratives of chronic illness are evocatively rendered while also revealing of the intersectional nature of discourses that converge within medical history, it is crucial to remember that they were not unique. Many hundreds of men and women experimented with traditional and alternative medicine and recorded—whether in published accounts or in private letters and diaries—their experiences. Edward Bulwer-Lytton was not the first, nor the last, "water-patient"; Harriet Martineau was one among many to experience and write about confinement to a sick-room; Robert Louis Stevenson was representative of many others whose respiratory ailments took them abroad "in search of health." It is worth emphasizing, though it should be obvious, that Bulwer-Lytton, Martineau, and

Stevenson each had resources sufficient to their needs and purposes. One finds peppered throughout Victorian fiction moving accounts of how the men and women of the working classes dealt with debility and disease. One can find in the autobiographical documents produced by the British working classes—letters and diaries primarily—many accounts of protracted ill health experienced within families.

It is striking that Bulwer-Lytton, Martineau, and Stevenson each foregrounded in their narratives the myriad ways that they found and experienced agency as patients. While each, of course, had medical care at given points in their experiences (Bulwer-Lytton and Stevenson both reference physicians overseeing their treatment regimens at the institutions where they sought relief or remedy, in fact), their narratives focus readers' attention instead on the ways that the chronically ill are essentially in charge of their experiences. They do not do so in a sophistic "attitude is everything" way; rather, they explore the multifarious ways that a person inhabits and manages the experience of protracted illness and adapts "the sick role" to his or her purposes.

In their shared focus on agency, these narratives, like the hundreds that surrounded them, complicate and make more nuanced our understanding of the relation of chronic illness to the history of disability. Reflecting the nineteenth-century embrace of the ideal of *mens sana in corpore sano* (a healthy mind in a healthy body), they construct understandings of the challenges posed to a healthy mind by bodies that have seemingly malfunctioned, or to healthy bodies by minds wracked with stress or anxiety. They demonstrate how incomplete would be a history of disability that focused exclusively on experiences of physical impairment limited to one bodily function (e.g. hearing or eyesight) or to the loss of use of limbs (as is explored in William Dodd's 1841 account of himself as a "factory cripple"). Work such as Dodd's account or Martineau's "Letters to the Deaf" circulated within a broader and variegated tapestry of texts devoted to representing the fundamental interconnectedness of mind and body in experiences of chronic affliction.

Perhaps most importantly, the three documents showcased in this chapter reveal well the fraught but fascinating relationship of pain to the history of chronic illness. In her informative study of Victorian pain, Rachel Ablow points out that the development of anesthetics and improvements in analgesic medicine combined with new understandings of nerve function to mean that "for the first time, pain came to seem potentially eradicable" (2017: 2). It makes sense, then, that as Roy Porter noted, the medical community came over the course of the century to understand chronic pain less as a sign of psychosomatic disorder, or "the mark of the malingerer," and instead developed the idea of the syndrome, with "intermediate explanatory categories such as neuralgia, spinal irritation, or functional disorder" (Porter 1993). From the vantage point of the patient, not the professional, however, pain would seem to belong instead to the realm of the acute, even if construed within the experience of one chronically ill. Pain has a precise trajectory—it erupts; it peaks; it subsides; it becomes a memory or is forgotten. The realm of the chronic would seem to have no certain place for pain, at least insofar as the arc of pain loses its definition within the far more diffuse experience of protracted, chronic illness. In her study of the representation of pain in late nineteenth-century English culture, Lucy Bending concludes that "pain has no innate meaning, but rather is subject to the diverse social and political aims of those who chose to interpret it" (2000: 239). Within nearly every narrative of chronic illness one can locate discussion of pain, but, as Ablow (2017) argues, the emphasis is less to describe pain than to *use* it. The author of *Confessions of a Hypochondriac* claimed that the wet-sheets that were part and parcel of the water cure "transformed pain into pleasure" (1849: 107). Richard Lane, author of *Life at the Water Cure*, wrote of the treatment's potential to banish pain as well, but simultaneously recognized the capacity of the mind to anticipate and almost invite pain: "For the past month real cares and griefs have been whistled off, and, for the time, left me untouched: to-day, the very whisper of an *imaginary* ill has power to build up a formidable and heartfelt infliction" (1846: 251). In her meditation on temporality in *Life in the Sick-Room*, Martineau took care to distinguish a "day's illness" from that drawn out over "a succession of months and seasons" (1844: 44). Reflecting on incidences of pain within the protracted period of illness, she writes:

> during the year looked back upon, all the days, and most hours of the day, have had their portion of pain—usually mild—now and then, for a few marked hours of a few marked weeks, severe and engrossing; while perhaps, some dozen evenings, and half dozen mornings, are remembered as being times of almost entire ease.

After yet more tallying and consideration, she concludes as if solving a math problem, "This is the sum of the pains of the year, in relation to illness. Where are these pains now?—Not only gone, but annihilated. They are destroyed so utterly, that even memory can lay no hold upon them. The fact of their occurrence is all that even memory can preserve" (1844: 45). Martineau's point is less to emphasize what Elaine Scarry in her influential study *The Body in Pain* would posit as pain's radical subjectivity, but instead to lay stress on its relative transience (1985). She does so not to diminish it, but rather to accentuate what she believed endured in the experience of chronic illness—perspective to be gained, lessons to be learned, good to be shared with the wider world of the afflicted and the healthy. Many hundreds of nineteenth-century men and women felt similarly and were driven to chronicle their experiences with protracted ill health. They were beneficiaries of an increasingly literate public and a print culture that made finding readerships and outlets for their chronicles possible. Medical and cultural historians today, eager to understand how chronic illness was experienced and understood in this period, are in turn beneficiaries of a vast repository of material to work with.

CHAPTER FOUR

Blindness

Creating and Consuming a Nonvisual Culture

VANESSA WARNE

In 1863, *Temple Bar* magazine published an anonymous, firsthand account of a blind person's visit to the International Exhibition of 1862, the sequel to the Great Exhibition of 1851. While the essay's title, "How A Blind Man Saw the International Exhibition," is a knowing nod to the prioritization of the sense of sight in exhibition spaces, the essay shares a rich account of its author's nonvisual experience: of the vibration of the halls' wooden floors, the oily smell of the industrial section, and the sound of visitors' movements and conversations. The essayist enjoyed parts of the Exhibition, such as the international halls, where stall keepers invited him to touch items on display. He explains, however, that he felt conspicuous in the Exhibition's art galleries, where visitors commented on his presence, one person observing, "What good can he be doing here? He can't see the pictures" (1863: 234). An account of accommodation as well as ostracism, the essay is a valuable record of the sensory and social experiences of a blind person in Victorian Britain, a person who was both a consumer of nineteenth-century culture and, in his role as essayist, a contributor to it.

This chapter examines the cultural history of blindness in nineteenth-century Britain and, to a lesser extent, the USA. It pairs blind people's experiences and opinions, such as those shared in the *Temple Bar* essay, with sighted people's perceptions and depictions of blind people. I begin the chapter with an overview of definitions of blindness and medical responses to blindness, including interest in its causes and cure. I examine the educational history of blind people, including the proliferation of schools for blind students and the advent of the reading of books by touch. Exploring mainstream attitudes toward blindness, I offer readings of visual and literary depictions of blind people created by sighted people, depictions that typically identify blindness as a state of dependency and ineptitude, but that also associate blindness with compensatory gifts, such as unusual acuity of hearing and touch. I end the chapter with an exploration of the work of blind authors, including activists, whose self-representations challenge negative perceptions of blindness.

This survey will demonstrate that in the nineteenth century, as in other eras, the lived experience of blindness was influenced by the attitudes and actions of sighted people, including legislators, doctors, and educators. It will also show that the nineteenth-century history of blindness was shaped by a period-specific development: the introduction into the USA and the British Empire of methods for the printing of raised-print books that could be read by touch. These books and the spread of the skills required to read them—

products of the organized efforts of blind people—allowed visual disability to be both experienced and imagined in new ways. Literacy is consequently a dominant theme in what follows; additional themes include the cure or amelioration of blindness; blindness, paid work, and the value placed on productivity; and blindness and gender.

4.1. DEFINITIONS, CAUSES, AND CURES

In the nineteenth century, different expert groups proposed definitions of blindness, a term used in common parlance to refer to total blindness, but also to a range of visual disabilities and differences, including low vision. Professor Hugo Magnus, an influential German doctor, proposed that people who could not see and count fingers at a distance of three feet were blind. At the 1889 Royal Commission on the Blind, the Deaf and Dumb &c. of the United Kingdom, commissioners heard from over 100 experts, but only one speaker, a Dr. R. B. Carter, proposed a definition, suggesting that blindness be defined as "a state in which no occupation can be followed for which vision is required" (Abel 1983: 50). England's Elementary Education Act of 1893 guaranteed state-funded education for children who were "too blind to be able to read the ordinary school books used by children" (*An Act to Make Better Provision* 1893: ch. 15). Charitable organizations set their own policies regarding who qualified as blind. The managers of London's School for the Indigent Blind explained in an Annual Report that applicants who could distinguish between colors or could see more than the difference between light and darkness would not be admitted. While lawyers and legislators dealt with questions related to the determination or degree of blindness, the label "legally blind," first used in the USA in 1934, did not have a nineteenth-century equivalent.

Blind commentators on blindness seem, by comparison, uninterested in defining the term "blindness" or in limiting this label's application to specific kinds or degrees of visual disability. This is not to say that terms used to refer to blindness were not of interest to blind people. In her essay "A Few Words About Blindness," Alice King, a British blind person and author, rejected the use of the colloquial term "dark," which she observed was a "not at all uncommon way among the lower orders of speaking of a blind man or woman" (1884: 191). King also challenged sighted people's perception of blindness as an affliction when she referred to blind people as "the so-called afflicted" (1884: 191). Rejecting terms that perpetuate negative perceptions of blind people, King was not concerned with the development of a precise definition of blindness, but with the damage done by discriminatory language that identifies blindness with suffering.

Causes of blindness are, predictably, a focus of medical case studies, but they are also a feature of autobiographical writing from the period. James Downing, a British soldier, shared his experience of becoming blind while on campaign in Egypt in a long poem published as a book that he sold to earn money. Downing explains that he was returning to camp one evening when "A blast of wind blew in my eyes / Which seemed like burning coals" (1821: 91). His eyes became swollen and painful and, by the next morning, Downing was unable to see. Other soldiers in the camp had the same symptoms, and Downing walked with them, each holding another's coat, to get medical help. Blisters, poultices, and drops failed to relieve Downing's pain or to restore his sight. He returned to England in 1801 as a blind person, one of hundreds of British soldiers who became blind in the first decades of the century, not from a sand-borne infection unique to Egypt, as many speculated and as Downing proposes in his poem, but from ophthalmia, an infection that was venereal in origin and could be transmitted by touch to the eyes. Misattributed to exposure to a foreign land—quite literally, to Egypt's injurious sand—blindness was one of several disabilities associated with the work of empire, a price paid by soldiers whose vision loss while on campaign disqualified them from military service.

As historians of medicine, including Luke Davidson, have shown, the prevalence of ophthalmia was a catalyst for the development of the specialization of ophthalmology.[1] Toward the end of the century, an American doctor, L. Webster Fox, reflected on the medical community's commitment to both preventing and curing blindness. Webster Fox observed, "probably at no time in the history of the science of medicine has there been so much attention given to the effort to prevent blindness, correcting visual defects, or operations devised for the restoration of vision, than at the present day" (1889: 422–3). Ophthalmia neonatorium, which injured the eyes of newborns exposed to it in the birth canal, was another significant and closely studied cause of vision loss. Contagious diseases, such as smallpox and measles, were also significant and widely reported-on causes. In addition to disease, medical professionals treated and documented the loss of vision due to workplace accidents; they were likewise concerned with the damage done to workers' eyesight by the demands of occupations such as weaving, engraving, and needle-making. While blindness was by no means a class-specific experience, class status did shape experiences of blindness. Vision loss frequently led to financial crises for employed people, including working-class men who were viewed as unemployable if they lost their sight, a societal attitude that impoverished workers and their families.

The new experts in eye health were supported in their work by the founding of institutions dedicated to the treatment of eye conditions, and also by Charles Babbage's mid-century invention of the ophthalmoscope, a tool for illuminating and examining by sight the interior of the eye. Medical professionals shared new knowledge of the anatomy of the eye in clinical publications. Treatments for blindness, both successful and unsuccessful, were documented by both doctors and their patients. British author and illustrator George du Maurier described the loss of sight in his left eye when he was an art student as "the most tragic event of my life," claiming that "it poisoned all my existence" (Sherard 1895: 398). du Maurier traveled to Germany to consult with oculists and incorporated his medical experiences there into his semiautobiographical novel, *The Martian* (1897), in which the protagonist, who is also blind in one eye, is directed to drink mercury and apply leeches behind his ears to prevent the onset of total blindness.

In contrast to ineffectual treatments like these, cataract removal operations had higher success rates in this era than in previous ones. Medical reports on successful cataract surgery often stress the impact on patients' ability to work. British surgeon Charles Bell Taylor reported in *The Lancet* that his patients had gained "very useful vision" (1870: 654), noting that his female patients could, for example, earn money from fine sewing. Known as couching, cataract removal surgery not only changed the lives of some blind people, but also changed attitudes toward blindness, redefining blindness in the popular imagination as a surgically curable condition.[2] Optimism about surgical cure played a catalyzing role in what Georgina Kleege identifies as Western culture's fascination with "The Hypothetical Blind Man," a phrase she adopts from Elisabeth Gitter to explore sighted people's investment in philosophical speculation about the sensations, emotions, and abilities of blind people who experience sight for the first time as a result of surgery (Kleege 2005).

4.2. READING BY TOUCH AND NEW SCHOOLS FOR BLIND STUDENTS

Not unlike cataract surgery, reading by touch changed the lives of some blind people while simultaneously challenging sighted people's ideas about blindness. Blind people began to read books by touch following the introduction into Britain and the USA of embossed printing methods that had originated in France in the 1780s. Though it took several decades for French educator Valentin Haüy's successful experiments in teaching reading by touch to blind students to find traction in Anglo-American culture, public interest in this practice was significant, and the entry into literacy of the first generation of blind readers was perceived by commentators as a significant amelioration of the perceived suffering of people with inoperable eye conditions—indeed, as a kind of cure.[3] W. W. Fenn, a blind person and professional author, enthused, "give ... the blind man in his fingers an equivalent for his eyes, and the darkness in which he lives is dispelled" (1886: 478). Fenn proposed that "the Fingers of the intelligent and skillful blind can be trained to afford very fair compensation for sight." They can, Fenn asserts, "be made to light up a darkened world" (1886: 478). The pioneering and controversial American educator of blind students Samuel Gridley Howe noted in 1846 the strong feelings experienced by both blind readers and sighted observers:

> The moment [the blind students] take their books, and, running their fingers along the lines, begin to read aloud, there is a mingled feeling of relief and admiration, which shows itself in smiles and tears. There is hardly a person who can witness this, for the first time, without deep emotion. (Klages 1999: 115)[4]

Writing for *Household Words*, Harriet Martineau shared her enthusiasm regarding the expansion of the reading public to include blind people, announcing, "the blind can now read—a good many of them—and all will, by and by" (1854: 424). In reality, many blind people lacked opportunities to learn to read, and even affluent and educated blind people did not always choose to read by touch. The British statesman and academic Henry Fawcett, for example, preferred to employ a sighted secretary, a privilege of his class status.

Personal accounts of reading by touch express deep appreciation for the opportunity to read. An Englishman who became blind in his late twenties described the arrival by mail of a package of raised-print reading materials, explaining, "before they came to hand, I had dull, desponding, and indolent feelings, with very dark prospects for this life; but when the means of improvement, comfort, and usefulness was presented, they tended much to relieve my mind" (Bull 1859: 212). Similar reflections on the benefits of reading by touch describe the importance of embossed printing to academic study, the value of unmediated access to religious scripture, and the pleasures and social benefits of a private correspondence.

While the system of raised dots proposed by Louis Braille in 1824 was taken up by some Anglophone educators and readers, blind people's print culture in nineteenth-century Britain and the USA was characterized by the coexistence and rivalry of different raised-print scripts. Some scripts, including braille, used raised dots; some took the form of radically simplified versions of the Roman alphabet; others replicated closely the shapes of ink-print letters read by sighted people. The coexistence of script systems limited the variety of books available to blind readers because core texts, such as the Gospels, were reprinted in different scripts. The proliferation of scripts also cost some readers time and energy, as they sometimes mastered the reading of one script system only to find the institution with which they were affiliated had decided to switch to a different system. The blind activist Thomas Rhodes Armitage described the situation as a "Babel of systems" (1886: 37). Convinced of the need for a universal script system for blind readers, Armitage, together with colleagues at the British and Foreign Blind Association (BFBA), launched a research program to learn about readers' preferences and to test their accuracy and speed while reading different scripts. The result of this research was, beginning in 1868, an organized and ultimately successful campaign for the adoption of braille as the dominant if not universal script of blind readers.

Initially limited in their choice of reading materials to short religious tracts or excerpts of the Gospels, blind people secured by the century's end access to editions of Dickens' novels, the poems of Tennyson and Browning, and even weekly news magazines.[5] The high cost of raised-print books made private collection impractical for most, but circulating libraries developed to address the needs and preferences of the blind readership. The largest and most significant library for blind patrons in Britain was the Lending Library for the Blind in London. Founded in 1882 by Martha Arnold, a blind person and teacher, the Library's subscription charge was a penny a week and, by 1899, the Library was circulating 3,200 volumes among 300 members (Leach 1984: 1). In 1906, American librarian E. E. Allen worried about the underservicing of blind readers and recommended that raised-print books circulate by mail with no charge for the mailing costs. Convinced that "lending libraries for the blind must become sending libraries," Allen insisted, "the blind of any community have the same right to a proportionate amount of free reading matter as have other citizens of the community" (1906: 644).

Institutions for the vocational training of blind people predated by decades the introduction into Britain and the USA of reading by touch. The first school for blind people in the UK was the School for the Indigent Blind in Liverpool, founded in 1791. Initially focused on training in skills such as knitting, basket making, and brush making, these schools extended their mandate in the course of the century to include reading and writing, as well as math, geography, and science.[6] By 1870, the number of educational institutions for blind people in England had grown to nineteen. In the USA, the Perkins School, founded in 1829 and still extant, was the first dedicated school for blind students.

In the USA, many blind students attended government-funded residential schools in their home states. In a poem published in 1844, Frances Jane Crosby expressed gratitude for her education at the New York Institution for the Blind:

> Go gentle reader, back with me
> A few short years, and thou shalt see
> The blind, in mental darkness, left
> Their way to grope, and many reft
> Of all that rendered life most dear,
> Without one beam of hope to cheer
>
> Their stricken hearts. (Crosby 1844: 21)

Crosby's portrait of a recent past when uneducated blind people were obliged to "grope" their way epitomizes a conventional identification of blindness with a tragic state of ignorance.[7] While schools for blind students were lauded as an almost miraculous amelioration of the perceived suffering of blind people, some blind people questioned the benefits of an education that did not improve their chances of paid employment. Blind activist W. H. Levy urged schools to operate workshops staffed by former students as, he asserted, "instruction without employment is almost useless" (1872: 494).

In both Britain and the USA, private donors were important supporters of schools. Administrators consequently welcomed visits from curious sighted people. Visitors to schools for blind students included Charles Dickens, who visited Laura Bridgman, a celebrated deaf-blind person, at the Perkins School in 1842; Dickens wrote about her in *American Notes*, discussed below.[8] Helen Keller, a second celebrated deaf-blind graduate of Perkins and the heir to Bridgman's fame, published the first of her twelve books, *The Story of My Life*, in 1903. Living a public life as an activist until her death in 1968, Keller campaigned for social change, including improved access for blind people to educational opportunities and paid work.

4.3. SOCIETAL ATTITUDES

A contributor to *The Youth's Magazine* began a mid-century essay with a confident assertion:

> There is no class of our suffering fellow-men, who meet with more universal sympathy than those who are deprived of their sight. When we consider all the sources of pure and exquisite pleasure of which the eye is the medium of communication to the mind, we can never attempt to realize the privation of the sense of seeing, without the utmost commiseration for those so afflicted. ("The Blind" 1850: 157)

This powerfully ocularcentric assessment encapsulates the widely held perception of blindness as a tragic state and of blind people as deserving objects of sympathy. Building on Martin Jay's term for and theorization of Western culture's privileging of vision over the other senses, both Rosemarie Garland-Thomson and David Bolt have explored the role of ocularcentrism in the history and cultural construction of disability (Garland-Thomson 2009; Bolt 2014). Bolt has examined the relationship between ocularcentrism—the belief in the dominance of visual perception—and what he terms "ocularnormativism," which Bolt defines as "the perpetuation of the conclusion that the supreme means of perception is necessarily visual" (Bolt 2014: 14). While blind people's ability to read demonstrated the information-gathering potential of touch, the perception of sight as the foremost sense and a related association of blindness with ineptitude proved tenacious. Charles Baker, an expert on the education of blind people, observed in *Chambers's Encyclopaedia* that "the man who loses his sight after having had full use of it for years is profoundly to be pitied. He has lost not merely that great gateway of knowledge, but it frequently happens that the loss of sight, for a time at least, shatters and enfeebles mental energy, and weakens the remaining senses and powers" (Baker n.d.: 224). Charles Bell Taylor, an eye surgeon, struck a similarly ocularcentric note when he closed a report on a successful cataract operation by explaining, "it is quite certain that now and again apparently hopeless cases—such as the one I have recorded—may be restored to all the blessings attendant upon the exercise of that function without which life itself is worth little" (1897: 653).

Writing in 1884, the aforementioned blind writer Alice King challenged the perception of blindness as tragic. Targeting the belief that blind people lived isolated lives, denied of social contact and unaware of their surroundings, she explains, "In most minds there seems to exist a notion that the blind man goes about the world shut up in a sort of terrible iron cage, like the Tartar king of old renown" (1884: 189). Images of imprisonment noted by King are a convention of nineteenth-century writing on blindness. Dickens' now widely critiqued description of Laura Bridgman is one of the more memorable: "there she was, before me; built up, as it were, in a marble cell, impervious to any ray of light, or particle of sound; with her poor white hand peeking through a chink in the wall, beckoning to some good man for help, that an Immortal soul might be awakened" (Dickens 2000: 39). King's response to this kind of characterization of blindness is unambiguous: "no idea is more mistaken than this. Blind men or women have to the full as much enjoyment, in their own peculiar way, of the glories and beauties of nature, and of the sweetnesses of social intercourse, as those who can see" (1884: 189).

Given both the inadequacy of employment opportunities and of state-funded welfare provisions for blind people, individuals and institutions may have strategically portrayed blindness as calamitous, perpetuating negative stereotypes in order to encourage charitable giving. Some religious blind people, eager to reconcile biblical depictions of blindness with their lived experience of blindness, understood blindness as part of a divine plan but insisted that blindness was not a barrier to a productive and happy life. W. H. Levy, for example, proposed that parents tell their blind children that

> God has enabled some people to tell things with their eyes, and that others cannot do so ... that God who made both the sighted and the blind, gave to each of them the means of doing that for which He made them, and that if he, the child, use his hands and ears rightly, and if he employ his thoughts properly, he will by-and-by become a happy and a good man. (1872: 31)

A belief in divine compensation for a lack of vision, taking the form of gifts such as musical talent, literary inspiration, and a refined sense of touch, was widespread, and was reinforced by the perception of reading by touch as a kind of miracle. Some commentators insisted that blind people could tell the colors of fabric or of shards of glass by touch; a Canadian journalist asserted that brain matter had been discovered in the fingertips of blind people during autopsies (Ontario Institution 1899: 2). Whereas the ability to read by touch was understood by some observers as evidence of blind people's highly sensitive touch, blind people and sighted educators of blind students insisted that tactile acuity was a product of effort and education and was not a compensatory gift.

4.4. LOOKING AT BLINDNESS

In 1858, the *Illustrated London News* published an engraving of the Association for Promoting the General Welfare of the Blind in London. Titled *Work-School for the Blind, Euston Road*, it shows the Association's workshop, where blind adults sit at tables or on the floor making brushes and baskets (Figure 4.1). A salesman enters at one door and, at the center of the workshop, a man sits on a bundle and reads a book by touch. Possibly reading to himself or, seated as he is at the center of the workshop, entertaining his companions as they work, the reader holds one of the more than 100 volumes that made up the Association's library. Energetic in their efforts to secure public support, the Association's blind founder, Elizabeth Gilbert, and its manager, W. H. Levy, arranged to have the illustration reproduced, on a much enlarged scale, as an oil-painted billboard that hung outside the workshop.[9]

A portrait of blind people working and reading, this widely circulated and proudly displayed image can be read as a refutation of the culturally dominant image of the blind beggar. As studies of journalist Henry Mayhew's depiction of blind people in *London Labour and the London Poor* (1861–2) by Martha Stoddard Holmes and others have

FIGURE 4.1 "Work-School for the Blind, Euston Road."

shown, blind beggars were part of a larger community of blind street sellers and performers who inspired a range of responses that include pity, disgust, and fascination (Holmes 2004). Pairing interviews of blind street people with engraved portraits, Mayhew was an influential contributor to the conversation on blindness and its relationship to work and poverty. In Mayhew's interviews and reports, as in the broader culture, the blind beggar is sometimes associated with gullibility or dishonesty but is largely tolerated by a culture that perceived blindness as an unsurpassable barrier to wage-earning work.

Sir John Everett Millais' *The Blind Girl* (1856) is one of period's best-known images of a blind beggar (Figure 4.2). The painting depicts two girls sitting on the edge of a highway. Covered by a shawl that has shielded her from a rainstorm, the older girl has a small note pinned on her dress that reads "Pity the Blind," confirmation of a fact communicated by a number of visual clues. The girl's inability to see is suggested by her closed eyes, by her careful examination by touch of the grass beside her, and, most obviously, by her failure to turn and view the visual spectacle that has attracted the attention of her sighted companion. Featuring paired rainbows and a striking contrast of storm cloud, sky, and field, Millais' colorful landscape attracts both the companion's attention and the gaze of viewers of the painting, who experience a pleasure in it that cannot be shared by the blind girl. A portrait of blindness that stimulates and satisfies a range of visual appetites, Millais' painting is a compelling measure of the value Victorians placed on vision. As Kate Flint has noted, Millais "reminds the spectator of the importance of a higher, inward vision," as "the dominance of the material and visible world is called into question" (2000: 66). Though, as Flint demonstrates, there is much more at stake in this painting

FIGURE 4.2 John Everett Millais, "The Blind Girl." 1856.

than a sympathetic portrayal of a blind beggar, Millais' painting forcefully identifies visual disability with deprivation and dependency.

Images of middle-class and socially prominent blind people challenged the association of blindness with begging. Britain's blind Postmaster General, Henry Fawcett, sat for numerous photographers and for Ford Madox Brown, who painted a dual portrait of Fawcett with his wife, Millicent Garrett Fawcett (Figure 4.3). The portrait shows Fawcett

FIGURE 4.3 "Henry Fawcett; Dame Millicent Fawcett." 1872.

wearing his academic gowns and seated in an armchair, with his wife beside him. Fawcett gestures at a letter, written in ink, to which he points with his index finger; his wife holds a pen, indicative of her role as amanuensis. The portrait depicts Fawcett speaking, characterizing Fawcett as an active mind, positioning him as the intellectually dominant partner of a companionate marriage, who, though unable to read an inked letter, points to a passage in a letter in a fashion that suggests, surprisingly, that he can both see it and read it. This painting could in fact be mistaken for an image of a sighted man who has closed his eyes to better consider and comment on the contents of a letter he holds in his hand. Whereas in photographs Fawcett is shown wearing dark glasses, for this portrait Fawcett's eyelids are closed; this is also the case for a bronze bust of Fawcett, created by Mary Grant, one of Britain's leading female sculptors. This bronze, part of a memorial fountain to Fawcett, was, the monument's inscription states, erected "by his grateful countrywomen" in 1886 in London's Victoria Embankment Gardens, an expression of appreciation for Fawcett's progressive thinking on women's issues. Open to being read as an early example of public art designed with accessibility in mind, the fountain's design makes available a tactile portrait of a blind person, installed within reach of people who visit it.

Consistent with the example of Fawcett's depiction, portraits of blind people typically depict their subjects with eyes closed or covered by dark glasses. Like the use of prosthetic eyes, another facet of the nineteenth-century material history of blindness, this practice signals the sighted majority's unease with visible signs of ocular difference. Significantly, blind commentators expressed concern not about the social pressure to cover a portion of their faces, but with sighted people's perception of the faces of blind people as expressionless. Pierre Villey, a scholar and blind person, felt that the visual appearance of blindness played a role in the sighted population's underestimation of the intellectual potential of blind people. Villey explained, "The first inclination is to suppose that behind these sightless eyes, this lifeless countenance, everything is quiet—intelligence, will, sensations—that all the faculties are torpid and, as it were, benumbed" (1909: 683). There was no dominant public face of blindness in the nineteenth century, no representative depiction, but, as Villey's comments suggest, the faces of blind people were studied by sighted people, and blind people were conscious of, and concerned about, the sighted majority's scrutiny.

4.5. LITERARY PERSPECTIVES

The diversity of messages communicated by visual art about blindness is matched by the diversity of attitudes expressed in literature. Like the visual record, the literary record emphasizes connections between visual disability and paid work. "Eyes that Saw not: A Story," a short story by Onoto Watanna (the penname of Winnifred Eaton) and Bertrand W. Babcock, published in *Harper's Magazine* in 1902, is one of dozens of stories about blindness that circulated in the Anglo-American periodical press. Its protagonist, John Swinnerton, is a newspaper reporter who, after becoming blind, decides to try his hand at fiction. John, a competent journalist, is a failure as a creative writer. Overly confident about his talent, John is, however, easily deceived by a well-intentioned sighted woman, Elizabeth, who, working as John's secretary, recognizes the poor quality of his work and decides, when his submissions are rejected, to secretly rewrite his stories before sending them for publication. As the revised stories are published, John, buoyed by a false sense of his success, proposes to Elizabeth, explaining that he does so in the knowledge that he is "a strong, successful man, an author blind, but with insight into the human heart" (Watanna and Babcock 1902: 34). The couple marry and are happy until a successful surgery restores John's sight. The climactic scene of the story features John reading a book he thought he had authored and discovering that the words in it, though published under his name, are not his own. A story about failed literary ambition, "Eyes that Saw not" portrays a blind man as talentless and delusional, representing his potential as limited, both creatively and financially. What is more, the depiction of John as an unknowing participant in the coauthorship of a body of fiction, his work very extensively rewritten by his wife, differs pointedly from the circumstances of Eaton and Babcock, the sighted pair who published this story under both their names.

Negative repercussions from successful sight restoration surgery are a central concern of Wilkie Collins' *Poor Miss Finch* (1872). Collins' novel, in which the title character's temporarily successful cataract surgery imperils her romantic relationship and happiness, is an attempt, Collins proposes in his preface, at "exhibiting blindness as it really is" (1995: xxxix). The novel's depiction of Lucilla as a highly capable, sexual, and financially independent upper-middle-class blind woman has attracted significant critical attention. Tabitha Sparks has explored Collins' depiction of corrective surgery as a threat to the domestic realm, and Samuel Gladden has argued for the importance of blindness to the novel's treatment of secrecy and sexuality. Martha Stoddard Holmes has explored the novel's investigation of "the appropriate place of disabled women in the realms of sexuality, marriage, and reproduction" (2003: 60). Noting Lucilla's identity as a happily married mother at the novel's end, a powerful contrast to tragic plots featuring blind women in melodrama, Holmes proposes that "the most sensational thing about this novel may be how conventional a heroine Lucilla Finch finally is" (2004: 89).

As with *Poor Miss Finch*, the gender politics of blindness feature prominently in Charlotte Brontë's novel *Jane Eyre* (1847) and in Elizabeth Barrett Browning's verse novel *Aurora Leigh* (1856). As critics, including Mary Wilson Carpenter, have shown, the similarities in these texts' depictions of the dependency of a blind man on a capable and independent woman suggest that blinding was a useful plot device for reforming arrogant or overly dominant male love interests. Both Edward Rochester and Romney Leigh are chastened by blindness, a change that permits strong and independent heroines to marry them. While connections between the two texts are noteworthy, critics have also offered rich treatments of them in isolation. Romney Leigh loses his sight after being hit by a falling beam as Leigh Hall burns, an injury whose impact on his vision seems intensified by the impact of the twinned traumas of his failure as a social reformer and his witnessing of the destruction of his ancestral home. Carpenter notes that feminist readings of Browning's verse novel by critics such as Angela Leighton and Susan Friedman interpret the blinding of Romney as "a gendered act of symbolic violence, a metaphor for feminist vengeance directed at masculinist power" (2006: 55). Elizabeth Barrett Browning, in contrast, insisted on the metaphoric nature of Romney's blindness, explaining in a letter that "he had to be blinded, observe, to be made to see" (Carpenter 2006: 53), an idea voiced by Romney when he thanks God "who made me blind, to make me see!" (Browning 1996: bk 9, ln 830).[10] Rochester's injuries at the end of Brontë's novel, which include diminished eyesight and the amputation of his right hand, are a central concern of *The Madwoman and the Blindman: Jane Eyre, Discourse, Disability*, a collection edited by David Bolt, Julia Miele Rodas, and Elizabeth J. Donaldson (2012b).

The collection's explorations of blindness include Essaka Joshua's (2012) essay on biblical narratives of blindness, Holmes' (2012) essay on film depictions of Rochester, and Bolt's (2012) essay on the novel's gendered treatment of blindness. These essays demonstrate, through their attention to both *Jane Eyre* and its cultural afterlife, the extent to which disability significantly curtails the social power—and also the sexual threat—of a character otherwise privileged by masculinity and wealth.

Portraits of blindness are so numerous in the nineteenth-century literary record that it is difficult to identify well-known authors who did not at least touch on the experience of visual disability. George Eliot created the blind scholar, Bardo, for her novel *Romola* (1863). Charles Dickens' 1845 Christmas story *A Cricket on the Hearth* depicts a young woman excluded from the courtship and marriage plots that structure the lives of her sighted friends.[11] Rudyard Kipling's 1891 novel *The Light That Failed* maps the decline of a painter who becomes blind, a narrative arc Bolt reads in the context of the period's not infrequent literary depiction of suicidal blind people.[12] Alfred Tennyson's "Tiresias" (1885) offers a mythological treatment of blindness, examining the tragedy of the blind seer, while William Wordsworth's blind beggar in Book VII of *The Prelude* is one of numerous poetic portrayals of blind street people.

Records of the reception by blind people of these literary works are difficult to locate, perhaps because many of the texts that portrayed blind people were unavailable to people who read by touch. That blind people pushed back against damaging depictions of blind people in conversation, if not in print, is suggested by at least one anecdote. Richard Rowe, the sighted author of a *Good Words* essay on London's blind community, attended a meeting of blind people with the intention of writing a second piece on blindness. Rowe discovers that his work was "rather angrily discussed at meetings of the Poor Blind in London" (1881: 323). Indeed, he overhears his work criticized by a blind woman who asserts, "it was too bad of 'Good Words' to make the blind out to be worse than they are" (1881: 326). This complaint may have given Rowe pause, but did not silence him on the topic. Indeed, the woman's anger provided him with another interesting anecdote about blind people to share with sighted readers.

4.6. SELF-REPRESENTATIONS

Alice King, a professional author and blind woman, reflected that: "many great authors have striven to portray, in their word pictures, blind men and women; many great thinkers have put on paper weighty sayings about blindness in the abstract; but very rare have been the blind people who themselves have said anything in print on the subject" (1884: 189). While King's assessment of an imbalance in the conversation on blindness is valid, the publication of blind people's writing became less rare in the course of the century. The publication of blind people's memoirs has been explored by Mary Klages, whose pioneering analysis of autobiographical writing about blindness focuses on two American women's memoirs, S. Helen deKroyft's *A Place in Thy Memory* (1849) and Mary L. Day's *Incidents in the Life of a Blind Girl* (1859). While not all blind writers chose to write on the subject of blindness, many did, and their work is a valuable repository for information on the lived experience of visual disability.

One such writer was Emoline Ann Warne, a British singer and lecturer who supported her family by giving "Services of Sacred Songs." Warne's book describes her travels around England in search of audiences, her mother's and brother's invalidism, and the importance of her income to her family. Like similar books published by subscription, it contains a list of the names of people who funded its publication. Warne addresses her subscribers when she writes, "I trust the Lord will bless this little book to all who may purchase it, and that our dear friends will pardon all mistakes" (1884: 55). Part fundraising endeavor, part advertisement, the book includes a list of the topics in Warne's repertoire; they include "Drink as an Evil" and "The Blind Restored to Sight."

The publication of autobiographies by subscription was supported by blind people's improved access to education but was necessitated by their underemployment. Whereas Warne authored her own story, some blind people delegated the task. This was the case for James Ure Campbell, who lost his job as a railway worker when he lost his sight. Campbell drafted a memoir, but his friends judged it too poorly written for publication. His biography, *The Story of a Working Man's Blindness*, was authored instead by a sighted man, Johnston Ross, and Campbell traveled around England selling the book door-to-door. American Henry Hendrickson also earned money by selling his story, an autobiography titled *Out from the Darkness* (1879). Hendrickson, who worked as a musical instrument salesman, hoped his book would open the door to a new career as a lecturer. While Hendrickson proposes that "the adventures of a blind man, if truly told, cannot be made picturesque by glowing delineations of wood, mountain, river and sea" (1879: 10), he is confident that "there are worlds of thought and action into which the landscape does not enter, which the mind alone may grasp; and the seals of that vast library are open alike to the sightless and the seeing" (1879: 10).

Poetry was an important genre for autobiographical writing by blind people. Edmund White, a railway conductor who became blind, authored and sold long poems to support himself and his family. Ambitious in style and scope, two of these poems, *Blindness: A Discursive Poem in Five Cantos* (1856) and *The Genius of the Blind* (1859), reflect on his experiences as a blind person and were, as their title pages announce, "Composed in total Blindness." *Blindness*, which is more than 100 pages long and written in heroic couplets, opens with White's hope that "Milton's classic fire" (White 1856: 2) will inspire White, who opts to intersperse his retelling of the fall of Adam and Eve with accounts of traumatic moments in his own life. While references to Milton's blindness and quotations from his writings about blindness are a commonplace of sighted authors' writing on blindness in this era, for blind authors such as White, Milton not only influenced the content and style of their work, but also validated their decision to become writers.

While some blind authors published by subscription or sold books door-to-door, others sold their work to periodicals or established publishers. James Holman was one of the most successful and celebrated travel writers of the early nineteenth century. Known as "the blind traveller," Holman authored *The Narrative of Journey* (1822), a book about his extensive travels in Europe, and a four-volume collection, *A Voyage Round the World* (1834–5), describing trips through Africa, Asia, and Australia.[13] W. W. Fenn also enjoyed a successful career as an author—in his case, of essays and short stories. Fenn, a landscape painter who turned to writing after becoming blind, was a regular contributor to journals, including *Good Words*, *All the Year Round*, and the *Illustrated London News*. He republished his essays and stories in collections whose titles advertised the fact of his blindness: the two-volume *Half Hours of Blind Man's Holiday* (1878 and 1879) and *Woven in Darkness* (1885). Fenn reflected on his blindness in his essay "My Own Story," but chose to write on a wide range of subjects. In doing so, he frustrated at least one reviewer who wished Fenn had made blindness the central theme of his work. The reviewer asks, "Could he not give us more, still very much more than he has given us, of the special 'experiences' of a cultivated man in fitting himself to his new and painful position—some kind of autobiography of blindness, in fact?" (Review of W. W. Fenn's *Half Hours of Blind Man's Holiday* 1878–9: 204).

Frances Browne (1816–79) had even less to say about blindness in her published work than Fenn did. Author of the children's story collection *Granny's Wonderful Chair* (1857), Browne contributed to leading periodicals, including the *Athenaeum* and *Tait's*, and published a critically acclaimed long poem, *The Star of Atteghei* (1844). Details about her life as a blind person were shared in the preface to *The Star of Atteghei* by Browne's editor, who claimed to be presenting information taken from a letter Browne wrote to a friend, this in the absence of material prepared by Browne to share with her readers.[14] William Artman and L. V. Hall noted of Browne's career, "It is most remarkable that, in her whole collection of poems, there is not a word about blindness. The most probable reason that we can assign for this is, Miss Brown did not wish the sympathy which her supposed unhappy condition might awaken, either to enhance or diminish the intrinsic value of her productions" (1862: 159–60). Browne also wrote two novels, the first of which, *My Share of the World* (1861), features a heroine who commits suicide after becoming blind.

Artman and Hall dedicated their book *Beauties and Achievements of the Blind* (1862) to the promotion of the accomplishments of blind people, including blind authors. Examples of similar projects by blind authors and editors include the second half of W. H. Levy's *Blindness and the Blind* (1872), in which Levy describes the lives of accomplished blind people, and James Wilson's *Biography of the Blind* (1821), in which Wilson celebrates the lives of a diverse group of blind people, including poet Thomas Blacklock and natural philosopher Henry Moyes. Artman and Hall, whose collection pairs information about blind authors' lives with samples of their work, rejected the sympathetic or lenient assessment of disabled authors' work. They asserted:

> We utterly abominate and detest every remark or insinuation that tends to hold up in the light of sympathy the literary efforts of a class, who have in every age worn the fairest laurels, and enriched the commonwealth of letters. It has been our object in the present work, to point out to the blind, and the public in general, the achieving abilities of our order. (1862: 12)

The publication of pamphlets and books by blind authors on issues of concern to blind people was an important tool of blind campaigners for social reform. Hippolite Van Landeghem published on problems with specialized residential schools for blind students, which she relabeled "exile schools." She condemned asylum schools for, among other failings, their separation of blind children from their families. Armitage (quoted above), a blind person and leader in London's blind activist community, published *The Education and Employment of the Blind: What is has been, is, and ought to be*, an extended analysis of the problems faced by blind people. Armitage, a founder of the BFBA, was a vocal advocate for improved employment and educational opportunities for blind people. While he addressed sighted audiences effectively in speeches, in letters to *The Times*, and in his books, Armitage was committed to the position that blind people needed to independently conduct research on issues of importance to them and to campaign collectively for change. By the end of the century, community leaders used publications such as the National League of the Blind's monthly newssheet, *The Blind Advocate*, to share news and engage readers in their campaigns.

4.7. CONCLUSIONS

This chapter opened with a description of an anonymous essay, "How a Blind Man Saw the International Exhibition." The essay is just one example of the multifaceted ways in which blind people participated in nineteenth-century culture, in this case, in the twinned roles of exhibition goer and essayist, cultural consumer and commentator. It is worth noting both that this essay had an international readership and that at least one reader questioned the truthfulness of the essay, doubting a blind person's ability to attend an exhibition and write an engaging account of it. In the *Daily Southern Cross*, a New Zealand paper, a reviewer suggested that the essay may not have been written by a blind man, noting that the essay lacked "the undoubted stamp of truth" ("English Magazines" 1863: 3). Apparently reluctant to recognize the erudite author as a blind person, the reviewer explains, "we confess we have experienced some doubts about the author's blindness at times as we read. Be this however as it may, the descriptions are highly ingenious, and, if not by a blind man, argue a great power of throwing the mind into an imaginary situation in no common degree" (1863: 3). The reviewer questions the fact of an author's visual disability, but modern-day readers of this and of other nineteenth-century documents about blindness have an opportunity to respond differently, not with skepticism about the reality or degree of an author's blindness, but instead with an appreciation of what the cultural record can tell us about the cultural lives and contributions of visually disabled people.

As the innovations, images, and texts discussed above suggest, experiences of blindness were shaped not only by societal attitudes about disability, but also by class and gender identity and by widely held beliefs about work, education, health, pleasure, and social connection. It is worth noting by way of conclusion that the anonymous essayist, a member of the first generation of blind readers, examined at the International Exhibition a display of raised-print books, a display that, he explained, made "peculiar claims upon my notice" (1863: 231). One indication of the significance of blind people's literacy to the lived experience and cultural history of blindness—the inclusion in a Victorian-era exhibition of raised-print books to be read by touch and not by sight—now makes its claim on our notice.

CHAPTER FIVE

Deafness

Representation, Sign Language, and Community, ca. 1800–1920

ESME CLEALL

The catalogue of infirmities and calamities to which human nature is liable, exhibits, perhaps, no case of our fellow creatures (insanity excepted), which more forcibly, or more justly excites our commiseration than that of the uneducated deaf and dumb, for although blindness may and does claim a readier sympathy, from the deep interest it excites, yet, on attentively comparing these two great calamities, we cannot fail to discover that the former possesses the heavier privations. (Binham 1845: 2)

5.1. INTRODUCTION

Writing in 1845, a teacher of deaf children, H. B. Binham, summed up some of the ambivalent associations with deafness in nineteenth-century Western Europe and North America. While many deaf activists have argued that deafness is not, in fact, an impairment at all, but the basis of a linguistic minority, in the nineteenth century it was uniformly discussed as a "defect" or, as here, a "great calamity" (Davis 1995a: 881–2; Lane 2002: 356–79). Yet the "deaf-mute" did not epitomize the pitiable figure in sentimental Victorian discourse as did the blind person or "cripple." Instead, deaf people were perceived as unable to hear the "word of God" and thus were often labeled "irreligious." Linking deafness with insanity was also very common in the nineteenth century because, due to their perceived lack of language, deaf people were seen as unable to reason. Over the course of the nineteenth century, other associations with deafness started to emerge, particularly fears regarding hereditary deafness, which became such a concern that some even started worrying about the creation of a "deaf variety of the human race" (Bell 1884). The first part of this chapter, on social and cultural attitudes toward deafness, will trace some of the developments and shifts in the largely negative imagery associated with deafness throughout the period.

If, however, the deaf were seen as experiencing heavy privations and deserving commiseration, it was not a condition that was seen as completely without amelioration. While medical and technological treatments for deafness were limited, education was highly prized as a means of "reaching," "treating," or "saving" the deaf. The second part of this chapter will look at the way in which deafness was treated and responded to in this period, particularly focusing on the emergence and growth of deaf education. Here, my argument is that, in constructing deafness as a problem that hearing people might solve, the experience of deafness itself was constructed as undesirable and something to be mitigated. Building on this, the third section of the chapter will focus on the most contentious debate in deaf education: the question as whether best to educate deaf children using the "manual" method (a language of hand gestures, whether a recognized sign language—the native language of a particular deaf community—or an artificial language created by hearing people for the purposes of education) or the "oral" method (lip-reading the vernacular). As I shall explain, this debate, which originated in Europe and came to a head in the infamous 1880 Congress of Milan, had global ramifications. The fourth and final section of this chapter (section 5.5) will explore how deaf people responded to these developments. I shall argue that, as well as active discrimination against deaf people, this period also saw the rise of deaf identity through deaf associations, the deaf press, and imaginations of a deaf future.

When contemporaries spoke about "the deaf," they were not usually talking about anyone with a hearing loss, but rather those who were also without speech; that is, those who were called "deaf and dumb," or as the century progressed, "deaf-mutes." It is on this group—which we might think about today as nonverbal deaf people—that this chapter focuses. I will not, therefore, be specifically discussing those with hearing loss related to aging, who were considered to be in quite a different category, free from many of the negative associations that the term "the deaf" evoked. I try to use terms that now have offensive connotations, such as "dumb," only sparingly in this chapter, but I do not avoid them completely. This is because the terms were essential to how deafness was constructed and how deaf people came to see and name themselves. I have decided not to follow the distinction, introduced by the linguist James Woodward in 1972 and since widely accepted among many scholars of deafness, to capitalize "deaf" when using it as an identity and use lower-case letters when using it adjectively. As the scholar of American deafness Douglas Baynton remarks, this distinction is not always possible to make when discussing nineteenth-century figures (Baynton 1996: 11–12). When I discuss "sign language," I mean distinct languages that have developed among deaf people such as American Sign Language (ASL) in the USA, British Sign Language (BSL) in Britain, Langue des Signes Française (LSF) in France, or Auslan in Australia, and not manually encoded versions of spoken vernaculars.

Quantifying deafness is difficult due to changing terminology, shifting measurements of hearing loss, and the lack of correspondence between degree of hearing loss (in decibels) and its social impact (e.g. on a person's ability to follow spoken conversation or to speak orally). British Census officials, who started enumerating deaf people from 1851 onwards, put the numbers of deaf people in England and Wales in 1851 at 18,306, or 1 in every 979 people. By 1901, they recorded 25,317, or 1 in every 778 (Census Reports). But these figures, as well as being limited geographically, are very unreliable. As Census officials themselves recognized, deafness was widely underreported due to the stigma associated with it, and, further, the categories used to tabulate deafness ("deaf and dumb," "deaf-mute," or "deaf") changed throughout the period, making comparison difficult (Census Report 1861; see also Söderfeldt 2013: 29–90). Certainly, deafness was more common in the nineteenth century than it is in contemporary Western Europe and America due to higher rates of illnesses causing deafness (scarlet fever, mumps, chicken pox, influenza, measles, encephalitis, meningitis, and rubella) and poor-quality audio-enhancing technology (which was also prohibitively expensive).

5.2. IMAGINING THE DEAF: SOCIAL ATTITUDES AND CULTURAL REPRESENTATIONS

As a group, "the deaf and dumb" attracted much attention in the nineteenth century, and this attention came from varied quarters: deaf characters appeared in jokes, stories, plays, and satires; sermons were preached on the "plight of the deaf and dumb"; and charities and societies for deaf people proliferated. The deaf population also played a formative role in thinking about disability more broadly, and their perceived otherness defined them as a distinct social category. The link long drawn in Western philosophy between language and thought meant that, without speech, deaf people were imagined as unable to think or reason. In some cases, deaf people were refused property rights, unable to inherit, denied access to the courts, deemed unable to give evidence, excluded from education, discouraged from marrying, and forcibly institutionalized (Ackers 1880: 164; Ward 2012: 3–20). These exclusions and interventions were justified on the grounds that deaf people did not qualify for full personhood; deaf people were, in Jan Branson and Don Miller's memorable phrase, "damned for their difference" (2002). Some even argued that deaf people were more like animals than human beings; one observer wrote that deaf people were "not much above the animal creation," and that the deaf person was "a creature … little removed from other dumb creatures" (quoted in Joyner 2004: 13).

One of the key ways in which deaf people were constructed as "other" involved ideas about religion and irreligion (Cleall 2013: 590–603). In Britain and America, the "Deaf, who on that account do not attend Church" were identified as a community unable to hear the Word of God (SPCK 1864). Their perceived lack of subjectivity was troubling: if those "without a voice" could not reason, could they exercise free will, or even believe in God? Opinions abounded as to whether deaf people could be considered part of the Christian community or, among other things, understand marriage vows (Cockayne 2003: 505). Writing of deaf people in 1864, the author of *Children of Silence* described their lives as consisting of "perpetual and cheerless silence" (Anon. 1864: 5–6). In so doing, the author makes a common association between deafness and silence, which was often used to suggest that being deaf was a poignant position. In ignoring the sounds that deaf people may hear or make, such portrayals contributed to the metaphorical silencing of the deaf throughout the period. "To be 'Deaf'," the author writes, "is to be cut off from enjoying the melody of nature, the pleasures of social intercourse and the persuasive sound of the preacher's voice calling men to hear the Word of God" (5–6). To be "deaf and dumb" was considered even worse: "if the affliction should have come in early life, it renders the faculties of the mind dormant, confining the nobler part of the child as in a dark prison-house without any ray of hope to illuminate the path." Indeed, the author continues, "it may be said of persons in this lamentable state, 'Eyes have they, but they see not; ears have they, but they hear not.'" Religious contexts reoccur in this image of deaf isolation: "God is not in all their thoughts" (5–6). Thus, in both predominantly Catholic countries and Protestant countries, the deaf were constructed as morally suspect (Martins 2009: 109).

While the construction of deaf people as unchristian was a discourse of otherness, it was one often articulated through the language of pity. This was not the relatively straightforward kind of pity evoked by other disabled figures in this period, notably the blind person and the "cripple." Indeed, there is a rarity of sentimental representations of deafness, with the deaf and hard of hearing more often presented as figures of fun or misanthropes. Instead, it was a pity for the "heathenism" deaf people represented and, thus, the moral danger they might pose. A man identified solely as Mr. Gordon, writing about the "instruction of the deaf and dumb" in Dublin, was one of many who adopted a pitying tone and framed deaf people as suffering beings in need of rescue. "The sympathies of our nature must be awakened" for the "uneducated deaf mute," he wrote, because "he must be forever excluded in this life ... doomed to pine away his years in solitary misery, incapable of ameliorating his condition in the slightest degree by any exertions of his own" (Gordon 1831: iv). Typically, Gordon linked the supposed passivity of deaf people with social transgression and exclusion. Ignoring the varied and often effective means of communication deaf and hearing people improvised at community levels, he depicted the deaf as thoroughly isolated from human contact. Gordon believed that, when finding that "his rude language of gestures" is "ill-adapted" to communicating "with his family or his neighbours," the deaf person's "continual vexations soon call up the evil passions in his breast," and "as is generally the case where the impetus to virtue, religious instruction, is wanting" and one is "ignorant" of "all the great truths of natural and revealed religion," a "propensity to evil has ... full scope" (iv). In such circumstances, he concluded, "well it is, if along with being a burdensome, he does not become a troublesome and mischievous member of society" (Gordon 1831: iv). Here, Gordon constructs deaf irreligion as a signifier of their victimhood. Scriptural imagery, practical forms of religious exclusion, the undermining of deaf subjectivity, critiques of sign language, and pity for their "heathenism" all led to the construction of deaf people as religious others.

Even portrayals of deafness as sympathetic, rather than simply pitiable, could feed into the construction of its perceived otherness. In Charles Dickens's *Doctor Marigold*, for example, sign language, as used by the novella's heroine, Sophy, is represented fairly positively. Furthermore, in the representation of Sophy as the mother of a hearing child (a plot line at odds with the strong link between deafness and heredity in "scientific" discourse), we might see a progressive interpretation of deafness in the 1860s, one that ran counter to some of the fears that the idea of deafness generated elsewhere (Dickens 1865). The novella ends with the eponymous Marigold's "happy, yet pitying tears" at his realization that Sophy's child is hearing. These tears, as Martha Stoddard Holmes so effectively argues, reinforce associations between disability, tragedy, and loss (Holmes 2009: 53–64). Yet, at the same time, as Christine Ferguson points out, the cause of the pity in this context is complex, relating to the grief around childhood death (a different storyline) and abuse rather than disablement (Ferguson 2008: 20). Fiction also provided a vehicle for rather more romanticized versions of deafness, or particularly muteness, as an idealized form of womanhood. As Elisabeth Gitter asserts, "mute" and "angelic" heroines, as popularized in Daniel Auber's *La Muette de Portici* or *Masaniello* (1828) and John Farrell's *The Dumb Girl of Genoa* (1827), were such a feature of mid-nineteenth-century theatre as to earn ridicule in Bernard Bayle's farce *The Dumb Belle* (1841) (Gitter 1992: 185). Most famously, perhaps, the deaf-mute heroine is found in Wilkie Collins's Madonna (*Hide and Seek*, 1854), whose feminized silence helped to construct her as an angelic type (Gitter 1992: 188–9).

In her excellent study of deafness in Victorian Britain, Jennifer Esmail has argued that, toward the end of the nineteenth century, there was a shift in attitudes regarding deafness: it stopped being a "private issue," an individual misfortune, and became a "public threat" (Esmail 2013: 141). One of the ways in which we can see this shift happen is in the increasing notice that eugenicists, such as Alexander Graham Bell, paid to questions of deafness. Born in 1847 in Edinburgh, Bell had an international career. He emigrated to Canada with his family in 1870. He then moved to the USA, where he became a naturalized citizen in 1882, and later he returned to Nova Scotia, where he died in 1922.

Best known as an inventor—he is famously credited with inventing the telephone—Bell had a wide range of interests, including science, eugenics, linguistics, and deaf education. His interest in the latter was something of a family tradition. His father, Alexander Melville Bell, was an educator who worked to create a system of "visible speech" for deaf students. His mother, Eliza, née Symonds, was almost completely deaf and, later, Alexander Graham Bell married one of his own students, a young deaf woman called Mabel Hubbard. Using his father's methods, Bell taught in deaf schools in Scotland, Canada, and the USA, and was passionate about the oral method of deaf education.

It is for his *Memoir on the Formation of a Deaf Variety of a Human Race* that Bell is best remembered among scholars of deafness. In this paper, originally a lecture delivered at Yale University in 1883 and published the following year, Bell started from the selective reproduction of breeds of domestic animals, extrapolating from them that "if we could apply selection to the human race we could also produce modifications or varieties of men" (Bell 1884: 3). His central thesis was that "if the laws of heredity that are known to hold in the case of animals also apply to man, the intermarriage of congenital deaf-mutes through a number of successive generations should result in the formation of a deaf variety of the human race" (4). And this, he argued, was a strong possibility, as "in this country [the USA] *deaf-mutes marry deaf-mutes*" (4, emphasis in original). With deaf people forming clubs, socializing with one another, and, worst of all in his opinion, marrying other deaf people, Bell believed that the creation of a "deaf race" was well underway. While deaf people were not alone in representing "inferior racial stock," their distinctive communities made the problem more pressing: "We do not find epileptics marrying epileptics, or consumptives knowingly marrying consumptives," Bell wrote (3). As an antidote to deaf communities, he emphasized the supposed benefits of assimilation. The majority of what became a treatise of nearly 100 pages was a careful statistical analysis of patterns of the inheritance of congenital deaf-mutism, and the marriage patterns resulting, Bell believed, from deaf education, socialization, and, in particular, sign language (Baynton 1996: 28).

Deaf people as well as hearing people could perpetuate negative stereotypes of deafness. John Kitto, whose 1845 memoir, *The Lost Senses*, provides an illuminating insight into the physicality and emotionality of the experience of deafness in this period, using an "uneducated" boy only conversant in sign language as an example of the kind of deaf person that Kitto himself was not: impoverished, isolated, and ignorant (Kitto 1845: 115). Indeed, as Holmes has noted in her analysis, Kitto seems convinced that deaf people suffered "disqualifications" from many of the walks of life in which he himself excelled (Holmes 2004: 158–64). Further, Kitto claimed to have always "abominated" sign language—the visible marker of deaf identify. He was deeply offended to have been connected with the Deaf and Dumb Institution and strove to distinguish himself from "deaf-mutes" (Cleall 2015c: 132–3).

Given the negative connotations attached to deafness and the prominent place it occupied in the public sphere, it is unsurprising that many attempted to "save," "civilize," and "reform" the deaf through medical or technological cure or through education and spiritual salvation.

5.3. "SAVING" THE DEAF: MEDICINE AND EDUCATION

Deafness was something that doctors, encouraged by Enlightenment developments in biomedicine, had become increasingly determined to "cure." But, in the age of empires, the cure still largely eluded them. Physicians drilled holes through deaf children's jaws, poured caustic substances into their ears, pierced eardrums, applied white-hot metal, and, in some cases, fractured their skulls behind the ear (Carpenter 2009: 115). Such procedures invariably failed to induce hearing and were not infrequently fatal. While the development of certain instruments, such as the cephaloscope (an aural instrument designed to test the circulation of air in the inner ear), contributed to the professionalization of the discipline of aural surgery, quackery still remained widespread (Virdi-Dhesi 2013: 347–77). The aforementioned deaf traveler and missionary, John Kitto, recorded how doctors "poured into my tortured ears various infusions, hot and cold; they bled me, they blistered me, leeched me, physicked me; and, at last, they put a watch between my teeth, and on finding that I was unable to distinguish the ticking, they gave it up as a bad case, and left me to my fate" (Kitto 1845: 12). Fiction presented more positive interpretations of surgery, as in W. Fletcher's *The Deaf and Dumb Boy* (1843), where surgery apparently cures the congenitally deaf Jack, and he becomes a hearing partner in a law firm (Miller 1992: 46). Various technologies, from "ear spectacles" to "ear trumpets," were used to mitigate the effects of deafness, but, despite some famous advocates (the writer, traveler, and sociologist Harriet Martineau was perhaps one of the most well-known users of the ear trumpet), such innovations were rudimentary; there was a large contingency of deaf people whom they did not help at all, and the costs of such technologies put them beyond the reach of many ordinary people (Virdi-Dhesi 2016).

The main way through which deafness was "treated" in the nineteenth century was education. While early attempts at deaf education had been pioneered in Spain, these did not really spread in Western Europe until the end of the eighteenth century, when there was a profound shift in the way in which deaf people were seen and responded to (Van Cleve and Crouch 1989: 10–16). While deaf people had long been seen as "uneducable," techniques for teaching the deaf were slowly developed in this time period by teachers, missionaries, parents, and deaf people themselves. In 1760, the Royal Institution for the Deaf and Dumb was opened in Paris by Abbé de l'Épée, a French priest who, having observed deaf Parisians communicate with each other, was inspired to adapt and codify this "language of signs" for the purpose of teaching deaf people about the life of Christ. At more or less the same time, Thomas Braidwood, a mathematics teacher based in Edinburgh, was approached by the father of a deaf boy anxious for his son to be educated. Braidwood developed his own techniques (about which he was secretive, considering them to represent commercially sensitive information) for deaf education and established the Braidwood Academy for the Deaf and Dumb in Edinburgh later in 1760. The first permanent school for the deaf in America was the American School for the Deaf (originally the Connecticut Asylum for the Education and Instruction of Deaf and Dumb Persons), which was founded in 1817 by Mason Fitch Cogswell (the determined father of a deaf daughter, Alice), Thomas Hopkins Gallaudet (a talented congregational minister who had studied at the Royal Institution for the Deaf and Dumb in Paris), and Laurent Clerc (a deaf teacher at the Royal Institution who came to the USA with Gallaudet) (Van Cleve and Crouch 1989: 30).

Following these early moves, and some tentative first steps, deaf schools started to flourish throughout Western Europe and North America. The Edinburgh Institution for the Deaf and Dumb, founded in 1810 by Thomas Braidwood's grandson, John, after the original Academy relocated to London, was one of the largest of such institutions. Its object, reiterated yearly in its annual reports, was "to remedy one of the most calamitous and affecting imperfections, to which human nature is liable" (Edinburgh Institution

1815: 3). In a mixture of religious and secular aims typical of deaf education, it aimed "to withdraw that evil" by which the minds of deaf people had been "rendered inaccessible to the lights of truth and reason, and to the blessed light of religion" (Edinburgh Institution 1815: 3). "Industrial training" was an important part of the curriculum of many of these schools, with students trained in a variety of skills, from printing to brush-making. Susan Plann records the daily *labores* Spanish girls did in the Spanish National Deaf School in Madrid, where they were trained, among other things, to compete in a marriage market in which their deafness was presumed to disadvantage them (Plann 2007: 167–76). In America, the success of schooling for deaf children contributed to demands for a Deaf College, where higher levels of education could be achieved. The opening of the National Deaf Mute College in 1864 was an important moment, hailed by John Carlin in its inauguration ceremony as "a bright epoch in deaf mute history" (Van Cleve and Crouch 1989: 71–86).

As well as being places where deafness was defined and treated by hearing people, schools were also important sites for the formation of deaf identity. Schools were often the first places where deaf children encountered other deaf people, and many expressed profound feelings of connectedness when they realized there were other children like them. One pupil at the Edinburgh Institution of the Deaf and Dumb, George Tait, described his "delight" on entering the schoolroom for the first time when he saw "a number of boys and girls" of whom he states, "like myself none of them could either hear or speak" (Tait 1878: 6). Alexander Atkinson, an older pupil at the institution, also commented on being "sensibly affected when I saw that I became the glanced of fifty young eyes, hailing enough to say, 'Oh! Come to us, for we are all deaf and dumb, like you'" (Atkinson 1865: 11). In North America, too, school experiences were bonding and formative (Winzer 1997: 363).

Schools for deaf people also developed elsewhere in the Anglophone world, sometimes coupled with institutions for blind people. By the beginning of the twentieth century, deaf schools in Canada included institutions in Halifax, Nova Scotia, and Fredericton, New Brunswick, which, in their origin and praxis, followed along similar lines to schools in Britain (Board of Education 1901a: 292, 1901b:342; Cleall 2015a). The Institution for the Deaf and Dumb and the Blind in New South Wales was opened in 1869 by Thomas Pattison, a deaf and dumb Scottish immigrant (Board of Education 1901b: 238). In Tasmania, the Blind, Deaf and Dumb Institution opened in North Hobart in 1898 with the intention of providing education and industrial training. The Brisbane Institution for the Instruction of the Blind, Deaf and Dumb catered for those in Queensland and was founded in 1883. In southern Africa, meanwhile, education for the deaf was provided by church and missionary organizations rather than civic philanthropic endeavors. The Irish Dominican Order established the first School for the Deaf, the Dominican Grimley Institute (also known as St. Mary's), in Cape Town in 1863 and, unlike schools in Australia and Canada, which were essentially European enterprises, it was open to indigenous Africans as well as European settlers (Aarons and Akach 2002: 301).

Charting the development of deaf education beyond the Western world is difficult due to sketchy and disparate evidence, though excellent preliminary work by M. Miles suggests that attitudes were as varied as might be anticipated (2000: 115–34, 2001: 291–315, 2004: 531–45). With the scarcity of English-language sources on the topic, indigenous constructions of disability are beyond the scope of this chapter, which focuses instead on the way in which these constructions were understood by European and American writers. Certainly, we should be wary of assuming, as did some nineteenth-century British missionaries, that the absence of European involvement meant that those with impairments were simply excluded or abused.

The most significant work among deaf people in the late nineteenth-century British Empire was done by missionary societies. The Church of England Zenana Missionary Society was particularly active in establishing schools for the deaf in Palamcottah, India (opened 1897), Madras, India (opened 1913), and Mount Lavinia, Ceylon (opened 1912). Another notable establishment was the Institution for Deaf Mutes in Bombay. The then Vicar Apostolic of Bombay, Bishop Meurin, had established the institution in 1884, having been approached by members of his congregation with deaf children. A Catholic institution in its origin and management, the school was nonetheless planned as "open to children of every caste and of every religious denomination," with "no attempt to wound in any way the religious susceptibilities of non-Christian scholars," and with "the strictest religious neutrality … observed with regard to pupils not belonging to the Christian communion" (Walsh 1890). Given the rates of deafness in Bombay, however, the number of students was surprisingly low, and the principal of the school, Mr. T. A. Walsh, believed that many potential students were kept away due to the suspicions of their parents that the school was an instrument of proselytization. Elsewhere, the development of deaf education was more limited. Some missionaries attempted to work with the individual deaf people they encountered. Reverend Colden Hoffman, for example, taught basket-weaving to a Liberian deaf boy, baptized Harvey Peet. These efforts were ad hoc throughout the period (Miles 2004: 537–8).

5.4. MANUALISM VERSUS ORALISM: THE BATTLE OVER SIGN LANGUAGE

The most contentious—indeed, vitriolic—debate that characterized the development of deaf education was whether the manual system (sign language) or the oral system (lip-reading) should be used. This brings us to sign language, perhaps the heart of deaf identity. While the aforementioned Abbé de l'Épée is often credited with first attempting to codify sign language, signed languages had, of course, been used all over the world both by groups of deaf people and by deaf individuals to communicate with their families and communities. When contemporaries talked about "signs," they were actually talking about several different things. Sometimes they were discussing gestures used by hearing and deaf people alike (like pointing or beckoning). Sometimes they were talking about sign systems improvised for communication between deaf individuals, particularly in a community where several people were deaf. Sometimes they were talking about an "artificial" sign system, usually "invented" by hearing people (Abbé de l'Épée's system was a version of this). And sometimes they were talking about an organic language, developed within deaf communities, which today we would discuss as BSL in the British case or ASL in America. These are separate languages with separate grammars and vocabularies. The blurring between these categories was essential in denigrating sign language.

From the beginnings of deaf education in the late eighteenth century, there were always some differences of opinion regarding the "best" pedagogical method of teaching deaf children. "Manualism" (sometimes called the French method) embraced the sign languages indigenous to deaf communities, supplementing and altering them with sign systems codified by hearing teachers (Figure 5.1). At the same time, another system developed, "oralism" or the "German method," which focused on articulation and speech-reading the vernacular. "Oralists" abhorred sign languages, which they believed

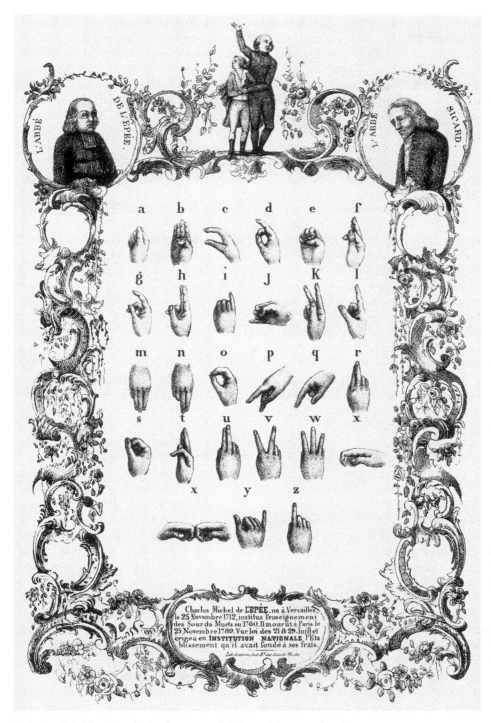

FIGURE 5.1 The French sign language alphabet with ornate border.

to be fundamentally primitive. They discouraged (and sometimes forcibly restrained) deaf children from using sign language, and encouraged them instead to focus on pronouncing and speech-reading spoken language. A variety of methods were used to do so, such as tying the hands of deaf children behind their backs so they could not sign and tediously teaching them the micromechanics of oral pronunciation. In the early nineteenth century, manualism and oralism coexisted reasonably peacefully, but, by the mid-nineteenth century, these two distinct forms had hardened into opposing camps. Manualism was favored in France and the USA, while oralism was increasingly used in Germany. Spain, the Netherlands, and the Scandinavian countries did not have a fixed position—rather, different schools used different methods—and in Britain, some schools used what they called the "combined system," where both were deployed (Van Cleve and Crouch 1989: 107–8).

The debate over which form of deaf education was better intensified into an important philosophical discussion about the limits of language and "civilization." By the mid-nineteenth century, it was felt that these methods could no longer coexist, and there were heated arguments between teachers and schools within countries and internationally about which system was superior. With individuals, schools, and missionaries petitioning different European governments, two international conventions in 1878 and 1880 were convened in order to establish once and for all which system would be considered preferable.

The second of these conferences, the Congress of Milan, held in 1880, is the most notorious point in deaf history and is associated with the deliberate suppression of sign language. From the outset, the conference displayed bias. Out of the twelve speakers, nine spoke in favor of oralism, compared to only three who championed manualism (the Gallaudet brothers from the USA and Richard Elliott, a teacher from England). The conference was chaired by the Italian Abbé Guilio Tarra, who was a strong advocate in favor of oralism. There were almost no deaf people present.

Again and again, it was argued that only oralism would properly equip deaf people for participation in hearing society. Oralists contended that "the mouth was positively exalted": "of all movements for the expression of ideas, those of the lips are the most perfect. All is comprehended in that wonderful instrument, the mouth, played upon by the hand of the Deity" (President 1880: 24). Signs were repeatedly derided: "Symbols and signs are metals absolutely base" (Kinsey 1880: 12). The president of the congress claimed that only oralism could convey abstract thought and that signs only left his pupils "in possession of grossly material images" (1880: 26). Those arguing in favor of the "German method" also fused oralism with masculinity. "In the school room begins the 'redemption' of the deaf mute," stated the president of the congress: "he is waiting to be made a man of by his teacher. Let the pupil be taught to move his lips in speech, not his hands in signs." In such a statement we see sign language users excluded both from the category of "man" as representative of humanity and from adult manhood, the gendered category of those treated as political actors. Others argued that manualism made deaf education needlessly expensive. But the central argument was that signing made deaf people different. M. Hugentobler from Lyons, for example, argued that "deaf mutes are born with the same faculties as hearing children. They differ from the rest of mankind only when they are taught signs. Moral development is then prevented" (1880: 34). Difference was increasingly intolerable, and difference became embodied in the sign language debate.

These debates had huge consequences for the way in which deaf people were educated. Teachers and pedagogues across Britain, Europe, and America turned away from the use of sign language and toward "Pure Oralism." The Congress of Milan has been seen by deaf scholars and activists as crushing deaf culture and ushering in a "dark age" of deaf education. Children, forced laboriously to learn articulation, were denied access to education beyond the mere rudiments of speech. The conference is etched on the memory of the deaf community as a moment of cultural demolition.

So why did oralism rise with such devastating effect? Douglas Baynton argues that, in the case of the USA, the turn away from manualism can be explained by a reconfiguration of the "problem" of deafness from one of religious belonging to one of national belonging (1996). Before the 1860s, Baynton explains, deafness was seen as isolating because it cut people off from the Christian community. After the 1860s, he continues, this was no longer paramount. Instead, the hearing community became increasingly concerned that deaf people were cut off from English-speaking American culture and thus could not belong to the nation (Baynton 1992: 216–43; 1996: 15). Baynton provides two explanations for this shift. Firstly, he argues that sign language came to be linked with primitivism. Secondly, he states that the shift occurred in response to renewed nationalism in the wake of the Civil War and the anti-immigration rhetoric that developed in this milieu. Although Baynton's thesis is constructed about American culture, a similar shift occurred in the British context. In Britain, too, sign language became increasingly linked with primitivism.

One of the ways in which sign language was denigrated was through placing it in the same analytic frame as "race," to which attitudes were also hardening over the nineteenth century. Anthropologists were one group who, in drawing on the notions of language and civilization, helped to articulate disabled others and racialized others in shared discursive terms, not least through subjecting both the deaf and the colonial other to the same "scientific" gaze. Edward Burnett Tylor, the first professor of Anthropology at Oxford University, who had previously studied Mexico and the Mexicans, wrote extensively about "the gesture language of the deaf and dumb" in his *Researches into the Early History of Mankind* (Tylor 1865). Tylor drew on research conducted in a range of deaf institutions in Britain and Germany and his friendship with BSL users to list numerous examples of what he discussed as "picture signs" and to detail the different grammatical aspects of sign language, such as word order and tense use. Tylor placed considerable importance on establishing the independence of sign language from speech; he emphasized that "the real deaf-and-dumb language of signs" should be distinguished from finger-spelling and artificial grammatical additions to it by hearing teachers of the deaf (1865: 16–17): "The gesture language is not, like the finger alphabet, an art learnt in the first instance from the teacher, but an independent process originating in the mind of the deaf-mute, and developing itself as his knowledge and power of reasoning expand under instruction" (1865: 17–18). The "gesture language," Tylor argued, was the "mother tongue" of the deaf and, just "as a foreigner is not fit to teach a Frenchman French, so the speaking man has no business to meddle with the invention of signs, giving them abstract values" (Tylor 1865: 19). While, in many ways, Tylor defended the use of sign language, by placing it in the same analytic frame as race and by discussing it in terms of national identity, he opened the doors to suggestions that those who used sign language did not belong to the nation state.

As the nineteenth century wore on and evolutionary discourses gained hold, the association between sign language and "savagery" contributed to the decline of manual education for the deaf and the rise of oralism. As Baynton demonstrates, oralist educators such as Gardiner G. Hubbard, president of the Clarke Institution for Deaf-

Mutes, one of the first oral schools in America, claimed that the sign language of deaf people "resembles the languages of the North American Indian and the Hottentots of South Africa." Further, the British oralist Susanna E. Hull claimed in an article in the *American Annals of the Deaf* that to teach children sign language was to "push them back in the world's history to the infancy of our race" (Baynton 1996: 43). Here, we can see important intersections between disability, colonialism, and race that characterized the construction of deafness more widely (Cleall 2015b: 22–36).

5.5. BEING DEAF: DEAF ASSOCIATIONS, COMMUNITIES, PUBLICATIONS, AND COLONIES

So far, this chapter has focused on images of and social attitudes toward deaf people predominantly propagated by hearing people, but deaf people were also active in constituting their own image as projected in the public sphere and in forging their own communities and identities.

Throughout the nineteenth century, deaf people created organizations to enable them to come together, share the experience of being deaf, and advocate on behalf of other deaf people. In Britain, the Association in Aid of the Deaf and Dumb was established in 1841 and was one of the largest of such organizations. This organization (the Royal Association in Aid of the Deaf and Dumb [RAADD] from 1873 on) was formed to assist adult deaf people who, it was argued, had been omitted from the first wave of philanthropy directed at deaf children. The RAADD was behind the creation of a deaf church, St. Saviours, on Oxford Street, London, which opened in 1875 and both reflected and contributed to the sense of the deaf as a discrete community (Pemberton 2004: 60) (Figure 5.2). The RAADD also supported a wide range of activities, including a debating society, evening lectures, soirées, bazaars, spelling bees, plays, and impersonated black "minstrel" shows (Pemberton 2004: 60) (Figure 5.3).

While the RAADD was always headed by a hearing man, the National Deaf and Dumb Society and the British Deaf and Dumb Association (BDDA) were British organizations run by deaf people for deaf people. The BDDA was the brainchild of Francis Maginn, a deaf Irishman who had been educated in England and at the National Deaf Mute College in Washington, DC. His experience of the American deaf community and subsequent involvement in the International Congress of the Deaf and Dumb in Paris in 1889 inspired him to try to establish an empowering deaf organization back in Britain (Grant 1990: 19). The American deaf community, which Maginn had found so influential, certainly had a deep tradition of deaf activism. As Van Cleve and Crouch argue, the prominent American deaf associations—such as the National Fraternal Society of the Deaf, the American Athletic Association of the Deaf, the National Congress of the Jewish Deaf, and the American Professional Society for the Deaf—are striking because of the extent to which "in the United States deaf people created their own associations, funded them and controlled them" (1989: 87). Nonetheless, in France, deaf associations, such as the Société des Sourds-Muets de Bourgogne, were also established in the wake of the Congress of Milan to defend the use of sign language (Mirzoeff 1995: 182). In Germany, meanwhile, associations, clubs, and other groups were also key to the spread of the deaf movement (Söderfeld 2013: 145–218).

Deaf publications were an important means through which deaf communities were imagined, constituted, and bound together. The earliest deaf publications took off in the mid-nineteenth century, a period in which decreases in the stamp duty and technological

FIGURE 5.2 A vicar using sign language.

FIGURE 5.3 A Christmas entertainment, presented in sign language.

advances enabled cheaper production and distribution of periodicals and the rapid increase of a reading public fueled the demand for specialist publications. One of the most striking things about deaf newspapers is the sheer number of them. In America, there were vast numbers of the publications known collectively as "Little Papers" or the "Little Paper Family," which tended to be produced and managed by schools that acted as hubs for the deaf community (Van Cleve and Crouch 1989: 98). Raymond Lee calculates that since the first known magazine for the deaf was published in Edinburgh in 1839 until 2004, there was a "minimum count" of 356 known journals for the deaf published in Great Britain (2004: 131). And, in France, as many as fourteen periodicals and journals were established by and about the deaf between 1883 and 1899 (Mirzoeff 1995: 182). The proliferation of publications points to the enthusiasm for such papers as ways of sharing news in the deaf community, creating jobs for deaf artists and journalists, training deaf students, and raising money for the deaf community. It also reflects the difficulties in sustaining such papers. Because it was difficult to break even, many fell into financial collapse, and some were absorbed into others.

Early papers were not originally aimed at a deaf readership, but rather were geared toward supporters or potential supporters of the deaf cause. But this soon changed. *A Magazine Intended Chiefly for the Deaf and Dumb*, which was established in 1873 and edited by the Reverend Samuel Smith (of the RAADD), was the first British magazine intended principally for the deaf themselves and included "Pictures from Scripture History," sermons, explanations of scripture doctrine, "The Lives of Good Men" (especially those that were deaf), and long compositions by deaf readers, especially on religious topics (1873: 1–16). Early American publications to be edited by deaf people included the *Deaf Mutes' Friend*, edited by William B. Swett and William M. Chamberlain, which contained stories told by the former to the latter in ASL and then translated by Chamberlain into written English (Edwards 2012: 110). The first British magazine to be edited by a deaf person was the *Deaf and Dumb Herald and Public Intelligencer*, which was edited by Ralph Clegg, who had been deaf from childhood. The editorship was self-consciously deaf, emphasizing the benefits of a publication being edited "by one of their own flock" (1876: 1, 32).

As Jennifer Esmail has argued, "the print culture of deaf periodicals was transatlantically entwined," and, from their earliest days, these magazines had a transnational scope (2013: 24). Back in 1843, the *Edinburgh Quarterly Messenger* encouraged publications from continental Europe and the USA, and later on, extracts appeared about the deaf community further afield, particularly in Australia (*The Edinburgh Quarterly Messenger* 1843: 1; *The Deaf and Dumb Magazine* 1880: 182–4; *The British Deaf Mute* 1895: 168). In 1891, in its first year of existence, the Leeds-based *Deaf and Dumb Times* published contributions from teachers of the deaf stationed in Britain, Australia, China, Nova Scotia, Paris, and California (*Deaf and Dumb Times* 1891). *The Deaf Chronicle* also had global ambitions; its editorials began, "To our readers throughout the world" (1892: 1). The *American Annals for the Deaf* was perhaps the most widely read paper of its type internationally and is still in existence today. Considerable intertextuality meant that information was repeated across different periodicals and a deaf community woven transnationally. Articles roamed over a wide variety of topics, from the manualism/oralism debate to reports from schools to biographies of significant members of the deaf community.

Some deaf people, however, felt that it was not satisfactory for them to always be what historian of American deafness R. A. R. Edwards describes as a "scattered and minority culture in a hearing world" (2012: 112). During the nineteenth century, deaf identity also started to be expressed in terms of a desire for a land of their own, where deaf people could live together free from hearing influence altogether. In the 1820s, Laurent Clerc, the so-called "Apostle of the Deaf in America," had suggested using some of the land Congress had given in Alabama to the American Asylum as a location where deaf people could settle (Krentz 2000: 161). In the 1830s, a group of graduates of the American Asylum talked of purchasing land "out west" so that they could continue living close to each other (Krentz 2000: 161). Acting as a "sort of secret society," they had planned to "form a nucleus around and within which others of our class might in process of time, gather" (Booth to Flournoy, in Krentz 2000: 177). In Martha's Vineyard, where there was a high concentration of deaf people and where deaf and hearing people used sign language, a community already existed and was an inspiration for others (Groce 1988). In Australia, there were several schemes (some of which were realized) for large-scale deaf farms, where the deaf could live collectively (Flynn 1984: 45–65). There were also deaf separatist movements throughout the nineteenth century in Britain and in France (Krentz 2000: 161–4).

The most well-known demand for a separatist deaf territory came from John Flournoy, a slave-owner from Georgia, who, in 1855, proposed that a "Deaf State" should be created in the USA. Outraged at the discrimination he faced as a deaf man and by the passing of recent legislation in Georgia "to make deaf and dumb people idiots in the law and to provide them guardians," Flournoy wanted to "secure the government and offices of a small territory or State, to the mute community" (quoted in Krentz 2000: 165). In a pamphlet circulated to deaf people across North America and Europe, he demanded that deaf people be allowed to purchase land in the American West and establish their own state there, "colonizing some small territory ... with a population of mutes" (quoted in Krentz 2000: 165). In the ongoing discussion, various places were named as potential sites for the deaf state, which he believed could be the size of Rhode Island or Connecticut (Krentz 2000: 166). He variously discussed this scheme as the creation of a "deaf state," "empire," "colony," or "commonwealth." The scheme attracted much attention in the deaf press and was extensively debated for the rest of the century. Deaf people wrote both in support of and against the deaf territory, which some mockingly suggested might be called Deaf-Mutia or Gesturia (Flournoy's own choice was Gallaudetia) (John Carlin, in Krentz 2000: 192; Flournoy, in Krentz 2002: 199). Criticism notwithstanding, Flournoy felt convinced of the "practicability and utility" of the scheme (quoted in Krentz 2000: 184).

While Flournoy's plan never got off the ground, another plan for a deaf colony did make some progress. In 1884, Jane Groom, a deaf British woman, traveled to Canada with ten deaf men, intending to settle a "colony" for the deaf in the Canadian northwest (Cleall 2016: 39–61). Groom had been a missionary to the deaf in London and, horrified by the discrimination and poverty she encountered there, she determined to help deaf people start anew in Canada. "I have noticed so much distress among the deaf and dumb," she wrote, "that I feel perfectly sad at witnessing it, and I am sure that nothing can be done for them here to establish them satisfactorily. My opinion on this subject is that the only scheme to accomplish their ultimate well-being is to carry out my scheme of emigration to Canada" (in H. H. 6). Over the next ten years, Groom established twenty-four more deaf settlers and their families in Canada, much to the outrage of local hearing settlers, who claimed that the "deaf-mutes" would be unable to support themselves and would soon be reliant on charity. There were also other traditions of deaf settlement in the Canadian prairies, including a steady flow of deaf homesteaders to Saskatchewan during the early twentieth century. From 1905, the deaf homesteaders inaugurated the tradition of the annual picnic, which helped them to maintain a deaf community. Cliff Carbin notes that there were so many deaf people proportionately that "the merchants, lawyers, doctors, farmers and even the 'red-coated' Policemen in the area learned to converse with these labourers by using the manual alphabet and some signs" (1996: 238). This demonstrates not only that there were considerable numbers of deaf people present, but also that they were able to exercise some degree of cultural power, dictating the terms of communication.

International conferences were another way of establishing a global deaf community. In 1834, a new annual tradition had been founded in France: a banquet to honor the birthday of Abbé de l'Épée. The banquets were celebrations of signed languages and an opportunity to celebrate a shared deaf history and heritage (Mottez 1993: 143–4). Right from the start, the banquets had an international element, with visitors invited from the deaf communities in Britain, Italy, and Germany. Women, however, were excluded until the 1880s (Mottez 1993: 145). Eighteen international meetings of deaf people were held across Europe and North America between 1873 and 1912 (Murray 2007: 60).[1] The largest was the 1893 Chicago meeting, which had 1,000 delegates, but the 1905 Liège conference and 1912 Paris conference had the largest numbers of nations represented by participants, at nineteen countries each (Murray 2007: 60). The congresses created forums through which to share and explore issues of common concern, including the two highly contentious topics of inter-deaf marriage and deaf education (Murray 2007: 257–9). The experience of participating in these grand gatherings could be transformative. The congresses offered a space where deaf people, all too aware of their habitual position as a minority group in a hearing world, could "enjoy the privileges of temporary majority status" as large numbers of deaf people gathered together (Murray 2007: 43). They offered an opportunity of giving visibility and public validation to sign language, bestowing on it the authority of an official language at an international gathering. Continuity of delegates from one congress to the next offered the opportunity for acquaintances and connections made at these gatherings to be consolidated into real friendships and transient communities. Perhaps most significantly, there arose at these congresses the possibility for deaf people to contemplate shared experiences with other deaf people that overrode national affiliations. As historian Joseph Murray puts it, "at these Congresses, Deaf leaders found points of comparison in one another's lives, a commonality of experience lacking in interactions with their national auditory counterparts" (2007: 66). While other identities would usurp and intersect with deafness at other points, the congresses offered an opportunity to privilege that aspect of identity in the "here and now" (Murray 2007: 66).

5.6. CONCLUSION

Writing in 1897, a contributor to the deaf periodical *The British Deaf Monthly* reflected on the huge leaps forward deaf education had seen in the nineteenth century: "Really, we exaggerate little, if at all, if we say that the deaf have made more progress during the past sixty years, than the world at large in the past 60,000!" Continuing in an imperialist vein, the author states: "Barely a hundred years ago, the deaf and dumb were generally, and not unjustly regarded as little, if at all, better than savages. At the present day, the educated deaf are recognized by all persons of intelligence, as their equals" (*British Deaf Monthly* 1897). While we might be wary of so triumphalist a narrative chartering "progress" and "civilization," the nineteenth century certainly saw a huge amount of change in the way in which deafness and deaf people were represented and treated, as well as how they saw themselves. This chapter has traced some of these changes by examining the ways in which deafness was represented and treated by hearing people, the vitriolic debate over sign language, and the ways in which deaf people constituted themselves in the public sphere.

CHAPTER SIX

Speech

Dysfluent Temporalities in the Long Nineteenth Century

DANIEL MARTIN

This chapter explores the medicalization of speech impediments in the nineteenth century, focusing on contestations over knowledge about the causes and cures for speech blocks, repetitions, and hesitations. A disability studies approach to speech—and primarily stammering or stuttering—examines the therapeutic techniques that elocutionists, doctors, and researchers developed throughout the century to articulate both a cause and cure. Beginning in the 1830s, throughout Europe, elocutionary claims that training the voice through vocal gymnastics could produce fluent speech intersected uncomfortably with medical approaches that emphasized neurogenic or psychogenic causes. In other words, there was considerable uncertainty during this period about how best to "cure" stuttered speech. Was it strictly a physiological "problem" requiring elocutionary exercises for "proper" vocal production or were dysfluent speech patterns the result of brain chemistry or nervous disposition? Despite medical efforts to "cut the knot" of "entangled speech" (Wright 1843: 24) through surgical procedures in the early 1840s or various therapeutic "systems," popular elocutionary theories of cause and cure would persist throughout the century as a seemingly ineradicable belief in a panacea for stuttered speech.[1] If, as Josephine Hoegaerts suggests, the nineteenth century was the "age of the stammerer" (2015: 746), the era's primary insistence was that people with speech dysfluencies conform to standardized vocal rhythms in the name of cure, a goal that led to the widespread public mockery of dysfluent voices in print throughout the last two centuries. That stuttering today still has no definitive cause or cure demonstrates the impossibility of achieving this conformity.

In nineteenth-century elocutionary and medical contexts, this demand that people who stutter conform to "healthy" or "natural" vocal rhythms was itself distinctly modern in its emphasis on standardized time frames. In virtually all published work on stuttered speech, therapeutic techniques attempted biopolitical training of speaking bodies, in that they emphasized a regulation of not merely the particular experiences of individuals, but also the management of populations through standardized theories of cause and therapeutic techniques.[2] Michel Foucault claims that modern disciplinary techniques of the period were "no longer simply an art of distributing bodies, of extracting time from them and accumulating it, but of composing forces in order to obtain an efficient machine" (1995: 164). What this means is that the century's techniques for training and regulating the human body's rhythms in schools, prisons, hospitals, asylums, and even speech clinics, or "homes," insisted that all embodied experiences conform to efficiencies and technically precise processes of control and order. The century's insistence on fluent rhythms informed virtually all experts in both etiology and therapeutics, and even had ramifications in public cultures of the voice in religion, politics, and entertainment. Perhaps the best example of this biopolitical insistence that the person who stutters be subjected to "fluent" or efficient time frames is the fact that the medicalization of dysfluency at mid-century frequently appropriated the time-based therapeutic techniques promoted by the same elocutionists that medical experts labeled "quacks" (Hunt 1870: 212), even while they rejected elocutionary theories of the physiological causes of dysfluency.

The following pages include three sections, focusing in order on historical developments and social attitudes, cultural expressions, and theoretical implications. At the outset, a focus on definition and terminology will be helpful as a way of understanding nineteenth-century intellectual tensions about the origins and cures for dysfluent speech. Precision in terminology is foundational to current "dysfluency studies" (Eagle 2014: 4) because, unlike the broader concept of disability, which has legally binding terminology regarding who and who does not qualify as disabled, speech dysfluencies vary widely across individual case studies. While the concepts of "stuttering" and "stammering" refer to clinically diagnosed issues in speech production, the broader term "dysfluency" covers a wide range of both "normal" and "pathological" symptoms of speech that all humans experience at some point or another, especially during childhood.[3] In this regard, the plural concept of "dysfluencies" refers to a spectrum of speech symptoms that may or may not be "pathological" at any given time depending on the context of the utterance. Speech experts from early in the century, and even into the early twentieth century, were frequently split in their definitions and diagnoses of stammering and stuttering, and there was no real consensus on a conceptual difference between the two. However, some experts did claim symptomatic differences. For example, British medical expert James Wright argued in a published lecture in *The Lancet* that stammering is a "purely mental impediment," whereas stuttering is "not only a mental, but also, and principally, a physical interruption" (Wright 1851: 20). British accounts throughout the century were especially drawn to this distinction between mental stammering and physiological stuttering, although such a difference was by no means standard, especially in popular elocutionary textbooks and home remedy manuals.[4] And yet, the difference between mental hesitations and physiological blocks and repetitions that result in "painful stoppages of breath, and wry motions of the body" (Wright 1851: 21) aligned stuttered speech more broadly with other physical disorders, such as epilepsy and St. Vitus' Dance.[5] While accounts of such distinctions are compelling from a historical point of view, debates over terminology perpetuate a medical model of diagnosis and classification that is anathema to the critical work of disability studies, so this chapter will rely on both terms interchangeably, while privileging "stuttering" because of its historical connotations with the intersections and tensions between voice and body.

The nineteenth century witnessed numerous developments in thought about a range of speech-related disorders, such as lisping, rhotacism, aphasia, coprolalia, echolalia, and, most notably, stammering and stuttering. As Chris Eagle observes, the discoveries of both Broca's area and Wernicke's area, two regions of the brain primarily responsible for speech, revolutionized scientific study by linking vocal production to particular hemispheres of the brain (Eagle 2013: 4–5, 36). As compelling as such scientific studies were, nineteenth-century textbooks and treatises on speech focused less extensively on disorders resulting from brain injuries and more on the enigmatic causes of stuttering. Injury-induced dysfluencies or deafness had seemingly clear etiologies, as did the "normal" dysfluencies of early childhood. Stuttering that persisted beyond childhood, however, has always been mired in mysterious and unknown causes, and was especially troubling for nineteenth-century experts in the science of vocal production.

While histories of nineteenth-century speech science and rehabilitative techniques prioritize progressive models of the "search" or "quest" for a cure (Rockey 1980; Bobrick 1995; Wingate 1997), a disability studies approach requires analysis and critique of the tensions in the century between vocal "choreographies" (Paterson 2012: 171; St. Pierre 2015b: 50) that emphasized normative rhythmic fluencies and a range of cultural expressions of the "melancholic" or "grotesque" embodiments of people who stutter. Elocutionists would persist throughout the century in promoting systems of cure premised on simplistic theories of cause, such as a failure of the lungs to supply sufficient air during vocal enunciation (McCormac 1828) or a spasmodic inability to keep the glottis open at all times during speech (Arnott 1827: 608). Elocutionary systems of cure included such other techniques as uttering a vowel sound before each blocked consonant, choral singing, reciting poetry, speaking in iambic pentameter rhythm, or speaking to a uniform beat.[6] Such remedies, however, also had their uncanny effects when people who stuttered attempted to speak fluently. As mid-century medical expert Henry Monro argued in *On Stammering, and Its Treatment*:

> if [sufferers are] told to persist in uttering er [before anticipated difficult words], or to sing or roar out [their] words on all occasions, and trust to these as [their] infallible remedies, [they] will probably fail, for the remedies are so much more than the disease that all sensitive minds would instinctively shun them with horror, and despond the more in consequence. (1850: 14–15)

While such medical challenges to the elocutionary tradition were persistent, they were still fraught with their own problematic assumptions about where to locate the cause of stuttered speech: in the immediate physiology or neurology of the speaking subject or "elsewhere" in the social interactions between bodies.[7] Current historical accounts emphasize the development of therapeutic techniques and advancements in the pursuit of a definitive cause, but this chapter approaches the problems introduced by the therapeutic reliance on uniform time frames through the century's many sympathetic accounts of the melancholia introduced by the stutter's status as an irritant in broader cultural demands for fluent vocal communication.

6.1. HISTORICAL DEVELOPMENTS AND SOCIAL ATTITUDES

This first section explores historical developments and social attitudes to speech dysfluencies, focusing initially on early-century elocutionary theories of cause and cure, then on the medicalization of stuttering beginning roughly in the 1840s. This chronology is primarily for the purposes of convenience because contestations over knowledge about causes and cure were not as linear as they might first appear. Available histories of nineteenth-century stuttering and stammering emphasize positivist narratives of the development of aid for people with dysfluencies. Denyse Rockey brackets the century's developments between the work of British romantic poet turned elocutionist John Thelwall early in the century and the late-century work of physician John Wyllie, both of whom developed clinical approaches to the study of speech disorders (1980: 15). This persistence of primarily physiological approaches to the study of speech dysfluencies from Thelwall to Wyllie is useful for understanding the historical progression from simple elocutionary theories focusing on correct rhythm, breathing, and intonation to more complex medical theories that prioritized the complex vocal mechanics of the human body. However, disability studies perspectives on historicism assume the persistence of dense, competing networks of knowledge and power across a range of texts and contexts that impact the experiences of people with disabilities (Davis 1995b: 128). The period's social attitudes to dysfluent speech were far more genealogical than a straightforward history might suggest. Genealogical viewpoints allow for the possibility of multiple intersecting causes and relationships among phenomena without resorting to a single point of origin or linear development of thought. Even while medical models began to replace elocutionary principles in the competition for professional legitimacy, elocutionary techniques would be central to the entire century's popular knowledge about dysfluencies. Moreover, the slowed-down and inward-turning rhythms of melancholia persisted as the century's primary diagnosis of the person who stutters' disposition. Out of sync with the rhythms of the outside world, both vocally and psychologically, the person who stutters persisted as a challenge to the century's assumptions about the values of fluent communication between bodies.

A study of dysfluency rhythms outside the context of medical and clinical progress, however, does not so much disrupt standard historical accounts as it reveals the myriad ways in which nineteenth-century thought about speech dysfluencies coalesced anxiously around the temporal rhythms of "normal" or "healthy" speech. While Foucault's analysis of modern biopower focuses primarily on the body as a site of power relations, the voice also underwent extensive biopolitical training throughout the nineteenth century.[8] The nineteenth century produced an extraordinarily vast range of written materials about the causes, cures, and cultural implications of dysfluent speech, in similar fashion to the century's "incitement to discourse" about sexuality (Foucault 1990: 17–35).[9] Elocutionary and medical thought corresponded to transformations in the temporal experiences of both public and private life. Like factory systems, with their manufacture of predictable and reproducible rhythms, or the emerging European railway network, vocal utterances were increasingly subjected to external demands to eliminate accidental or inefficient "defects" of speech. These demands were consistent throughout the century, regardless of various contestations over knowledge by elocutionists, medical practitioners, psychologists, surgeons, and phonologists. As Kevin Paterson argues, the "taken-for-granted and negotiated choreography of everyday life" and its "temporal norms" frequently set people with speech impairments at a disadvantage, resulting in "exclusion and estrangement" (2012: 171). The best example of this exclusion is the American voice movement beginning toward the end of the century. Influenced by the French expert in vocal gesture, François Delsarte, American textbooks on voice and public speaking frequently ignored considerations of dysfluent speech in their promotion of "healthy" vocal production for all students. Such works as J. Harry Wheeler's *Vocal Physiology, Vocal Culture and Singing*, Elsie M. Wilbor's *Delsarte Recitation Book and Directory*, and Oskar Guttmann's *Gymnastics of the Voice for Song and Speech* contributed implicitly to eugenic and racial discourses. Dysfluent speech was not an explicit agenda of European or American eugenic systems of thought, but once the voice became integral to national health through the pedagogy of public speaking, dysfluencies became residual concerns.

Various "quack" experts were complicit in the century's proliferation of systems and techniques for producing fluency in dysfluent speakers. Quack elocutionists were especially reliant on the rhetoric of sympathy in their accounts of the melancholic experiences of people who stutter. In the 1820s, Henry McCormac's *Treatise on the Cause and Cure of Hesitation of Speech* claimed that people who stutter tend to become "melancholy, passionate, or morose, from a sense of their degradation, and their deprivation of the greatest blessing of humanity – oral communication with their fellow-creatures" (1828: 14). Moreover, McCormac claimed, people who stutter are "for ever severed from the pleasures of eloquence, and the delights of oral communication with their fellow-creatures" (1828: 32). Although associated with quackery, McCormac's diagnosis of the person who stutters was nevertheless unchallenged in elocutionary, medical, and cultural expressions throughout the century.

While early British and American elocutionists of the 1820s and 1830s marketed easy-step systems of cure, French experts in speech defects were developing early statistical data for an emerging science of dysfluent speech. Even so, their respective techniques for cure emphasized primarily elocutionary or mechanical processes. Mechanical systems of cure focused on re-habituating the speaking body within uniform speaking rhythms. The French expert Jean Itard believed that inserting a metallic fork into the mouth to keep the tongue in its proper place while speaking could retrain the vocal rhythms of people who stutter. Itard's instrumental cure is reminiscent of well-known accounts of the ancient Greek orator Demosthenes, who famously inserted pebbles into his mouth while speaking in order to cure his stutter. Demosthenes was, and still is, one of the most persistent characterizations in the broader historical narrative of the *heroic* overcoming of disability (Rose 2003: 50; Shell 2005: 32; Dolmage 2014: 119). This strategy of inserting various objects into the mouth would persist throughout the century in a range of practices, but, more importantly, Itard's work set the stage for the emergence of surgical operations beginning in the early 1840s.

In similar fashion to the British and American elocutionists, Itard's work insisted on non-psychogenic or non-neurogenic causes. Itard's contemporary, Marc Colombat de l'Isère, introduced another instrumental means through which medical experts early in the century legitimized their work. Colombat's *muthonome*—a version of Johann Maelzel's *metronome* adapted for the purposes of rhythmic speech exercises—applied elocutionary principles to the pursuit of standardized vocal time frames.[10] Colombat's "orthophonic exercises" included counting syllables during speech. Such exercises, premised on speaking fluently according to a uniform beat, were influential throughout the century, even encroaching on medical theories later in the century. For example, in the 1870s, the Austrian clinician Moritz Rosenthal classified stuttering as a disease of the nervous system. A central figure in late nineteenth-century clinical work on hysteria and neurosis, Rosenthal claimed that patients who stutter were victims of an "insubordination of the organs of speech" (1879: 401). Rosenthal promoted the curative value of French therapeutic techniques, such as orthophonic exercises, vocal gymnastics, speaking to the beat of a metronome, crescendo and decrescendo exercises, and speaking in poetic meter and four-quarter time. Echoing his predecessors in elocution and the science of speech patterns, Rosenthal claimed that dysfluent speech was the result of a body out of time with what experts believed to be the natural rhythms of speech. Such elocutionary and mechanical techniques for treating an essentially out-of-tune speaking body posited the elocutionist or speech expert as a mechanic or engineer of language. Lacking the harmony that occurs in the habitually unconscious rhythms of fluent speech, people who stuttered, elocutionists believed, could relearn—and fundamentally retrain—their "ugly" or "grotesque" speech habits.[11]

Although dismissed by medical experts beginning in the 1830s and 1840s, elocutionary principles proved to be discursively resilient and adaptable, as Rosenthal's work in the 1870s attests. Early in the century, Thelwall's foundational elocutionary principles emphasized a distinctly English "rhythmus" and claimed that any gains in fluency must begin with a careful analytical reduction of fluent speech to its elementary sounds, each recited in rhythmic successions. Thelwall's clinical work contributed to an implicit ideology of Britishness that would return persistently throughout the century as "good" speech became associated with not only individual physical health and fitness, but the general well-being of the nation. Walter K. Fobes' *Elocution Simplified* suggested to readers who wanted to improve their speaking voices that they "must have health, strength, and elasticity of body" (1877: 85), echoing claims from a few decades earlier by stuttering advocates such as Charles Kingsley, whose essay "The Irrationale of Speech" championed James Hunt's system of cure because it allowed the person who stutters to "betake himself to all manly exercises which will put him into wind, and keep him in it" (1859: 11). Kingsley's application of Hunt's work to the tenets of the muscular Christianity movement in Britain reflects broader assumptions of the time that dysfluent speech was not merely a melancholic disorder of the individual, but also had widespread cultural urgency in Britain's promotion of healthy masculinity.[12]

Such emphasis on the health and vigor of the speaking body was consistent in contemporary elocutionary and phonetic textbooks, especially in wide-ranging emphases on vocal "gymnastics" and "exercises," culminating in the American voice movement's prioritization of vocal gesture as a technique for general health. John Millard's *Grammar of Elocution* promoted, like many other elocution textbooks, various exercises for "removing" (1884: 113) stuttered speech. Like the acclaimed work of Alexander Melville Bell, whose son Alexander Graham Bell invented the telephone, Millard's treatises included tables and charts of consonant sounds for practice with proper elocutionary vocal technique. Correlations between healthy voices and healthy bodies were thus premised on a widespread assumption that devoted practice with such elocutionary or phonetic exercises could restore "natural" speaking habits in people who stutter. Elocutionists were also prepared to promote their theories through carefully constructed rhetoric about the person who stutters' loss of "natural" vocal rhythms. For example, Charles John Plumptre's *King's College Lectures on Elocution* claimed that stuttered speech was analogous to "a man walking irregularly, and not keeping time" (1881: 233). Similar claims span the extensive body of work on stuttered speech throughout the century. From as early as Thelwall's claims about a distinctly English rhythmus, the stutter became a symptom of a melancholic inability to locate in the body a "natural" account of time that had been lost at some point in childhood. Elocutionists and phoneticians fundamentally reinforced Kingsley's claim that Hunt's system of cure taught patients "to speak consciously, as other men spoke unconsciously" (1859: 9). Problems remained, however, especially considering Monro's claim in 1850 that elocutionary therapeutic techniques had a peculiar effect of being just as disagreeable as a stutter. In the name of "cure," people who stuttered were subjected to vocal exercises that effectively turned their speech into mechanical repetitions of nonsense words.

From the point of view of the material history of the mediated voice (Picker 2003; Kreilkamp 2005; Connor 2014; Camlot 2015), it might seem strange to view elocutionary recourse to charts of consonantal combinations for the purposes of speech practice as a strategy for a return to "natural" speech. Media historians instead see in nineteenth-century elocution systems the origins of a modern "interface" between the natural expressions of the human voice and its reproduction in technical systems and machinery (Camlot 2015: 19). For example, Melville Bell's work in vocal phonetics was influential in the development of the Edison phonograph in the 1870s and other contemporary speaking or talking machines (Emmott 2017; Radick 2007: 93). Melville Bell's contributions are compelling because his reputation was premised on his pursuit of "visible speech"—a universal system of phonetic symbols, each representing the correct position of the mouth, lips, and tongue during articulation (Bell 1867). What often goes unnoticed, however, is the extent to which Melville Bell envisioned his work with phonetics as a mechanism for removing dysfluencies from the realm of vocal utterance. Disability scholars and historians of American education systems have increasingly recognized Melville Bell's body of work as not simply a system of "universal alphabetics" with emancipatory potential for people with speech disabilities, but also a standardization of speech that had eugenic and racist implications (Kates 2001: 60; Esmail 2013: 101, 134).

Trained through standardized rhythms for the purposes of rediscovering a supposedly lost affinity with nature, people who stuttered were brought into a mechanical universe of simple sounds and articulations—first single syllables, then two-syllable words, and moving slowly toward more and more complex word-phrases, culminating in reciting poetry and then prose. At the same time, the elocutionary and medical literature identified in the experience of the stutter a profoundly melancholic relationship with communication and the temporal rhythms of modern society. Underlying the distinctions between ugly speech and hegemonic fluency were seemingly incommensurate temporal registers. The stutter exploded fluid lines of communication through an undoing of seemingly natural human impulses toward communication, introducing asynchronous temporalities into human interactions; corrective techniques sought to return dysfluent vocal disruptions back within "normal" temporal rhythms. Rosemarie Garland-Thomson's influential account of "normate" (1997: 8) embodied subject positions finds its vocal counterpart in nineteenth-century speech experts' ideological fantasies of a fluent voice that was free from perceived defects. Like the "normate" body that "describes only a minority of actual people" (Garland-Thomson 1997: 8), "normal" or "fluent" speech became a kind of impossible return to "natural" vocal utterances and expressions. As elocutionary principles expanded into general health movements, their emancipatory aspirations gave way to normate technical procedures for managing and regulating all voices under the auspices of a supposedly universal fluency.

British elocutionary texts emphasized the melancholia of the "stammerer" or "stutterer" in order to sell their systems of cure, but the result was far more than merely promotional. Paradoxically, despite contestations between the elocutionary principles and medical expertise, the diagnosis of melancholia introduced the possibility for a medical model of cause and cure that sutured individual accounts of melancholic or depressive states with epidemiological considerations of public health. Psychologists realized that melancholia essentially slowed curative processes because of complex psychogenic or traumatic causes. Melancholia's "oneness of thought" (Hunt 1870: 292) forced mid-century medical experts to recognize the challenging—near-impossible—work of curing stuttered or stammered speech that had been internalized by adults who were unable to surmount the origins of dysfluent speech in childhood. In this context, Hunt's work anticipates Sigmund Freud's psychoanalytic claims that the repression of childhood wishes is compulsory for any "normal" adult development, and that repressed content returns through various symptoms in neurotic and hysterical patients.[13] In the seventh edition of his major work, *Stammering and Stuttering: Their Nature and Treatment*,

Hunt cited the French expert on mental health, Jean-Étienne Dominique Esquirol, in his diagnosis of the essentially melancholic dispositions of people who stutter (1870: 292). In melancholic temporal registers, every stuttering event is infused with haunting reminders of previously unsuccessful attempts at communication. For this reason, mid-century medical experts included both traumatic and anticipatory vocal rhythms into an already complicated choreography of speech for people who stutter. Medicalization resulted in an "incitement to discourse" (Foucault 1990: 17–35) that produced the stutterer as a personage with a challenging melancholic inability to overcome childhood vocal traumas. In this regard, medicalization of dysfluent speech coincided with contemporary thought about traumatic neurosis; both were premised on the realization that traumatic experiences, in childhood especially, could return through various related symptoms at any time after an initial trauma. Medical experts in dysfluencies thus contributed to modern medical revelations that psychical experiences of trauma could produce physical symptoms in the body, even in the absence of a physical wound or infliction.[14] Yet, as medical experts began to realize, especially in the 1840s and 1850s, the lack of a definitive cause of stuttered speech directly within the body, brain, or nervous system necessitated a hybridization of techniques. Medical experts and elocutionists alike prioritized time and rhythm as strategies for managing dysfluency. The fundamental difference between elocutionary and medical models were disagreements over the speed of recovery and the extent to which therapy was bound with complex neurogenic causes. As Hunt claims about the melancholic disposition of the person who stutters, "to think of applying one method of instruction, or one special treatment, to the whole range of defects constituting stammering, would be as senseless and paradoxical as is the boast of quacks" (1870: 212).

One of the first sustained movements in the century's medicalization of stuttering resulted from surgical procedures by the German surgeon Johannes Dieffenbach, whose treatise, *Memoir on the Radical Cure of Stuttering*, received widespread praise in medical communities after its English translation in 1841. British surgeon James Yearsley popularized Dieffenbach's surgical methods in London, becoming one of the primary targets of Wright's treatise, *The Stutterer's Friend*, which campaigned against the abuses resulting from dangerous surgical operations in the name of cure. Even though Yearsley's surgical theories were extensions of medical thought in the early 1840s, his published work on stuttered speech nevertheless prioritized elocutionary techniques of cure. His essay from *The Lancet* declares, for example, that "[a]ll pleasant and agreeable speakers are good timists, and masters of rhythm" (1844: 248). Yearsley suggests that all elocutionists who treat people who stutter make their patients recite blank verse because of its rhythmical measure. "It is not the mere motion which produces the good result," Yearsley writes, "but any action of the kind is a powerful auxiliary in establishing the rhythm first in the mind, and through it on the speech" (1844: 248).

Although *The Stutterer's Friend* campaigned against the "ruinous and barbarian novelty of experimenting with the knife" (1843: vii) resulting from Dieffenbach's influence on British surgeons, Wright essentially agreed with Dieffenbach's account of a stuttering child's traumatizing "phonophobia" (1841: 12).[15] Dieffenbach argued that surgery could alleviate fears and anxieties resulting from early childhood terrors involving speech. His foundational narrative of childhood trauma involved "the presence of a stranger" that terrified a young patient (1841: 11). Unable to overcome a traumatic moment of vocal choreography with another speaker, the boy stuttered, and the terror had resulted in traumatic reenactments of this primal traumatic scene later in his childhood: "the same painful scene was thus again and again renewed" (1841: 11–12). In his protest against surgical procedures, Wright argued that people who stutter lack a sense of order in the coordination of speech organs. The will and the organs of enunciation, Wright claims, "seem to act contrary to each other" (1843: 22). "Sufferers" must rehabituate themselves to the natural mechanisms of fluid speech. In this claim, Wright perpetuates elocutionary principles and techniques. Stuttering occurs, he argues, from a "lack of harmony" (1843: 20) of all of the major organs and muscles of the speech apparatus, often in domestic settings in which parents and household staff intentionally or unintentionally berate children who stutter for their errors in speech. Wright thus introduced the possibility of merging seemingly traumatic encounters with other speaking bodies with the practical, eugenically tinged good sense of British middle-class domestic etiquette and conduct.

Wright was by no means alone in his claim that the family home could be a dangerous site for children with a propensity toward dysfluent speech. His critique of the "indolence or ignorance of persons concerned in the management of children" (1843: 41) promoted an image of the British middle-class home as one fraught with potentially violent encounters coalescing around the production of "healthy" speech. Throughout the century, one of the most persistent medical claims—one that Wright's work anticipated—was that speech dysfluencies could be contracted through unconscious imitation or conscious mockery of other people who stutter. This widespread theory of the stuttering child's "imitative propensity" (Hunt 1870: 87) was premised on an essentially epidemiological model of the infectious transmissions of dangerous speech habits.[16] The imitation theory situated the cause of stuttered speech in the intersubjective choreographies between children and other speaking bodies.[17] It also relied on a neurogenic understanding of dysfluency, anticipating contemporaneous theories of neurosis and hysteria by Jean-Martin Charcot, Josef Breuer, and Freud in the 1880s and 1890s. Any cure for the melancholia of people who stutter required careful attention to each specific iteration of speech symptoms and their origins in traumatic childhood experiences. Challenging common claims throughout the century that stuttering could be hereditary (Monro 1850), Hunt argued that close attention to stuttering reveals imitation as more often than not the real cause. Some of his contemporaries in speech "assert that [functional speech defects] may be inherited, in the shape of organic defects," but Hunt suggests, "in my opinion, they are in most such cases owing chiefly to imitation; thus whole families are sometimes noticed as affected with a peculiar species of stammering" (1870: 195). Adding further to the analogy of stuttering's disease-like transmission, Hunt claims that "one stammerer or stutterer in a family ... is quite sufficient to infect others; and so rapid is the contagion to a susceptible child, that I know of more than one case in which the infirmity was contracted by a single interview with a stutterer" (1870: 252).

Interwoven within epidemiological theories in the 1840s and 1850s, stuttering became subject to implicit and explicit eugenics practices. Whereas statistical sciences could increasingly articulate an average or "normal" body through anthropometric data and measurements, the voice remained conceptually challenging to regulate and render "fluent" at the level of public health. The distinctly modern appeal of such concepts as vocal eloquence, composure, and authority certainly explains the widespread cultural and domestic appeal of elocutionary systems in Britain and the USA. Hunt's work was especially fraught with anxieties about balancing competing epistemologies of the voice, and the result was a closing chapter that situates the medicalization of stuttered speech within statistical claims about national difference and contemporary debates about whether or not cultures and languages outside of Europe contained documented accounts of stuttered speech. The recourse in *Stammering and Stuttering* to statistics is by no means surprising, given the extensive work on the demographics of stuttered speech throughout the century. As Lennard J. Davis argues, "statistics is bound up with eugenics," and its fundamental "aim" is to "norm the nonstandard" (2016: 3). And yet, despite his primary focus on data, Hunt concludes his chapter with a curious section on "stuttering among savages." Acknowledging that earlier editions of his book refused to consider that stuttered speech was prevalent among "savage" peoples in Africa and the Americas because of a widespread belief that dysfluencies were affectations of speech produced only in "civilized" societies, Hunt accepts the presence of stuttering in Africa in the light of documented anthropological evidence, but remains convinced that stuttered speech is primarily a product of "civilized" society. Hunt speculates that if stuttering does exist among the "savages," it is most certainly a direct result of African peoples imitating the "fashionable" stammered speech of Europeans in the region (Hunt 1870: 351). Such speculations about the impact that civilization has on the "natural" rhythms and intonations of human speech would return problematically in later eugenic thought influenced by Hunt's work. The important point here is that toward the end of the century medical theories about stuttered speech would become integrated within competing networks of thought about civilization, physical and public health, and general notions of cultural, economic, racialized, and gendered concepts of vocal "fitness." Hunt's role as the President of the London Anthropological Society in the 1860s and his racist belief in polygenesis—that human races have different origins—are indicative of a complex intertwining of the period's thoughts about vocal health within broader cultural beliefs about human experiences of time and rhythm.[18]

6.2. CULTURAL EXPRESSIONS

Although extraordinarily preoccupied—technically, scientifically, aesthetically, and morally—with the vocal rhythms of "normal" speech, the nineteenth century produced only a handful of literary explorations that treated the experiences of people who stutter with the same level of sympathy as elocutionists and medical experts did. As Jeffrey K. Johnson writes, prior to the twentieth century, "a person who stuttered was almost never shown to be a three-dimensional character and often was merely seen as the embodiment of a speech impediment" (2012: 11). Instead, scholars with interests in the intersections of literature, popular culture, and disability have uncovered a vast catalogue of comedic, grotesque, or allegorical popular representations of dysfluent speakers that confirms Johnson's claim (Shell 2005; Goldmark 2006; Johnson 2008; Hoegaerts 2015). In British and American literature especially, characterizations of dysfluency include the stuttering wit of the essayist Charles Lamb and the infamous shyness of the celebrated children's author Lewis Carroll (two of the century's most celebrated people who stutter), various humorous and grotesque minor characters who stutter in the literature of Charles Dickens, Wilkie Collins, and other popular writers of the period, and the eponymous character in Herman Melville's *Billy Budd*, perhaps the century's most well-known literary allegorization of stuttered speech.[19] These are but a few of many cultural expressions of dysfluent speech throughout the century in which stuttering came to represent something more than its particular symptomatology, "whether about the personality of the character or about the nature of language itself" (Eagle 2013: 159).

This brief catalogue does not include the extensive historical record of American and British humor on stuttering, nor popular music at the end of the century that adopted

FIGURE 6.1 "A Sense of Proportion" (1888), Punch, 94, 28 Jan.: 40.

the cadences of stuttered speech for humorous effect. The extensive volumes of *Punch Magazine*, for example, included numerous instances of satire or wit directed at people who stutter, some of which played on cultural perceptions of the stutterer's poor timing (Figure 6.1). *Wit and Humor of the Age*, an American anthology edited in part by Mark Twain, likewise included various short pieces on the humor of stuttered speech, as did numerous other anthologies throughout the second half of the century. Hoegaerts argues that the popular appeal of stuttering songs at the turn of the century is evidence of the "multiplicity of modernity" (2015: 754), because they often portrayed marginalized stuttering speakers, especially women and African Americans, who were then associated positively with privileged popular musical preferences for stuttered syncopations and rhythms. At the same time, humorous cultural expressions of the "stutterer" or "stammerer"—such as the short tale of Rueben Rammer in the annual *Good Things for the Young of All Ages* (1873: 649) or William Denton's satirical narrative of Moses' stutter in the poem "The Plagues of Egypt" (1881: 118–45)—reflected the complexities of modern time frames in a popular context.[20] Throughout the century, humorous caricatures of people who stutter frequently exploited the comedy of speaking bodies perpetually out of rhythm with "normal" speech.

Humorous characterizations were not the only means through which dysfluencies became normalized as defining characteristics of modernity. Toward the end of the century, Lucas Malet's popular novel, *The Wages of Sin*, characterized people who stutter as embodiments of the supposedly dangerous impulses of modern culture, including sexual interactions between men and women and the perceived ill effects of excessive devotion to aesthetic creativity. Malet situates the stuttered speech of her male protagonist-artist as a violent—and at times sadistically attractive—expression of artistic impulses.[21] In similar fashion, theories of aesthetic degeneracy in the 1890s—most notably in the work of conservative social critic Max Nordau—also situated stuttered speech as symptomatic of "degenerative" cultural and aesthetic forces.[22] The extent to which these literary works allegorize the stutter as a symptom of cultural tensions is itself indicative of the transgressive rhythms that the stutter introduced into social thought and expression. For artists and social critics at the fin de siècle, the stutter signified a constellation of cultural symptoms as a result of modernization's perceived hesitant, accelerated, and asynchronous rhythms.

While specific literary and cultural references to dysfluency remained relatively sparse throughout the century, literary texts by the century's most celebrated authors and poets frequently adopted voice markers indicating stuttered speech (he stuttered, she stammered) to express a wide range of character tendencies, motivations, and flaws. While it is tempting to follow Gilles Deleuze's argument that such markers separate poor writers from those who have an intensive awareness of all language systems' intrinsic capacities for stuttered rhythms and concatenations (1998: 107), the century's frequent reliance on dysfluent voice markers tended to represent the stutter as something metaphorical or symptomatic rather than as a disorder of speech. This is not just a problem with the representation of speech in nineteenth-century cultural texts; current literary and cultural theory is also complicit in continuing the nineteenth century's privileging of stuttering as a representation of the hesitant, circumlocutory, and grotesque rhythms of modern life and its problematic insistence that stuttering be symptomatic of something insidious and pathological, despite the breadth of elocutionary and medical claims that rejected such accounts. For example, without any significant training in—or reference to—medical histories of stuttering, biographies and interpretations of Carroll's literature and personal correspondence tend to read his lifelong stutter as a symptom of repressed pedophilic desires or childhood sexual abuse (Wallace 1990: 116; Hollander 1997: 200; Zornado 2001: 107). In reiterating such problematic assumptions that stuttered speech must be symptomatic of some buried or "unspeakable" trauma or repression, literary and cultural scholarship perpetuates Deleuze's privileging of writers that "make language as such stutter" and know how to produce "an affective and intensive language" rather than simply an "affectation of the one who speaks" (1998: 107). Stuttering becomes in such models a product of complex systems of language and cultural expression, while the actual person that stutters is often effaced from cultural expression.

Disability studies approaches to dysfluencies are thus crucial to reconsidering the ways in which scholarship perpetuates troubling metaphors of stuttered speech. The emergence of modern culture in the nineteenth century coincided with irreconcilable tensions between a demand to make language systems and their literary/cultural effects more rhythmically modern and an equally powerful systemic erasure of the bodies and voices of people who actually stutter. In current literary and cultural criticism, stuttering seems to emancipate itself from the body, resulting in a systemic neglect of the history of speech dysfluencies and therapeutics.[23] Despite a rich tradition of nineteenth-century intellectual labor about dysfluencies, cultural and literary representations routinely disavowed the complex temporal, psychosomatic, and interrelational processes and negotiations at work in the day-to-day lives of people who stutter. The fact that this absence of dynamic characterizations of the lives of people who stutter is at play in both nineteenth-century literature and current literary and cultural criticism is indicative of broader systemic tensions around the very concept of speech and voice.

Nineteenth-century elocutionary and medical knowledge about dysfluency sought to liberate stuttered speech from disagreeable speech symptoms and countless cultural stereotypes—like those mentioned above—that seemed to have no sympathy for the melancholic experiences of people who stutter. In British literature especially, didactic representations of people who stutter often adopted the pleas of the period's elocutionists in order to advocate for the rights of dysfluent speakers. Popular poet Martin Farquhar Tupper's "The Stammerer's Complaint" was often excerpted in elocutionary and medical textbooks throughout the century, as were his other poetic musings on his own experience with stuttered speech (Hunt 1861: 3; Lewis 1902: 161). Literary critics disapproved of "The Stammerer's Complaint" because of its excessively mechanical iambic pentameter lines and heavy-handed concluding revenge fantasy, involving the inevitable suicide of a confident male blowhard forced to live one day with a debilitating stutter.[24] Despite its poetic drawbacks, "The Stammerer's Complaint" became well-known as an expression of a dysfluent speaker's melancholic complaint about being barred from "the proper glorious privilege of Speech" (1838: 1.4). In his memoir, Tupper wrote of his own experiences of being treated by what he called his many "Galens" (1886: 73) throughout his lifelong pursuit for an effective system of cure.[25]

In similar fashion to Tupper's didactic poetry, Melville Bell's poetic work, *The Tongue: A Poem*, argued didactically for the need to resurrect the heroic oratorical voices of past ages. Relying on a tinge of eugenic anxiety about the modern age's stuttering, broken rhythms, the poem suggests that dysfluencies are symptoms of an overly prosaic age given over to global networks of newspapers and dull parliamentary reports and proceedings. Such modern communicative rhythms, Melville Bell argues, have destroyed the "natural" and "heroic" powers of the human voice and its ability to communicate the sublimity of the human soul. Melville Bell's early poetic account of his phonetic and elocutionary work thus reinforced claims in the period that therapeutic techniques have the capacity to return a once-powerful vocal capacity to its proper place in modern culture.

Two minor novels from the 1850s also reflect the breadth of elocutionary and medical thought about the experiences of people who stutter. Edward Bulwer-Lytton's *What Will He Do With It?* (1858) features a struggling clergyman barred from his profession because of a "debilitating" stammer. Like his real-life counterpart, Carroll, who also struggled at Oxford because of his stammered speech, Bulwer-Lytton's failed parish preacher gives up his position because of his stutter. His fortunes change when he meets the novel's central protagonist, a retired actor with a personal secret—one that sets the novel's plot in motion—and a self-professed talent for curing stuttered speech through elocutionary techniques. While actual instances of stuttered speech are sparse in the novel, Bulwer-Lytton's characterization nevertheless reflects the persistent novelty of elocutionary techniques and their perennial appeal throughout the century. In similar fashion, James Malcolm Rymer's *The Unspeakable: Or, the Life and Adventures of a Stammerer* adapts the period's elocutionary and medical concerns about stuttered speech to the domain of literary representation. Rymer's fictional autobiography narrates the lifelong experiences of a young boy who acquires a stutter during an encounter with a dysfluent step-uncle, who proceeds to haunt him literally and figuratively throughout the rest of his life. *The Unspeakable* is especially noteworthy because of its didactic fictionalization of Hunt's system of cure. The novel even adopts the imitation theory as its primary traumatic childhood cause of stuttered speech. Rymer's protagonist narrates his experiences from early childhood when he acquired his stammer to his early adult life, when he begins an exhaustive search for an "expert" to help him fix his stammered speech. All of the protagonist's fortunes change, the novel suggests, upon his discovery of Hunt's system of cure.

These literary works each emphasize the debilitating melancholy of stuttered or stammered speech. While Bulwer-Lytton and Rymer remain optimistic about the possibilities of a cure and generally treat dysfluent speech as an innovative narrative device, Tupper's poem more accurately reflects the cultural mood of nineteenth-century thought about the impossible position people who stutter faced in the spoken communities of the modern world. Despite their significant limitations as works of literature, they nevertheless articulate a subject position for people who stutter that did not perpetuate damaging or cruel stereotypes of the grotesque, nervous, and ugly stutter that were widespread throughout the century. And yet, even in their didactic claims and expressions, they nevertheless insisted that the melancholic temporal rhythms that impacted people who stutter resulted in an inescapable experience of being perpetually out of sync with "normal" vocal communication.

6.3. THEORETICAL IMPLICATIONS

Assaulted by a systemic standardization of time and rhythm in a rapidly advancing industrial age, stuttering voices frequently appeared in nineteenth-century literary and cultural discourse as grotesque or humorous tropes for addressing the tensions between modernity's seemingly morbid and "degenerate" effects on human experience and its economic insistence on uniformity and standardization. Even dynamic characterizations that relied on the trope of melancholia prioritized disjunctions in the temporal rhythms between and within bodies. Nineteenth-century narratives of speech trauma, invasion, and contagion may seem outmoded within the context of current scientific research about the causes of developmental stuttering, but they are instructive in terms of framing how scholarship about disability interrogates normative speech and vocal rhythms.

They may also reveal a problem within disability studies itself. James Berger claims that disability studies' emphasis on spatial geographies of exclusion results in a struggle to account for the traumatizing rhythms of dysfluent speech (2014: 173). Nineteenth-century demands for rational systems of cure that could provide a panacea for stuttered speech imagined the origins of speech-language pathology as institutional techniques rooted in biopolitical training. But, as this chapter has suggested, speech clinics and "homes" were themselves promoted primarily as sites of rhythmic and temporal attunement to standardized time frames. Contestations between elocutionary and medical thought introduced the possibility of situating stuttered speech intersubjectively or epidemiologically in the encounters—or choreographies—between bodies. As Joshua St. Pierre argues, "parameters of how fast, evenly, and clearly bodies can speak—and are *expected* to speak—are generated from so-called basic similarities that reflect the dominant able-bodied mode of temporal existence" (St. Pierre 2015b: 53). St. Pierre's claim here echoes a similar argument by Paterson that people who stutter are consistently "estranged by the dominant choreography of everyday life" (2012: 171), which demands that all vocal utterances conform to efficient speech techniques. As such claims attest, dysfluent voices have all too often been measured or assessed according to rhythms that bear the influence of ideology and normative vocal production.

The emancipatory claims of disability studies, which are dominated, as Paterson argues, "by a topography/geography of oppression" (2012: 165), often struggle to account for the arrhythmic dysfluencies present in the exchange of words between bodies. In such topographical paradigms, there is often no space for considering the temporal embodiments and rhythms of people who stutter. Sometimes, this is merely an oversight or a failure to consider stuttering as "disabled" speech in the first place.[26] As Caitlin Marshall argues, "while it is a central tenet of disability studies that material and ideological built environments, *not* bodies, are disabling, neither crip theory nor disability studies has extended this foundational premise to speech, voice, or communication disability" (2014: n.p.). Any emancipatory project for people who stutter must begin by challenging the normalizing time frames of the social world, rather than strictly its spatial or topographical barriers. As this chapter attests, biopolitical emphasis on both optimizing fluency through management and eliminating dissenting or dysfluent voices through speech regulation originated in nineteenth-century thought and practice.

From a disability studies perspective, the dearth of dynamic characterizations of people who stutter in nineteenth-century literature and cultural expression reflects modern culture's discomfort with inarticulate, dysfluent, broken, hesitant, or resistant expressions of vocal communication. Research in voice studies has interrogated the ways in which "acousmatic" voices—those that are heard but not always visually accounted for—condition sonic experiences of modernity (Chion 1999) and the extent to which the poetics of the stutter introduce radical accounts of vocal embodiment (Migone 2011; Labelle 2014). Adding to the complex negotiations at work in any cultural analysis of the voice is the tendency of the modern age to produce a proliferation of "object voices" in literature and new media (Dolar 2006; Sacido-Romero and Mieszkowski 2015) that seem to introduce a "mysterious jump in causality, a breach, a limping causality, an excess of the voice-effect over its cause" (Dolar 2006: 10). The proliferation of "ugly" voices throughout nineteenth-century literature and popular culture reinforced a hegemonic privileging of fluent articulation and a casting out of unwanted or uncanny voices. Current studies of the voice, especially in a literary context, privilege a positive development of ideologically and discursively "normal" speech, rather than accounting for transgressive, unwanted, and broken vocal disarticulations and dysfluencies. And yet, cultural and textual histories of the nineteenth century are steeped in the privileging of the dysfluent rhythms of modern economic life. Fundamentally, the stutter itself serves as a limit point for critical engagement with modernity's economic, cultural, and aesthetic rhythms. One of the positives of current voice and sound studies is their potential to unsettle normative assumptions about the voice's relation to meaning, truth, and authenticity. Another positive is the inverse of this potential: to challenge misguided cultural assumptions that dysfluencies of all kinds are symptoms of anxiety, deception, secret desires and ambitions, repression, and sinister intentions. There exists in this unsettling of the normative rhythms of the voice a transgressive and emancipatory potential, especially through the stutter's ultimate refusal to conform to standardized rhythms and time frames.

CHAPTER SEVEN

Learning Difficulties

The Transformation of "Idiocy" in the Nineteenth Century

PATRICK MCDONAGH

When an apparently feral boy was carried from the woods of Aveyron in southern France to the salons of Paris in 1800, his presence created a philosophical debate that was to have a lasting impact. The boy, who had reportedly been living in the wild for several years, was examined by some of France's leading intellects, and physician Philippe Pinel spoke for most of them when, after listing the boy's characteristics and deficiencies, he concluded that "the child ought to be categorized among the children suffering from idiocy and insanity, and that there is no hope whatever of obtaining some measure of success through systematic and continued instruction" (quoted in Lane 1977: 69). But Jean Itard, a student of Pinel's, disagreed, suggesting instead that the boy's apparent "idiocy" resulted from deprivation and that, untouched by instruction or, indeed, society, he presented a perfect opportunity to study how humans acquire knowledge. The story of the wild boy of Aveyron crystallizes several themes connected to the idea of what was known as "idiocy" at the start of the nineteenth century: the characteristics of idiocy, both as a concept and when applied to individuals; the place of idiocy, and people identified as idiots, in society; and the symbolic functions and associations of the image of idiocy. This chapter will address these themes by focusing on the state of affairs at the start of the nineteenth century, when Itard begins the training of the wild boy; at the middle years of the century, when the idea of idiocy has shifted dramatically; and finally during the century's final decades, when anxieties that idiocy, imbecility, and feeble-mindedness would contribute to societal and racial degeneration led to the long-term segregation of people so diagnosed.

What, precisely, is an intellectual disability? What, in the nineteenth century, was idiocy? The concepts of intellectual disability and such precursor notions as folly, idiocy, deficiency, and retardation pose an interpretative challenge to historians and non-historians alike—and indeed, this is an important indicator of their conceptual and representational instability. The physician John Haslam, writing in 1823 to clarify the legal use of such terms as "unsoundness of mind," asserted that "generally speaking, the state of idiotcy [sic] is well understood" (18), and that the condition was unproblematic in legal matters. But fifty years later, another physician, John Charles Bucknill, the founder of the *Asylum Journal* (later the *Journal of Mental Science*), in addressing the Governors of the newly formed Birmingham and Midland Counties Asylum for Idiots in 1873, recounted an "influential magistrate making the earnest inquiry—'Who can tell me what an idiot really is?'" Bucknill confessed that, although he knew what an idiot was, "I shall not myself find this question an easy one to answer ..." (1873: 169–70).

While in one sense idiocy seemed uncomplicated, its boundaries as well as its core features proved challenging to define and describe. Indeed, lay, legal, and medical definitions remained closely entwined, with lay definitions providing a foundation for these more ostensibly professional evaluations (Jarrett 2018). The English physicians Martin Duncan et al. lamented that "The terms used in the literature of idiocy complicate the first steps of practical inquiry greatly, and different writers, regardless of the necessity for unanimity, use the same words to describe various classes of idiots" (1861: 236). This fluid terminology has often appeared as both an obstacle to understanding the condition and as an indication of its universality. Édouard Séguin suggests the latter when he opens his 1846 *Traitement Moral, Hygiène et Éducation des Idiots* with a multilinguistic and cross-cultural list of synonyms for "idiocy," but twenty years later, in 1866, he observes that "[idiocy's] definitions have been so numerous, they are so different from one another, and they have so little bearing on the treatment ..." (39). Even today, the multiplicity of terms remains a characteristic of what we sometimes call intellectual disability, learning disability/difficulty, developmental disability, or cognitive impairment—each variation expressing a particular medical, psychological, or philosophical concept. Throughout this chapter, I do not replace "idiocy" or other historical terms with more acceptable contemporary ones for the simple reason that the current terms do not indicate the same understanding of intellectual difference, the same forms of intellectual difference, or even where such difference might be thought to exist. Despite these terms being conceptual kin, the terminological slippage or instability identified by Séguin, Duncan and Lond, and others is particularly notable across decades, or centuries, so it would be an error to assign a one-to-one relationship between nineteenth-century "idiocy," twentieth-century "mental retardation," and twenty-first-century "intellectual disability" or "learning difficulty." Instead, I alternate between some variation of the "people identified as having ..." formulation preferred by advocacy groups such as People First when referring to the actual human beings judged "idiotic" or diagnosed as "intellectually disabled," and whatever designation—"idiot," "innocent," etc.—is used in the text or period being cited when referring to the concept itself. The tensions underlying the creation of labels and concepts are underscored when none is given priority as a more correct or accurate form of signification, so I will be replicating the historical terms, as well as diagnoses, as I find them in source texts.

7.1. PHILOSOPHY, EDUCATION, AND THE WILD BOY OF AVEYRON

At the end of the eighteenth century, idiocy was perceived as a constant, unchanging state and functioned as a primary marker of identity, but the feral boy from Aveyron would prove a catalyst for transforming these notions. Upon arriving in Paris in 1800, the boy was housed at the Institution Impériale des Sourds-Muets, headed by the renowned Abbé Roch-Amboise Sicard, whose efforts in teaching sign language to deaf pupils had made him a celebrity. In addition to becoming a media sensation, the "enfant sauvage" was also briefly the center of attention for the recently formed Société des Observateurs de l'Homme, where he fell under the professional examination of Philippe Pinel, the leading psychiatrist of the day, who asserted that the boy was an idiot, likely abandoned by his parents.

But others, most notably the young Jean Itard, then the physician at Sicard's Institution, believed the boy to offer the proverbial *tabula rasa*, or blank slate, described by John Locke. Locke had argued that we are born not with innate ideas bequeathed by God, as René Descartes had proposed, but instead acquire knowledge initially through impressions from the physical senses that are then analyzed and codified by the increasingly conscious mind. Drawing on Locke, Étienne Bonnot, Abbé de Condillac, had proposed as a thought experiment the idea of a sculpture coming to life and, acquiring one sense at a time, developing knowledge and a consciousness of self (Lane 1977; Shattuck 1980; Stainton 2018). Itard perceived the wild boy as the Lockean blank slate or Condillac's animate sculpture, and he insisted in the preface to his first report that the child's apparent idiocy stemmed from deprivation:

> If it was proposed to resolve the following metaphysical problem, viz. "to determine what would be the degree of understanding, and the nature of the ideas of a youth who, deprived, from his infancy, of all education, should have lived entirely separated from individuals of his species": I am strangely deceived, or the solution of the problem would give to this individual an understanding connected only with a small number of his wants, and deprived, by his insulated condition, of all those simple and complex ideas which we receive from education, and which are combined in our minds in so many different ways, by means only of our knowledge of signs. Well! the moral picture of this youth would be that of the Savage of Aveyron, and the solution of the problem would give the measure and the cause of his intellectual state. (1972 [1801]: 99)

Itard's first report, *De l'Éducation d'un Homme Sauvage ou des Premiers Développements Physiques et Moraux du Jeune Sauvage de l'Aveyron*, published in 1801, is organized around his initial attempts to solve the riddles of the human intellect posed by the wild boy, whom he named Victor (Figure 7.1). Itard established a series of social and educational goals for the boy, which he describes in detail. But after working with Victor for less than a year, he draws only preliminary conclusions.

Itard's writings present Victor not only as the subject of a philosophical and pedagogical experiment, but also as a figure shaped by the artistic discourses of the early nineteenth century. Indeed, theatrical discourses are central to the representation of the wild boy. In *Le Journal de Paris*, the journalist Gabriel Feydel proposed that "the so-called wild boy of Aveyron is only a little actor playing his role moderately well" (Gineste 2004: 199), and referred to the boy as the "young mime from Aveyron" (Gineste 2004: 201; my translations). Itard also relies heavily on poetic and theatrical imagery to describe Victor and his progress, drawing in part upon representations of the figure of the mute that was central to much contemporary French melodrama (McDonagh 2013). Itard describes Victor's behavior as evoking the language of the melodrama's gestural expression, and he draws upon theatrical metaphors to illustrate certain events. When Victor runs away from the Institution Impériale des Sourds-Muets, he is picked up by the police and eventually retrieved by his governess:

> A number of inquisitive bystanders gathered to watch their most touching reunion. Scarcely had Victor seen his *gouvernante* than he turned pale and lost consciousness for a moment; but when he felt her arms about him, he quickly came to his senses and showing his joy by shrill cries, the convulsive clasping of hands and a radiant face, he

FIGURE 7.1 An Historical Account of the Discovery and Education of a Savage Man.

offered to the eyes of all not so much a fugitive forcibly returned to his keeper as an affectionate son gladly running to the open arms of the one who had given him birth. (1972 [1806]: 170)

While not present at this event, Itard renders it in dramatic detail: the presence of an audience, the expressive gestures and facial expressions, and the lack of language all shape this episode as a melodramatic performance. A final theatrical influence can be found in the boy's name. Itard writes that he selected "Victor" because the child had learned to pronounce the "o" sound ending that name, but it is likely that the boy was also named for the protagonist of the renowned dramatist Guilbert de Pixérécourt's 1798 play *Victor ou l'enfant de la forêt*, based on François-Guillaume Ducray-Dumenil's 1787 novel of the same name. *Victor*, one of Pixérécourt's greatest successes, ran for over 400 performances, while two other adaptations of the novel were also mounted in Parisian theaters (Gineste 2004). In this narrative, Victor is the son of a bandit, but his upbringing has raised him far above the state of his father, making him an endorsement of the power of moral and rational education. It is not difficult to see in the fictional Victor's story the outcome Itard must have desired for his own forest-child.

If literature and the theater helped shape how Itard and others perceived and responded to Victor, the wild boy also provided fresh material for poems and plays. Among the contemporary works exploiting his fame was a melodrama by Dupaty, Maurice, and Chazet entitled *Le Sauvage du departement de l'Aveyron ou Il ne faut jurer rien* (*The Wild Boy of Aveyron, or You Never Can Tell*); that same year, the English poet Mary Robinson, in "The Savage of Aveyron," presents a "wild boy" who is not an abandoned child, but rather the witness of his mother's murder and survivor of attempts on his own life.

By the time of Itard's second report in 1806, Victor's fame had subsided, and Itard declared his experiment's failure, noting that he had not succeeded in educating Victor into proper young manhood and conceding that perhaps Pinel was correct and the boy may indeed have been "disgraced by nature" (1972 [1806]: 115)—that is, born an "idiot." But in Victor's story, others would eventually perceive an outcome that Itard missed: a means of educating such apparently ineducable individuals.

7.2. EARLY NINETEENTH-CENTURY LITERARY AND ARTISTIC REPRESENTATIONS OF IDIOCY

The appearance of idiot characters in the literature of the time did not depend upon Victor, the wild boy, for inspiration. William Wordsworth's poem "The Idiot Boy" (published as part of *Lyrical Ballads*, his seminal 1798 collaboration with Samuel Taylor Coleridge) features Johnny Foy, the "idiot boy," as an expression of a natural romantic poet, at one with nature and subject to the transformative power of poetry (Ronell 2002; McDonagh 2008). In this comic poem, Betty Foy sends "him whom she loves, her idiot boy" (11) on a quest to fetch a doctor for her ailing neighbor, Susan Gale, thus trusting him with both her neighbor's life and his own well-being. But Johnny does not return when expected, and the bulk of the poem narrates Betty's growing fears and her attempts to find her son, along with the narrator's hypotheses of what fates may have waylaid him. The frantic mother, Betty, abandons Susan's bedside to search for her wayward son, going herself to the doctor, only to learn that Johnny had never arrived there. Exotic fears present themselves to her imagination, as well as that of the narrator, but Betty eventually finds her son, sitting still on the pony, which has wandered into a field to graze. Meanwhile, Susan Gale's anxiety over Betty and Johnny overwhelms her illness and sends her into the night in search of her friends, so that concern for them becomes as strong a cure as the doctor's medicine could. The links that Wordsworth draws between Johnny, the natural world, the pony, maternal love, and the rural community argue for the curative powers of sympathy as governed by forces found in nature, love, and friendship. While Johnny Foy is an idiot boy, he is also, by the end of the poem, a version of Wordsworth's solitary poet (Bewell 1989; Ronell 2002), as his final lines transform his evening hours spent listening to owls hooting in the moonlight into a world existing in the imagination:

> The cocks did crow to-whoo, to-whoo,
> And the sun did shine so cold. (460–1)

Another (considerably less famous) poem, published two months before *Lyrical Ballads* came out, represents the "idiot" in a much different form. Robert Southey's "The Idiot" was accompanied by a note claiming that "The Circumstances Related in the Following Ballad Happened Some Years Since in Herefordshire." In Southey's poem, Ned is "A thing of idiot mind. / Yet to the poor, unreasoning man / God hath not been unkind" (1798: 2–4). God's kindness is evident in the fact that Ned's mother, Sarah, with whom he lives, "lov'd her helpless child," so that "life was happiness for him / Who had no hope nor fear" (5, 7–8). But when Sarah dies, Ned is not only bereft, but also incapable of understanding mortality. He attends her funeral, but later returns to her grave, digs up her body, and takes it home with him to place in its accustomed chair; then he gazes at his mother and asks, "Why, mother, do you look so pale, / And why are you so cold?" (55–6). Soon, however, God calls the son to join his mother in eternal bliss. Southey's macabre narrative expresses a deep anxiety about the nature of idiocy. While both his idiot adult and Wordsworth's idiot boy are informed by an aesthetic tradition that locates in idiocy a divine naiveté and innocence, Johnny Foy is a participant in his community, part of the range of human possibilities, and, indeed, a variant of the Wordsworthian poet, the idiot as artist and everyman. Southey's Ned, in contrast, is a "thing of idiot mind" existing on the fringes of human society with his mother and fully isolated from it upon her death.

While Wordsworth's poem links Johnny Foy to his community and Southey's distances Ned from his, George Crabbe's 1810 poem depicting village life, "The Borough," includes an "idiot" character linked explicitly to her mother's sin. This long poem includes the story of Ellen Orford, one of the "poor of the Borough," who is seduced by a wealthy, unfaithful lover and gives birth to a daughter who is both beautiful and an idiot. While Crabbe identifies Ellen's faithless lover as a primary cause of her predicament, he also emphasizes the idiot girl's role as a symbolic reprimand. As Ellen recounts,

> Four Years were past; I might again have found
> Some erring Wish, but for another Wound:
> Lovely my Daughter grew, her Face was fair,
> But no Expression ever brighten'd there;
> I doubted long, and vainly strove to make
> Some certain Meaning of the Words she spake;

> But Meaning there was none, and I survey'd
> With dread the Beauties of my Idiot-Maid. (l. 210–17)

Ellen interprets her daughter's condition as a warning to caution her from taking another lover, so that for the narrator and the reader, the idiot girl is linked with Ellen's "erring Wish." At the same time, the daughter is physically attractive, her identity being defined by and expressed through the twin characteristics of her idiocy and her sexuality. The narrative follows Ellen's marriage and the deaths of her husband and sons, but these sorrows are followed by yet another, when the "Idiot-Girl, so simply gay before," is impregnated—likely raped by her "sick-pale Brother"—and dies in childbirth (ll. 309, 314). Throughout, the unnamed daughter remains morally innocent, and her association with sexuality, Ellen's "erring wish," is passive, as a woman more easily exploited and abused than others.

Each of these early nineteenth-century images of idiocy performs a distinct representational function, but all share a common feature: the condition of idiocy is unalterable. In this, literary representations aligned with scientific and medical beliefs of the time. However, these were about to change.

7.3. THE TRANSFORMATION OF IDIOCY IN THE MID-NINETEENTH CENTURY

"The moral manifestations of mind are ... deficient in a complete idiot," asserted physician Alexander Morison in 1843. "He has no religious sentiment, no desires or aversions, no affections, and consequently is unconscious of the social relations; in short, he has no reason to control his will, no desires or inclinations to excite it, and no will to be controlled or excited" (218). But even as Morison wrote, such dismal prognoses were being challenged. During the mid-1840s, a series of reports brought word of new pedagogical explorations to English readers. In 1843, another physician, William Twining, traveled to Johann Jakob Guggenbühl's facility in Switzerland and reported on this visit in *Some Accounts of Cretinism and the Institution for its Cure on the Abendberg*, summarizing Guggenbühl's instructional methods, seeking to direct English philanthropy for Guggenbühl's work, and helping establish the cretin-idiot as an object of sympathy. In 1845, John Conolly, superintendent of the Middlesex Lunatic Asylum, visited educational facilities established by Édouard Séguin at the Bicêtre in Paris, and he wrote in the *British and Foreign Medical Review* that "nothing more extraordinary can well be imagined" (1845: 292). He reports on one Charles Émile, a fifteen-year-old who had been at the Bicêtre for three years. According to Conolly, upon arrival in the institution, the boy

> was wholly an animal. He was without attachment; overturned everything in his way, but without courage or intent; possessed no tact, intelligence, power of dissimulation, or sense of property; and was awkward to excess. His moral sentiments are described as null, except for the love of approbation, and a noisy instinctive gaiety, independent of the external world. (1845: 294)

With this unpromising material, the teachers of the Bicêtre have "redeemed" the boy "from the constant dominion of the lowest animal propensities; several of his intellectual facilities are cultivated, some have even been called into life, and his better feelings have acquired some objects and some exercise" (1845: 294). On returning to England, Conolly launched his own program for the education of idiots at the Middlesex Asylum (Wright 2001: 27). Samuel Gaskell, medical superintendent of the Lancaster Lunatics Asylum, followed Conolly to the Bicêtre a year later and published his laudatory impressions in three short articles that appeared in *Chambers's Edinburgh Journal* early in 1847 (Gaskell 1847a, 1847b, 1847c).

In England, these reports generated a rapid response. The first British training school, the Institution for Idiot Children, and Those of Weak Intellect, was founded in Bath in 1846 by Charlotte White, a teacher. Like later, larger institutions, the school emphasized reading, writing, and arithmetic, with (as its 1850 report notes) "religious knowledge and moral culture ... directly or indirectly kept in view in every pursuit" (quoted in Carpenter 2000a: 170). Other small schools were established around Bath (Carpenter 2000b), stimulated by White's initiative and by the reports from abroad of successful new pedagogies. Larger initiatives also followed these European examples. In London, the Asylum for Idiots at Park House, Highgate—also known as the National Asylum for Idiots—was established in 1847, the result of the collaborative efforts of Conolly and the nonconformist reverend Andrew Reed, already renowned for establishing orphanages (Barrett 1986; Wright 2001).

While Christian philanthropy was essential to the operation of asylums, soliciting this philanthropy resulted in a representational tension between the bestial idiot and the guiltless innocent. The rhetoric used to garner public and political support for the asylums and their attempt to extend the benefits of education and rational thought—or raising the inmates "to the level of humanity" ("Idiot Asylums" 1865: 70)—creates an important problem in representations of "idiocy," and especially of "innocence." If the innocent idiot is favored by God, then why must he be "reclaimed"? What happens to the divine favor offered to the "idiot" if he is no better than a brute animal?

The early asylum proponents may have been prepared to offer hard answers to these questions in private, among fellow professionals, but the public image of the "idiot" was very much linked to the sentimental notion of the "innocent," and asylum advocates sought to invoke a Christian pity for that traditional character to gain public support. "The innocent" figures heavily in an 1869 booklet soliciting support for the Royal Albert Asylum, which included previously published works representing the place of the idiot in the family of God. Notable among them is Caroline Bowles Southey's "Harmless Johnny," first published in 1824 in *Blackwood's Magazine* as part of her "Chapters in Churchyards" series. In it, Johnny, a seventy-year-old "innocent," is described as "one for whom no heart was tenderly interested" (319), and the absence of family provides much of the story's pathos. But Johnny's status in the community, while marginal, is secure: the narrative emphasizes his role in performing odd tasks, his pleasure in dressing in military clothing and playing with the village children, and his tearful response to music (except in church, where with great effort he controls himself). But he is now dead to all music, notes the narrator, as she brings the readers back to the present, where Johnny sleeps undisturbed in the graveyard

> till the call of the last trumpet shall awaken him, and the mystery of his earthly existence shall be unfolded, and the soul, emerging from its long eclipse, shall shine out in the light of immortality. (320)

Here, the "unoffending innocent" (320) is given his Christian reward, providing a striking contrast to representations such as Conolly's description of Charles Émile as a loathsome subhuman who requires the intervention of dedicated Christian physicians and teachers to become a responsible moral being.

The rise of asylums led to a new configuration of the "idiot" in literary, journalistic, and other writings, and indeed gave birth to a short-lived journalistic subgenre, the asylum travelogue, in which visitors to asylums reported on their experiences, usually describing the astonishing transformations taking place among the asylum's inmates (McDonagh 2018). As Charles Dickens wrote in "Idiots," documenting his 1853 visit to the National Asylum for Idiots at Park House, "the main idea of an idiot would be of a hopeless, irreclaimable, unimprovable being," but in recent years,

> a closer study of the subject has now demonstrated that the cultivation of such senses and instincts as the idiot is seen to possess, will, besides frequently developing others that are latent in him but obscured, so brighten those glimmering lights, as immensely to improve his condition, both with reference to himself and to society.
> (1853: 313)

Similarly, in "On the Education of the Imbecile," Dora Greenwell, a poet and social activist, attempts to merge some of the qualities of the "innocent" and the "bestial" idiot: "amongst the abnormal conditions of humanity, imbecility, at first sight so repulsive, so barren of all suggestion, will appear, when we come to look at it more closely, to be rich in analogical reference and full of tender poetry," she writes (1868: 76). As Greenwell argues, only a deep engagement with the apparently bestial idiot will reveal his true innocence, while also allowing new creative and intellectual insights for those willing to make this engagement.

No longer a static figure, the idiot was showing the capacity for transformation. Dickens' 1841 novel *Barnaby Rudge* offers a case in point. As the novel opens, we meet most of the main characters, including Barnaby, who, we learn, was born an idiot because his father, bloodied from committing a murder, confronted his pregnant wife, who collapsed in fright and gave birth to an idiot son. The second and main portion of the novel begins five years later and concerns the Gordon riots in opposition to Catholic emancipation in the late eighteenth century. Barnaby becomes an unlikely riot leader, and the novel then follows the riots, their consequences, and the various fates of the participants (Figure 7.2).

Barnaby is largely peripheral to the novel's main action, but Dickens saw fit to name the book after him because of his symbolic usefulness. The significance of idiocy in *Barnaby Rudge* lies in its relation to the debate over the proper expression of paternalism in government and society. Barnaby, infantilized as an eternal child, is associated with the rioters, and by extension, in the political context of 1841, with the working-class Chartist movement, also (in Dickens' view) a rebellious mob abandoned by proper paternal guidance. This association foregrounds a belief in the inherent inability of the working classes to be fully self-governing; like Barnaby, they would always require a strong but caring paternalist authority to guide and rule them. At the novel's conclusion, Barnaby is incorporated into a benevolent post-riot community and saved from the moral degeneration afflicting other participants in the riots by his natural innocence. Barnaby also gains in rationality when he and his mother are incorporated into a larger community symbolically presided over by the novel's true hero, Gabriel Varden. Barnaby, himself an obvious subject for paternal guidance, becomes the perfect symbol of a people in need of good government. At the same time, Dickens' Barnaby is also a harbinger of efforts to educate idiots and to bring them more fully into society.

FIGURE 7.2 "Barnaby in Newgate," by Hablot Knight Browne ("Phiz"), in *Barnaby Rudge* (1841).

7.4. EXPLAINING IDIOCY: HYPOTHESES AND ANXIETIES

In *Barnaby Rudge*, Barnaby's idiocy is credited to "maternal fright": the theory, largely discredited by Dickens' time, that idiocy could sometimes be traced to the pregnant woman's emotional response to a disturbing experience. While this source proved symbolically useful for Dickens, most physicians looked elsewhere for causes, which proved legion, but were often culturally specific. Duncan et al., summarizing Samuel Gridley Howe's 1848 *Report made to the Legislature of Massachusetts, on Idiocy*, concluded that "it would appear that the statistics of one nation will not apply to the idiots of another, unless the social and climatic conditions are the same"; instead, they note, the report's "fairest conclusions become doubtful when they are examined and tested by our experience amongst our own countrymen," and "in America there is hardly a case whose [familial] history does not bear upon its cause; here it is quite the opposite" (1861: 237). Conversely, the anonymous writer of "Cretins and Idiots" in the 1858 *Atlantic Monthly* noted that most residents of Britain's Royal Earlswood Asylum (Figure 7.3) were not, in fact, "idiots" as the term was understood in America, but that "the greater part of the admissions ... are from the pauper and poor laboring classes; and the simple substitution of wholesome and sufficient food for a meager and innutritious diet is alone sufficient to effect a marked change in them" (417); the asylum may be a force for benevolence, but "these youth are not idiots, and no such analogy exists between them and idiots as would enable us to infer with certainty the successful treatment of the latter from the comparatively rapid development of the former" (417). This conflict is important for understanding idiocy's social-symbolic function. To the British writer, American "idiocy" is rooted in a perverse familial lineage, whereas the American writer perceives a British "idiocy" connected to class—associations that reproduce fundamental sites of social conflict and anxiety in these cultures.

Just as identifying people as idiots could prove challenging, so could identifying the fundamental characteristics of their condition. The anonymous author of "Idiot Asylums" wrote in 1865 that

FIGURE 7.3 "The Royal Earlswood Asylum (The National Asylum for Idiots)."

> the body is but the instrument, the mind of the unseen musician, and the strings must be in tune or no harmony can be produced by the most skillful hand. Thus the corporeal state of the idiot being disordered, discord results from the agency of the mind upon it. All that can be said of what the idiot really is terminates in this—that an idiot is one wanting in power, greater or less, to develop and manifest the normal human faculties by reason of organic defects. ... the nerves of motion and sensation are without due action. (46)

This passage draws on the authority of Édouard Séguin, whose major writings reiterated the argument that the bodily organization of the idiot was deficient and that consequently such individuals needed careful stimulation and discipline to learn how to properly receive and act upon sensations.[1] His method of physiological and moral education is meant to address this apparent incapacity. Séguin developed a "trinitarian hypothesis" proposing that "man ... is artificially analyzed ... into his three prominent vital expressions, activity, intelligence, and will." According to this schema, the idiot is "a man infirm in the expressions of his trinity," requiring that one "educate the activity, the intelligence, the will ... not with a serial object in view ... but with a sense of their unity in one being" (1866: 83).

This "trinitarian" treatment was intended to be, in a sense, holistic: the corporeal idiot is treated in conjunction with the intellectual and moral being. As Séguin writes, "Moral treatment involves employing every means available to develop and regulate the activities, intelligence and passions of the idiot" (1846: 642). In effect, as Murray Simpson argues, Séguin's pedagogy demands that all activity be "moralized": that a moral function be applied to basic activities such as eating meals, in which "control over the appetite must be learned through the intimacy of family-sized eating areas and the judicious timing of serving" (2014: 234), and in labor, which must be "linked to production, immediately visible and tangible" (2014: 235). Séguin's method was tremendously influential, his impact reflected by a publishing boom in books, articles, and pamphlets on the education of idiots. The review article "Idiot Asylums," appearing in the July 1865 issue of the *Edinburgh Review*, covers fourteen works published between 1846 (Séguin's *Traitement*) and 1864, with half coming after 1860 and all drawing heavily upon Séguin's work.

Séguin, like Itard before him, developed an approach to treatment that addressed a philosophical problem, and like Itard, his interest lay in pedagogy rather than medical treatment or a search for causes. But before long, interest shifted to searching for the roots of idiocy. Samuel Gridley Howe achieved fame as head of the Massachusetts Asylum for the Blind in Boston and educator of the deaf and blind prodigy Laura Bridgman, and in 1846, inspired by reports of Séguin's work in Paris and Conolly's in England, he began to advocate similar facilities in Massachusetts and was appointed to chair a commission on idiocy, leading to his 1848 report to the Massachusetts Legislature. This report was accompanied by the supplement *On the Causes of Idiocy*, penned by Howe, which, with the report itself, made his a particularly strong voice in shaping dominant notions of idiocy, especially in the USA. Howe proclaimed:

> We regarded idiocy as a disease of society; as an outward sign of an inward malady. ... It appeared to us certain that the existence of so many idiots in every generation *must* be the consequence of some violation of the *natural laws*;—that where there was so much suffering there must have been sin. We resolved, therefore, to seek for the sources of the evil, as well as to gauge the depth and extent of the misery. (1972 [1848]: vi)

Howe and his committee then identified the deviant practices that seemed associated with idiocy, which formed the basis of *On the Causes of Idiocy*. While accepting that "the whole subject of idiocy is new [...]. Science has not yet thrown her certain light upon its remote, or even its proximate causes," Howe follows Séguin in noting that causes "are to be found in the CONDITION OF THE BODILY ORGANIZATION ... If any bodily peculiarities, however minute, always accompany peculiar mental conditions, they become important; they are the finger-marks of the creator, by which we read his work" (1972 [1848]: ix, emphasis in original). Locating idiocy in physiology provided a means to link the physical state of the idiot child with that of the degenerate parent. Howe listed five primary factors leading to idiocy: poor physical organization, intemperance, masturbation, marriage between close relations, and failed attempts at abortion. The first (and most all-encompassing) of these categories anticipates later arguments concerning the enfeebling qualities of urban environments:

> It is said by physiologists, that among certain classes of miserably paid and poorly fed workmen, the physical system degenerates so rapidly, that the children are feeble and puny, and but few live to maturity; that the grandchildren are still more puny; until, in the third or fourth generation, the individuals are no longer able to perpetuate their species. ... It would seem that startled nature, having given warning by the degenerated condition of three or four generations, at last refuses to continue a race so monstrous upon the earth. (1972 [1848]: 25)

Scrofula, with its broad range of symptoms, is a constant in his case histories, and, while it is "difficult to describe exactly the marks which characterize this low organization," Howe stresses that "the eye of a physiologist detects it at once" (25). Idiocy is closely linked to immoral behavior in his second cause, intemperance, for which he cites a study of 359 idiots identifying 99 as the children of alcoholics; his third cause, masturbation, he does not support with statistics, but characterizes as "a monster so hideous in mien, so disgusting in feature, altogether so beastly and loathsome, that, in very shame and cowardice, it hides its ugly head by day, and, vampire-like, sucks the very life-blood from its victims by night" (29). Similarly, a concern with disciplining sexual practices also frames Howe's final two categories: idiocy stemming from closely related parents and that caused by attempts to procure abortions. Idiocy, he concludes, is a consequence of sins against God and nature.

7.5. EVOLUTION, DEGENERATION, AND IDIOCY

The idea of idiocy and its apparent connection to degeneration found a new conceptual framework following the 1859 publication of Charles Darwin's *On the Origin of Species by Means of Natural Selection*. Victorians linked the ideas of evolution and progress closely, but this association also implied the possibility of regress—and not simply at the level of individual bloodlines, but also of entire communities, societies, or even species. As early as 1861, the British physician W. A. F. Browne had written that idiocy endemic to "a particular community or locality," or that "attributable to the habits and modes of life of a particular race or district," should prompt research into its causes in order to address questions of human degeneration.

The new asylums, bringing together an idiot population in unprecedented numbers, provided ample opportunity for carrying out this essential research. John Langdon Down, the Royal Earlswood Asylum's medical superintendent from 1858 to 1868, played a central role in advancing the medical study of idiocy, frequently publishing papers in *The Lancet* and *The Journal of Mental Science*; in 1867, Down, George Shuttleworth, Fletcher Beach, and William Ireland—Britain's four leading medical figures concerned with idiocy—met in what would be the first medical conference on idiocy (Wright 2001), and, in that same period, Down published his most famous work, "Observations on an Ethnic Classification of Idiots." After studying Earlswood's residents, Down reached a startling conclusion:

> I have been able to find among the large number of idiots and imbeciles which come under my observation ... that a considerable portion can be fairly referred to one of the great divisions of the human family other than the class from which they have sprung. (1867: 121–2)

Drawing on the five-part racial division of eighteenth-century anatomist Johann Friedrich Blumenbach, Down hypothesized that many forms of idiocy were genetic throwbacks, avatars of less evolved races: while he observes that "there are numerous representatives of the great Caucasian family," he describes the others—the Ethiopian, the Malay, the Native American and the Mongolian—in more detail, identifying each "race" according to its "typical" physical features, and focusing on the Mongolian, the most common variation, for the second half of his paper. Indeed, he writes, "a very large number of congenital idiots are typical Mongols. So marked is this that, when placed side by side, it is difficult to believe that the specimens compared are not children of the same parents" (1867: 122). He concludes that "there is no doubt that these ethnic features are the result of degeneration" (1867: 122).

For many mid-Victorians, a kind of inherent evolutionary and intellectual inferiority was assigned to people whose ethnic and cultural heritage was not primarily Anglo-Saxon. After the popularization of Darwinian natural selection, evolution—figured as progress—and degeneration quickly entered the mainstream of nineteenth-century discourse. Ernst Haeckel's 1866 proposal of "recapitulation theory," in which "ontogeny recapitulated phylogeny"—that is, the individual repeats in its own growth the progress of the phylum—offered what seemed to some a feasible system to explain degeneration as Darwin's natural selection had explained evolution (Gould 1977). While Down's division of "idiots" into representatives of different "recapitulated" races was unique, it shared with the theories advanced by many of his peers some deep roots in a degeneration theory influenced by Darwinian natural selection.

Down's use of recapitulation theory was its first elaborate application to idiocy, and the "European negroes" and others described in his article remained in the realm of undeveloped theory rather than acquiring the status achieved by "Mongolism," the only category to be widely adopted.[2] This use of recapitulation theory quickly merged with the pervasive belief that degeneracy was the consequence of both moral and physiological weakness, entering a much larger discussion about the apparent association between idiocy and racial degeneration carried out in professional and popular arenas alike.

One frequent claim echoed Down's notion that the "idiot" was in some ways comparable or analogous to other, supposedly more "primitive" expressions of humanity. European brains, Henry Maudsley argued in his 1879 article "Materialism and its Lessons," stand in relation to "Bushmen" brains as they do to microcephalic idiots, and he suggests:

> If we were to have a person born in this country with a brain of no higher development than that of the low savage—destitute, that is, of the higher nervous substrata of

thought and feeling—if, in fact, our far remote prehistoric ancestor were to come to life among us now—we should have more or less of an imbecile, who could not compete on equal terms with other persons, but must perish, unless charitably cared for, just as the native Australian perishes when he comes into contact and competition with the white man. (1879: 254)

As a prominent physician and editor of *The Journal of Mental Science* from 1863 to 1878, Maudsley exerted an especially powerful influence on degeneracy theory from the 1860s to the 1890s (Pick 1989), but the analogy he draws between "savage" and "idiot" brains had been gaining medical legitimacy for some time; in 1867, John Marshall had published "On the Brain of a Bushwoman; and on the Brains of two Idiots of European Descent," perceiving signs of the "structural inferiority" (102) of the Bushwoman brain in comparison to the European brain, even though "no suspicion either of idiocy or other defect exists as concerns the Bushwoman" (103). Marshall does not directly compare these brains, but their analysis is assumed to be a study of inferior forms of intelligence, with the aim of throwing light on the later development of complexity in the brains of Europeans.

European racist discourses had long posited the Caucasian (and, in England, the Anglo-Saxon) as the pinnacle of human development, with other "races" lingering below, and ideas of idiocy and degeneration were inserted smoothly into these discourses, as these examples (of many possible) suggest. Thus, idiocy became not simply an individual problem or an issue that could be addressed by the support and education of people labeled as idiots. Instead, it was increasingly to be seen as an indicator of societal degeneration, much as Howe had perceived it several decades earlier—but with the moral outrage underlying Howe's analysis of causes replaced by medical and scientific theory.

7.6. IDIOCY, DEGENERATION, AND GENDER

With the rise of degeneration theory, certain long-held associations of idiocy and gender became particularly significant. From the sixteenth century, literary (and, for that matter, non-literary) representations of "idiocy" and related concepts exhibit clear gender associations: that is, writers representing female "idiot" characters are likely to associate them with sexual behavior or bodily appetite; by contrast, male "idiot" characters were most often represented as being incapable of managing money and authority. These notions remain vigorous throughout the nineteenth century and well into the twentieth, especially in relation to anxieties over societal degeneration.

For example, Mr. Dick, described as "simple" in Charles Dickens' *David Copperfield* (1985 [1850]: 720), is cared for by Betsy Trotwood, Copperfield's aunt, who also allows him to carry change like other men; however, he was "only allowed to rattle his money, and not to spend it" (1985 [1850]: 307), his manhood being an illusion supported by Betsy Trotwood's generosity. And in "Letter XVIII" of George Crabbe's long 1810 poem depicting village life, *The Borough*, the narrator describes an "ancient widow" and her son:

> With her an harmless idiot we behold
> Who hoards up Silver Shells for shining Gold;
> These he preserves, with unremitted care,
> To buy a Seat, and reign the Borough's Mayor ... (ll. 40–3)

These are representative of many other examples that could be mined from the history of representations of idiocy—male idiot characters consistently embodied a debased form of masculinity barred from patriarchal power due to their incapacity to manage the markers of that authority.

Female idiot characters, on the other hand, posed a threat to masculine power through their undisciplined sexuality. Crabbe's narrative of Ellen Orford, discussed earlier, provides a clear association between idiocy and transgressive female sexual activity. In many writings, "idiot" women are portrayed as being sexually unstable, and, as such, present a threat to idealized notions of femininity, while their sexual availability endangered the ideal of a rational and well-regulated masculinity. However, for much of the nineteenth century, female "idiot" characters embodied a paradox in that they were often represented as sexual innocents, thus warranting the protection of masculine authority. Maggy of Dickens' *Little Dorrit* is a twenty-eight-year-old woman who is intellectually like a child and physically both adult and like an infant, "with large bones, large features, large feet and hands, large eyes and no hair" (1985 [1857]: 142) (Figure 7.4). Maggy also serves as a double to Amy Dorrit, embodying those things (including a physical appetite) that Amy (also "childlike") cannot admit she desires, and both are, in the end, offered the protection of the masculine protagonist Arthur Clennam. In the second half of the nineteenth century, some women writers also redrew the female "idiot" character to critique masculine power. In Margaret Oliphant's *Salem Chapel* (1863), an unscrupulous father abducts his beautiful idiot daughter to sell her into prostitution while at the same time misleading the girl's virtuous guardian with a promise of marriage: the female character is still associated with sexuality, but the concern has shifted onto her oppression and exploitation. As with the representations of male characters described as idiots, these are resilient associations, and they can be found in cultural products reaching back at least until the sixteenth century.

These associations gain new social significance toward the end of the nineteenth century, when "mentally deficient" women will be seen as sexually promiscuous conduits of degeneration, and "mentally deficient" men as potential criminals due to their incapacity to earn and maintain an honest living.

7.7. A GREATER DANGER TO THE STATE

In the late nineteenth century, these fears of degeneration, crime, and pauperism led to the enlarging of the concept of idiocy to embrace the "feeble-minded," a term increasingly used to designate those apparently inferior beings with a disquieting capacity to pass as "normal." *The British Medical Journal* noted in an 1894 editorial, "The Borderland of Imbecility," that "those inhabiting the borderland of imbecility"—that is, the "feeble-minded"—were "more to be pitied, and certainly … a greater danger to the State, than the absolutely idiotic" (1894: 1264). This conception of "feeble-mindedness" is borne of degeneration theory and the pathologizing of poverty, indicating a growing anxiety about the burgeoning numbers of unemployed poor and casual laborers, as well as fears of increased criminal activity (Jackson 2000). Scientific, social, and cultural discourses fused to shape a new image of a dangerous urban idiot, threatening racial decline as well as social order: an economic burden, a petty criminal and innocent tool for the more ambitious criminals, and, perhaps worst of all, a progenitor of more of the same, promising ever-accelerating social decay.

FIGURE 7.4 "Little Mother," by Hablot Knight Browne ("Phiz") in *Little Dorrit* (1857).

In England, the threat of degeneration was closely connected to urban environments, with its conceptual home lying in the impoverished slums and rookeries of London and other major cities, places often represented as lairs of depravity from which only degraded humans issued forth. In 1889, physician J. Milner Fothergil discerned recapitulation among Londoners:

> while the rustic remains an Anglo-Dane, his cousin in London is smaller and darker, showing a return to the Celtic-Iberian race. ... The cockney, reared under unfavorable circumstances, manifests a decided reversion to an earlier and lowlier ethnic form. In appearance, the East-Ender ... bears a strong resemblance as to figure and feature, to the small and ugly Erse who are raised in the poorer districts of Ireland. (1985 [1889]: 113–14)

He concludes that "the deterioration, both physical and mental, of town bred organisms, is a matter not meant for the philanthropist, but for the social economist" (1985 [1889]: 114). In this and similar analyses, feeble-mindedness is bred in the perverse hothouse of urban life, the inevitable consequence of the blend of immoral acts facilitated by close living in the noxious environments that characterized urbanity.

In America, idiocy, while occasionally urban, was as likely to fester in remote rural communities where unchecked vice was thought to run rampant. This fear is documented in family-history studies such as Richard Dugdale's 1877 *The Jukes*, which claimed to demonstrate the conjoined nature of criminality, immorality, and mental deficiency, although Dugdale was cautious on asserting a role for heredity in this equation (Trent 1994). Arthur Estabrook's 1916 follow-up study, *The Jukes in 1915*, demonstrates a significant shift, however, locating heredity as the source of the Jukes' criminal behaviors and feeble-mindedness; Henry H. Goddard's 1912 study, *The Kallikak Family*, also presents the Kallikaks as representative of the dangers of hereditary feeble-mindedness; the study received wide attention before being discredited many years later (Zenderland 2004).

Anxiety around this decline was exacerbated by other factors. For instance, in England, the 1870 Education Act established a national system of elementary schools, meaning that for the first time all poor and working-class children appeared in formal classrooms; however, many did not prosper as well as hoped in this environment (Simmons 1978; Thomson 1998). The sheer numbers of struggling students hinted that the apparently deficient were more plentiful than suspected, and, even more worryingly, many seemed to have been traveling through life otherwise unnoticed, passing their tainted constitutions to their offspring. The Charity Organisation Society (COS), founded in 1869 to organize and assign charitable assistance throughout London, was prompted by the rising numbers of unsuccessful students to commission a report produced in 1893 under the title *The Feeble-Minded Child and Adult*, which argued that the children facing difficulties in the compulsory classrooms were "all probable social failures—now at the child-stage" (quoted in Simmons 1978: 389), who needed immediate attention in order to avoid costing society dearly in later years. By the turn of the century, the COS and others were calling for the "permanent support"—that is, the segregation—of the feeble-minded, an approach thought necessary both to maintain social order and to ensure the biological health of the race. The facilities needed for initiatives such as these at the national level could not be supported solely by philanthropy: government assistance would be necessary. In 1904, after much energetic lobbying by the COS and its allies, the government appointed a Royal Commission on the Care and Control of the Feeble-

Minded, which, after four years of inquiry and meetings, recommended the creation of a system of institutions for the permanent segregation of the feeble-minded. An abstract of the multivolume report, published in 1909 under the name *The Problem of the Feeble-Minded*, made its research and recommendations available to a broad readership, and it particularly stressed the threat of immoral behavior, including promiscuity, drunkenness, and criminal activities. "Feeble-minded" women were portrayed as threats to the health of the state, bringing forth a flood of mentally deficient offspring who would overwhelm the nation's healthy sons and daughters. Clearly, the fears of social and racial degeneration had overwhelmed the optimism of the mid-nineteenth century, and idiocy had become a convenient screen onto which to project a range of fears and anxieties afflicting society, growing especially from urban population growth, immigration, and poverty.

These concerns would shape responses to idiocy, mental deficiency, and mental retardation from the end of the nineteenth century and through much of the twentieth century, providing fuel for eugenicist movements in Britain, Europe, and America. A. F. Tredgold, Medical Expert to the Royal Commission, argued that "modern civilization" no longer weeds out the feeble, as this natural process is "thwarted by sentiment, which ignores the race in its concern for the individual," but that "it becomes imperative ... to devise such social laws as will ensure that these unfit do not propagate their kind" (1909: 101). In Britain, the 1913 Mental Deficiency Act defined four levels of "mental defectives"—idiots, imbeciles, feeble-minded persons, and moral imbeciles—thus broadening the concept of idiocy and embracing many individuals who may well have escaped the ignominy of such notice sixty years earlier. Indeed, the Act replaced "idiocy" with an alternative term, "mental defective," as a general designation, with mental defectives at all levels being liable, under appropriate circumstances, to be committed to segregated homes or asylums.

The Royal Commission's 1908 Report, the 1913 Act, and eugenic proclamations regarding feeble-mindedness had a profound impact on the way idiocy—or, now, mental deficiency—was understood, and they expressed a pervasive cultural anxiety that was then projected onto those individuals identified as idiots, imbeciles, feeble-minded, or mentally defective. By the end of the nineteenth century, the asylums originally erected to reclaim the "poor idiot" to humanity were adapting to a new role as exile colonies for an unwanted and purportedly dangerous population—and new institutions were being constructed for this same purpose. The idea of idiocy in cultural, social, and medical discourses had completed its second dramatic transformation of the long nineteenth century. Its first metamorphosis saw it shift from a constant, unchanging, and unproblematic state to one that could, with enlightened pedagogies and appropriate structures, be at least in part alleviated, enabling the idiot to participate more fully in society. This second movement—almost a complete reversal—saw the potentially productive idiot become instead an expression of a powerful and pervasive force that threatened social and racial degeneration—and thus requiring removal from that society.

CHAPTER EIGHT

Mental Health Issues

Alienists, Asylums, and the Mad

ELIZABETH J. DONALDSON

In *Madness and Civilization: A History of Insanity in the Age of Reason* (1965), Michel Foucault infamously linked the Enlightenment with what he called the large-scale "great confinement" of mad people in institutions. However, some historians of medicine and psychiatry have remained skeptical of Foucault's timeline, as well as other components of his theses regarding madness, noting that if there were a great confinement it began much later, in the nineteenth century, with the dramatic increase of patients populating newly formed state-supported asylums (e.g. see Shorter 1997: 6; Porter 2002: 92–100; Pietikainen 2015: 77–82). This chapter traces the developing discipline of psychiatry in the long nineteenth century, often referred to as the Age of the Asylum, using the scaffold of that development to discuss a broader cultural history of madness that includes the experiences of people with mental illnesses, with subsections dealing specifically with gender and race, crime, and institutionalization. During this period, public asylums devoted to the care of mentally ill people were established and the treatment and diagnosis of mental illness underwent dramatic changes. These two major developments cross-fertilized nineteenth-century literature and culture. Earlier religious and Hippocratic humoral balance models of madness gave way to new somatic and medical models, with emphases on cure, treatment, and restoring a patient's reason and self-control. But this new attention to cure and treatment did not always have the desired effect, and some of the major issues that concern disabled people, disability rights advocates, and disability scholars today (e.g. the hyper-medicalization and criminalization of mental illness) are legacies of these nineteenth-century innovations.

This chapter begins with an examination of moral treatment and the new asylum movement in England and the USA, which includes brief discussions of major figures such as the influential physician Phillipe Pinel, the Quaker advocate of moral treatment Samuel Tuke, and the asylum reformer Dorothea Dix. Section 8.2 begins with the quintessential nineteenth-century madwoman, *Jane Eyre*'s Bertha Rochester, and then moves on to discuss African-American mental health via W. E. B. Du Bois' *The Souls of Black Folk*. Section 8.3 deals with changing concepts of criminal insanity in the English courts, with special emphasis on the major precedent-setting legal cases of the nineteenth century: the trials of James Hadfield and Daniel M'Naghten. Section 8.3 also includes a discussion of how medicolegal concepts such as monomania and partial insanity found their way into popular literature through Edgar Allan Poe's short stories. Section 8.4 discusses efforts by ex-patient Elizabeth Packard and reformer Nellie Bly to challenge the asylum system's excesses and failures, and it ends with physician/writer Anton Chekhov's criticism of the cultural and social power of medical diagnoses in his short story "Ward No. 6."

8.1. MORAL TREATMENT AND THE AGE OF THE ASYLUM

In the nineteenth century, as Andrew Scull has noted, the mad became a "medical problem" (1993: 4), or objects of a medical gaze, as medicine itself moved toward greater professionalization in the wake of the eighteenth-century Age of Reason. Yet psychiatry as a discipline did not yet exist, and in Britain and America physicians who treated the mad were known as "alienists," after their French counterparts, *aliénistes*. Terms such as "madness," "lunacy," and "insanity" were used interchangeably to refer to people who were experiencing serious mental distress. Older categories of madness, such as melancholy and mania, persisted but were reconceived as disorders of the nerves and their respective under- or over-activity (melancholy and mania were broad categories that gestured toward respective passivity or energy, rather than having the current association with mood). Throughout this chapter, I use nineteenth-century terms, while noting that in some cases these coincide with current language that has different connotations. In keeping with a developing medical materialism (discussed below), immaterial states of mind became physiologically based diseases demanding professional attention from mad-doctors, or alienists.

These alienists developed new ways of treating the mad. In 1801, French physician Philippe Pinel published the highly influential *Traité medico-philosophique sur l'alienation mentale* (translated into English as *A Treatise on Insanity* in 1806), which introduced "moral treatment" to a wide and receptive audience of fellow practitioners. Pinel, who is infamous for freeing his female patients from their chains at the Salpêtrière hospital, advocated for more humane treatment of the mad, in part by focusing on case histories and the curative, therapeutic relationship between physician and patient. "Before the advent of moral treatment in the early nineteenth century," historian Petteri Pietikainen writes, "madhouses were not usually expected to cure their patients or clients. They functioned mostly as shelters that provided physical security, often coupled with religious instructions, not as institutes of medical treatment" (2015: 83). Yet new conceptions of madness as a curable condition and the increasing professionalization of medicine helped to change this. Pinel was a major figure in this transformation, and he is often credited with founding the field of psychiatry: "In most conventional histories of the subject, modern psychiatry begins with Pinel" (Shorter 1997: 12). Pinel has become an almost mythical figure in this history, as shown in Tony Robert-Fleury's painting *Pinel a la Salpêtrière* (Figure 8.1). In this romanticized portrayal of Pinel freeing the insane from their chains, a grateful inmate kisses the hand of her liberator.

Pinel's moral treatment of madness was highly gendered in practice: the women of Salpêtrière may have been freed from their chains, but they were in turn bound to new forms of medical control and surveillance. André Brouillet's *Une leçon clinique à la Salpêtrière* shows neurologist Jean-Martin Charcot demonstrating his ability to induce an epileptic fit in his hypnotized female subject, Blanche Wittmann, while his colleagues observe (Figure 8.2). Based in part on her reading of this portrait as well as hospital photographs (see Figure 8.3), Amanda Finelli has argued that the "photographic and physical spaces of the Salpêtrière encourage a pornographic gaze" (2015: 127). The gendered power dynamics of Salpêtrière remained even if the physical restraints were removed.

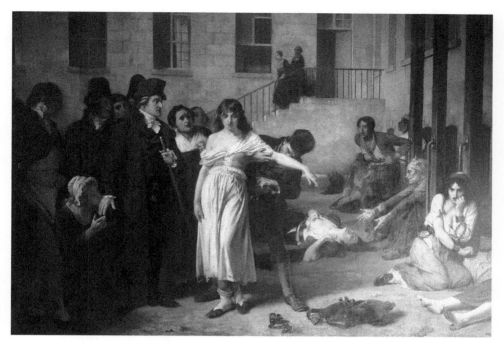

FIGURE 8.1 "Pinel à la Salpêtrière."

FIGURE 8.2 "Une leçon clinique à la Salpêtrière."

FIGURE 8.3 "Attitudes Passionelles: Extase."

It is also important to note here that the concept of moral treatment did not solely begin with Pinel. In Italy, physician Vincenzio Chairugi opened a therapeutic hospital for mentally ill patients in 1788 and several years later published his multivolume *On Insanity*, which described his program of humane asylum medical care. In England in 1796, Quaker William Tuke opened the York Retreat, a private asylum that combined religious study, work therapy, a healthy diet, and outdoor exercise in a bucolic country setting. At the York Retreat, patients were rarely restrained, and most medical interventions were eschewed in favor of Quaker moral and religious instruction (Digby 1985). Although the York Retreat was small, it had a significant impact: Tuke's grandson, Samuel Tuke, described the York Retreat's successes in his book, *Description of the Retreat* (1813), which in turn inspired others to create similar therapeutic communities.

In its most ideal form, moral treatment signaled a movement away from the heroic medical interventions of the past—such as bloodletting—and away from the indiscriminate violence of the past—such as flogging and chaining—toward a new emphasis on the therapeutic, humane relationship between physician and patient. In *A Treatise on Insanity*, Pinel calls for a definitive break with this past:

> Public asylums for maniacs have been regarded as places of confinement for such of its members as are become dangerous to the peace of society. The managers of those institutions, who are frequently men of little knowledge and less humanity ... have been permitted to exercise toward their innocent prisoners a most arbitrary system of cruelty and violence; while experience affords ample and daily proofs of the happier effects of a mild, conciliating treatment, rendered effective by steady and dispassionate firmness. (1806: 3–4)

Pinel describes how formerly "furious and dangerous" maniacs change after experiencing moral treatment: "upon being received with affability, soothed by consolation and sympathy, and encouraged to expect a happier lot, [they] suddenly subsided into a placid calmness, to which has succeed a rapid convalescence" (Pinel 1806: 67). As Pinel notes and Samuel Tuke confirms, physical treatments like bloodletting and potions have had poor success: in his chapter on "Medical Treatment," Tuke writes, "I regret that it will be the business of the present chapter, to relate the pharmaceutic means which have failed, rather than to record those which have succeeded" (1813: 71). Moral treatment was instead a psychological approach: patients, believed to be alienated from reason, needed guidance to help rule their passions. The alienists working in the moral treatment mode helped return patients to reason by fostering the patients' self-regulation of their passions.

This break with the old asylum treatment of the past was not only ideological; it also required a reconceptualization of the asylum in a literal sense. The architecture of the asylum was reimagined to enable the types of healthful activities that moral treatment advocated. The York Retreat, for example, was designed and built to resemble a family farm, "favorable to longevity," with gardens, light-filled day rooms, and expansive views of the countryside (Tuke 1813: 62). There were also courtyards with animals: "These creatures are generally very familiar with the patients: and it is believed that they are not only the means of innocent pleasure; but that the intercourse with them, sometimes tends to awaken the social and benevolent feelings" (Tuke 1813: 63). Alienists realized that the architecture of asylums could be a significant factor in promoting the health of patients, and in the USA fellow Quaker Thomas Story Kirkbride also became an influential advocate of thoughtful asylum design (Tomes 1994). Kirkbride hospitals were vast, perfectly balanced structures with a bat-like shape: long patient wings, designed to maximize light and air ventilation, extended from a core building for administration.

With their new emphasis on the health and well-being of the patient, the Kirkbride asylums and Tuke's private York Retreat provided a stark contrast to the relatively ancient Bethlem Hospital in London, which was quickly becoming a source of public embarrassment and concern. Bethlem, or "Bedlam" as it was known colloquially, was rife with scandal and controversy at the time. In 1815, the House of Commons special committee for the "Better Regulation of Madhouses in England" investigated the conditions at Bethlem and brought the sad case of James (also known as William) Norris to light:

FIGURE 8.4 William Norris restrained by chains at the neck and ankles.

he stated himself to be 55 years of age, and that he had been confined about 14 years ... a stout iron ring was rivetted round his neck, from which a short chain passed through a ring made to slide upwards and downwards on an upright massive iron bar, more than six feet high, inserted into the wall. Round his body a strong iron bar about two inches wide was rivetted; on each side of the bar was a circular projection; which being fashioned to and enclosing each of his arms, pinioned them close to his sides. (Sharpe 1815: 47)

Norris quickly became a "poster child" for Bethlem's abuses and inhumane treatment: an artist's engraving of Norris in his iron harness circulated widely and helped to garner public support for reforms (Figure 8.4). A fellow inmate of Norris's, Urbane Metcalfe, also went public with his exposé, *The Interior of Bethlem Hospital Displayed* (1818), a self-published threepenny pamphlet that provided further evidence and may be "the single surviving patient's description" of Bethlem during this time (Peterson 1982: 75).

Public outrage over the conditions at Bethlem helped to move asylum reform forward in England. Earlier legislation—the 1774 Act for Regulating Private Madhouses—required yearly licenses and inspections for private madhouses, which were a thriving business until the mid-nineteenth century. But for the poor who could not afford the services of private madhouses, options were limited to family care, the workhouse, and the prison. The County Asylum Act ("Wynn's Act") of 1808 allowed local governments to create asylums for the insane, but it did not compel them to do so. It was not until 1845, when the County Asylum Act and Lunacy Act were jointly passed, that counties were required to establish asylums with local funds and to hire medical officers. And it was not until 1874, when the British government began to partially fund county asylums, that counties began investing in earnest in asylums for the mentally ill poor (Pietikainen 2015: 88–9).

In the USA, the development of public asylums and moral treatment followed a different pattern. Benjamin Rush, "the father of American psychiatry" (Barton 1987: 16), published the first US textbook on mental illness, *Medical Inquiries and Observations upon the Diseases of the Mind*, in 1812. "The cause of madness," Rush speculated, "is seated primarily in the blood-vessels of the brain, and ... depends upon the same kind of morbid and irregular actions that constitute other arterial diseases" (1812: 17). For Rush, treatment options were often divided into two categories: those "applied to the mind, through the medium of the body," such as bloodletting and purging for mania, and those "applied to the body through the medium of the mind," such as small acts of kindness delivered by the physician (usually relief from a prior punishment or "painful remedy") or diverting manic patients' attention away from their "ruling" passions through conversation (1812: 179–204). As historian Edward Shorter points out, "Rush's partisans have argued that his occasional musings on moral suasion anticipated later psychotherapies. Yet psychological sensitivity is difficult to detect in his practice" (1997: 15). Manic patients were kept locked in small cells in the basement of the Philadelphia Hospital that Rush led, and Rush's somatic treatments were often quite harsh. "It would appear Rush and his staff," Pietikainen writes, "looked upon themselves as animal tamers who ascribed bestial nature to the mentally ill" (2015: 92).

At the beginning of the nineteenth century, when Rush was practicing, there were few asylums, either public or private, in the USA, and the mentally ill poor might find themselves in deplorable conditions, imprisoned in workhouses and jails if their families were no longer able or willing to support them. In towns with limited resources, the poor would be sold by auction to the lowest bidder for yearly service, which could be especially traumatic for people with severe mental illness (Pietikainen 2015: 92). Dorothea Dix, a writer and former schoolteacher, wanted to change these conditions. Inspired in part by her friendships with reformers like Samuel Tuke and in part by her experiences teaching at Sunday school to women in East Cambridge Jail, Massachusetts, Dix canvassed the state, visiting as many almshouses and jails that she could, in search of incarcerated people with mental illness (Parry 2006: 624–5). Dix reported her findings to the state legislature in an impassioned speech that she later published as a pamphlet, *Memorial to the Legislature of Massachusetts* (1843). In her testimony, Dix described case after case of neglect and abuse. Dix framed her appeal, which was rather shocking in its details, in terms of her sensitive female nature and the legislature's paternalist power and obligation to protect the weak:

> I shall be obliged to speak with great plainness, and to reveal many things revolting to the taste, and from which my woman's nature shrinks with peculiar sensitiveness. But truth is the highest consideration. ... If I inflict pain upon you, and move you to horror, it is to acquaint you with sufferings which you have the power to alleviate, and make you hasten to the relief of the victims of legalized barbarity. (1843: 1–2)

In one example, Dix described "a young woman in a state of complete insanity [who] was confined entirely naked in a pen or stall in a barn. There, unfurnished with clothes, without bed and without fire, she was left—but not alone. Profligate men and idle boys had access to the den, whenever curiosity or vulgarity prompted" (1843: 23). Dix's "peculiar sensitiveness" as a woman and her fact-driven testimony as an eyewitness were a powerful combination. Furthermore, as one historian speculates, Dix, who had periods of ill health, depression, and nervous exhaustion throughout her life, "may have had personal experience of mental instability that drove her to focus on the issue of asylum reform" (Parry 2006: 624). By the time Dix died in 1887, her mission to create hospitals dedicated to serving people with mental illness was largely realized: according to the 1880 US census, approximately 140 institutions served nearly 41,000 patients (Grob 1983: 4).

For critics of the asylum system like Foucault, numbers such as these are evidence of oppression, not success: the increased number of asylum inmates illustrates the increasing power of the state over individuals. And, indeed, there is plenty to criticize here. The ideals of moral treatment symbolized by the small York Retreat (sixty-two patients on eleven acres, with a staff–patient ratio of one to ten) would not live up to the pressures of increased scale (Tuke 1813: 64; Pietikainen 2015: 91). By the end of the nineteenth century, the problems that reformers like Dix attempted to address were being replicated in the very asylums designed as solutions to those problems.

8.2. GENDER, RACE, AND MENTAL HEALTH

This section uses two literary texts—Charlotte Brontë's *Jane Eyre* and W. E. B. Du Bois' *The Souls of Black Folk*—to discuss gender, race, and mental health in England and the USA, respectively. While reformer Dorothea Dix advocated for better treatment of people with mental illness and their release from workhouses and jails, it is worth noting that she did not advocate for their complete freedom: "I admit that public peace and security are seriously endangered by the non-restraint of the maniacal insane. I consider it in the highest degree improper that they should be allowed to range the towns and country without care or guidance" (Dix 1848: 8). Dix's warning about the dangers of the "maniacal insane" invites comparison to literature's most famous nineteenth-century madwoman, Bertha Rochester from Charlotte Brontë's *Jane Eyre* (1847), the story of a plain governess (Jane Eyre) who falls in love with her employer, Edward Rochester. To protect others from her scandalous behavior and her violence (qualities that mark her as insane), Bertha the madwoman is kept secretly imprisoned in her husband's attic, under the care of her alcoholic and negligent keeper, Grace Poole. When she is first revealed to readers, Bertha is barely recognizable as human:

> In the deep shade, at the farther end of the room, a figure ran backwards and forwards. What it was, whether beast or human being, one could not, at first sight, tell: it grovelled, seemingly, on all fours; it snatched and growled like some strange wild animal: but it was covered with clothing, and a quantity of dark, grizzled hair, wild as a mane, hid its head and face. ... The maniac bellowed; she parted her shaggy locks from her visage, and gazed wildly at her visitors. (Brontë 1847: ch. 26)

Later in the novel, Bertha Rochester (née Mason) sets a fire that physically disables her estranged husband and destroys the estate. She leaps from the burning house and kills herself.

Bertha Rochester typified maniacal insanity for Victorian readers, and even helped to shape contemporary clinical discourse. In *The Female Malady: Women, Madness, and English Culture, 1830–1980*, Elaine Showalter notes that "Bertha's violence, dangerousness and rage, her regression to an inhuman condition and her sequestration became such a powerful model for Victorian readers, including psychiatrists, that it influenced even medical accounts of female insanity" (1985: 68). Moreover, Bertha's violence was used to support arguments that "insane women should be treated at asylums rather than at home" (Showalter 1985: 68). This last point is especially noteworthy. Although Brontë's portrayal of Bertha certainly seems unkind by today's standards, Brontë's treatment of mental illness in the novel may be more perceptive and compassionate than it first appears. As disability studies scholar Chris Gabbard notes, attitudes toward caring for people with mental illness were changing at the time the novel was written. Asylums and moral treatment were hailed as more progressive solutions to the problem of madness. Gabbard writes, "Rochester implicitly makes choices about Bertha's care that a portion of Brontë's audience in the late 1840s would have recognized as inadequate and outdated" (2012: 101). Brontë, Gabbard argues, critiques Edward's system of "custodial care" and advocates for a different system of "caring labor" in *Jane Eyre* (2012: 92). And plain, sane Jane provides this type of caring labor to the maimed and melancholy Edward Rochester after mad Bertha's manic death.

Whether Brontë intended it or not, Bertha Rochester has become "the madwoman in the attic," a literary icon of female madness and rebellion for later generations (Gilbert and Gubar 1979). Bertha has inspired a large body of feminist criticism in her wake, and she has been interpreted as a compelling example of how the patriarchal oppression of women can lead to madness. However, sometimes these later readings have the ironic effect of dampening critical attention to Bertha's mental disability, especially when the madwoman in the attic becomes a metaphor that represents female oppression under patriarchy in a general sense.[1] In *Charlotte Brontë and Victorian Psychology*, Sally Shuttleworth (1996) has redirected attention back to the historical contexts of physiognomy and phrenology, noting how nineteenth-century concepts of medical materialism and madness inform

Brontë's fiction. As Shuttleworth argues, phrenological theories of self-control shape both Jane's struggle to rule her emotions and Bertha's fall into madness.

In *Jane Eyre*, Bertha's madness is just as linked to her race as it is to her gender. Her intersectional madness is produced by a system of European imperialism and colonial slavery—it is an inheritance from her racially mixed mother (see also Rhys 1966; Spivak 1985). Edward Rochester points to this murky history and their arranged marriage in Bertha's native Jamaica in order to justify and explain his secret imprisonment of his wife: "Bertha Mason is mad; and she came from a mad family; idiots and maniacs through three generations! Her mother, the Creole, was both a madwoman and a drunkard!" (Brontë 1847: ch. 26). Bertha's madness is inextricably connected to her Creole origins, and her illness is presented as an inevitable family heritage—three continuous generations of maniacs. (This is eerily similar to Oliver Wendell Holmes's statement, "three generations of imbeciles are enough," in the US Supreme Court case *Buck v. Bell* [1927], permitting the involuntary sterilization of a mentally disabled woman.) That Bertha's family history and race would affect how Edward Rochester treated Bertha's mental illness is in keeping with the thinking of the time. Even the humanitarian Pinel noted that in practice moral treatment would not translate into treating all mentally ill people equally:

> To apply our principles of moral treatment, with undiscriminating uniformity, to maniacs of every character and condition in society, would be equally ridiculous and unadvisable. A Russian peasant, or a slave of Jamaica, ought evidently to be managed by other maxims than those which would exclusively apply to the case of a well bred irritable Frenchman, unused to coercion and impatient of tyranny. (Pinel 1806: 66)

One might generously interpret this passage in Pinel as a precursor to the idea of cultural competency in medical care (the concept that health care should be tailored to the culturally specific needs of the patient). However, it is clear from the context that Pinel's focus is on providing the "irritable Frenchman" the proper standard of care, which seemingly requires more finesse and attention—and less coercion and tyranny—than the care provided to peasants and slaves.

Perhaps nowhere is the thinking about race and madness more convoluted at this time than in the USA. By the mid-nineteenth century, the national conversation about slavery and its abolition was nearing fever pitch and would eventually lead to the Civil War (1861–5). Increasing support for public asylums and moral treatment for mental illness uneasily mixed with a robust tradition of scientific racism. Racial difference was widely perceived as biological difference, and even some abolitionists described the system of slavery as one that destroyed the morals and mental health of both whites and blacks, while still holding views that blacks were an inferior race. For example, the "father of American psychiatry," Benjamin Rush, noted that slavery begat vice: "All the vices which are charged upon the Negroes in the southern colonies ... Idleness, Treachery, Theft, and the like, are the genuine offspring of slavery" (quoted in Reed 2014: 123). Yet Rush also theorized that blackness was a pathological and contagious skin condition that required strict segregation of the races in his 1797 paper "Observations Intended to Favour a Supposition that the Black Color (As It Is Called) of the Negroes Is Derived from the Leprosy" (Reed 2014: 125). Nineteenth-century phrenologists and craniologists turned their attention to the skull and brain in works like George Combe's *The Constitution of Man* (1828) and Samuel George Morton's *Crania Americana* (1839): according to these theories, the shape of the skull revealed the development of the different organs of the brain that it contained. In comparison with the Caucasian skull, Combe and others argued, the particular shape of an African skull left little room for the mental organs of reason and intellect to develop and too much room for the organs of sentiment and feeling (Cooley 2001: 60–3, 176).

Then, in 1840, the USA conducted its sixth census, a potentially groundbreaking survey with significant ramifications for public policy about disability. For the very first time, the census would collect data about mental disability, including mental illness and developmental disability, under the broad category of the "insane and idiots." The census "gave promise of an accurate enumeration of the mentally handicapped in America, with invaluable bases for statistical comparison between the white and Negro populations, the free and the slave" (Deutsch 1944: 471). The results were shocking. As measured by the survey, mental disability among whites varied little between the North and South: 1 out of 995 and 1 out of 945, respectively. But the rates of mental disability among Negroes of the North versus the South were dramatically different: 1 out of 145 versus 1 out of 1,558, respectively (Deutsch 1944: 472). Freedom, therefore, was judged mentally disabling. "Here is proof," argued former vice president John C. Calhoun, "of the necessity of slavery. The African is incapable of self-care and sinks into lunacy under the burden of freedom. It is a mercy to him to give him the guardianship and protection from mental death" (quoted in Deutsch 1944: 473). An 1843 article in *The Southern Literary Messenger* repeated this appeal to white paternalism in the context of mental health: once free blacks of the North appear to be as happy as slaves, then "the subject of general emancipation will be entitled to more consideration. But so long as they furnish little else but materials for jails, penitentiaries and madhouses; warned by such examples, we cannot desire to be the destroyers of the dependent race" (quoted in Deutsch 1944: 473).

The 1840 census had a long-term effect on both public and professional perceptions of the mental health of African-Americans, and it is significant for disability scholars of mental health because it is an example of pernicious bias and the importance of accurate data in shaping public policy. The report was, as historian Albert Deutsch states, "one of the most amazing tissues of statistical falsehood and error ever woven together under government imprint" (1944: 475). Edward Jarvis, a physician and statistician, found sweeping internal inconsistencies and flaws in its data regarding the Northern population: he declared the document so "heavy with its errors and misstatements" that it is a "bearer of falsehood to confuse and mislead" (quoted in Deutsch 1944: 476). The numbers of "insane Negros" were simply fabricated in some cases or grievously miscalculated. James McCune Smith, an African-American physician and statistical expert, examined the Southern data, which he correctly suspected of undercounting the numbers of mentally ill slaves. Smith's analysis also revealed "that the census's methodology was so deeply flawed that it was tantamount to libel regarding the health and mental status of African Americans" (Washington 2006: 149).

Proof of the census' flaws did little to prevent the use of its false data by proslavery apologists. If freedom caused insanity, then, by a certain logic, the desire to escape slavery could also been seen as pathological. And hence "manifestations of the blacks' rejection of the institution of slavery were fitted into the medical model of insanity," such as physician Samuel A. Cartwright's concept of "drapetomania," the slave's pathological desire to run away (Gilman 1985: 138). The 1840s census data also supported the somehow complementary but contradictory belief that African-Americans in general lacked the mental capacity to become mentally ill or suicidal. This inability to adequately conceptualize mental illness in the black population led to even more problems after emancipation. Historian John S. Hughes points out, for example, that the Kirkbride Plan for asylum architecture did not account for the presence of black patients in a segregated society. Kirkbride himself did not approve of integrated wards: "The idea of mixing up all colors and all classes ... as is seen in one or two institutions of the United States, is not what is wanted in our hospitals for the insane" (quoted in Hughes 1992: 440). And so asylum superintendents would preserve the orderly and balanced Kirkbride architecture for their white patients and build haphazard separate structures behind the main hospital for black patients. As Hughes states, "blacks occupied a reality literally beyond (and behind) the ideals espoused" by the leaders of the moral treatment movement (1992: 441). Furthermore, "an unexplored irony of the formal policy of moral treatment," with its focus on work therapy, deference to authority, and structured daily routines, was that it "shared similarities with idealized notions of the antebellum slave system" (Hughes 1992: 443).

The legacy of scientific racism and the errors of the 1840 census still echo in the USA today (Deutsch 1944: 481; see also Metzl 2009; Jarman 2012). In his 1903 *The Souls of Black Folk*, civil rights activist W. E. B. Du Bois countered this legacy of racist psychiatry with a description of black mental life that was rich and complex:

> the Negro is a sort of seventh son, born with a veil, and gifted with second-sight in this American world,—a world which yields him no true self-consciousness, but only lets him see himself through the revelation of the other world. It is a peculiar sensation, this double-consciousness, this sense of always looking at one's self through the eyes of others, of measuring one's soul by the tape of a world that looks on in amused contempt and pity. One ever feels his two-ness,—an American, a Negro; two souls, two thoughts, two unreconciled strivings; two warring ideals in one dark body, whose dogged strength alone keeps it from being torn asunder. (Du Bois 1903: ch. 1)

Du Bois' cauled "seventh son" inverts discourses of degeneration and posits a resilient black mind that has special powers of insight and a "double-consciousness" that is born out of the intergenerational trauma of slavery and racism. "Double consciousness," as Du Bois knew, was also a nineteenth-century medical term describing split personality cases, like Mary Reynolds, who woke up one day with an altered personality and no memory of her previous life (Bruce 1992: 300, 303). Reynolds, like others with this condition, would shift back and forth from her original consciousness to a second consciousness. In Reynolds' case, "commentators noted her intellectual acuity in both states, as well as the fact that, settling permanently in her second state, she nevertheless spent her remaining years as a productive, respectable, and respected member of society" (Bruce 1992: 305). For Du Bois, the term's medical meaning captured both the extraordinary position of African-Americans and the sense of two fully functioning but opposing personalities in battle. And it also captured the suffering caused by not having a "true self-consciousness": "All the accounts of double consciousness reported its sufferers' great anguish, their real unhappiness upon becoming aware of their condition, their desire to possess a single individual self" (Bruce 1992: 306). Du Bois' use of double consciousness to describe the psychosocial production of internalized racism and the rich but conflicted inner life of African-Americans is a powerful reinterpretation of psychiatric discourse. It also highlights the potentially productive fluidity of diagnostic categories and psychiatric language at this historical moment.

8.3. CRIME AND INSANITY

During the nineteenth century in England, several high-profile criminal cases prompted the development of medicolegal definitions of insanity, and the role of medical experts in the courtroom expanded. This section traces the development of this language in two important cases—Hadfield and M'Naghten—and ends with a discussion of how these courtroom concepts informed literary representations of mental illness, with a special emphasis on Edgar Allan Poe's work.

Nineteenth-century cases of insanity pleas differed markedly from earlier cases. In *Witnessing Insanity: Madness and Mad-Doctors in the English Court*, Joel Peter Eigen notes, "Before the nineteenth century, a medico-legal literature was virtually nonexistent, lectures on the subject were not offered until the late 1700s, and the status of the medical witness was anything but exalted" (1995: 113). The legal definition of insanity also underwent important challenges during the long nineteenth century, beginning in 1800 with the trial of James Hadfield, who attempted to assassinate King George III. At trial, Thomas Erskine, Hadfield's counsel, effectively contested the "wild beast" standard of insanity established in *Rex v. Arnold* (1724), which stated that, for a man to be considered insane, he "must be totally deprived of his understanding and memory, so as not to know what he is doing, no more than an infant, a brute, or a wild beast." Hadfield, Erskine argued, should be considered insane because of his delusional thinking: although Hadfield was not frenzied and could reason, his reasoning began from premises that were completely false. Erskine also argued that Hadfield's disordered thinking was a result of a head injury incurred in war—a piece of his skull was sliced off by a sword—and he showed the jury the exposed membrane of Hadfield's brain (Moran 1985: 504). Several physicians testified as part of Hadfield's defense and reinforced Erskine's argument that Hadfield "became insane through '*violence to the brain, which permanently affects its structure*'" (Moran 1985: 504, emphasis in original). Hadfield was ultimately acquitted by reason of insanity. Yet although Hadfield won and was saved from the death penalty, this legal success had long-term detrimental effects on the rights of people with mental illness.

In one respect, Hadfield's acquittal was an important judgment that expanded the legal definition of insanity from a narrow sense of a frenzied "wild beast" to a more nuanced awareness of how a person's actions can be influenced by delusional thoughts. It is potentially a more humane response to crimes involving insanity, especially since Hadfield was not sentenced to death. However, in the aftermath of this acquittal, the House of Commons moved quickly to pass the Criminal Lunatics Act (1800), which gave the state far-reaching powers to indefinitely detain criminally insane defendants. This legislation was retroactively applied to Hadfield, who spent the rest of his life imprisoned (Moran 1985: 516).

This pattern of acquittal and lifelong commitment is repeated in another pivotal case in the history of the insanity plea: the trial of Daniel M'Naghten. In 1843, M'Naghten attempted to kill Prime Minister Robert Peel, but mistakenly shot and killed his assistant instead. Like Erskine's earlier defense of Hadfield, M'Naghten's defense rested on convincing jurors that delusional thinking was a significant factor in mitigating his criminal responsibility for the murder. According to expert medical witnesses, M'Naghten was experiencing monomania, or a partial insanity. In other words, while M'Naghten may have been capable of rational thought concerning other subjects, he had a fixed delusion regarding the Tory Party, which he believed was persecuting him. The defense argued that the murder "flowed from those delusions" and that "he was not under the ordinary restraint by which persons in general are bound in their conduct; his moral liberty was destroyed" (quoted in Eigen 1991: 45). The jury was convinced, and M'Naghten was acquitted.

The use of monomania in expert court testimony was relatively brief historically, but influential nonetheless. Its use in high-profile court cases meant that the somewhat obscure diagnostic category would become better known by the public, and its appearance in creative fiction would also help to establish its place in the public imaginary. The idea of a person being suddenly seized by an ungovernable impulse was of great interest to gothic writers like Edgar Allan Poe, who first mentions monomania in his short story "Berenice," published in 1835. In "Berenice," the narrator becomes obsessed with his cousin/fiancée's teeth. As the narrator tells his story, he describes the onset of his "disease" ("for I have been told that I should call it by no other appellation"), when Berenice, whose body has been ravaged by a mysterious illness, smiles at him: "Then came the full fury of my monomania, and I struggled in vain against its strange and irresistible influence" (Poe 1835: 333).

Poe's "The Tell-Tale Heart" also has a narrator with a singular obsession: the cloudy Evil-Eye of an old man, whom he murders. This story has even clearer connections to forensic psychiatry: it is framed as a post-arrest conversation the narrator is having with either a lawyer or a medical examiner. It begins with the narrator disputing his diagnosis: "You fancy me mad. Madmen know nothing. But you should have seen me. You should have seen how wisely I proceeded—with what caution—with what foresight—with what dissimulation I went to work!" (1843: 29). In this passage, Poe evokes the old "wild beast" standard of insanity—"madmen know nothing"—and illustrates the challenge that monomania or partial insanity presents to ideas of criminal culpability.

Monomania has also been famously depicted in Herman Melville's *Moby-Dick* (1851) as Ahab's singular focus on pursuing the whale (Smith 1978). In Emily Brontë's *Wuthering Heights*, Heathcliff has a "monomania on the subject of his departed idol" (1870: ch. 13). In Fyodor Dostoyevsky's *Crime and Punishment*, Raskolnikov is described as having a "perfect monomania" (1866: ch. 5). And, in George Eliot's *Middlemarch* (1871–2) and *Daniel Deronda* (1876), monomania and murder are linked (During 1988; Jones 2016). All of these fictional examples use the concept of monomania to connect madness with cruelty and violence. Even though monomania as a psychiatric term would eventually die out, the legacy of this association between madness and crime persists, with madness often used as a shorthand to describe acts of violence that are not otherwise immediately legible.

8.4. INSTITUTIONALIZATION AND THE ROOTS OF ANTI-PSYCHIATRY

This section discusses efforts by ex-patient Elizabeth Packard and reformer Nellie Bly to challenge the asylum system's excesses and failures, and ends with physician/writer Anton Chekhov's criticism of the cultural and social power of medical diagnoses in his short story "Ward No. 6." Under a diagnosis of "monomania on the subject of religion," Elizabeth Packard was involuntarily committed in June 1860 at the request of her husband, a local pastor (Carlisle 2010: 74). This committal had been slowly brewing. Packard's husband had become increasingly frustrated with her participation in a bible-study group, which, after she was asked to join, had grown from six to forty-six members. The bible-study group and Packard's spirited discussions were a source of concern to church deacons, who saw them as a potential threat to the congregation (Carlisle 2000: 45). Packard's husband insisted that she quit, under his strict conditions, and she refused, citing her liberty of consciousness (Packard 1868: 17). Fairly soon after, her husband "enlisted the aid of the local sheriff and two doctors (both members of the Bible class)," broke into her locked bedroom with an ax, and carried her away to an asylum while her children and neighbors watched (Carlisle 2000: 45). For the next three years, Packard was a reluctant patient at the Illinois State Asylum and Hospital for the Insane in Jacksonville, IL, an institution that, in many ways, embodied the promises of reformers in moral treatment: it was built following the Kirkbride Plan and it was established through Dorothea Dix's advocacy work (Carlisle 2010: 63, n. 20). The Jacksonville superintendent, Dr. Andrew McFarland, was also a well-respected physician and psychiatric expert—he even evaluated former first lady Mary Todd Lincoln, at the request of her son, while she was committed (Emerson 2007: 100). Yet despite being built with good intentions and despite McFarland's credentials, the Jacksonville Insane Asylum was hardly a therapeutic experience for Packard, who maintained throughout her incarceration that she was sane and was simply being punished for holding religious views that were contrary to her husband's. When Packard finally gained her freedom, she quickly published her memoirs and then spent the next twenty years as an ardent and effective advocate for reforms.

Packard is a significant figure in the early history of ex-patient protest literature, and her story illustrates the intersection of civil rights discourses with disability rights, abolition rhetoric, and women's rights. In some ways, Packard's asylum writings are fairly typical: as Benjamin Reiss notes, "Nearly every former patient who published a memoir protested that his or her incarceration in an asylum was a matter of disciplining deviant political and/or religious views" (2008: 169). Yet Packard distinguished herself not simply because she was one of the most effective advocates of her day, but also because of her unique perspective and the terms of her dissent. Her civil rights work focused primarily on the rights of married women, and her fight against laws of coverture in marriage was the basis for her fight for the rights of people with mental illness, or perceived mental illness, who were facing involuntary committal. Before Packard's advocacy, the laws of committal to an asylum were more relaxed for married women. While all other people who were facing committal to an asylum needed to go before a judge and have a hearing, the laws in Illinois at the time suspended that requirement for married women and required only the consent of the husband and two doctors. This relaxed requirement, as Packard's case illustrates, opened the door to abuses: "Intended to shield married women from public humiliation in a court proceeding, the amendment instead gave husbands a means for legal subjugation of unsubmissive wives" (Carlisle 2000: 46–7). Packard's tale of involuntary committal captured the public imagination and revealed the precarious legal position of married women; it was like something out of novel—a real-life counterpart to Wilkie Collins' novel, *The Woman in White*, in which a scheming husband imprisons his disobedient wife in an asylum.

As a result of her committal and her status as a married woman, Packard lost her freedom, her access to her husband's property, and her children. Packard viewed her battle with her husband in a larger context of religious freedoms and civil rights in the USA:

> My husband and I have grown apart—he conservative, and I radical—he Calvinistic, and I Christian. … So the South and North have grown apart, instead of together—slavery and freedom—oppression and human rights. (quoted in Carlisle 2000: 59)

The Packards' civil union became a civil war. Packard relied on slavery rhetoric often in her writing, comparing the plight of married women to slaves. The title of her first book was in part *Exposure on Board the Atlantic & Pacific Car of Emancipation for the Slaves* of Old Columbia. ... With an Appeal to the Government to Emancipate the Slaves of the Marriage Union (1864); it was subtitled "Edited by a Slave, Now Imprisoned in the Jacksonville Insane Asylum" (Carlisle 2000: 48). In her later work, this conflation of wife and slave becomes even more pronounced:

> I have given my narrative to the public, hoping that my more tangible experiences may draw the attention of the philanthropic public to a more just consideration of married woman's legal disabilities; for since the emancipation of the negro, there is no class of American citizens, who so much need legal protection, and who receive so little, as this class. (Packard 1868: xii)

Packard would also compare asylum inmates to slaves, bound in service to the asylum superintendent/overseer and to the state. Packard notes that the asylum's focus on work therapy is not simply a therapeutic one and that, because of the structure of the institution, there is no incentive to release a patient who is a productive laborer. And she explicitly accuses McFarland of keeping cured patients longer so that he can extract their labor. In one case, he "breaks" a physically abused wife until she begs to be returned to her violent, alcoholic husband, but even then she is not quite fully cured: "She has not yet performed her share of unrequited labor for the State of Illinois, as its slave; and if she is a good and efficient workman, there may be weeks, months, years of imprisonment yet before her, ere her cure is complete!" (122). Packard's attacks on McFarland were returned in kind, and the two were lifelong foes, although Packard's issue with McFarland was not that their relationship demanded her submissiveness, but that he did not fulfill his duty to protect the dependents in his care adequately.

As a result of Packard's advocacy work, several states passed "Packard Laws," which required more stringent commitment hearings and limited the powers of asylum

FIGURE 8.5 "Popular Mode of Curing Insanity!."

superintendents to admit and hold patients (Reiss 2008: 173). Packard was also successful in passing legislation regarding married women's custody and property rights. As a result, she was able to regain custody of her children and to keep the money she earned from publishing her books (which otherwise could have become the property of her estranged husband). Packard's work marks the early stages of a long tradition of ex-patient critiques of psychiatric treatment and psychiatric power (see Figure 8.5). But it is worth remembering, as Ben Reiss notes, that "like most of the other asylum protests," Packard "did not call for the abandonment of the asylum system," but only for reform (Reiss 2008: 173). And Packard always insisted on her fundamental sanity: she did not belong in an asylum because she was sane. There were other women in her same situation—"pseudo 'lunatics,'" who were unjustly committed, but sane (Packard 1868: 33). On the other hand, there were those she saw as truly insane, and Packard's close association with "the filthy maniacs" of the asylum was "humiliating in the extreme" (Packard 1868: 260). Packard's mission was mainly focused on her fellow "pseudo-lunatics." This is somewhat ironic, since through the years her sanity was still questioned, even after a week-long trial and a jury found her "sane" (Carlisle 2000: 53). Packard acknowledged the stigma and erasure of rights associated with mental illness—"what is an insane person's testimony worth? Nothing" (Packard 1868: 122)—but she did not fight that stigma and worked hard to distance herself from the insane.

Packard's well-known exposé of US asylum life would be followed decades later by another famous work, Nellie Bly's *Ten Days in a Mad-House* (1887). Bly, an investigative reporter on assignment with the *New York World* newspaper, faked symptoms of mental illness and was sent to the Insane Asylum at Blackwell's Island. Even though Bly faked symptoms to get into the asylum, she dropped most of these pretenses (except for an impaired memory regarding her identity) once she was in the asylum: "I talked and acted just as I do in ordinary life. Yet strange to say, the more sanely I talked and acted the crazier I was thought to be by all except one physician" (1887: ch. 1). Bly's malingering predated, by over eighty years, the infamous Rosenhan experiment in which pseudo-patients feigned an auditory hallucination in order to be hospitalized (Rosenhan 1973). Like Bly, the Rosenhan patients acted "normally" after admission. And, like Bly, they were treated as insane. Bly's story, like Rosenhan's study, was deeply critical of doctors' inability to recognize the difference between sanity and insanity. But the truly scandalous portion of Bly's exposé concerned the abhorrent living conditions, the abusive staff and attendants, and the lack of real medical treatment, other than sedating drugs, for the patients. Bly's descriptions of the meager amounts of spoiled food allotted to the patients, the lack of heat and adequate clothing and linen, and the unsanitary and unhygienic conditions were shocking to readers. She described patients, including patients with infectious skin conditions, bathing one after another in the same unchanged bath water and sharing the same single towel. The female ward attendants were skilled at expectorating tobacco juice and beating patients. There was nothing for patients to do on the ward but sit silently on benches. It was an environment better designed to produce than cure madness:

> What, excepting torture, would produce insanity quicker than this treatment? Here is a class of women sent to be cured. I would like the expert physicians who are condemning me for my action, which has proven their ability, to take a perfectly sane and healthy woman, shut her up and make her sit from 6 A. M. until 8 P. M. on straight-back benches, do not allow her to talk or move during these hours, give her

> no reading and let her know nothing of the world or its doings, give her bad food and harsh treatment, and see how long it will take to make her insane. (Bly 1887: ch. 12)

While Bly does describe madness as socially or environmentally produced here, it is not clear that she believes that all cases of madness can be attributed to such causes, and, like Packard, she is quick to distinguish the truly mad from the falsely incarcerated.

The mad themselves appear to be a species apart from Bly. On watching a rope gang of violent patients pass, Bly gets caught staring:

> One who had blue eyes saw me look at her, and she turned as far as she could, talking and smiling, with that terrible, horrifying look of absolute insanity stamped on her. The doctors might safely judge on her case. The horror of that sight to one who had never been near an insane person before, was something unspeakable. (1887: ch. 12)

While Bly has sympathy for the inmates of Blackwell, she also has a palpable fear of mad people and the experience of madness: "Mad! what can be half so horrible? My heart thrilled with pity when I looked on old, gray-haired women talking aimlessly to space. One woman had on a straightjacket, and two women had to drag her along. Crippled, blind, old, young, homely, and pretty; one senseless mass of humanity. No fate could be worse" (1887: ch. 12). Bly acknowledges the indiscriminate nature of madness—the great equalizer—and its ability to strike anyone and dissolve the individual into the homogenous "senseless mass." In Bly's narrative, madness is also potentially contagious. Earlier in her story, before she begins to play the part of a mad girl, she takes one last look at her sane self in the mirror: "who could tell but that the strain of playing crazy, and being shut up with a crowd of mad people, might turn my own brain, and I would never get back" (1887: ch. 2) (see Figure 8.6).

These themes of contagion and the seemingly arbitrary division of the sane from the insane (or, rather, the ability of the asylum to produce and maintain insanity) are infamously represented in Anton Chekhov's "Ward No. 6" (1892). In this story, the physician Andrey Yefimitch Ragin, who has until now been reliably neglectful of the hospital and the patients in his charge, discovers a kindred spirit in his patient Ivan Dmitrich Gromov and spends increasing amounts of time in the psychiatric ward talking philosophy with him. Eventually, the physician's unusual behavior is scrutinized by his colleagues. He enters into "an enchanted circle which there is no getting out of": "When you are told that you have something such as diseased kidneys or enlarged heart, and you begin being treated for it, or are told you are mad or a criminal—that is, in fact, when people suddenly turn their attention to you—you may be sure you have got into an enchanted circle from which you will not escape" (1892: section XVI). In this diagnostic echo chamber, Andrey Yefimitch is labeled mad, and there is simply no way to become un-mad. He transitions from physician to patient and is imprisoned in the same ward with Ivan Dmitrich. Here, Andrey Yefimitch must confront the absurdity of his old ideas. He had previously consoled his patient by encouraging him to be "philosophical": "There is no real difference between a warm, snug study and this ward. ... A man's peace and contentment do not lie outside a man, but in himself" (1892: section X). After one night deprived of his clothes and his liberty, and after a brutal beating from the ward attendant, this false belief is corrected. Now he must face his failure as a physician and his inability to recognize the reality that was before him:

> He bit the pillow from pain and clenched his teeth, and all at once through the chaos in his brain there flashed the terrible unbearable thought that these people, who seemed

NELLIE PRACTICES INSANITY AT HOME.

FIGURE 8.6 "Nellie Practices Insanity at Home."

now like black shadows in the moonlight, had to endure such pain day by day for years. How could it have happened that for more than twenty years he had not known it and had refused to know it? (1892: section XVIII)

He dies of an apoplectic stroke the next night. Thomas Szasz, who is well known for his association with anti-psychiatry thinking, has called this story "arguably, the most discerning and most powerful condemnation of the practice of therapeutic coercion and its inevitable consequence, psychiatric slavery" (2009: 159). Chekhov's story and the non-fictional exposés by Packard and Bly are critiques of institutionalization that contain seeds of thought that would develop later in the 1960s as anti-psychiatry, a many-pronged movement that collectively criticizes the power of psychiatry as a discipline, challenges the accuracy of psychiatric diagnoses and the existence of the field itself, and holds psychiatry responsible for patient abuses and forcible treatments.

8.5. CONCLUSION

The nineteenth century was the Age of the Asylum, when a public mental hospital system emerged out of high-minded ideals of moral treatment and therapeutic care. And then that system metastasized: overpopulation and the stasis of routine turned moral treatment into custodial care, and care became neglect, and worse. Professional authority moved from alienists, to superintendents, to neurologists and psychiatrists. Professional associations that began in the asylum, such as the Association of Medical Officers of Asylums and Hospitals and the Association of Medical Superintendents of American Institutions for the Insane, would eventually break with the concepts of the nineteenth century and develop into their twentieth-century forms: the Royal College of Psychiatrists and the American Psychiatric Association. The evolving professionalization in medicine in the nineteenth century generated new models of mental illness. Some, like Jean-Étienne Esquirol's monomania, would fall into oblivion; others, like Emil Kraepelin's dementia praecox, would live on in mutating forms (schizophrenia). At the turn of the century, ex-patients would continue to battle against the authority of their doctors: Charlotte Perkins Gilman's short story "The Yellow Wall-Paper" (1892) was a scathing critique of physician Silas Weir Mitchell's rest cure treatment. But other spaces opened up for ex-patients to form alliances with leaders in psychiatry: Clifford Beers' *A Mind That Found Itself* (1908), his compelling autobiographical account of his breakdown and asylum experiences, brought Beers into a fruitful partnership with the leading American psychiatrist of the day, Adolf Meyer. Beers became one of the first prominent advocates for asylum reform who did not deny that he was mentally ill when he was committed, and he founded and eventually led advocacy groups for mental hygiene initiatives.[2] And, while Adolf Meyer pursued research into biopsychosocial models of mental illness at the newly opened Phipps Clinic (the first psychiatric teaching clinic in the USA) at Johns Hopkins Hospital, Freud was presenting the Clark Lectures (1909), bringing his theories of psychoanalysis to an appreciative American audience. And a new age began.

NOTES

INTRODUCTION

1. For more exploration of Frankenstein and disability, see Mossman 2001; Marchbanks 2010; Holmes 2014; Rodas 2016; Wang 2017; and Friedman and Kavey 2018.
2. See also Foucault, *Birth of the Clinic* (1963: 34).
3. See, for example, Romantic poet William Wordsworth's famous claim in "Ode: Intimations of Immortality from Recollections of Early Childhood" (1807) that "Heaven lies about us in our infancy!" As Marah Gubar notes, however, "the 'otherness' of children was not a settled fact during the nineteenth century but the subject of a long, drawn-out fight" (2009: 152).
4. The Enlightenment focus on reason also stood to increase the marginality of mentally or learning-disabled adults, as Tobin Siebers argues in *Disability Theory* (2008: 12).
5. For a fuller discussion of these fears, see Gallagher (1987).
6. For a discussion of nineteenth-century fears of vaccination, including Gillray's cartoon, see Kudlick (2014).
7. See Holmes (2007).
8. See also Holmes (2009).
9. For a partial list of characters with disabilities in Victorian literature, as well as a further discussion of both Mayhew and life-writing, see Holmes (2004).
10. For an excellent example of a reading that includes all of these, see Eltis (2002).
11. In their foundational work on patterns of disability and narrative, Mitchell and Snyder trace how disability repeatedly serves as a "deviance or marked difference" that is revealed, explained, brought to the center, and then removed—through "cure," "rehabilitation," purification, extermination, and other forms of erasure. They note that "since what we now call disability has been historically narrated as that which characterizes a body as deviant from shared norms of bodily appearance and ability, disability has functioned throughout history as one of the most marked and remarked upon differences that originates the act of storytelling" (53–4).
12. See Susan Coolidge's *What Katy Did* (1872; discussed by Bourrier in Chapter 2 of this volume), George MacDonald's *The Princess and the Goblin* (1872), Dinah Mulock Craik's *The Little Lame Prince and His Travelling Cloak* (1875), Johanna Spyri's *Heidi* (1881), Kate Douglas Wiggin's *The Birds' Christmas Carol* (1886), Robert Louis Stevenson's *Treasure Island* (1883), J. M. Barrie's *Peter and Wendy* (1911), and Francis Hodgson Burnett's *The Secret Garden* (1910).
13. See also Maria Edgeworth's *The Parents' Assistant: Stories for Children* (1796), political economy tales that feature ill and disabled adults whose presence in the lives of sometimes careless children spurs the moral development of child characters and readers.

CHAPTER 1

1. A sustained search of the catalogues of the Wellcome Library and the British Library, as the well as the London *Times*, reveals that the term first appears in this context in Britain around 1900 and is used widely only during and after the First World War.

2   These photographs were purchased by the Natural History Museum, London, at a sale of Owen's effects. They were then pasted into the museum's copy of Cull (1856), where they remain to this day.

CHAPTER 2

1   Although the stare of an able-bodied woman like Oliphant may seem oppressive, disability studies scholar Rosemarie Garland-Thomson argues that staring is an "interrogative gesture" that can be generative as well as oppressive; staring "asks what's going on and demands the story" (2009: 3).
2   I first explored this advertisement, as well as texts by Aspinall and Martineau, at greater length in *Nineteenth-Century Disability: Cultures and Contexts* (Bourrier 2015b).
3   I explore the relationship between George and Dinah Craik at greater length in my biography of Dinah Craik, *Victorian Bestseller: A Life of Dinah Craik*, forthcoming from the University of Michigan Press.
4   For an extended analysis of this trope, see Bourrier (2015a).

CHAPTER 3

1   Many in the nineteenth century used the word "invalid" to refer obliquely to any person experiencing severe enough suffering to be rendered incapable of routine functioning. The term was capacious enough to encompass chronic suffering of a relatively minor sort and chronic suffering that might leave one bedridden. Throughout this chapter, I will make use of terminology like "invalid" and "invalidism" that reflects the ordinary usage in medical and social discourse of the period. Whereas a term like "affliction" carried with it little judgment, but now seems dated, a term like "malingering" clearly connoted some level of moral judgment. My occasional use of the terms "sufferers" and "suffering" seeks not to deny the many ways that people had productive and fulfilling lives while also experiencing chronic illness, but rather to acknowledge the reality of those whose experiences with chronic illness or pain resulted in or included some level of suffering.
2   "Water-patient" was a familiar term used by nineteenth-century men and women to refer to those undergoing hydrotherapy (or "the water cure"), typically at a spa and under some medical (or pseudo-medical) supervision.
3   In Greek and Roman mythology, Hygieia was the goddess of health.
4   Mesmerism, also known as animal magnetism, was a now discredited form of alternative medicine introduced by the German doctor Franz Mesmer in the latter half of the eighteenth century. Mesmer and other advocates of mesmerism believed that one could incite "invisible forces" within a person to aid in healing. By the middle of the nineteenth century, the heyday of mesmerism had passed.

CHAPTER 4

1   For discussions of ophthalmia's place in the medical history of blindness, consult Davidson (1996) and Carpenter (2010).
2   Consult Carpenter (n.d.) for an informative discussion of cataract surgery.
3   For more detailed analysis of the history of blind people's reading experiences in nineteenth-century Britain, consult Warne (2011, 2015).

4   For an important discussion of Samuel Gridley Howe's research on raised printing methods and his work with blind students, consult Klages (1999: 28–55). Consult also Gitter (2001).
5   Consult Tilley (2011) for an analysis of the raised-print publication of Dickens' *Old Curiosity Shop*.
6   For important studies of the educational and state welfare history of British blind people, consult Oliphant (2007, 2009) and Phillips (2004). For a useful study of blindness and history in France in the early nineteenth century, consult Paulson (1993).
7   For more on Crosby, consult Cohen (2017).
8   Consult Bourrier (2009) for a discussion of the role played by reading by touch in Dickens' portrait of Bridgman.
9   For a different reading of this *Illustrated London News* illustration and of two of the three paintings discussed below, consult Tilley (2018).
10   For a discussion of Elizabeth Barrett Browning's relationship with the blind poet Hugh Stuart Boyd, consult Rodas (2007).
11   For discussions of blindness in *A Cricket on the Hearth*, consult Rodas (2004) and Holmes (2004).
12   For more on Kipling and blindness, consult Bolt (2004).
13   For more on Holman, consult Bar-Yosef (2009).
14   For discussions of Browne's reputation as a blind poet, consult Tilley (2009) and McLean (2003).

CHAPTER 5

1   International meetings of deaf people were held in Berlin (1873), Vienna (1874), Dresden (1875), Leipzig (1878), Prague (1881), Stockholm (1884), Paris (1889), Hannover (1892), Chicago (1893), Geneva (1896), London (1897), Stuttgart (1899), Paris (1900), St. Louis (1904), Liège (1905), Hamburg (1911), Rome (1911), and Paris (1912) (Murray 2007: 60).

CHAPTER 6

1   In this regard, the high frequency of systems of easy or quick cure promoted throughout Europe and the USA reflects our own twenty-first-century promotion of easy-step solutions or cures, either online or in print.
2   For an extensive introduction to this concept of biopower or the biopolitical, see Part 5 of *The History of Sexuality, Volume One* (Foucault 1990: 135–59). In this foundational discussion of the shift in modern Western culture from the sovereign's right to take life to new administrative means of controlling, regulating, and administering bodies, Foucault introduces a foundational theoretical framework for understanding how disability functioned in the nineteenth century as an administrative and institutional "problem" that required disciplinary management.
3   In recent years, advocates for the "stuttering pride" movement, transfluency, and neurodiversity have also raised compelling questions about the distinctions between "disfluency" and "dysfluency" in current scientific literature, the latter of which marks a transgression rather than a negation in its choice of prefix. While these two terms have been relatively interchangeable in practice, their differences in prefix are an important reminder of how language choice impacts thought about disability. This chapter adopts the term "dysfluency" because the prefix "dys-" marks a transgression rather than a lack.

Transgressions have the potential for agency and choice. For more on this distinction, see St. Pierre (2015a).

4 For more on nineteenth-century distinctions between stammering and stuttering, see Rockey (1980: 15).

5 Nineteenth-century medical experts frequently drew similarities between stuttering and such bodily disorders; see Monro (1850: 27), Poett (1856: 20), and Hunt (1870: 316).

6 For a detailed account of early nineteenth-century elocutionary theories, see Hunt (1870). Hunt's posthumous edition of *Stammering and Stuttering; Their Nature and Treatment* is, even by today's standards, the most comprehensive compendium of the history of thought about stuttering from the ancient Greeks to Hunt's contemporaries in the 1850s and 1860s.

7 This concept of an etiological "elsewhere" is prominent in current cultural and philosophical studies of the voice, especially those influenced by the psychoanalytic theories of Jacques Lacan; see Dolar (2006) and Connor (2014).

8 For a theoretical account of the biopolitics and hegemony of dysfluency, see St. Pierre (2017).

9 The connection between masculinity and speech was especially prominent throughout the century, especially considering that nineteenth-century statistics reflect current ratios of three to four men who stutter to every woman who stutters. For more on the intersections of dysfluency and masculinity studies, see Lee (2008), Eagle (2013), and St. Pierre (2015b).

10 Maelzel's *metronome* was patented in 1815. For a detailed study of the metronome's place in the history of Western music, see Grant (2014). It is perhaps no coincidence that metronomic training is still a common therapeutic strategy in research on occupational/physical therapy and language/reading impairment.

11 For specific usage of the "ugly," "disagreeable," or "grotesque" in nineteenth-century elocutionary/medical literature on stuttering, see Monro (1850: 43, 54), Rymer (1855: 20), Hunt (1870: 310), and Lewis (1902: 47).

12 For more on Kingsley's work on stuttering and its application to the muscular Christianity movement, see Lee (2008).

13 Freud wrote little about psychoanalytic theories of stuttered speech throughout his career, but psychoanalysts after Freud frequently associated stuttered speech with conflicts at the oral or anal stages of childhood development.

14 For a further discussion of trauma studies and its bearing on speech dysfluencies, see Müller (2012). Berger claims that disability studies does not yet contain a methodological framework for analyzing the causes of stuttered speech in traumatic childhood intersubjective experiences (2014: 173–9).

15 For a speculative and theoretical account of this concept of "phonophobia," see Connor (2014: 22).

16 While this concept of a capacity in children for imitating "poor" or "unhealthy" speech has had no medical or pedagogical merit since the early twentieth century, it is a significant theory for any historical understanding of nineteenth-century medical accounts of dysfluency.

17 Hunt's work was highly regarded, owing especially to his treatment of some of the century's most well-known writers and intellectuals who stuttered, including Charles Kingsley and Lewis Carroll. While Kingsley was a devout advocate of Hunt's system of cure, the same cannot be said of Carroll, whose relationship with Hunt was inconsistent; see Woolf (2010: 76).

18 For more on Hunt's racist beliefs in polygenesis and his work as President of the Anthropological Society, see Pande (2010: 40–1) and Challis (2013: 43–4).

19 Melville's *Billy Budd* is arguably the century's most mercurial cultural representation of stuttered speech. As such, it has undergone extensive interpretative scrutiny by literary

critics. For an effective review of criticism of the novella focusing on a disability studies perspective, see Berger (2014: 45–51).
20. Like the Greek rhetorician Demosthenes, the biblical account of Moses' speech is a common historical reference point in scholarship about speech dysfluencies; see Shell (2005: 102–36).
21. Lucas Malet was a pseudonym for the writer Mary St. Leger Kingsley, the daughter of Charles Kingsley. Given her intimate familiarity with her father's stuttered speech and his proud championing of "healthy" speech, it is surprising that *The Wages of Sin* takes such a thematic or interpretive stance on the aesthetics of stuttering.
22. Infamously, Nordau criticizes British and French aesthetic and decadent poetry of the 1850s onward for its tendency toward "senseless stammering and babbling" and "idiotic echolalia" (1895: 43, 271). Nordau's frequent reference to echolalia borrows from claims in the period that people suffering from dementia and idiocy produced echolalic speech that merely echoed the vocal utterances of others.
23. More evidence of this systemic erasure exists in the fact that only a handful of historical accounts of stuttering and stammering have appeared in print since Rockey (1980).
24. For an example of one such review, see Wilson (1838).
25. Tupper mentions in *My Life as an Author* that "The Stammerer's Complaint" was printed in a medical book by one of the experts he consulted throughout his life. Which "Galen" Tupper refers to here is unknown.
26. Marc Shell (2005: 2) suggests that even classic texts in the field of disability studies often appropriate metaphors of stuttering in their emancipatory claims.

CHAPTER 7

1. Séguin's first major works were published in French—*Hygiène et Éducation des Idiots* (1843) and the much larger and more influential *Traitement Moral, Hygiène et Éducation des Idiots* (1846)—but in 1850 he left France for the USA, and in 1866 published his major English-language work, *Idiocy: And Its Treatment by the Physiological Method*, under the anglicized name Edward Seguin.
2. Of course, this "Mongolism" is today known as Down (or Down's) syndrome, or trisomy 21, and it is caused by the appearance of a third copy of the twenty-first chromosome.

CHAPTER 8

1. In my essay, "The Corpus of the Madwoman: Toward a Feminist Disability Studies Theory of Embodiment and Mental Illness," I argue that the use of Bertha to symbolize female rebellion in contemporary feminist criticism can be a harmful distraction from historically based readings of her mental disability (Donaldson 2012).
2. Beers was, of course, not the first ex-patient who acknowledged that he was mentally ill while hospitalized. In *From Under the Cloud: Personal Reminiscences of Insanity*, Anna Agnew described her suicide attempts and her attempt to kill one of her children before she was admitted into the asylum. Agnew's narrative, however, is a difficult one to assimilate into the usual disability studies canon of asylum protest literature. As Kathleen M. Brian notes, Agnew aligned "herself with evolutionary science and asylum medicine," and her narrative is an example of "one of the earliest and most troubling sites for the articulation of a eugenicist rationale" (2011: 283).

REFERENCES

Aarons, Debra, and Philemon Akach (2002), "South African Sign Language: One Language or Many?" in Rajend Mesthrie (ed.), *Language in South Africa*, 127–47, Cambridge: Cambridge University Press.
Abel, Rhoda (1983), "The Identification of the Blind, 1834–1968: A Study of the Establishment of the Blind Register and the Registration Process," PhD diss., London School of Economics.
Ablow, Rachel (2017), *Victorian Pain*, Princeton: Princeton University Press.
Ackers, John (1880), "Historical Notes on the Education of the Deaf," *Transactions of the Royal Historical Society*, 8: 163–71.
Adams, Bluford (1997), *E Pluribus Barnum: The Great Showman and the Making of U.S. Popular Culture*, Minneapolis: University of Minnesota Press.
Adams, Rachel (2001), *Sideshow USA*, Chicago: University of Chicago Press.
Agnew, Anna (1886), *From Under the Cloud: Personal Reminiscences of Insanity*, Cincinnati: Robert Clark & Co.
Alberti, Samuel J. M. M. (2011), *Morbid Curiosities: Medical Museums in Nineteenth-Century Britain*, Oxford: Oxford University Press.
Allen, E. E. (1906), "Library Work for the Blind," *Charities and the Commons: A Weekly Journal of Philanthropy*, 15: 641–5.
Amato, Joseph H. (2004), *On Foot: A History of Walking*, New York: New York University Press.
"American Jack the Frog Man" (1888), Guildhall Library, London, Playbills Folder (Miscellaneous): American Museum.
Ames, Eric (2004), "From the Exotic to the Everyday: The Ethnographic Exhibition in Germany," in Vanessa Schwarz and Jeannene M. Przyblyski (eds), *The Nineteenth-Century Visual Culture Reader*, 313–27, London: Routledge.
"An Act to Make Better Provision for the Education of Blind and Deaf Children in England and Wales" (1893), Ch. 42, Section 15, Sept. 12.
"Annual Report for 1885" (1885), School for the Indigent Blind, London.
Anon. (1864), *Children of Silence or the Story of a Deaf and Dumb Child*, London: William Macintosh.
Armitage, T. R. (1886), *The Education and Employment of the Blind: What Has Been, Is, and Ought to Be*, 2nd edn., London: Harrison & Sons.
Arnott, Neil (1827), *Elements of Physics*, 2nd edn., London: Thomas and George Underwood.
Artman, William and L. V. Hall ([1854] 1862), *Beauties and Achievements of the Blind*, Dansville: Published for the Authors.
Aspinall, W. B. (1865), *San Remo as a Winter Residence*, London: John Churchill and Sons.
Atkinson, Alexander (1865), *Memoirs of My Youth*, Doncaster: Deaf History Society.
"The Aztecs and the Earthmen" (1854), John Johnson Collection, Bodleian Library, Oxford University, Entertainments Folder 6.

Bailin, Miriam (1994), *The Sickroom in Victorian Fiction: The Art of Being Ill*, Cambridge: Cambridge University Press.

Baker, Charles (n.d.), "Blind," in *Chambers's Encyclopaedia*, vol. II, 224–30, London: William and Robert Chambers.

Ballantyne, J. W. (1892), *The Diseases and Deformities of the Foetus*, vol. II, Edinburgh: Oliver and Boyd.

Bancel, Nicholas, Pascal Blanchard, Eric Deroo, and Sandrine Lemaire (eds.) (2009), *Human Zoos: Science and Spectacle in the Age of Colonial Empires*, Liverpool: Liverpool University Press.

Barker-Benfield, Ben (1978), "The Spermatic Economy: A Nineteenth-Century View of Sexuality," in Michael Gordon (ed.), *The American Family in Social-Historical Perspective*, 33–71, New York: St. Martin's Press.

Barnes, Colin (2013), The Disability Archive UK (http://disability-studies.leeds.ac.uk/library/), Leeds: University of Leeds.

Barrett, Michael Anthony (1986), "From Special Education to Segregation: An Inquiry into the Changing Character of Special Provision for the Retarded in England, c. 1846–1918," PhD diss., University of Lancaster.

Barton, Walter E. (1987), *The History and Influence of the American Psychiatric Association*, Washington, DC: American Psychiatric Press.

Bar-Yosef, Eitan (2009), "The 'Deaf-Traveller,' the 'Blind Traveller,' and Constructions of Disability in Nineteenth-Century Travel Writing," *Victorian Review*, 35 (1): 133–54.

Bashford, Alison (2004), *Imperial Hygiene: A Critical History of Colonialism, Nationalism and Public Health*, Basingstoke: Palgrave.

Baynton, Douglas C. (1992), "'A Silent Exile on This Earth': The Metaphorical Construction of Deafness in the Nineteenth Century," *American Quarterly*, 44 (2): 216–43.

Baynton, Douglas C. (1996), *Forbidden Signs: American Culture and the Campaign Against Sign Language*, Chicago: University of Chicago Press.

Baynton, Douglas C. (2001), "Disability and the Justification of Inequality in American History," in Paul K. Longmore and Lauri Umansky (eds.), *The New Disability History: American Perspectives*, 33–57, New York: New York University Press.

Baynton, Douglas C. (2016), *Defectives in the Land: Disability and Immigration in the Age of Eugenics*, Chicago: University of Chicago Press.

Beers, Clifford W. (1908), *A Mind That Found Itself*, London: Longmans, Green.

Bell, Alexander Graham (1884), *Memoir Upon the Formation of a Deaf Variety of the Human Race: A Paper Presented to the National Academy of Sciences at New Haven, November 13, 1883*, National Academy of Sciences, Internet Archive (original in Gallaudet University Library). Available online: https://archive.org/details/gu_memoirformati00bell.

Bell, Alexander Melville (1867), *Visible Speech: The Science of Universal Alphabetics*, London: Simpkin, Marshall & Co.

Bending, Lucy (2000), *The Representation of Bodily Pain in Late Nineteenth-Century English Culture*, Oxford: Clarendon Press.

Berger, James (2014), *The Disarticulate: Language, Disability, and the Narratives of Modernity*, New York: New York University Press.

Bewell, Alan (1989), *Wordsworth and the Enlightenment: Nature, Man, and Society in the Experimental Poetry*, New Haven: Yale University Press.

Binham, H. B. (1845), *Essays by the Pupils at the College of the Deaf and Dumb, Rugby, Warwickshire*, London: Longman.

Bird, M. (1909), "Our Blind Citizens," in *The Lady's Realm*, XXV: 627–36, Nineteenth-Century Collections Online.

Black, C. Allan, (1867), *An Essay on Conduct of a Physician in a Sick Room*, Philadelphia: University of Pennsylvania.

Blackie, Daniel (2014), "Disability, Dependency, and the Family in the Early United States," in Susan Burch and Michael Rembis (eds.), *Disability Histories*, 17–34, Urbana: University of Illinois Press.

Bland Sutton, John (1930), *The Story of a Surgeon*, London: Methuen.

"The Blind" (1850), *Youth's Magazine*, 157–65.

"The Blind and their Limitations" (1856), *Universalist and Quarterly Review*, April, 147–61.

Bly, Nellie (1887), *Ten Days in a Mad-House*, New York: Ian L. Munro. Available online: http://digital.library.upenn.edu/women/bly/madhouse/madhouse.html.

Board of Education (1901a), *Special Reports on Educational Subjects: Vol. 4, Educational systems of the chief colonies of the British Empire* (Dominion of Canada; Newfoundland; West Indies), London.

Board of Education (1901b), *Special Reports on Educational Subjects: Vol. 5, Educational Systems of the Chief Colonies of the British Empire* (Cape Colony; Natal Commonwealth of Australia; New Zealand; Ceylon; Malta), London.

Bobrick, Benson (1995), *Knotted Tongues: Stuttering in History and the Quest for a Cure*, New York: Simon & Schuster.

Bogdan, Robert (1988), *Freak Show*, Chicago: University of Chicago Press.

Bolt, David (2004), "Caught in the Chasm: Literary Representation and Suicide Among People With Impaired Vision," *British Journal of Visual Impairment*, 23 (3): 117–21.

Bolt, David (2012), "The Blindman in the Classic: Feminisms, Ocularcentrism, and *Jane Eyre*," in David Bolt, Julia Miele Rodas, and Elizabeth J. Donaldson (eds.), *The Madwoman and the Blindman: Jane Eyre, Discourse, Disability*, 32–50, Columbus: Ohio State University Press.

Bolt, David (2014), *The Metanarrative of Blindness: A Re-reading of Twentieth-Century Anglophone Writing*, Ann Arbor: University of Michigan Press.

Bolt, David, Julia Miele Rodas and Elizabeth J. Donaldson (2012a), "Introduction" to *The Madwoman and the Blindman: Jane Eyre, Discourse, Disability*, 1–9, Columbus: Ohio State University Press.

Bolt, David, Julia Miele Rodas and Elizabeth J. Donaldson (eds.) (2012b), *The Madwoman and the Blindman: Jane Eyre, Discourse, Disability*, Columbus: Ohio State University Press.

Bolton, George Buckley (1830), *On the United Siamese Twins*, London: Richard Taylor.

"The Borderland of Imbecility" (1894), *British Medical Journal*, 1264.

Boster, Dea H. (2013), *African American Slavery and Disability: Bodies, Property, and Power in the Antebellum South, 1800–1860*, New York: Routledge.

Botting, Fred (2008), *Limits of Horror Technology, Bodies, Gothic*, Manchester: Manchester University Press.

Bourrier, Karen (2009), "Reading Laura Bridgman: Literacy and Disability in Dickens's *American Notes*," *Dickens Studies Annual*, 40: 37–60.

Bourrier, Karen (2014), "Orthopaedic Disability and the Nineteenth-Century Novel," *Nineteenth-Century Contexts*, 36 (1): 1–17.

Bourrier, Karen (2015a), *The Measure of Manliness: Disability and Masculinity in the Mid-Victorian Novel*, Ann Arbor: University of Michigan Press.

Bourrier, Karen (ed.) (2015b), *Nineteenth-Century Disability: Cultures and Contexts*, NINES. Available online: http://www.nineteenthcenturydisability.org/.

Bradley, Ian (1976), *The Evangelical Impact on the Victorians*, New York: Macmillan.

Bradshaw, Michael (ed.) (2016), *Disabling Romanticism*, London: Palgrave Macmillan.
Branson, Jan and Don Miller (2002), *Damned for Their Difference: The Cultural Construction of Deaf People as Disabled*, Washington, DC: Gallaudet University Press.
Braun, Marta (2012), *Eadweard Muybridge*, London: Reaktion Books.
Brett, Robert, (1851), *Devotions for the Sick Room and for Times of Trouble: Compiled from Ancient Liturgies and the Writings of Holy Men*, 4th edn,. London: Masters.
Brewer, William D. (2016), "Mary Robinson's Paralysis and the Discourse of Disability," in Michael Bradshaw (ed.), *Disabling Romanticism*, 105–26, London: Palgrave Macmillan.
Brian, Kathleen M. (2011), "The Reclamation of Anna Agnew: Violence, Victimhood, and the Uses of 'Cure,'" *Journal of Literary & Cultural Disability Studies*, 5 (3): 279–302.
British Deaf Monthly, 1897.
The British Deaf-Mute and Deaf Chronicle (1895).
Brontë, Charlotte (1847), *Jane Eyre*, London: Smith, Elder & Co.
Brontë, Charlotte ([1847] 2006), *Jane Eyre*, London: Penguin Classics.
Brontë, Emily (1870), *Wuthering Heights*, London: Smith, Elder & Co.
Brooks, Peter (1995), *The Melodramatic Imagination: Balzac, Henry James, Melodrama, and the Mode of Excess*, New Haven: Yale University Press.
Brown, Michael (2010), *Performing Medicine: Medical Culture and Identity in Provincial England, c. 1760–1850*, Manchester: Manchester University Press.
Browne, Frances (1844), *The Star of Atteghei*, London: Edward Moxon.
Browne, Frances (1857), *Granny's Wonderful Chair, and Its Tales of Fairy Times*, London: J. M. Dent.
Browne, Frances (1861), *My Share of the World, An Autobiography*, 3 vols., London: Hurst and Blackett.
Browne, W. A. F. (1861), "Endemic Degeneration," *Journal of Mental Science*, 7: 61–76.
Browning, Elizabeth Barrett (1996), *Aurora Leigh and Other Poems*, London: Penguin Classics.
Bruce, Dickson D., Jr. (1992), "W. E. B. Du Bois and the Idea of Double Consciousness," *American Literature*, 64 (2): 299–309.
Buchan, William (1874), *Domestic Medicine, or a Treatise on the Prevention and Cure of Diseases*. Philadelphia: Joseph Crukshank, Robert Bell, and James Muir.
Bucknill, John Charles (1873), "Address on Idiocy," *Journal of Mental Science*, 19: 169–83.
Bull, Thomas (1859), *The Sense Denied and Lost*, London: Longman, Green, Longman and Roberts.
Bulwer-Lytton, Edward (1845), "Confessions and Observations of a Water Patient," *New Monthly Magazine*, 75 (Sept.): 1–16. Available online: https://archive.org/stream/b24921622/b2491622_djvu.txt.
Bulwer-Lytton, Edward (1858), *What Will He Do with It?*, Edinburgh and London: William Blackwood and Sons.
Burney, Ian A. (2003), "Medicine in the Age of Reform," in Arthur R. Burns and Joanna Innes (eds.), *Rethinking the Age of Reform: Britain, 1780–1850*, 163–81, Cambridge: Cambridge University Press.
Bynum, W. F. (1994), *Science and the Practice of Medicine in the Nineteenth Century*, Cambridge: Cambridge University Press.
Camlot, Jason (2015), "Historicist Audio Forensics: The Archive of Voices as Repository of Material and Conceptual Artefacts," *19: Interdisciplinary Studies in the Long Nineteenth Century*, 21: n.p.
Campbell, James Ure (1898), *The Story of a Working Man's Blindness*, Glasgow: John Calder and Company.

Carbin, Clifton F., ed. Dorothy L. Smith (1996) *Deaf Heritage in Canada: A Distinctive, Diverse, and Enduring Culture*, Toronto: McGraw-Hill Ryerson.

Carlisle, Linda V. (2000), "'New Notions and Wild Vagaries': Elizabeth Packard's Quest for Personal Liberty," *Journal of the Illinois State Historical Society*, 93 (1): 43–66.

Carlisle, Linda V. (2010), *Elizabeth Packard: A Noble Fight*, Champaign: University of Illinois Press.

Carpenter, Mary Wilson (2006), "Blinding the Hero," *differences: A Journal of Feminist Cultural Studies*, 17(3): 52–68.

Carpenter, Mary Wilson (2009), *Health, Medicine and Society in Victorian England*, California: Praeger.

Carpenter, Mary Wilson (2010), "Blindness," in *Health, Medicine, and Society in Victorian England*, 128–48, Santa Barbara: Praeger.

Carpenter, Mary Wilson (n.d.), "A Cultural History of Ophthalmology in Nineteenth-Century Britain," in BRANCH: *Britain, Representation and Nineteenth-Century History*, Dino Franco Felluga (ed.), Available online: https://www.branchcollective.org/.

Carpenter, Peter (2000a), "The Bath Idiot and Imbecile Institution," *History of Psychiatry*, 11: 163–88.

Carpenter, Peter (2000b), "The Victorian Small Idiot Homes Near Bath," *History of Psychiatry*, 11: 383–92.

Census Report (1861).

Chadwick, Edwin (1842), *Report on the Sanitary Conditions of the Labouring Population of Great Britain*, London: W. Clowes and Sons.

Chadwick, Ellen ([1903] 1912), *Echoes from a Sick Room. Ellen Chadwick: The Famous Manchester Invalid*, London: Keywood.

Challis, Debbie (2013), *The Archaeology of Race: The Eugenic Ideas of Francis Galton and Flinders Petrie*, London: Bloomsbury.

Cheering Texts for Days of Trial: A Companion for Invalids (1873), London: Book Society.

Chekhov, Anton (1892), "Ward No. 6," *Russkaya Mysl*, 11.

Chemers, Michael M. (2005), "Introduction: Staging Stigma: A Freak Studies Manifesto," *Disability Studies Quarterly*, 25 (3). Available online: dsq-sds.org/article/view/574/751.

Chemers, Michael M. (2008), *Staging Stigma: A Critical Examination of the American Freak Show*, New York: Palgrave Macmillan.

Chen, Mia (2008), "'And There was No Helping It': Disability and Social Reproduction in Charlotte Yonge's *The Daisy Chain*," *Nineteenth-Century Gender Studies*, 4 (2). Available online: http://ncgsjournal.com/issue42/chen.htm.

Chion, Michael (1999). *The Voice in Cinema*, Claudia Gorbman (trans.), New York: Columbia University Press.

Clark, James (1841), *The Sanative Influence of Climate: With an Account of the Best Places of Resort for Invalids in England, the South of Europe, &c. From the 3rd London Edition*, Philadelphia: Waldie.

Cleall, Esme (2013), "'Deaf to the Word': Gender, Deafness and Protestantism in Nineteenth-Century Britain and Ireland," *Gender and History*, 25 (3): 590–603.

Cleall, Esme (2015a) "Deaf Connections and Global Conversations: Deafness and Education in and Beyond the British Empire, c. 1800–1900," *Journal of Colonialism and Colonial History*, 16 (1). Available online: http://eprints.whiterose.ac.uk/90897/3/Deaf%20 connections.pdf.

Cleall, Esme (2015b) "Orientalising Deafness: Race and Disability in Imperial Britain," *Social Identities*, 21 (2015): 22–36.

Cleall, Esme (2015c), "Producing and Managing Deviance in the Disabled Colonial Self: John Kitto, the Deaf Traveller," in Emily Manktelow and Will Jackson (eds.), *Subverting Empire: Deviance and Disorder in the British Colonial World*, 126–44, Basingstoke: Palgrave.

Cleall, Esme (2016), "Jane Groom and the Deaf Settlers: Empire, Emigration and the Agency of Disabled People in the Late Nineteenth-century British Empire," *History Workshop Journal*, 81 (1): 39–61.

Cockayne, Emma (2003), "Experiences of the Deaf in Early Modern England," *The Historical Journal*, 46 (3): 493–510.

Cohen, Laurence J. (2017), "Seeing Inward: The Blind Seer, Fanny Crosby, and the Education for the Blind in the Nineteenth Century," *Journal of Literary and Cultural Disability Studies*, 11 (1): 53–68.

Coleridge, Samuel Taylor ([1800] 2017), "This Lime-tree Bower My Prison," in Marc R. Plamondon (ed.), *Representative Poetry Online*, Edition 6.0, University of Toronto Libraries. Available online: https://rpo.library.utoronto.ca/poems/lime-tree-bower-my-prison.

Collins, Wilke ([1872] 1995), *Poor Miss Finch*, Oxford: Oxford University Press.

"Comfort for Invalids" (1856), *The Lancet*, March 22, 330.

Confessions of a Hypochondriac: Or, The Adventures of a Hypochondriac in Search of Health (1849), By M. R. C. S., London: Saunders and Otley.

Connell, Raewyn (2014), "Southern Bodies and Disability: Rethinking Concepts," in Helen Meekosha and Karen Soldatic (eds.), *The Global Politics of Impairment and Disability: Processes and Embodiments*, 1–14, London: Routledge.

Connor, Steven (2014), *Beyond Words: Sobs, Hums, Stutters and Other Vocalizations*, London: Reaction.

Conolly, John (1845), "Notices of the Lunatic Asylums of Paris," *British and Foreign Medical Review* 19: 281–98.

Cook Jr., James W. (1996), "Of Men, Missing Links, and Nondescripts: The Strange Career of P.T. Barnum's 'What is It?' Exhibition," in Rosemarie Garland-Thomson (ed.), *Freakery: Cultural Spectacles of the Extraordinary Body*, 139–57, New York: New York University Press.

Cook, James W. (2001), *The Arts of Deception: Playing With Fraud in the Age of Barnum*, Cambridge, MA: Harvard University Press.

Cooley, Thomas (2001), *The Ivory Leg in the Ebony Cabinet: Madness, Race, and Gender in Victorian America*, Amherst: University of Massachusetts Press.

Coolidge, Susan ([1872] 2010), *What Katy Did*, New York: Puffin Classics.

Crabbe, George (1907), *Poems*, Adolphus William Ward (ed.), 3 vols., Cambridge: Cambridge University Press.

Craik, Dinah Mulock (1861), Letter to Ben Mulock, Mulock Family Papers, Charles E. Young Research Library, UCLA.

Craik, Dinah Mulock ([1856] 2005), *John Halifax, Gentleman*, ed. Lynn M. Alexander, Peterborough: Broadview Press.

Craik, Dinah Mulock (n.d.), Letter to Ben Mulock, September 20, Mulock Family Papers, Charles E. Young Research Library, UCLA.

Crais, Clifton, and Pamela Scully (2009), *Sara Baartman and the Hottentot Venus: A Ghost Story and a Biography*, Princeton: Princeton University Press.

Craton, Lillian (2009), *The Victorian Freak Show: The Significance of Disability and Physical Differences in 19thc Fiction*, Amherst: Cambria Press.

"Cretins and Idiots: What Has Been Done and What Can Be Done for Them" (1858), *Atlantic Monthly*, 47–65.

Crockford, Ally (2012), "Spectacular Medical Freakery: British 'Translations' of Nineteenth-Century European Teratology," in Anna Kérchy and Andrea Zittlau (eds.), *Exploring the Cultural History of Continental European Freak Shows and "Enfreakment"*, 112–28, Newcastle: Cambridge Scholars Publishing.
Crosby, Frances Jane (1844), "The Rise and Progress of the New York Institution for the Blind," in *The Blind Girl and Other Poems*, 20–6, New York: Wiley & Putnam.
Cull, Richard (1856), "A Brief Notice of the Aztec Race," *Journal of the Ethnological Society of London*, 4: 120–8.
Dao, Duc, and Shale Preston (eds.) (2015), *Queer Victorian Families: Curious Relations in Literature*, New York: Routledge.
Davey, Herbert ([1914] 1981), *The Law Relating to the Mentally Defective*, New York: Da Capo.
Davidson, Luke (1996), "'Identity Ascertained': British Ophthalmology in the First Half of the Nineteenth Century," *Social History of Medicine*, 9 (3): 313–33.
Davie, Neil (2005), *Tracing the Criminal: The Rise of Scientific Criminology in Britain 1860–1918*, Oxford: Bardwell.
Davis, Lennard J. (1995a), "Deafness and Insight: The Deafened Moment as a Critical Modality," *College English*, 57 (8): 881–900.
Davis, Lennard (1995b), *Enforcing Normalcy: Disability, Deafness, and the Body*, New York, Verso.
Davis, Lennard J. (2016), "Introduction: Disability, Normality, and Power," *The Disability Studies Reader*, 5th edn., Lennard J. Davis (ed.), New York: Routledge.
The Deaf Chronicle (November 1891), 1 (1).
The Deaf Chronicle (October 1892), 1 (12).
The Deaf and Dumb Herald and Public Intelligencer (April 1876), 1 (1).
The Deaf and Dumb Magazine (December 1880), 8 (96).
Deaf and Dumb Times (1891).
Dean, Clarence (1899), *The Official Guide. Book of Marvels in the Barnum and Bailey Greatest Show on Earth with Full Descriptions of the Human Prodigies and Rare Animals*, London: Barnum and Bailey.
Deleuze, Gilles (1998), "He Stuttered," in *Essays Critical and Clinical*, Daniel W. Smith and Michael A. Greco (trans.), New York: Verso.
Denison, Lord Albert (1849), *Wanderings in Search of Health*, London: Printed for Private Circulation.
Dennett, Andrea Stulman (1997), *Weird and Wonderful: The Dime Museum in America*, New York: New York University Press.
Denton, William (1881), *Radical Rhymes*, 3rd edn., Wellesley: Denton Publishing.
Deutsch, Albert (1944), "The First US Census of the Insane (1840) and Its Use as Pro-Slavery Propaganda," *Bulletin of the History of Medicine*, 15 (5): 469–82.
Dickens, Charles (1853), "Idiots," *Household Words*, 167: 313–17.
Dickens, Charles (1865), *Doctor Marigold*, Christmas edn., *All the Year Round*.
Dickens, Charles ([1841] 1973), *Barnaby Rudge, a Tale of the Riots of '80*, Harmondsworth: Penguin.
Dickens, Charles ([1850] 1985a), *David Copperfield*, Harmondsworth: Penguin.
Dickens, Charles ([1857] 1985b), *Little Dorrit*, Harmondsworth: Penguin.
Dickens, Charles ([1845] 1994), *The Cricket on the Hearth and Other Christmas Stories*. New York: Dover Thrift.
Dickens, Charles ([1850] 1996), *David Copperfield*, ed. Jeremy Tambling, New York: Penguin.

Dickens, Charles ([1853] 1998a). *Bleak House*, ed. Stephen Gill, New York: Oxford University Press.

Dickens, Charles ([1865] 1998b), *Our Mutual Friend*, ed. Michael Cotsell, Oxford: Oxford University Press.

Dickens, Charles ([1842] 2000), *American Notes for General Circulation*, ed. Patricia Ingham, London: Penguin.

Dickens, Charles ([1848] 2001), *Dombey and Son*, ed. Alan Horsman, New York: Oxford University Press.

Dickens, Charles ([1843] 2003), *A Christmas Carol*, ed. Richard Kelly, Peterborough: Broadview Press.

Dieffenbach, Johann (1841), *Memoir on the Radical Cure of Stuttering*, Joseph Travers (trans.), London: Samuel Highley.

Digby, Anne (1985), *Madness, Morality and Medicine: A Study of the York Retreat, 1796–1914*, New York: Cambridge University Press.

Digby, Anne (1994), *Making a Medical Living: Doctors and Patients in the English Market for Medicine, 1720–1911*, Cambridge: Cambridge University Press.

Dix, Dorothea L. (1843), *Memorial to the Legislature of Massachusetts*. Available online: https://archive.org/details/memorialtolegisl00dixd.

Dix, Dorothea L. (1848), *Memorial Soliciting a State Hospital for the Protection and Cure of the Insane, Submitted to the General Assembly of North Carolina*. Available online: http://docsouth.unc.edu/nc/dixdl/dixdl.html.

"Doctors Buy Freaks" (1910), *World's Fair*, July 30.

Dodd, William (1941), *A Narrative of the Experience and Sufferings of William Dodd, a Factory Cripple. Written by Himself*, 2nd edn., London: G. Seeley.

Dolar, Mladen (2006), *A Voice and Nothing More*, Cambridge, MA: MIT Press.

Dolmage, Jay Timothy (2014), *Disability Rhetoric*, Syracuse: Syracuse University Press.

Donaldson, Elizabeth J. (2012), "The Corpus of the Madwoman: Toward a Feminist Disability Studies Theory of Embodiment and Mental Illness," in David Bolt, Julia Miele Rodas, and Elizabeth J. Donaldson (eds.), *The Madwoman and the Blind Man:* Jane Eyre, *Discourse, Disability*, 11–31, Columbus: Ohio State University Press.

Dostoevsky, Fyodor (1866), *Crime and Punishment*, Moscow: Russian Messenger.

Down, John Langdon (1867), "Observations on an Ethnic Classification of Idiots," *Journal of Mental Science*, 13: 121–3.

Down, John Langdon ([1887] 1990), *On Some of the Mental Affectations of Childhood and Youth, Together with Some Other Papers*, London: MacKeith Press.

Downing, James (1821), *A Narrative of the Life of James Downing (A Blind Man)*, New York: John C. Totten.

Drenth, Annemieke van (2008), "Caring Power and Disabled Children: The Rise of the Educational Élan in Europe, in Particular in Belgium and the Netherlands," in Susan L. Gabel and Scot Danforth (eds.), *Disability and the Politics of Education: An International Reader*, 443–9, New York: Peter Lang.

Drenth, Annemieke van and Francisca de Haan (1999), *The Rise of Caring Power*, Amsterdam: Amsterdam University Press.

Du Bois, W. E. B. (1903), *The Souls of Black Folk*, Chicago: A. C. McClurg & Co. Available online: https://www.gutenberg.org/files/408/408-h/408-h.htm.

du Maurier, George (1897), *The Martian*, London: George Bell and Sons.

Dugdale, Richard (1877), *The Jukes: A Study in Crime, Pauperism, Disease and Heredity*, New York: Putnam.

Duncan, P. Martin, and William Millard (1866), *A Manual for the Classification, Training and Education of the Feeble-Minded, Imbecile and Idiotic*, London: Longmans, Green & Co.

Duncan, P. Martin et al. (1861), "Notes on Idiocy," *Journal of Mental Science*, 7: 232–52.

Durbach, Nadja (2010), *Spectacle of Deformity: Freak Shows and Modern British Culture*, Berkeley: University of California Press.

During, Simon (1988), "The Strange Case of Monomania: Patriarchy in Literature, Murder in *Middlemarch*, Drowning in *Daniel Deronda*," *Representations*, 23: 86–104.

Eagle, Chris (2013), *Dysfluencies: On Speech Disorders in Modern Literature*, London: Bloomsbury.

Eagle, Christopher (ed.) (2014), *Literature, Speech Disorders, and Disability: Talking Normal*, New York: Routledge.

Earl, Dave (2017), "Australian Histories of Intellectual Disabilities," in Roy Hanes, Ivan Brown, and Nancy E. Hansen (eds.), *The Routledge History of Disability*, 308–19, New York, Routledge.

Edinburgh Institution (1815), *Report of the Institution for the Education of Deaf and Dumb Children for 1814*, Edinburgh.

The Edinburgh Quarterly Messenger, Being a Record of Intelligence Regarding the Deaf and Dumb (October 1843), 1.

Edwards, R. A. R. (2012), *Words Made Flesh: Nineteenth-Century Deaf Education and the Growth of Deaf Culture*, New York: New York University Press.

Ehrenreich, Barbara, and Deirdre English (1973), *Complaints and Disorders: The Sexual Politics of Sickness*, New York: The Feminist Press.

Eigen, Joel Peter (1991), "Delusion in the Courtroom: The Role of Partial Insanity in Early Forensic Testimony," *Medical History*, 35 (1): 25–49.

Eigen, Joel Peter (1995), *Witnessing Insanity: Madness and Mad-Doctors in the English Court*, New Haven: Yale University Press.

Eliot, George ([1871–2] 1985), *Middlemarch*, Harmondsworth: Penguin.

Eliot, George ([1876] 2014), *Daniel Deronda*, ed. Graham Handley and K. M. Newton, New York: Oxford University Press.

Ellis, Havelock (1912), *The Task of Social Hygiene*, London: Constable.

Eltis, Sos (2002), "Corruption of the Blood and Degeneration of the Race: Dracula and Policing the Borders of Gender," in John Paul Riquelme (ed.), *Dracula: A Case Study in Contemporary Criticism*, 450–65, Boston: Bedford/St. Martin's.

Emerson, Jason (2007), *The Madness of Mary Lincoln*, Carbondale: Southern Illinois University Press.

Emmott, James (2017), "Performing Phonographic Physiology," in Lara Karpenko and Shalyn Claggett (eds.), *Strange Science: Investigating the Limits of Knowledge in the Victorian Age*, Ann Arbor: University of Michigan Press.

"England's Native Wonder, Field Marshall Tom Thumb" (1846), Wellcome Library, London, Broadsides BF 24b/5.

"English Magazines for January" (1863), *Daily Southern Cross*, April 8: 3.

Esmail, Jennifer (2013), *Reading Victorian Deafness: Signs and Sounds in Victorian Literature and Culture*, Ohio: Ohio University Press.

Esmail, Jennifer (2014), "'The Little Dog Is Only a Stage Property': The Blind Man's Dog in Victorian Culture," *Victorian Review*, 40 (1), 18–23.

Estabrook, Arthur (1916), *The Jukes in 1915*, Washington, DC: Carnegie Institution of Washington.

Fahy, Thomas (2000), "Enfreaking War-Injured Bodies: Fallen Soldiers in Propaganda and American Literature of the 1920s," *Prospects*, 25: 529–63.

Fawcett, Trevor (1998), "Chair Transport in Bath: The Sedan Era," *Bath History*, 2: 113–38.
Fenn, W. W. (1878), *Half-Hours of Blind Man's Holiday*, London: Sampson Low, Marston, Searle & Rivington.
Fenn, W. W. (1880), *After Sundown; or, The Palette and the Pen*, London: Sampson Low, Marston, Searle & Rivington.
Fenn, W. W. (1885), *Woven in Darkness*, London: Kelly and Company.
Fenn, W. W. (1886), "The Welfare of the Blind," *Fortnightly Review*, April: 472–9.
Ferguson, Christine (2008), "Sensational Dependence: Prosthesis and Affect in Dickens and Braddon," *Lit: Literature Interpretation Theory*, 19 (1): 1–25.
Fiedler, Leslie (1996), *Tyranny of the Normal*, Boston: David R. Godine.
Figlio, Karl (1978). "Chlorosis and Chronic Disease in Nineteenth-Century Britain: The Social Constitution of Somatic Illness in a Capitalist Society," *Social History*, 3 (May): 167–97.
Finelli, Amanda (2015), "'*Attitudes Passionelles*': The Pornographic Spaces of the Salpêtrière," in Thomas Knowles and Serena Trowbridge (eds.), *Insanity and the Lunatic Asylum in the Nineteenth Century*, 115–33, London: Pickering & Chatto.
FitzGerald, William G. (1897), "Side-Shows," *Strand Magazine*, April: 407–16.
Fletcher, W. (1843), *The Deaf and Dumb Boy: with Some Account of the Mode of Educating the Deaf and Dumb*, London: John Parker.
Flint, Kate (2000), "Blindness and Insight," in *The Victorians and the Visual Imagination*, 64–92, Cambridge: Cambridge University Press.
Flynn, John (1984), *No Longer by Gaslight: the First Hundred Years of the Adult Deaf Society of Victoria*, Melbourne: Adult Deaf Society of Victoria.
Fobes, Walter K. (1877), *Elocution Simplified; With an Appendix on Lisping, Stammering, Stuttering, and Other Defects of Speech*, Boston: Lee and Shepard.
Fothergill, J. Milner ([1889] 1985), *The Town Dweller: His Needs and His Wants*, New York: Garland.
Foucault, Michel (1965), *Madness and Civilization: A History of Insanity in the Age of Reason*, New York: Random House.
Foucault, Michel (1990), *The History of Sexuality: An Introduction*, vol. 1, Robert Hurley (trans.), New York: Vintage.
Foucault, Michel ([1963] 1994), *The Birth of the Clinic: An Archaeology of Medical Perception*, A. M. Sheridan Smith (trans.), New York: Vintage.
Foucault, Michel (1995), *Discipline and Punish: The Birth of the Prison*, Alan Sheridan (trans.), New York: Vintage.
Foucault, Michel (1999), *Abnormal: Lectures at the Collège de France 1974–1975*, New York: Picador.
Fracis, M.D. (1886), *An Interesting Treatise on the Marvellous Indian Boy Laloo Brought to this Country by M.D. Fracis*, John Johnson Collection, Bodleian Library, Oxford University, Human Freaks Box 2.
Frawley, Maria H. (2004), *Invalidism and Identity in Nineteenth-Century Britain*, Chicago: University of Chicago Press.
"Freaks in Council" (1899), *The Era*, January 14: 19.
Friedman, Lester D., and Allison B. Kavey (eds.) (2018), "Chemistry, Disability, and *Frankenstein*," special issue, *Literature and Medicine* 36 (2).
Gabbard, Chris (2012), "From Custodial Care to Caring Labor: The Discourses of Who Cares in *Jane Eyre*," in David Bolt, Julia Miele Rodas, and Elizabeth J. Donaldson (eds.), *The Madwoman and the Blind Man:* Jane Eyre, *Discourse, Disability*, 91–110, Columbus: Ohio State University Press.

Gallagher, Catherine (1987), "The Body Versus the Social Body in the Works of Thomas Malthus and Henry Mayhew," in Catherine Gallagher and Thomas Laqueur (eds.), *The Making of the Modern Body: Sexuality and Society in the Nineteenth Century*, 83–106, Berkeley: University of California Press.

Garland-Thomson, Rosemarie (1996), "Preface" and "Introduction" in Rosemarie Garland-Thomson (ed.), *Freakery: Cultural Spectacles of the Extraordinary Body*, xvii–19, New York: New York University Press.

Garland-Thomson, Rosemarie (1997), *Extraordinary Bodies: Figuring Physical Disability in American Culture and Literature*, New York: Columbia University Press.

Garland-Thomson, Rosemarie (1999), "Narratives of Deviance and Delight: Staring at Julia Pastrana, the 'Extraordinary Lady,'" in Timothy B. Powell (ed.), *Beyond the Binary: Reconstructing Cultural Identity in a Multicultural Context*, 81–106, New Brunswick: Rutgers University Press.

Garland-Thomson, Rosemarie (2005), "Staring at the Other," *Disability Studies Quarterly*, 25 (4). Available online: dsq-sds.org/article/view/610/787.

Garland-Thomson, Rosemarie (2009), *Staring: How We Look*, New York: Oxford University Press.

Garry, Mary Anne (2016), "Sedan Chairmen in Eighteenth-Century London," *The Journal of Transport History*, 37 (1): 45–63.

Gaskell, Samuel (1847a), "A Visit to the Bicêtre," *Chambers's Edinburgh Journal*, 20–2.

Gaskell, Samuel (1847b), "Education of Idiots at the Bicêtre," *Chambers's Edinburgh Journal*, 71–3.

Gaskell, Samuel (1847c), "Education of Idiots at the Bicêtre," *Chambers's Edinburgh Journal*, 105–7.

Gerber, David (1990), "Pornography or Entertainment? The Rise and Fall of the Freak Show," *Reviews in American History*, 18 (1): 15–21.

Gerber, David (1996), "The 'Careers' of People Exhibited in Freak Shows," in Rosemarie Garland-Thomson (ed.), *Freakery: Cultural Spectacles of the Extraordinary Body*, 38–54, New York: New York University Press.

Gigante, Denise (2000), "Facing the Ugly: The Case of Frankenstein," *ELH*, 67 (2): 565–87.

Gilbert, Elizabeth (1874), "The Welfare of the Blind," *Charity Organisation Reporter*, November 11: 321.

Gilbert, Pamela K. (2007), *The Citizen's Body: Desire, Health, and the Social in Victorian England*, Columbus: Ohio State University Press.

Gilbert, Sandra, and Susan Gubar (1979), *The Madwoman in the Attic: Women Writers and the Nineteenth-Century Literary Imagination*, New Haven: Yale University Press.

Gilman, Charlotte Perkins (1892), "The Yellow Wall-Paper. A Story," *The New England Magazine*, 11 (5): 647–57.

Gilman, Sander L. (1985), *Difference and Pathology: Stereotypes of Sexuality, Race, and Madness*, Ithaca: Cornell University Press.

Gineste, Thierry (2004), *Victor de l'Aveyron: dernier enfant sauvage, premier enfant fou*, Paris: Hachette.

Gitter, Elisabeth (1992), "Deaf-Mutes and Heroines in the Victorian Era," *Victorian Literature and Culture*, 20: 179–97.

Gitter, Elisabeth (1999), "The Blind Daughter in Charles Dickens's *Cricket on the Hearth*," *SEL: Studies in English Literature*, 39 (4): 675–89.

Gitter, Elizabeth (2001), *The Imprisoned Guest: Samuel Howe and Laura Bridgman, the Original Deaf Blind Girl*, New York: Farrar, Straus and Giroux.

Gladden, Samuel Lyndon (2005), "Spectacular Deceptions: Closets, Secrets and Identity in Wilkie Collins's *Poor Miss Finch*," *Victorian Literature and Culture*, 33 (2): 467–86.

Goddard, Arthur (1898), "'EVEN AS YOU AND I' At Home with the Barnum Freaks," John Johnson Collection, Bodleian Library, Oxford University, Human Freaks Box 4.

Goddard, Henry H. (1912), *The Kallikak Family: A Study in the Heredity of Feeblemindedness*, New York: Macmillan.

Goldmark, Daniel (2006), "Stuttering in American Popular Song, 1890–1930," in Neil William Lerner and Joseph Nathan Straus (eds.), *Sounding Off: Theorizing Disability in Music*, 91–105, New York: Routledge.

Good Things for the Young of All Ages (1873), London: Henry S. King & Co.

Gordon, Mr. (1831), *Art of Instructing the Deaf and Dumb with Remarks on Existing Institutions for their Relief*, Dublin: O'Flanagan.

Gore, Clare Walker (2015), "'The Right and Natural Law of Things': Disability and the Form of the Family in the Fiction of Dinah Mulock Craik and Charlotte M. Yonge," in Duc Dao and Shale Preston (eds.), *Queer Victorian Families: Curious Relations in Literature*, 116–33, New York: Routledge.

Gould, George M., and Walter L. Pyle (1898), *Anomalies and Curiosities of Medicine*, Philadelphia: W. B. Saunders.

Gould, Stephen Jay (1977), *Ontology and Phylogeny*, Cambridge, MA: Harvard University Press.

Grant, Brian (1990), *The Deaf Advance. A History of the British Deaf Association, 1890–1990*, Edinburgh: Pentland Press.

Grant, Roger Matthew (2014), *Beating Time and Measuring Music in the Early Modern Era*, Oxford: Oxford University Press.

Greenwell, Dora (1868), "On the Education of Imbeciles," *North British Review*, 49: 73–100.

Grob, Gerald N. (1983), *Mental Illness and American Society, 1875–1940*. Princeton: Princeton University Press.

Groce, Nora (1988), *Everyone Here Spoke Sign Language: Hereditary Deafness on Martha's Vineyard*, Cambridge, MA: Harvard University Press.

Gubar, Marah (2009), *Artful Dodgers: Reconceiving the Golden Age of Children's Literature*, Oxford: Oxford University Press.

H. H. (1884), *An Evangelist among the Deaf and Dumb*, London.

Hagner, Michael (1999), "Enlightened Monsters," in William Clark, Jan Golinski, and Simon Schaffer (eds.), *The Sciences in Enlightened Europe*, 175–217, Chicago: University of Chicago Press.

Haley, Bruce (1978), *The Healthy Body and Victorian Culture*, Cambridge, MA: Harvard University Press.

Hall, Donald E. (1994), "Introduction" to *Muscular Christianity: Embodying the Victorian Age*, Cambridge: Cambridge University Press.

Hammerschlag, Keren (n.d.), "Animal Locomotion," in Karen Bourrier (ed.), *Nineteenth-Century Disability: Cultures & Contexts*, NINES. Available online: http://nineteenthcenturydisability.org/items/show/19.

Hampton, Jameel (2016), *Disability and the Welfare State in Britain: Changes in Perception and Policy 1948–79*, Bristol, Policy Press.

Haslam, John (1823), *A Letter to the Lord Chancellor*, London: R. Hunter.

Hawkins, Anne Hunsaker (1995), *Reconstructing Illness: Studies in Pathography*. West Lafayette: Purdue University Press.

Hendrickson, Henry (1879), *Out From The Darkness; An Autobiography*, Chicago: Western Sunday-School Publishing Company.

Herzl-Betz, Rachel (2015), "A Painfully 'Nice' Family: Reconstructing Interdependence in Wilkie Collins's *The Law and the Lady*," *Journal of Literary & Cultural Disability Studies*, 9 (1): 35–51.

Hinton, James (1861). "Health," *Cornhill Magazine*, March, 332–41.

Hix, Lisa, "Healing Spas and Ugly Clubs: How Victorians Taught Us to Treat People With Disabilities." Available online: https://www.collectorsweekly.com/articles/healing-spas-and-ugly-clubs-how-victorians-taught-us-to-treat-people-with-disabilities/.

Hodgkiss, A. D. (1991), "Chronic Pain in Nineteenth-Century British Medical Writings." *History of Psychiatry*, 2 (5): 27–40.

Hoegaerts, Josephine (2015), "S-s-s-syncopation: Music, Modernity, and the Performance of Stammering (ca. 1860–1930)," *Societies*, 5 (4): 744–59.

Hollander, John (1997), *The Work of Poetry*, New York: Columbia University Press.

Holman, James ([1822] 1834), *The Narrative of a Journey, Undertaken in the Years 1819, etc.*, 5th edn., London: Smith, Elder and Company.

Holman, James (1834–5), *A Voyage Round the World, including Travels in Africa, Asia, Australasia, America, etc., etc., from 1827 to 1832*, 4 vols., London: Smith, Elder and Company.

Holmes, Martha Stoddard (2001), "Working (with) the Rhetoric of Affliction," in James Wilson and Cynthia Lewiecki-Wilson (eds.), *Embodied Rhetorics: Disability in Language and Culture*, 27–44, Carbondale: Southern Illinois University Press.

Holmes, Martha Stoddard (2003), "'Bolder with Her Lover in the Dark': Collins and Disabled Women's Sexuality," in Maria K. Bachman and Don Richard Cox (eds.), *Reality's Dark Light: The Sensational Wilkie Collins*, 59–93, Knoxville: University of Tennessee Press.

Holmes, Martha Stoddard (2004), *Fictions of Affliction: Physical Disability in Victorian Culture*, Ann Arbor: University of Michigan Press.

Holmes, Martha Stoddard (2007), "Victorian Fictions of Interdependency: Gaskell, Craik, and Yonge," *Journal of Literary and Cultural Disability Studies*, 1 (2): 29–41.

Holmes, Martha Stoddard (2009), "'Happy and Yet Pitying Tears': Deafness and Affective Disjuncture in Dickens's 'Doctor Marigold,'" *Victorian Review*, 35 (2): 53–64.

Holmes, Martha Stoddard (2012), "Visions of Rochester: Screening Desire and Disability in *Jane Eyre*," in David Bolt, Julia Miele Rodas, and Elizabeth J. Donaldson (eds.), *The Madwoman and the Blindman: Jane Eyre, Discourse, Disability*, 150–74, Columbus: Ohio State University Press.

Holmes, Martha Stoddard (2014), "Disability in Two Doctor Stories," in Therese Jones, Lester Friedman, and Delese Wear (eds.), *Health Humanities Reader*, 63–76, New Brunswick: Rutgers University Press.

Horner, Jonah, M. D. (1855), *Instructions to the Invalid on the Nature of the Water Cure: In Connection with the Anatomy and Physiology of the Organs of Digestion and Nutrition*, London: Simpkin, Marshall.

"How a Blind Man Saw the International Exhibition" (1863), *Temple Bar*, January, 227–37.

Howe, Samuel Gridley ([1848] 1972) *On the Causes of Idiocy*, New York: Arno.

Howell, Michael, and Peter Ford (1983), *The True History of the Elephant Man*, London: Allison & Busby.

Huet, Marie-Helene (1993), *Monstrous Imagination*, Cambridge, MA: Harvard University Press.

Huff, Joyce L. (2008), "Freaklore: The Dissemination, Fragmentation and Reinvention of the Legend of Daniel Lambert, King of Fat Men," in Marlene Tromp (ed.), *Victorian Freaks: The Social Context of Freakery in Britain*, 37–59, Columbus: Ohio State University Press.

Hugentobler, M. (1880) *Report of the Proceedings of the International Congress on the Education of the Deaf Held at Milan, September 6th–11th 1880*, taken from the English Official Minutes, read by A. A. Kinsey, London: Allan & Co.

Hughes, John S. (1992), "Labeling and Treating Black Mental Illness in Alabama, 1861–1910," *The Journal of Southern History*, 58 (3): 435–60.

Hunt, James (1861), *Stammering and Stuttering, Their Nature and Treatment*, 5th edn., London: Longman, Green, Longman, and Roberts.

Hunt, James (1870), *Stammering and Stuttering: Their Nature and Treatment*, 7th edn., London: Longmans, Green & Co.

Hurley, Kelly (1996), *The Gothic Body: Sexuality, Materialism, and Degeneration at the Fin De Siècle*, Cambridge: Cambridge University Press.

"Idiot Asylums" (1865), *Edinburgh Review*, 122: 37–74.

The Invalid's Friend (1850–3), London: Society for the Promotion of Christian Knowledge.

Itard, Jean-Marc-Gaspard ([1801] 1972), "Of the First Developments of the Young Savage of Aveyron," in Lucien Malson (ed.), *Wolf Children and the Problem of Human Nature*, 91–140, London: NLB.

Itard, Jean-Marc-Gaspard ([1806] 1972), "Report on the Progress of Victor of Aveyron," trans. Joan White, in Lucien Malson (ed.), *Wolf Children and the Problem of Human Nature*, 141–79, London: NLB.

Jackson, Mark (2000), *The Borderland of Imbecility: Medicine, Society and the Fabrication of the Feeble Mind in Late Victorian and Edwardian Britain*, Manchester: Manchester University Press.

James, Henry (2009), *The Portrait of a Lady*, ed. Roger Luckhurst, New York, Oxford University Press.

Janechek, Jennifer (2015), "'This Curious Association of Objects': Dickens's Treatment of Chair-Transported Characters in *Dombey and Son* and *Bleak House*," *Dickens Studies Annual*, 46 (1): 147–65.

Jarman, Michelle (2012), "Coming Up from Underground: Uneasy Dialogues at the Intersections of Race, Mental Illness, and Disability Studies," in Christopher M. Bell (ed.), *Blackness and Disability Studies: Critical Examinations and Cultural Interventions*, 9–29, East Lansing: Michigan State University Press.

Jarrett, Simon (2018), "'Belief,' 'Opinion' and 'Knowledge': The Idiot in Law in the Long Eighteenth Century," in Patrick McDonagh, C. F. Goodey, and Tim Stainton (eds.), *Intellectual Disability: A Conceptual History 1200–1900*, 162–89, Manchester: Manchester University Press.

Jay, Martin (1993), *Downcast Eyes: The Denigration of Vision in Twentieth-Century French Thought*, Berkeley: University of California Press.

Jewson, N. D. (1976), "The Disappearance of the Sick-Man from Medical Cosmology, 1770–1870," *Sociology*, 10: 225–44.

Johnson, Jeffrey K. (2008), "The Visualization of the Twisted Tongue: Portrayals of Stuttering in Film, Television, and Comic Books," *Journal of Popular Culture*, 41 (2): n.p.

Johnson, Jeffrey K. (2012), "The Hero with a Thousand Dysfluencies: The Changing Portrayals of People Who Stutter," in Lawrence C. Rubin (ed.), *Mental Illness in Popular Media: Essays on the Representation of Disorders*, 11–24, Jefferson: McFarland & Co.

Jones, Christine Kenyon (2016),"'An Uneasy Mind in an Uneasy Body': Byron, Disability, Authorship, and Biography," in Michael Bradshaw (ed.), *Disabling Romanticism*, 147–67, London: Palgrave Macmillan.

Jones, David W. (2016), *Disordered Personalities and Crime: An Analysis of the History of Moral Insanity*, New York: Routledge.

Joshua, Essaka (2012), "'I Began to See': Biblical Models of Disability in *Jane Eyre*," in David Bolt, Julia Miele Rodas, and Elizabeth J. Donaldson (eds.), *The Madwoman and the Blindman: Jane Eyre, Discourse, Disability*, 111–28, Columbus: Ohio State University Press.

Joshua, Essaka (2016), "Picturesque Aesthetics: Theorising Deformity in the Romantic Era," in Michael Bradshaw (ed.), *Disabling Romanticism*, 29–48, London: Palgrave Macmillan.

Joshua, Essaka (2018), "Disability and Deformity in the Eighteenth Century," in Clare Barker and Stuart Murray (eds.), *Literature and Disability*, 47–61, Cambridge: Cambridge University Press.

Joyner, Hannah (2004), *From Pity to Pride, Growing Up Deaf in the Old South*, Washington, DC: Gallaudet University Press.

Kamenetz, Herman L. (1969), "A Brief History of the Wheelchair," *Journal of the History of Medicine and Allied Sciences*, 24 (2): 205–10.

Kates, Susan (2001), *Activist Rhetorics and American Higher Education, 1885–1937*, Carbondale and Edwardsville: Southern Illinois University Press.

Keith, Lois (2001), *Take Up Thy Bed & Walk: Death, Disability, and Cure in Classic Fiction for Girls*, New York: Routledge.

King, Alice (1884), "A Few Words about Blindness," *Argosy*, XXXVIII: 189–94.

Kingsley, Charles (1859), "The Irrationale of Speech," *Frasier's Magazine*, 60: 1–14.

Kinsey, Arthur A. (1880), "On the Education of the Deaf," a paper written for the International Congress at Milan, September, reproduced as an appendix in *Report on the Proceedings*.

Kitto, John (1845), *The Lost Senses: Deafness*, London: Charles Knight.

Klages, Mary (1999), *Woeful Afflictions: Disability and Sentimentality in Victorian America*, Philadelphia: University of Pennsylvania Press.

Kleege, Georgina (2005), "Blindness and Visual Culture: An Eyewitness Account," *Journal of Visual Culture*, 4 (2): 179–90.

Kochanek, Lisa (1997), "Reframing the Freak: From Sideshow to Science," *Victorian Periodicals Review*, 30 (3): 227–43.

Kreilkamp, Ivan (2005), *Voice and the Victorian Storyteller*, Cambridge: Cambridge University Press.

Krentz, Christopher (2000), *A Mighty Change: An Anthology of Deaf American Writing*, Washington, DC: Gallaudet University Press.

Kudlick, Catherine (2014), "Smallpox, Disability, and Survival in Nineteenth-Century France: Rewriting Paradigms from a New Epidemic Script," in Susan Burch and Michael A. Rembis (eds.), *Disability Histories*, 185–200, Urbana: University of Illinois Press.

LaBelle, Brandon (2014), *Lexicon of the Mouth: Poetics and Politics of Voice and the Oral Imaginary*, New York: Bloomsbury.

Lane, Harlan (1977), *The Wild Boy of Aveyron*, London: George Allen & Unwin.

Lane, Harlan (2002), "Do Deaf People Have a Disability?," *Sign Language Studies*, 2 (4): 356–79.

Lane, Richard (1846), *Life at the Water Cure: Or, A Month at Malvern*, London: Longman, Brown, Green and Longmans.

Leach, Allan (1984), "National Library for the Blind: Its Past, Present and Prospects," *Health Libraries Review*, 1: 1–7.

Lee, Louise (2008), "Voicing, De-Voicing and Self-Silencing: Charles Kingsley's Stuttering Christian Manliness," *Journal of Victorian Culture*, 13 (1): 1–17.

Lee, Raymond (ed.) (2004), *A Beginner's Introduction to Deaf History*, Middlesex: BSHS.

Lentz, John (1977), "The Revolt of the Freaks," *Bandwagon*, September–October, 26–9.

Levine, Philippa (2012), "Anthropology, Colonialism, and Eugenics," in Alison Bashford and Philippa Levine (eds.), *The Oxford Handbook of the History of Eugenics*, 43–61, Oxford: Oxford University Press.

Levine, Philippa, and Alison Bashford (2012), "Introduction: Eugenics and the Modern World," in Alison Bashford and Philippa Levine (eds.), *The Oxford Handbook of the History of Eugenics*, 3–25, Oxford: Oxford University Press.

Levy, W. Hanks (1872), *Blindness and the Blind or A Treatise on the Science of Typhology*, London: Chapman and Hall.

Lewis, George Andrew (1902), *The Practical Treatment of Stammering and Stuttering*, Detroit: George Andrew Lewis.

The Life and Adventures of Joseph Carey Merrick (ca. 1885), Leicester: H & A Cockshaw.

Life of Miss Alice Bounds, The Bear Lady (ca. 1911), National Fairgrounds Archive, University of Sheffield.

Lindfors, Bernth (1996), "Hottentot, Bushman, Kaffir: Taxonomic Tendencies in Nineteenth-Century Racial Iconography," *Nordic Journal of African Studies*, 5 (2): 1–28.

Lindfors, Bernth (ed.) (1999), *Africans on Stage: Studies in Ethnological Show Business*, Bloomington: Indiana University Press.

Lockhart, J. G. (1845), *Memoirs of the Life of Sir Walter Scott*, London: Robert Cadell.

A Magazine Intended Chiefly for the Deaf and Dumb (1873), 1 (1).

Magubane, Zine (2001), "Which Bodies Matter? Feminism, Poststructuralism, Race, and the Curious Theoretical Odyssey of the 'Hottentot Venus,'" *Gender and Society*, 15 (6): 816–34.

Mairs, Nancy (1986), Plaintext, Tucson: University of Arizona Press.

Malet, Lucas (Mary St. Leger Kingsley) (1891), *The Wages of Sin*, London: Swan Sonnenschein and Co.

Marchbanks, Paul (2010), "A Space, A Place: Visions of a Disabled Community in Mary Shelley's *Frankenstein* and *The Last Man*," in Ruth Bienstock Anolik (ed.), *Demons of the Body and Mind: Essays on Disability in Gothic Literature*, 21–34, Jefferson: McFarland.

Marsh, Jan, "Health and Medicine in the Nineteenth-Century," Victoria and Albert Museum. Available online: http://www.vam.ac.uk/content/articles/h/health-and-medicine-in-the-19th-century/.

Marshall, Caitlin (2014), "Crippled Speech," *Postmodern Culture*, 24 (3): n.p.

Marshall, John (1867), "On the Brain of a Bushwoman; and on the Brains of Two Idiots of European Descent," *Journal of Mental Science*, 12: 99–112.

Martin, Charles D. (2002), *The White African-American Body*, New Brunswick: Rutgers University Press.

Martin, William (1880), "Letter to the Editor," *Charity Organisation Reporter*, February 19, 44.

Martineau, Harriet (1845), *Letters on Mesmerism*, London: Edward Moxon.

Martineau, Harriet (1854), "Blindness," *Household Words*, XI: 421–5.

Martineau, Harriet ([1848] 1875), *Eastern Life, Present and Past*, London: Moxon.

Martineau, Harriet (1877), *Harriet Martineau's Auobiography, with Memorials by Maria Weston Chapman*, 3 vols., London: Smith, Elder.

Martineau, Harriet ([1834] 1996), "Letter to the Deaf," in A. Broomfield and S. Mitchell (eds.), *Prose by Victorian Women: An Anthology*, 52–65, New York: Garland.

Martineau, Harriet ([1844] 2003), *Life in the Sick-Room*, ed. Maria H. Frawley, Peterborough: Broadview Press.

Martins, Catarina S. (2009), "'Do You Hear With Your Ears or With Your Eyes?': The Education of the Deaf Pupils at Casa Pia de Lisboa (c. 1820–1950)," *Paedagogica Historica*, 45 (1–2): 103–16.

Mayhew, Henry ([1861–2] 1968), *London Labour and the London Poor*, 4 vols., New York: Dover.

Mayhew, Henry ([1851] 2009), *London Labour and the London Poor*, ed. Robert Douglas-Fairhurst, Oxford: Oxford University Press.

Maudsley, Henry (1873), *Body and Mind*, London: MacMillan.

Maudsley, Henry (1879) "Materialism and Its Lessons," *Fortnightly Review*, 26 (32 old series): 244–60.

McCormac, Henry (1828), *A Treatise on the Cause and Cure of Hesitation of Speech, or Stammering*, London: Longman, Rees, Orme, Brown, and Green.

McDonagh, Patrick (2008), *Idiocy: A Cultural History*, Liverpool: Liverpool University Press.

McDonagh, Patrick (2013), "The Mute's Voice: The Dramatic Transformations of the Mute and Deaf-Mute in Early Nineteenth-Century France," *Criticism*, 55: 655–75.

McDonagh, Patrick (2018), "Visiting Earlswood: The Asylum Travelogue and the Shaping of 'Idiocy,'" in Patrick McDonagh, C. F. Goodey, and Tim Stainton (eds.), *Intellectual Disability: A Conceptual History 1200–1900*, 211–37, Manchester: Manchester University Press.

McGann, Jerome (1985), *The Beauty of Inflections: Literary Investigation in Historical Method and Theory*, Oxford: Clarendon.

McHold, Heather (2002), "Diagnosing Difference: The Scientific, Medical, and Popular Engagement with Monstrosity in Victorian Britain," PhD diss., Northwestern University.

McHold, Heather (2008), "Even as You and I: Freak Show and Lay Discourse on Spectacular Deformity," in Marlene Tromp (ed.), *Victorian Freaks: The Social Context of Freakery in Britain*, 21–36, Columbus: Ohio State University Press.

McLean, Thomas (2003), "Arms and the Circassian Woman: Frances Browne's 'The Star of Atteghei,'" *Victorian Poetry*, 41 (3): 295–318.

McRuer, Robert (2006), *Crip Theory: Cultural Signs of Queerness and Disability*, New York: New York University Press.

Metzl, Jonathan M. (2009), *The Protest Psychosis: How Schizophrenia Became a Black Disease*, Boston: Beacon Press.

Michie, Helena (1999), "Under Victorian Skins: The Bodies Beneath," in Herbert F. Tucker (ed.), *A Companion to Victorian Literature and Culture*, 407–24, Oxford: Blackwell.

Migone, Christof (2011), *Sonic Somatic*, Kollwitzstrasse: Errant Bodies Press.

Mihm, Stephen (2002), "'A Limb Which Shall Be Presentable in Polite Society': Prosthetic Technologies in the Nineteenth Century," in Katherine Ott, David Serlin, and Stephen Mihm (eds.), *Artificial Parts, Practical Lives: Modern Histories of Prosthetics*, 282–99, New York: New York University Press.

Miles, M. (2000), "Signing in the Seraglio: Mutes, Dwarfs and Jesters in the Ottoman Court, 1500–1700," *Disability and Society*, 15: 115–34.

Miles, M. (2001), "Including Disabled Children in Indian Schools, 1790s–1890s: Innovations of Educational Approach and Technique," *Paedagogica Historica*, 37 (2): 291–315.

Miles, M. (2004), "Locating Deaf People, Gesture and Sign in African Histories, 1450s–1950s," *Disability and Society*, 19: 531–45.

Miles, M. (2011), *Blind and Sighted Pioneer Teachers in 19th Century China and India*, revised edn., *Independent Living*. Available online: https://www.independentliving.org/docs7/miles201104.html.

Millard, John (1884), *Grammar of Elocution*, 3rd edn., London: Longmans, Green & Co.

Miller, Jonathan (1992), "The Rustle of a Star: An Annotated Bibliography of Deaf Characters in Fiction," *Library Trends*, 41 (1): 42–60.

Mirzoeff, Nicholas (1995), *Silent Poetry: Deafness, Sign and Visual Culture in Modern France*, Princeton: Princeton University Press.

"Miss Julia Pastrana, The Nondescript" (1857), John Johnson Collection, Bodleian Library, Oxford University, Human Freaks Box 2.

Mitchell, Alexander (1860), *The Blind: Their Capabilities, Condition, and Claims*, London: G. Morrish.

Mitchell, Charlotte (2011), "Smedley, Francis Edward (1818–1864)," in H. C. G. Matthew and Brian Harrison (eds.), *Oxford Dictionary of National Biography*, New York: Oxford University Press. Available online: http://www.oxforddnb.com.ezproxy.lib.ucalgary.ca/view/article/25748.

Mitchell, David, and Sharon Snyder (2000), *Narrative Prosthesis: Disability and the Dependencies of Discourse*, Ann Arbor: University of Michigan Press.

Mitchell, David, and Sharon Snyder (2005), "Exploitations of Embodiment: *Born Freak* and the Academic Bally Plank," *Disability Studies Quarterly*, 25 (3). Available online: dsq-sds.org/article/view/575/752.

Mitchell, Sarah (2003), "Exhibiting Monstrosity: Chang and Eng, the 'Original' Siamese Twins," *Endeavour*, 27 (4): 150–4.

Monro, Henry (1850), *On Stammering, and Its Treatment*, London: John Churchill.

Moran, Richard (1985), "The Origin of Insanity as a Special Verdict: The Trial for Treason of James Hadfield (1800)," *Law & Society Review*, 19 (3): 487–519.

Morison, Alexander (1843), *Physiognomy of Mental Disorders*, London.

Moscoso, Javier (1998), "Monsters as Evidence: The Uses of the Abnormal Body During the Early Eighteenth Century," *Journal of the History of Biology*, 31 (3): 355–82.

Mossman, Mark (2001), "Acts of Becoming: Autobiography, *Frankenstein*, and the Postmodern Body," *Postmodern Culture*, 11 (3): para 1–34. Available online: http://pmc.iath.virginia.edu/issue.501/11.3mossman.html.

Mossman, Mark, and Martha Stoddard Holmes (2008), "Critical Transformations: Disability and the Body in Nineteenth-Century Britain," *Nineteenth-Century Gender Studies*, 4 (2). Available online: http://www.ncgsjournal.com/issue42/introduction/htm.

Mossman, Mark, and Martha Stoddard Holmes (2011), "Disability in Victorian Sensation Fiction," in Pamela Gilbert (ed.), *Blackwell Companion to Sensation Fiction*, 493–506, London: Blackwell.

Mottez, Bernard (1993), "The Deaf Banquets and the Birth of the Deaf Movement," in Renate Fischer and Harlan Lane (eds.), *Looking Back: a Reader on the History of Deaf Communities and Their Sign Languages*, 143–56, Hamburg: Signum.

"Mrs. Elizabeth Armitage" (c. 1846), Wellcome Library, London, Broadsides, BF 24b/11.

Müller, Patrick (2012), "'The Impediment that Cannot Say its Name': Stammering and Trauma in Selected American and British Texts," *Anglia*, 130 (1): 54–74.

Murray, Joseph (2007), "'One Touch of Nature Makes the Whole World Kin': The Transatlantic Lives of Deaf Americans, c. 1870–1924," unpublished PhD thesis, University of Iowa.

"Nature's Freaks With the Human Form" (1898), *Pearson's Weekly*, July 23, 23.

Nielsen, Kim E. (2012), *A Disability History of the United States*, Boston: Beacon Press.

Nordau, Max (1895), *Degeneration*, Boston: D. Appleton and Company.

Norman, Tom (1928), "Memoirs of Tom Norman," unpublished typescript, National Fairgrounds Archive, Sheffield University.

Norman, Tom, and George Barnum Norman (1985), *The Penny Showman: Memoirs of Tom Norman, "Silver King,"* London: Privately Published.

"Novels Past and Present" (1866), *Saturday Review*, April 14 (21.546): 438–40.

O'Connor, Erin (2000), *Raw Material: Producing Pathology in Victorian Culture*, Durham: Duke University Press.

Oliphant, John (2007), *Early Education of the Blind in Britain, ca. 1790–1900*, Lewiston: Edwin Mellen.

Oliphant, John (2009), "'Touching the Light': The Invention of Literacy for the Blind," *Pedagogica Historica*, 44 (1–2): 67–82.

Oliphant, Margaret ([1863] 1986), *Salem Chapel*, London: Virago.

Oliphant, Margaret ([1899] 2002), *The Autobiography of Margaret Oliphant*, ed. Elisabeth Jay, Peterborough: Broadview Press.

"Ontario Institution for the Blind, Brantford" (1899), *The Canadian Mute*, January 2, 7 (7): 2.

Oppenheim, Janet (1991), *"Shattered Nerves": Doctors, Patients, and Depression in Victorian England*, New York: Oxford University Press.

Ott, Katherine (2002), "Hard Wear and Soft Tissue: Craft and Commerce in Artificial Eyes," in Katherine Ott, David Serlin, and Stephen Mihm (eds.), *Artificial Parts, Practical Lives: Modern Histories of Prosthetics*, 147–70, New York: New York University Press.

"P.T. Barnum's Greatest Show on Earth" (1889), *Herald*, November 11. Available online: http://diginole.lib.fsu.edu/islandora/object/fsu%3A197825.

Packard, Elizabeth Parsons Ware (1868), *The Prisoners' Hidden Life, or Insane Asylums Unveiled*, Chicago: self-published; A. B. Case (printer).

Packard, Elizabeth Parsons Ware (1873), *Modern Persecution or Insane Asylums Unveiled*, New York: self-published; Pelletreau & Raynor (printer).

Pande, Ishita (2010), *Medicine, Race, and Liberalism in British Bengal: Symptoms of Empire*, New York: Routledge.

Park, Katharine, and Lorraine J. Daston (1981), "Unnatural Conceptions: The Study of Monsters in Sixteenth-Century France and England," *Past and Present*, 92: 20–54.

Parry, Manon S. (2006), "Dorothea Dix (1802–1887)," *American Journal of Public Health*, 96 (4): 624–5.

Parsons, Talcott (1951), *The Social System*, London: Routledge.

Paterson, Kevin (2012), "It's About Time!: Understanding the Experience of Speech Impairment," in Nick Watson et al. (eds.), *Routledge Handbook of Disability Studies*, 165–77, New York: Routledge.

Paulson, William R. (1993), *Enlightenment, Romanticism, and the Blind in France*, Princeton: Princeton University Press.

Peckham, Robert, and David M. Pomfret (2013), *Imperial Contagions: Medicine, Hygiene, and Cultures of Planning in Asia*, Hong Kong: Hong Kong University Press.

Pemberton, Neil (2009), "Deafness and Holiness Home Missions, Deaf Congregations, and Natural Language 1860–1890," *Victorian Review*, 35 (2): 65–82.

Pemble, John (1987), *The Mediterranean Passion: Victorians and Edwardians in the South*, Oxford: Clarendon.

Peterson, Dale (ed.) (1982), *A Mad People's History of Madness*, Pittsburgh: University of Pittsburgh Press.

Phillips, Gordon (2004), *The Blind in British Society: Charity, State and Community, c. 1780–1930*, Aldershot: Ashgate.

"Physical Curiosities" (1898), *The Lancet*, February 2, 451.

Pick, Daniel (1989), *Faces of Degeneration: A European Disorder, c. 1848–c. 1918*, Cambridge: Cambridge University Press.

Picker, John M. (2003), *Victorian Soundscapes*, Oxford: Oxford University Press.
Pietikainen, Petteri (2015), *Madness: A History*, New York: Routledge.
Pinel, Philippe (1806), *A Treatise on Insanity*, trans. D. D. Davis, Sheffield: Cadell and Davies.
Pixérécourt, René Charles Guilbert de (1799), *Victor ou L'Enfant du Forêt*.
Plann, Susan (2007), 'Deaf Lives: Nineteenth-Century Spanish Deaf Girls and Women," *Sign Language Studies*, 7 (2): 167–76.
Plumptre, Charles John (1881), *King's College Lectures on Elocution*, London: Trubner & Co.
Poe, Edgar Allan (1835), "Berenice," *Southern Literary Messenger*, 1 (7): 333–6.
Poe, Edgar Allan (1843), "The Tell-Tale Heart," *The Pioneer* 1 (1): 29–31.
Poett, J. H. Ayres (1856), *A Practical Treatise on Stammering*, London: John Churchill.
Poignant, Roslyn (2004), *Professional Savages*, New Haven: Yale University Press.
Poovey, Mary (1988), *Uneven Developments: The Ideological Work of Gender in Mid-Victorian England*, Chicago: University of Chicago Press.
Poovey, Mary (1995), *Making a Social Body: British Cultural Formation 1830–1864*, Chicago: University of Chicago Press.
Porter, Roy (1985), "The Patient's View: Doing Medical History from Below," *Theory and Society*, 14: 175–98.
Porter, Roy (1993), "Pain and Suffering," in Roy Porter and William Bynum (eds.), *Companion Encyclopedia of the History of Medicine*, vol. 2, 1574–91, London: Routledge.
Porter, Roy (2002), *Madness: A Brief History*, New York: Oxford University Press.
President (1880), *Report of the Proceedings of the International Congress on the Education of the Deaf Held at Milan, September 6th–11th 1880*, taken from the English Official Minutes, read by A. A. Kinsey, London: Allan & Co.
"The Psychology of Idiocy" (1865), *Journal of Mental Science*, 11: 1–32.
Qureshi, Sadiah (2004), "Displaying Sara Baartman, the 'Hottentot Venus,'" *History of Science*, 42 (2): 233–57.
Qureshi, Sadiah (2011), *Peoples on Parade: Exhibitions, Empire, and Anthropology in Nineteenth-Century Britain*, Chicago: University of Chicago Press.
Radick, Gregory (2007), *The Simian Tongue: The Long Debate About Animal Language*, Chicago: University of Chicago Press.
"Railway Accident" (1861), *London Times*, 7.
Ray, Sarah Jaquette, and Jay Sibara (2017), *Disability Studies and the Environmental Humanities: Toward an Eco-Crip Theory*, Lincoln: University of Nebraska Press.
Reed, Adam Metcalfe (2014), "Mental Death: Slavery, Madness and State Violence in the United States," PhD diss., University of California, Santa Cruz.
Reiss, Benjamin (2008), *Theaters of Madness: Insane Asylums and Nineteenth Century Culture*, Chicago: University of Chicago Press.
Report of the Royal Commission on the Blind, Deaf and Dumb, &c. of the United Kingdom (1889), London: Eyre and Spottiswoode.
Review of *Life in the Sick-Room* (1845), *The Christian Examiner*, March, 168–9, reprinted in Frawley, *Life in the Sick-Room*, 165, Peterborough: Broadview Press.
Review of W. W. Fenn's *Half Hours of Blind Man's Holiday* (1878–9), *The Contemporary Review*, XXXIV: 204.
Rhys, Jean (1966), *Wide Sargasso Sea*, New York: Norton.
Rintoul, Suzanne (2011), "'The Mysterious Woman and Her Legs': Scrutinizing the Disabled Body in *Barchester Towers*," *Nineteenth Century Gender Studies*, 7 (1): 119–35. Available online: http://www.ncgsjournal.com/issue71/rintoul.htm

Ritchie, J. M. (1930), *Concerning the Blind*, London: Oliver and Boyd.
Ritvo, Harriet (1997), *The Platypus and the Mermaid*, Cambridge, MA: Harvard University Press.
Robinson, Mary (2000), *Selected Poems*, Judith Pascoe (ed.), Peterborough, Ontario: Broadview.
Rockey, Denyse (1980), *Speech Disorder in Nineteenth Century Britain: The History of Stuttering*, London: Croom Helm.
Rodas, Julia Miele (2004), "Tiny Tim, Blind Bertha, and the Resistance of Miss Mowcher: Charles Dickens and the Uses of Disability," *Dickens Studies Annual*, 34: 51–97.
Rodas, Julia Miele (2007), "Misappropriations: Hugh Stuart Boyd and the Blindness of Elizabeth Barrett Browning," *Victorian Review*, 33 (1): 103–18.
Rodas, Julia Miele (2016), "Autistic Voice and Literary Architecture in Mary Shelley's *Frankenstein*," in Michael Bradshaw (ed.), *Disabling Romanticism: Body, Mind, and Text*, 169–90, London: Palgrave Macmillan.
Ronell, Avital (2002), *Stupidity*, Chicago: University of Illinois Press.
Roose, Robson (1886), "The Wear and Tear of London Life," *Fortnightly Review*, 230 (February): 200–8.
Rose, June (1970), *Changing Focus: The Development of Blind Welfare in Britain*, London: Hutchinson.
Rose, Martha L. (2003), *The Staff of Oedipus: Transforming Disability in Ancient Greece*, Ann Arbor: University of Michigan Press.
Rose, Sarah F. (2017), *No Right to Be Idle: The Invention of Disability, 1850–1930*, Chapel Hill: University of North Carolina Press.
Rosenhan, David (1973), "On Being Sane in Insane Places," *Science*, 179 (4070): 250–8.
Rosenthal, Moriz (1879), *A Clinical Treatise on Diseases of the Nervous System*, vol. 2, New York: William Wood.
Routh, C. H. F. (1886), *On Overwork and Premature Mental Decay: Its Treatment*, London: Bailiere, Tindall, & Cox.
Rowe, Richard (1881), "Pity the Poor Blind," in *Life in the London Streets*, 306–36, London: J. C. Nimmo and Bain.
Royal Commission on the Care and Control of the Feeble-Minded (1909), *The Problem of the Feeble-Minded: An Abstract of the Report of the Royal Commission on the Care and Control of the Feeble-Minded*, London.
Rush, Benjamin (1812), *Medical Inquiries and Observations upon the Diseases of the Mind*, Philadelphia: Kimber & Richardson.
Rymer, James Malcolm (1855), *The Unspeakable; Or, the Life and Adventures of a Stammerer*, London: Clarke & Beeton.
Sacido-Romero, Jorge, and Sylvia Mieszkowski (eds.) (2015), *Sound Effects: The Object Voice in Fiction*, Leiden: Brill Rodopi.
Scarry, Elaine (1985), *The Body in Pain: The Making and Unmaking of the World*, New York: Oxford University Press.
Schaffer, Talia (2016), *Romance's Rival: Familiar Marriage in Victorian Fiction*, New York: Oxford University Press.
Schweik, Susan M. (2009), *The Ugly Laws: Disability in Public*, New York: New York University Press.
Scull, Andrew (1993), *The Most Solitary of Afflictions: Madness and Society in Britain 1700–1900*, New Haven: Yale University Press.
Séguin, Édouard ([1846] 1978), *Traitement Moral, Hygiène et Éducation des Idiots*, Nendeln/Liechtenstein: Klaus Reprint.

Seguin, Edward ([1866] 1994), *Idiocy: And Its Treatment by the Physiological Method*, New York: Gryphon.

Sharpe, James Birch (ed.) (1815), *Report, Together with the Minutes of Evidence, and An Appendix of Papers from the Committee Appointed to Consider Provision Being Made for the Better Regulation of Madhouses in England*, London: House of Commons.

Shattuck, Roger (1980), *The Forbidden Experiment: The Story of the Wild Boy of Aveyron*, New York: Farrar Strauss Giroux.

Shell, Marc (2005), *Stutter*, Cambridge, MA: Harvard University Press.

Shelley, Mary ([1818] 2017), *Frankenstein or the Modern Prometheus*, Annotated for Scientists, Engineers, and Creators of All Kinds, eds. David H. Guston, Ed Finn, Jason Scott Robert, Cambridge, MA, and London: MIT Press.

Shepherd, Anna (2016), *Institutionalizing the Insane in Nineteenth-Century England*, London: Routledge.

Sherard, Robert (1895), "The Author of 'Trilby,'" *McClure's Magazine*, IV: 391–400.

Shorter, Edward (1997), *A History of Psychiatry: From the Era of the Asylum to the Age of Prozac*, New York: John Wiley & Sons.

Showalter, Elaine (1985), *The Female Malady: Women, Madness, and English Culture, 1830–1980*, New York: Pantheon.

"Shows We Have Sampled" (1898), *The Guyoscope*, November, 42–5.

Shuttleworth, Sally (1989), "Female Circulation: Medical Discourse and Popular Advertising in the Mid-Victorian Era," in Mary Jacobus, Evelyn Fox Keller, and Sally Shuttleworth (eds.), *Body/Politics: Women and the Discourses of Science*, 47–68, New York: Routledge.

Shuttleworth, Sally (1996), *Charlotte Brontë and Victorian Psychology*, Cambridge: Cambridge University Press.

Siebers, Tobin (2008), *Disability Theory*, Ann Arbor, University of Michigan Press.

Simmons, Harvey G. (1978), "Explaining Social Policy: The English Mental Deficiency Act of 1913," *Journal of Social History*, 11 (3): 387–403.

Simpson, Murray K. (2014), *Modernity and the Appearance of Idiocy: Intellectual Disability as a Regime of Truth*, Lampeter: Edwin Mellen.

Smiles, Samuel (1883), "Harriet Martineau," in *Brief Biographies*, 499–510, Chicago: Belford, Clarke, and Co.

Smith, Andrew (2004), *Victorian Demons: Medicine, Masculinity, and the Gothic at the Fin-de-Siècle*, Manchester: Manchester University Press.

Smith, Henry Nash (1978), "The Madness of Ahab," in *Democracy and the Novel: Popular Resistance to Classic American Writers*, 35–55, New York: Oxford University Press.

Society for the Propagation of Christian Knowledge (SPCK) (1864), *To the Deaf Who on That Account Do Not Attend Church*, London: SPCK.

Söderfeldt, Ylva (2013), *From Pathology to Public Sphere: The Germany Deaf Movement, 1848–1914*, Bielefeld: Transcript.

Southey, Caroline Bowles (1824), "Chapters on Churchyards. Ch. IV," *Blackwood's Magazine*, 16: 317–21.

Southey, Robert (1798), "The Idiot," *The Morning Post*, June 30.

Sparks, Tabitha (2002), "Surgical Injury and Narrative Cure in Wilkie Collins's *Poor Miss Finch* and *Heart and Science*," *Journal of Narrative Theory*, 32 (1): 1–31.

Spivak, Gayatri Chakravorty (1985), "Three Women's Texts and a Critique of Imperialism," *Critical Inquiry*, 12 (1): 243–61.

St Pierre, Joshua (2015a), "Disfluency vs. Dysfluency: What's in a Name?" *Did I Stutter?*, June 8. Available online: https://www.didistutter.org/blog/disfluency-vs-dysfluency-whats-in-a-name.

St Pierre, Joshua (2015b), "Distending Straight–Masculine Time: A Phenomenology of the Disabled Speaking Body," *Hypatia*, 30 (1): 49–65.
St Pierre, Joshua (2017), "Becoming Dysfluent: Fluency as Biopolitics and Hegemony," *Journal of Literary and Cultural Disability Studies*, 11 (3): 340–56.
Stainton, Tim (2018), "Sensationalism and the Construction of Intellectual Disability," in Patrick McDonagh, C. F. Goodey, Tim Stainton (eds.), *Intellectual Disability: A Conceptual History 1200–1900*, 104–27, Manchester: Manchester University Press.
Stallybrass, Peter, and Allon White (1986), *The Politics and Poetics of Transgression*, London: Methuen.
Stanback, Emily (2016), "Disability, Sympathy, and Encounter in Wordsworth's Lyrical Ballads (1798)," in Michael Bradshaw (ed.), *Disabling Romanticism*, 46–69, London: Palgrave Macmillan.
Starkowski, Kristen H. (2017), "Curious Prescriptions: Selfish Care in Victorian Fictions of Disability," *Journal of Literary & Cultural Disability Studies*, 11 (4): 461–76.
Stephens, Elizabeth (2005), "Twenty-First Century Freak Show: Recent Transformations in the Exhibition of Non-Normative Bodies," *Disability Studies Quarterly*, 25 (3). Available online: dsq-sds.org/article/view/580/757.
Stephens, Elizabeth (2006), "Cultural Fixions of the Freak Body: Coney Island and the Postmodern Sideshow," *Continuum: Journal of Media & Cultural Studies*, 20 (4): 485–98.
Stevenson, Robert Louis (1874), "Ordered South," *Macmillan's Magazine*, 30 (May): 68–73.
Stevenson, Robert Louis ([1881a] 1923), "Alpine Diversions," in *Sketches, Criticisms: Lay Morals and Other Essays. The Works of Robert Louis Stevenson*, vol. 24, 468–73, London: Heinemann.
Stevenson, Robert Louis ([1881b] 1923), "Davos in Winter," in *Sketches, Criticisms: Lay Morals and Other Essays. The Works of Robert Louis Stevenson*, vol. 24, 463–7, London: Heinemann.
Stevenson, Robert Louis ([1881c] 1923), "Health and Mountains" in *Sketches, Criticisms: Lay Morals and Other Essays. The Works of Robert Louis Stevenson*, vol. 24, 457–62, London: Heinemann.
Stevenson, Robert Louis ([1881d] 1923) "The Stimulation of the Alps," in *Sketches, Criticisms: Lay Morals and Other Essays, The Works of Robert Louis Stevenson*, vol. 24, 474–9, London: Heinemann.
Stevenson, Robert Louis ([1881e] 1988), "The Misgivings of Convalescence," in Jeremy Treeglown (ed.), *The Lantern Bearers and Other Essays*, 160–2, New York: Cooper Square Press.
Stevenson, Robert Louis (2005), "The Amateur Emigrant," in *Essays of Travel*, 1–44, Quiet Vision Publishing.
Stone, Deborah A. (1984), *The Disabled State*, Philadelphia: Temple University Press.
Strother, Z. S. (1999), "Display of the Body Hottentot," in Bernth Lindfors (ed.), *Africans on Stage: Studies in Ethnological Show Business*, 1–61, Bloomington: Indiana University Press.
Sussman, Herbert (1995), *Victorian Masculinities: Manhood and Masculine Poetics in Early Victorian Literature and Art*, Cambridge: Cambridge University Press.
Sussman, Herbert, and Gerhard Joseph (2004), "Prefiguring the Posthuman: Dickens and Prosthesis," *Victorian Literature and Culture*, 32 (2): 617–28.
Sweet, Matthew (2001), *Inventing the Victorians*, New York: St. Martin's Press.
Sweet, Ryan (2015), "Our Mutual Friend," in Karen Bourrier (ed.), *Nineteenth-Century Disability: Cultures & Contexts*, NINES. Available online: http://nineteenthcenturydisability.org/items/show/25.

Sweet, Ryan (2017), "'Get the Best Article on the Market': Prostheses for Women in Nineteenth-Century Literature and Commerce," in Claire L. Jones (ed.), *Rethinking Modern Prostheses in Anglo-American Commodity Cultures, 1820–1939*, 114–36, Manchester: Manchester University Press.

Szasz, Thomas (2009), *Antipsychiatry: Quackery Squared*, Syracuse: Syracuse University Press.

Tait, George (1878), *Autobiography of George Tait, a Deaf Mute*, Halifax: James Bowes and Sons.

Tankard, Alex (2018), *Tuberculosis and Disabled Identity in Nineteenth Century Literature*, London: Palgrave Macmillan.

Taylor, Charles Bell (1870), "Observations of an Improved Method of Cataract Extraction. With Illustrative Cases," *The Lancet*, 95 (April): 581–3.

Taylor, Charles Bell (1897), "Notes on a Case of Apparently Incurable Blindness in which Sight Was Restored," *The Lancet*, September, 653–4.

Tennyson, Lord Alfred (1885), *Tiresias and Other Poems*, London: MacMillan and Company.

Thomson, Mathew (1998), *The Problem of Mental Deficiency: Eugenics, Democracy, and Social Policy in Britain c. 1870–1959*, Oxford: Clarendon Press.

Tilley, Heather (2009), "Frances Browne, the 'Blind Poetess': Toward a Poetics of Blind Writing," *Journal of Literary and Cultural Disability Studies*, 3 (2): 147–61.

Tilley, Heather (2011), "The Sentimental Touch: Dickens's *Old Curiosity Shop* and the Feeling Reader," *Journal of Victorian Culture*, 16 (2): 226–41.

Tilley, Heather (2018), "Portraying Blindness: Nineteenth-Century Images of Tactile Reading," *Disability Studies Quarterly*, 38 (3). Available online: dsq-sds.org/article/view/6475/5096.

Tilley, Robert (1889), "What Can We Do to Induce the Government to Make the Census of 1890 Contribute Efficiently to a Clear Conception of the Causes of Blindness," *The Journal of the American Medical Association*, XIII (12): 409–11.

Tomes, Nancy (1994), *The Art of Asylum-Keeping: Thomas Story Kirkbride and the Origins of American Psychiatry*, Philadelphia: University of Pennsylvania Press.

Trask, Leonard (1858), *A Brief Historical Sketch of the Life and Sufferings of Leonard Trask, the Wonderful Invalid*, Portland: Tucker.

Tredgold, Alfred F. (1909), "The Feeble-Minded: A Social Danger," *Eugenics Review*, 1: 97–104.

Trent, James W. Jr. (1994), *Inventing the Feeble Mind: A History of Mental Retardation in the United States*, Berkeley: University of California Press.

Treves, Frederick (1885), "A Case of Congenital Deformity," *Transactions of the Pathological Society of London*, 36: 494–8.

Trollope, Anthony ([1857] 1996), *Barchester Towers*, ed. Michael Sadleir, New York: Oxford University Press.

Trombley, Stephen (1989), *Treves: The Extra-Ordinary Edwardian*, London: Routledge.

Tromp, Marlene (2008), "Introduction: Towards Situating the Victorian Freak," in Marlene Tromp (ed.), *Victorian Freaks: The Social Context of Freakery in Britain*, 1–18, Columbus: Ohio State University Press.

Tuke, Samuel (1813), *Description of the Retreat*, Philadelphia: Isaac Peirce.

Tupper, Martin Farquhar (1838), "The Stammerer's Complaint," *Geraldine, A Sequel to Coleridge's Christabel: with Other Poems*, 119–23, London: Rickerby.

Tupper, Martin Farquhar (1886), *My Life as an Author*, London: Sampson Low, Marston, Searle, & Rivington.

Twain, Mark, Josh Billings, Robert J. Burdette, Alex Sweet, and Eli Perkins (eds.) (1883), *Wit and Humor of the Age*, Chicago: Star Publishing.

Twining, Wiliam (1843), *Some Account of Cretinism: And the Institution for Its Cure, on the Abendberg, in Switzerland*, London: John W. Parker.
Tylor, Edward Burnett (1865), *Researches into the Early History of Mankind and the Development of Civilisation*, London: John Murray.
Van Cleve, John Vickrey, and Barry A. Crouch (1989), *A Place of Their Own: Creating the Deaf Community in America*, Washington, DC: Gallaudet University Press.
Van Lendeghem, Hyppolite (n.d.), *Charity Misapplied*, London: printed for the author.
Varul, Matthias Zick (2010), "Talcott Parsons, the Sick Role and Chronic Illness," *Body & Society*, 16 (2): 72–94.
Villey, Pierre (1909), "Intellectual Work Among the Blind," in *Annual Report Smithsonian Institution 1909*, 683–702, Washington, DC: Government Printing Office.
Virdi-Dhesi, Jaipreet (2013) "Curtis's Cephaloscope: Deafness and the Making of Surgical Authority in London, 1816–1845," *Bulletin of the History of Medicine*, 87 (3): 347–77.
Virdi-Dhesi, Jaipreet (2016), "Ear Spectacles for the Deaf: Making and Marketing Artificial Eardrums, 1850–1930," unpublished paper.
Vision of Britain Census Reports (n.d.). Available online: http://www.visionofbritain.org.uk/census/.
Vrettos, Athena (1995), *Somatic Fictions: Imagining Illness in Victorian Culture*, Stanford: Stanford University Press.
Wallace, Irving, and Amy Wallace (1978), *The Two*, New York: Simon and Schuster.
Wallace, Richard (1990), *The Agony of Lewis Carroll*, Melrose: Gemini Press.
Walsh, T. A. (1890), *Report on the Institution for Deaf-Mutes, Bombay, by Mr. T A. Walsh to the Director of Public Instruction, dated 17 Jan 1890. Report on the Institution for Deaf Mutes, Bombay Institution for Deaf-Mutes, Grant Road, 16 Jan 1890.* Education and training of the Blind, Deaf and Dumb and Idiots and Imbeciles in India IOR/L/PJ/6/295, File 202: January 14, 1891.
Wang, Fuson (2017), "The Historicist Turn of Romantic-Era Disability Studies, or *Frankenstein* in the Dark," *Literature Compass*, 14 (7): e12400.
"Wanted, High-Class Prodigies" (1899), *The Era*, March 4, 29.
Ward, A. B. (1888),"Hospital Life," *Scribner's Magazine*, 5 (January): 58–73.
Ward, Tony (2012), "Standing Mute," *Law and Literature*, 24 (1): 3–20.
Warne, Emoline Ann (1884), *A Brief Narrative of the Lives of Ephraim Angell and Emoline Ann Warne, The Blind Brother and Sister*, London: W. Speaight & Sons.
Warne, Vanessa (2009), "'To Invest a Cripple with Peculiar Interest': Artificial Legs and Upper-Class Amputees at Mid-Century," *Victorian Review*, ed. Jennifer Esmail and Christopher Keep, 35 (2): 83–100.
Warne, Vanessa (2011), "'So That the Sense of Touch May Supply the Want of Sight': Blind Reading in Nineteenth-Century Britain," in Colette Colligan and Margaret Linley (eds.), *Media, Technology, and Literature in the Nineteenth Century: Image, Sound, Touch*, 43–64, Farnham: Ashgate.
Warne, Vanessa (2015). "Blind Readers and Blind Writers," in Dino Franco Felluga, Pamela K. Gilbert, and Linda K. Hughes (eds.), *The Encyclopedia of Victorian Literature*, 140–7, Hoboken: Blackwell Publishing.
Warne, Vanessa (2017), "On Bridges and Streets: The Public Face of Raised-Print Readers," in Heather Tilley (ed.), *Touching the Book*, Online Exhibit. Available online: http://blogs.bbk.ac.uk/touchingthebook/2013/10/04/on-bridges-and-streets-the-public-face-of-raised-print-readers.
Washington, Harriet A. (2006), *Medical Apartheid: The Dark History of Medical Experimentation on Black Americans from Colonial Times to the Present*, New York: Anchor Books.

Watanna, Onoto, and Bertrand W. Babcock (1902), "Eyes That Saw Not. A Story," *Harper's Magazine*, June, 30–8.

Wear, Andrew (1985), "Interfaces: Perceptions of Health and Illness in Early Modern England," in Roy Porter (ed.), *Patients and Practitioners: Lay Perceptions of Medicine in Pre-industrial Society*, 55–100, New York: Cambridge University Press.

Webster Fox, L. (1889), "Blindness and the Blind," *Journal of the Franklin Institute*, 127 (6): 421–37.

White, Edmund (1856), *Blindness: A Discursive Poem in Five Cantos*, London: James Martin.

White, Edmund (1859), *The Genius of the Blind: A Poem in Five Cantos*, London: James Martin.

"The Wild Man of the Prairies" (1846), London Theatre Museum, Egyptian Hall 1845–1873 Folder.

Wilson, Dudley (1993), *Signs and Portents*, London: Routledge.

Wilson, James ([1821] 1838), *Biography of the Blind or the Lives of Such as Have Distinguished Themselves as Poets, Philosophers, Artists &c*, 4th edn., Birmingham: James Showell.

Wilson, John (1838), "Tupper's Geraldine," *Blackwood's Edinburgh Magazine*, 44: 835–52.

Wingate, Marcel E. (1997), *Stuttering: A Short History of a Curious Disorder*, South Hadley, MA: Bergin & Garvey.

Winter, Alison (1995), "Harriet Martineau and the Reform of the Invalid in Victorian England," *Historical Journal*, 38 (3): 597–616.

Winzer, Margaret (1997), "Deaf-Mutia: Responses to Alienation by the Deaf in the Mid-Nineteenth century," *American Annals of the Deaf*, 142 (5): 363–7.

Woolf, Jenny (2010), *The Mystery of Lewis Carroll: Discovering the Whimsical, Thoughtful, and Sometimes Lonely Man who Created Alice in Wonderland*, New York: St. Martin's.

Wordsworth, William (1807), "Resolution and Independence," in Marc R. Plamondon (ed.), *Representative Poetry Online*, Edition 6.0, University of Toronto Libraries. Available online: https://rpo.library.utoronto.ca/poems/resolution-and-independence.

Wordsworth, William ([1805] 1979), *The Prelude*, New York: W. W. Norton.

Wordsworth, William ([1798] 1991), *Lyrical Ballads*, R. L. Brett and A. R. Jones (eds.), London: Routledge.

"Work-School for the Blind, Euston-Road" (1858), *The Illustrated London News*, April 24, 428.

Wright, David (2001), *Mental Disability in Victorian England: The Earlswood Asylum, 1847–1901*, Oxford: Clarendon Press.

Wright, James (1843), *The Stutterer's Friend, or the Plea of Common Sense and Humanity, Against Two Publications*, 2nd edn., London: Sherwood, Gilbert, & Piper.

Wright, James (1851), "A Lecture on the Mental and Mechanical Obstacles Present in the Defects of Speech Termed Stammering and Stuttering," *The London Lancet*, 1: 20–6.

Wyllie, John (1894), *Disorders of Speech*, London: Oliver & Boyd.

Yearsley, James (1844), "On Stammering, Its Causes, Varieties, and Treatment," *The Lancet*, 1: 244–8.

Yonge, Charlotte ([1856] 1977), *The Daisy Chain*, New York: Garland.

Zenderland, Leila (2004), "The Parable of *The Kallikak Family*," in Steven Noll and James W. Trent, Jr. (eds.), *Mental Retardation in America: A Historical Reader*, 165–85, New York: New York University Press.

Zornado, J. (2001), *Inventing the Child: Culture, Ideology, and the Story of Childhood*, New York: Garland.

INDEX

A
Aarons, Debra 101
able-bodied, term (importance) 26–7
"acousmatic" voices 127
Act for Regulating Private Madhouses (1774) 155
agency, atypical body (relationship) 29–31
Age of Reason 150
Akach, Philemon 101
Albert, Edward 53–4
Alberti, Samuel J.M.M. 11
Alcott, Louisa May 20
alienists 149
Allen, E.E. 83
All the Year Round 92
"Amateur Emigrant, The" (Stevenson) 72
Amato, Joseph 49
American Annals for the Deaf 109
American Asylum 109
American Athletic Association of the Deaf 106
American Civil War
　"invalid corps," workforce entry 8
　visible amputees 51
"American Jack the Frog Man" 38
American Notes (Dickens) 84
American Professional Society for the Deaf 106
American School for the Deaf 100
American Sign Language (ASL) 96, 102
amputees 51–6
anesthesia, usage 6
Animal locomotion 50f
Animal Locomotion (Muybridge) 50
Anomalies and Curiosities of Medicine (Gould/Pyle) 36
anomalous body, medicalization 35–6
anti-psychiatry, roots 162–7
antiquity, monsters 26
antisepsis, development 44
antiseptic principles, usage 6
aphasia 114–15
"Apostle of the Deaf in America" 109
Armitage, Elizabeth 38

Armitage, Thomas Rhodes 83
Arnold, Martha 83
"artificial" sign system 102
Artman, William 93
Aspinall, W.B. 58
"assistive technology" 45–9
　term, usage 44–5
Association for Promoting the General Welfare of the Blind 85
Asylum for Idiots at Park House, Highgate 136
Asylum Journal 129–30
asylums 149
　age of asylum, moral treatment (impact) 150–6
　architecture, Kirkbride Plan 159–60
　operation, Christian philanthropy 136
Atkinson, Alexander 101
Attitudes Passionelles: Extase 152f
atypical bodies 23
　agency, relationship 29–31
　historicization 25–9
Auber, Daniel 98
"Australian Cannibal Boomerang Throwers" 30
autobiographies, publication 91–2
"Autumn Effect, An" (Stevenson) 72
average man 4–6
Aztecs 34f, 36
　Earthmen, pairing 33

B
Baartman, Saartje 11, 36
Babcock, Bertrand W. 89
Bailin, Miriam 57–8
Baker, Charles 84
Ballantyne, J.W. 36
Barchester Towers (Trollope) 43
Barker-Benfield, Ben 68
Barnaby in Newgate 138f
Barnaby Rudge (Dickens) 137
Barnum and Bailey, annual exhibition 40

INDEX

Barnum and Bailey Greatest Show on Earth 24f
Bartholomew Fair (London) 11
Bartola 34f
Barton, Clara 8
Bath chair 43
Bayle, Bernard 98
Baynton, Douglas 11, 12, 96, 105, 106
Beach, Fletcher 142
"Bear Lady" (Bounds) 38
Beauties and Achievements of the Blind (Artman/Hall) 93
"begging impostor," "deserving poor" (contrast) 52
Bell, Alexander Graham 5, 98–9, 118
Bell, Alexander Melville 99, 119, 125
"bell curve" 4–5
"benevolent paternalism," impact 10
Bentham, Jeremy 3
"Berenice" (Poe) 162
Berger, James 127
Bethlem Hospital (London) 154
"Better Regulation of Madhouses in England" 154
Bicêtre 135–6
Billy Budd (Melville) 122
Binham, H.B. 95
biopolitical training 127
Birmingham and Midland Counties Asylum for Idiots, formation 129–30
"Birthmark, The" (Hawthorne) 18
Blackie, Daniel 16
Blackwell's Island. *See* Insane Asylum
Bleak House (Dickens) 46–7
Blind Advocate, The 93
Blind, Deaf and Dumb Institution, opening 101
Blind Girl, The (Millais) 87f
blindness 79
　causes 80–1
　compensatory gifts, association 79–80
　cures 80–1
　examination 85–89
　literary perspectives 89–91
　portraits 90–1
　self-representations 91–3
　societal attitudes 84–5
　term, defining 80
　tragic, perception 84–5
Blindness (White) 92
Blindness and the Blind (Levy) 93

blind people
　employment opportunities/state-funded welfare provisions, inadequacy 85
　images, impact 88–9
　portraits, depictions 89
blind readers, underservicing 83
"Blind Restored to Sight, The" 92
blind street people, interviews (pairing) 86
blind students, new schools 82–4
"blind traveller" 92
Bly, Nellie 162, 165–7
　insanity, practice 167f
Boby, John 31, 32f
body (bodies)
　"anatomical" differences 33
　anomalous body, medicalization 35–6
　atypical bodies 23
　harm, susceptibility 13
　vocal mechanics 116
　vulnerability 13
body-state relationship 26
Bogdan, Robert 11, 28
Bolt, David 17, 84, 90
Bolton, George Buckley 36
Bonnot, Étienne (Abbé de Condillac) 131
"Borderland of Imbecility, The" 144
"Borough, The" (Crabbe) 134
Boster, Dea 12
Bounds, Alice 38
Bourrier, Karen 14
Braddon, Mary Elizabeth 57
Braidwood Academy for the Deaf and Dumb 100
Braidwood, John 100
Braidwood, Thomas 100
Braille, Louis 82–3
"brassfounder's ague" 6
Breuer, Josef 15, 121
Brewer, William D. 18, 45
Bridgman, Laura 8, 84, 140
　Dickens description 84–5
Brief Historical Sketch of the Life and Sufferings of Leonard Trask (Trask) 61
Brisbane Institution for the Instruction of the Blind, Deaf and Dumb 101
British and Foreign Blind Association (BFBA) 83, 93
British Deaf and Dumb Association (BDDA) 106
British Sign Language (BSL) 96, 102, 105
Broca's area, discovery 114–15
Brontë, Charlotte 90, 156–7

Brontë, Emily 162
Brooks, Peter 18
Brouillet, André 150
Browne, Frances 93
Browne, W.A.F. 141
Brown, Ford Madox 88
Browning, Elizabeth Barrett 90
Buchan, William 64
Bucknill, John Charles 129–30
Buck v. Bell 158
Bulwer-Lytton, Edward 65–9, 74, 126
Burke, Edmund 18
Burney, Fanny 46
"Bushmen" brains 142
Byrne, Charles 31
Byron, Lord 18
    clubfoot, treatment 56–7

C
Calhoun, John C. 159
Campbell, James Ure 92
Carbin, Clifton F. 110
caring 15–17
"caring labor" system 157
"caring power" 9
Carlin, John 101
Carpenter, Mary Wilson 90
Carroll, Lewis 122, 124
Carter, R.B. 80
Cartwright, Samuel A. 159
Catherick, Anne (Collins character) 20
Chadwick, Edwin 3–4, 64, 71
Chairugi, Vincenzio 153
Chamberlain, William M. 109
Chambers' Encyclopaedia 84
Chang and Eng ("Siamese Twins") 31, 36
Charcot, Jean-Martin 121, 150
Charity Organisation Society (COS), founding 146
Charlotte Brontë and Victorian Psychology (Shuttleworth) 157–8
Chase, Richard 17
Cheering Texts for Days of Trial 61
Chekhov, Anton 162, 166–7
chicken pox 96
children, educational provisions (growth). *See* disabled children
Children of Silence 97
"children's literature," classification 20
cholera
    epidemic 65
    outbreak 64

Christmas Carol, A (Dickens) 20, 25
Christmas entertainment, sign language presentation 108f
chronic (term, usage) 63–4
chronic, convalescence 75
chronic pain/illness 61
Church of England Zenana Missionary Society 102
Clarke, Edward 14
Clarke Institution for Deaf-Mutes 105–6
Clark, James 61
Clegg, Ralph 109
Clennam, Arthur (Dickens character) 144
Clerc, Laurent 109
Clever Woman of the Family, The (Yonge) 16
clubfoot, treatment 56–7
"Cockermouth and Keswick" (Stevenson) 72
Cogswell, Mason Fitch 100
cold-air climes, vigor 75
Coleridge, Samuel Taylor 18, 50, 133
    laudanum addiction 18
Collins, Wilkie 16, 90, 98, 122
colonial borders, management 13
Combe, George 158
commercial display, scientific space 40
Condillac, Abbé de. *See* Bonnot
Confessions and Observations of a Water-Patient (Bulwer-Lytton) 65–9, 74
"congenital deformity" 39–40
congenital mobility impairments 56–7
Congress of Milan 96, 104, 106
Connecticut Asylum for the Education and Instruction of Deaf and Dumb Persons 100
Connell, Raewyn 12
Conolly, John 135–6, 140
Constitution of Man, The (Combe) 158
Contagious Diseases Acts (Britain) 4
contagious diseases, significance 81
Coolidge, Susan 57
coprolalia 114–15
corporeal "deviance," forms 25
County Asylum Act (Wynn's Act) 155
"Cow Pock–or–the Wonderful Effects of the New Innoculation!" (Gillray) 13, 13f
Crabbe, George 134, 143–4
Crachami, Caroline 31
Craik, Dinah Mulock 55
Craik, George 55
Crania Americana (Morton) 158–9
"Cretins and Idiots" 139
Cricket on the Hearth, A (Dickens) 91

INDEX 203

Crime and Punishment (Dostoyevsky) 162
crime, insanity (relationship) 160–2
Criminal Lunatics Act (1800) 161
"crippled," mobility impairments 44–5
"Crippled Street Seller of Nutmeg Graters" 52, 4f
"cripple," term (reclamation) 44–5
Crosby, Frances Jane 83
cultural authority, process 40–1
cultural stigma, ugly laws (impact) 6
"custodial care," system (*Jane Eyre*) 157
Cuvier, George 35

D

Daisy Chain, The (Yonge) 57
"damned for their difference" 97
Daniel Deronda (Eliot) 56, 162
Darwin, Charles 5, 67, 141
David Copperfield (Dickens) 8, 20, 47, 143
Davidson, Luke 81
Davis, Lennard J. 5, 10, 122
"Davos in Winter" (Stevenson) 72, 75
Dawson, John 46
Day, Mary L. 91
deaf
    associations/colonies 106–11
    education 102–5
    journals, "minimum count" 108
    medicine/education 99–102
    privations/commiseration 95–6
    publications 106–11
    representation 97–9
    "saving" 99–102
    social attitudes/cultural representations 97–9
"deaf and dumb" 96
    instruction 98
Deaf and Dumb Boy, The (Fletcher) 100
Deaf and Dumb Herald and Public Intelligencer 109
Deaf and Dumb Institution 99
Deaf and Dumb Times 109
deaf communities 106–11
    establishment, international conferences 110–11
deaf-mute 95, 96
    marriage 99
    self-support 110
deaf mute, redemption 104
Deaf Mutes' Friend (Swett/Chamberlain) 109
Deaf-Mutia (Deaf-Gesturia) 110
deafness 95
    illnesses, impact 96
    portrayals 98
    "problem" 105
    "public threat" 98–9
    quantification 96
    representation/community 95
"Deaf State," proposal 109–10
"defectives"
    immigration 11
    institutions, growth 41
"deformed patients," treatment 56–7
"deformity" 12
"deformity aesthetics" 18
Degeneration (Nordau) 12
DeHaan, Francisca 9
"Dejection" (Coleridge) 18
deKroyft, S. Helen 91
De l'Éducation d'un Homme Sauvage ou des Premiers Développements Physiques et Moraux de Jeune Sauvage de l'Aveyron (Itard) 131
Deleuze, Gilles 124–5
Delsarte, Francois 116
Delsarte Recitation Book and Directory (Wilbor) 116
Demosthenes 117
Denton, William 124
dependency, embracing (Christian framework) 16
Derrida, Jacques 20
Descartes, René 131
Description of the Retreat (Tuke) 153
"deserving poor" 16
    "begging impostor," contrast 52
Deutsch, Albert 159
Dickens, Charles 8, 15, 25, 29, 46, 52, 91, 98, 122, 137, 143
    description 84–5
Dieffenbach, Johannes 120
disability. *See* intellectual disabilities; psychiatric disabilities
    aesthetics, cultural history 21
    concealment 54
    constructions, variation 2
    disability-based voting exclusions, passage 11
    fear, usage 12
    heroic overcoming, historical narrative 117
    Judeo-Christian frameworks/Victorian Christianity ideas 15, 16
    medical model 12
    public policy, ramifications 159

social nature 43–4
disability studies 125
    emancipatory claims 127
Disability Studies and the Environmental Humanities 21
disability, term (reference/usage) 2, 24–7
disabled children, educational provisions (growth) 8
disabled men, visible community (emergence) 41
disabled people, emotional capital 10
disabled, term (circulation) 26
Disabling Romanticism 17
disease, fear (usage) 12
Diseases and Deformities of the Foetus, The (Ballantyne) 36
"diseases of the chest," recuperative environment 58
distribution curve (Quetelet) 4–5
Dix, Dorothea 149, 156–7, 163
Dmitrich, Ivan 166
Doctor Marigold (Dickens) 98
"Doctors Buy Freaks" (article) 41
Dombey and Son (Dickens) 46
Dombey, Edith (Dickens character) 46
domestic angels 14–15
Domestic Medicine (Buchan) 64
Dominican Grimley Institute 101
Donaldson, Elizabeth J. 17, 90
Dorrit, Amy (Dickens character) 144
Dostoyevsky, Fyodor 162
Double-Bodied Hindoo Boy (Laloo) 37f, 38
"double consciousness" 160
Downing, James 80–1
Down, John Langdon 141, 142
Down syndrome 142, 173
Dracula (Stoker) 20
"drapetomania," concept 159
Drenth, Annemieke van 9
"Drink as an Evil" 92
"dual striptease," type (performance) 31
Du Bois, W.E.B. 149, 156, 160
Dugdale, Richard 146
Dumb Belle, The (Bayle) 98
Duncan, Martin 130
dysfluencies
    characterizations 122
    disability studies 125
    knowledge 116
    plural concept 114
    rhythms, study 116
"dysfluency studies" 114
dysfluent speech, medicalization 120

dysfluent temporalities 113
dysfluent vocal disruptions, corrective techniques 119

E
Eagle, Chris 114–15
"ear spectacles," usage 100
Earthmen/Aztecs, pairing 33
"ear trumpets," usage 100
East Cambridge Jail, women (teaching) 156
Eaton, Winnifred 89
Echoes from a Sick Room (Chadwick) 71
echolalia 114–15
Edinburgh Institution for the Deaf and Dumb, founding 100–1
education 8–10
    development (*See* special education)
    "special" education, influence 8–9
Education Act (1870) 146
Education and Employment of the Blind, The (Armitrage) 93
Edwards, R.A.R. 109
"Elastic Skinned Men" (Ballantyne) 36
Elementary Education Act (1893) 80
"Elephant Man" (Merrick) 12, 28, 38–40, 39f
Eliot, George 56, 64, 91, 162
Elliott, Richard 104
elocutionary principles 118
Elocution Simplified (Fobes) 118
"emasculated air," faults 76
Émile, Charles 135, 136
empire 11–13
encephalitis 96
"enfant sauvage" 130–1
Epée, Abbé de l' 100, 102, 110
epidemics, occurrence 6
Erskine, Thomas 161
Esmail, Jennifer 98–9
Esquirol, Jean-Étienne Dominique 120
ethnicity 11–12
ethnographic "specimens," exhibition 33
eugenic rhetoric 2
eugenics practices 121–2
"European negroes" 142
"euthanasia" 5
"exile schools" 93
ex-patient protest literature 163
Exposure on Board the Atlantic & Pacific Car of Emancipation for the Slaves of Old Columbia (Packard) 163–4
"Eyes that Saw not: A Story" (Watanna) 89–90

INDEX

F
Fawcett, Henry 88–9, 88f
Fawcett, Millicent Garrett 88–9, 88f
Feeble-Minded Child and Adult, The (COS) 146
"feeble-mindedness," conception 144
feeble-minded, "permanent support"/
    segregation 146–7
"feeble-minded" women, portrayal 147
female "cripple," damage/deviant sexuality
    (association) 45
Female Malady, The (Showalter) 157
Fenn, W.W. 82, 92
Ferguson, Christine 98
"Few Words About Blindness, A" (King) 80
Feydel, Gabriel 131
"Fiction Fair and Foul" (Ruskin) 21
Fiedler, Leslie 41
Finelli, Amanda 150
Fletcher, Phineas 55
Fletcher, W. 100
Flint, Kate 88
Flournoy, John 109–10
Fobes, Walter K. 118
foreign land, exposure (misattribution) 81
Fothergil, J. Milner 146
Foucault, Michel 3, 9, 113, 116, 149, 156
Fox, Edward 18
Fox, L. Webster 81
Foy, Betty 133–4
Foy, Johnny 134
Frankenstein (Shelley) 1, 18
    creature, stirrings 19f
Frawley, Maria 58
freak(s)
    active agents 29–30
    manager, relationship 30
    presentation 11
    "revolt of the freaks" 26 28, 33, 41
    shows, persistence 35–6
    term, usage 26
    "type," conflation 34–5
freak shows 11–12
    cultural work 23
French sign language alphabet 103f
Freud, Sigmund 15, 119, 121
Friedman, Susan 90
"fringe medicine" 67

G
"Galens" 125
Gale, Susan 133–4
Gallaudet, Thomas Hopkins 100
Galton, Sir Francis 5, 76
Garland-Thomson, Rosemarie 11, 12, 26, 84, 119
Gaskell, Samuel 135
Genius of the Blind, The (White) 92
"German method" 102–4
Gilbert, Elizabeth 16, 85
Gilbert, Pamela K. 3
Gilbert, Sandra 17
Gillray, James 13
Gitter, Elisabeth 81, 98
"Goblin Market" (Rossetti) 20
Goddard, Henry H. 146
Good Things for the Young of All Ages 124
Good Words (Rowe) 91, 92
Gordon, Mr. 97–8
Gordon riots 137
Gore, Clare Walker 17
Gould, George M. 36, 38
Grammar of Elocution (Millard) 118
Granite State Water-Cure 66f
Granny's Wonderful Chair (Browne) 93
Grant, Mary 89
Great Exhibition (1851) 79
Greenwell, Dora 137
"grinder's asthma" 6
Groom, Jane 110
Gubar, Susan 17
Guggenbühl, Johann Jakob 135
Guttmann, Oskar 116
Gymnastics of the Voice for Song and Speech (Guttmann) 116

H
Hadfield, James 149, 161
Haeckel, Ernst 142
Half Hours of Blind Man's Holiday (Fenn) 92
Halliday, Andrew 5
Hall, L.V. 93
Hammerschlag, Keren 50
"Harmless Johnny" (Southey) 136
Haslam, John 129
Haüy, Valentin 82
Hawthorne, Nathaniel 18
"Health and Mountains" (Stevenson) 72, 74
health essays (Stevenson) 72–6
health, masculinity (relationship) 14
heath, pursuit 2–4
Hendrickson, Henry 92
Henley, W.H. 70
Hertzl-Betz, Rachel 16
Heth, Joice 12

"High-Class Prodigies," advertisement 38
Hodgkiss, A.D. 65
Hoegaerts, Josephine 113, 124
Hoffman, Colden 102
Holman, James 92
Holmes, Martha Stoddard 14, 18, 20, 25, 52, 85, 86, 90, 98, 99
Holmes, Oliver Wendell 8, 158
Hood, Thomas 54–5
Horner, Jonah 61
"Hottentot apron" 35 36
"Hottentot Venus" 34–5
Household Words (Martineau) 82
Howe, Samuel Gridley 3, 5, 82, 139–41
Hubbard, Gardiner G. 105
Hubbard, Mabel 99
Huff, Joyce L. 8
Hugentobler, M. 104
Hughes, John S. 159–60
Hull, Susanna E. 106
"human abnormalities" 23
human diversity, visibility (repression) 5
human variation, "science" 35
human voice, natural expressions (interface) 118–19
"hunchback" 43
Hunt, James 118–22
    cure, system 126
Hurley, Kelly 20
hydropathic spas, usage 67
"Hypothetical Blind Man, The" 81

I
"idiocy"
    danger 144–7
    evolution/degeneration 141–3
    explanation, hypotheses/anxieties 139–41
    gender 143–4
    literary/artistic representations 133–5
    philosophy/education 130–3
    transformation 129, 135–7
    "trinitarian" treatment 140
"idiocy," degeneration 143–4
    threat 146
"idiot" asylums 9
"Idiot Asylums" 139 140
"Idiot Boy" (Wordsworth) 8, 17, 133
idiot girl 134–5
"Idiot-Girl" 135
"Idiots" (Dickens) 137
"Idiot, The" (Southey) 134
Illustrations of Political Economy (Martineau) 69–70

immobility, social construction 44
impairment
    female mind vulnerability 15
    medical nature 43–4
Incidents in the Life of a Blind Girl (Day) 91
indigenous Australians, abduction 30
individual autonomy, impact 11
indoor vehicles, self-propulsion 46
industrialization 6–8
"industrial training" 101
infants, clubfoot (treatment) 56–7
influenza 96
"In Hospital" (Henley) 70
Inland Voyage, An (Stevenson) 72
Insane Asylum (Blackwell's Island) 165
    inmates, sympathy 166
insanity
    crime, relationship 160–2
    curing 164f
    plea, history 161
    "wild beast" standard 161
Institution for Deaf Mutes in Bombay 102
Institution for Idiot Children, and Those of Weak Intellect 136
Institution for the Deaf and Dumb and the Blind in New South Wales, opening 101
Institution Impériale des Sourds-Muets 130, 131
Instructions to the Invalid on the Nature of the Water Cure (Horner) 61
intellectual disabilities 11
inter-deaf marriage 110–11
Interior of Bethlem Hospital Displayed, The (Metcalfe) 155
International Congress of the Deaf and Dumb 106
invalid chairs, comfort 49
"invalid corps," workforce entry 8
invalidism, mobility (relationship) 57–8
"invalid mind," idea (examination) 75
invalids, comfort 48f
Invalid's Friend, The 61
"Invalid's World, The" (Ward) 70
Ireland, William 142
Irish Dominican Order 101
"Irrationale of Speech, The" (Kingsley) 118
Island of Doctor Moreau, The (Wells) 20
Italian War of Independence, soldier (leg loss) 54
Itard, Jean 129–31

J
Jacksonville Insane Asylum 163–4
James, Henry 57

INDEX

Janecheck, Jennifer 46
Jane Eyre (Charlotte Brontë) 20, 90, 149, 156–8
Jarvis, Edward 159
Jay, Martin 84
Jewson, N.D. 63
John Halifax, Gentleman (Craik) 55
Johnson, Jeffrey K. 122
Jones, Annie 28
Jones, Christine Kenyon 18
Joshua, Essaka 18, 91
Jukes, The (Dugdale) 146

K
Kallikak Family, The (Goddard) 146
Keith, Lois 20
Keller, Helen 84
Kiba, Oguri 26
King, Alice 80, 84, 91
King George III, assassination attempt 161
King's College Lectures on Elocution (Plumptre) 118
Kingsley, Charles 14, 118, 141
Kingsley, Mary St. Leger. *See* Malet
Kipling, Rudyard 91
Kirkbride Plan 159–60
Kirkbride, Thomas Story 153–4, 160
Kitto, John 99, 100
Klages, Mary 91
Kleege, Georgina 81

L
Laloo (Double-Bodied Hindoo Boy) 37f
Lamb, Charles 122
"lame," mobility impairments 44–5
Lane, Richard 66
Langue des Signes Française (LSF) 96
Law and the Lady, The (Collins) 16
learning difficulties 129
Leigh, Romney (Browning character) 90
Leighton, Angela 90
Lending Library for the Blind in London 83
"Letter to the Deaf, A" 61
"levees" (exhibitions) 31
Levy, W.H. 84, 85, 93
l'homme moyen (ideal) 5
Life and Sufferings of Leonard Trask The 62f
Life at the Water Cure, Or, A Month at Malvern (Lane) 66
Life in the Sickroom (Martineau) 57, 61, 63, 69–72
    structure 71
Light That Failed, The (Kipling) 91

limbs, loss 51
Lincoln, Mary Todd 163
Lindfors, Bernth 35
lip-reading 102
l'Isère, Marc Colombat de 117
lisping 114–15
literary representations 17–20
Little Dorrit (Dickens) 144
"little elephant" 47
Little Mother 145f
"Little Paper Family" 108
"Little Papers" 108
Little Women (Alcott) 20
"Lives of Good Men, The" 108
"Living Skeletons" (Ballantyne) 36
Locke, John 131
Lombroso, Cesare 12
London Anthropological Society 122
London, Bartholomew Fair 11
London Labour and the London Poor (Mayhew) 17, 52, 85
Lost Senses, The (Kitto) 99
Lunacy Act 155
Lydgate, Tertius (Eliot character) 64–5
Lyrical Ballads (Wordsworth/Coleridge) 17, 134

M
madness 149
    institutionalization 162–7
    moral treatment (Pinel) 150
Madness and Civilization (Foucault) 149
Madwoman and the Blindman, The (Rodas/Donaldson/Bolt) 17, 90
"madwoman in the attic" 157–8
Magazine Intended Chiefly for the Deaf and Dumb 108
Maginn, Francis 106
Magnus, Hugo 80
Mairs, Nancy 44
Malet, Lucas (Mary St. Leger Kingsley) 124
manager, freak (relationship) 30
manic patients, lockup 155
mankind, races (differences) 33
manualism, oralism (contrast) 102–6
Marshall, John 143
Marsh, Jan 64
Martha's Vineyard, deaf people (concentration) 109
Martian, The 81
Martin, Charles 31
Martineau, Harriet 44, 57, 61, 69–72, 75, 82
    affliction 69

Masaniello (Auber) 98
masculinity
    concept 14
    health, relationship 14
Massachusetts Asylum for the Blind in Boston 140
"Materialism and its Lessons" (Maudsley) 142
Maudsley, Henry 142–3
Maurier, George du 81
Maximo 34f
Mayhew, Henry 16, 17, 52–3, 85
McCormac, Henry 117
McFarland, Andrew 163–4
McRuer, Robert 44
measles 96
    contagious disease 81
mediated voice, material history 118–19
Medical Act, The (1858) 64
Medical and Chirurgical Society 36
medical authority, rise 3–4
medical history, narratives 63
Medical Inquiries and Observations upon the Diseases of the Mind (Rush) 155
medicalization, impact 120
"medical opinion," embracing 74
medical perception, inventions (impact) 6
Mediterranean Passion, The (Pemble) 73
melodrama, Providential structure 18–19
Melville, Herman 18, 162
Memoir on the Formation of a Deaf Variety of a Human Race (Bell) 99
Memoir on the Radical Cure of Stuttering (Dieffenbach) 120
Memorial to the Legislature of Massachusetts (Dix) 156
meningitis 96
mental/bodily differences, disability (term) 2
"mental defective" term 147
Mental Deficiency Act (1913) 147
mental health
    crime, insanity (relationship) 160–2
    gender/race 156–60
    institutionalization 162–7
    issues 149
"mental retardation" 130
Merrick, Joseph. *See* "Elephant Man"
Metcalfe, Urbane 155
Michie, Helena 15
middle-class blind people, representations (impact) 88–9
middle-class tastes, development 3
middle-class women, confinement 15

Middlemarch (Eliot) 64, 162
Middlesex Lunatic Asylum 135
Miles, M. 9, 101, 102
Millais, Sir John Everett 87–8
Millard, John 118
Miller, Don 97
mind, harm (susceptibility) 13
"minstrel" shows 106
Mirzoeff, Nicholas 106, 108
miscarriage 45
"Misgivings of Convalescence, The" (Stevenson) 75
"Miss Kilmansegg and her Golden Leg" (Hood) 54
M'Naghten, Daniel 149, 161
    trial 161
mobility
    invalidism, relationship 57–8
    scientific/artistic study 50
    social construction 44
    themes (Romantic poetry) 49–50
mobility impairment 43, 50–1. *See also* congenital mobility impairments
    term, usage 44–5
Moby Dick (Melville) 18, 162
"Mongolism" 142
Monro, Henry 115
"monsters," observation 35
moral treatment, impact 150–6
Morel, Bénédict Auguste 12
Morison, Alexander 135
Morton, Samuel George 158–9
Moss, Henry 31
Mottez, Bernard 110
Moyes, Henry 93
Muette de Portici, La (Auber) 98
mumps 96
Murray, Joseph 110–11
muscular Christians 14–15
Muybridge, Eadweard 50
My Share of the World (Browne) 93

N
Narrative of Journey, The (Holman) 92
National Asylum for Idiots at Park House 137
National Congress of the Jewish Deaf 106
National Deaf Mute College 101, 106
National Fraternal Society of the Deaf 106
natural selection 5
"Negro Crossing-Sweeper, The" (Mayhew) 53
Neroni, Madeline (Trollope character) 43–6

"nervous system diseases" 67
New Poor Law 10, 68
Nielsen, Kim 11
Nightingale, Florence 8
non-normative bodies/minds
    accommodation 8
    pathologization 12
nonvisual culture, creation/consumption 79
Nordau, Max 12, 124
normalcy, negotiation 1
"normal," tyranny 41
Norman, Tom 28, 30, 39–40
"normate" body 119
Norris, James (William) 154
    chains, restraints 154f
    "poster child" 155
"novelties" 30

O
"Observations Intended to Favour a Supposition that the Black Color (As It Is Called) of the Negroes Is Derived from the Leprosy" (Rush) 158
"Observations on an Ethnic Classification of Idiots" (Down) 142
O'Connor, Erin 3, 6, 51
Old Curiosity Shop, The (Dickens) 29
Oliphant, Margaret 47, 144
Omer, Mr. (Dickens character) 47–8
"oneness of thought" 119–20
On Insanity (Chairugi) 153
On Overwork and Premature Mental Decay (Routh) 68
On Stammering, and Its Treatment (Monro) 115
"On the Brain of a Bushwoman; and on the Brains of two Idiots of European Descent" (Maudsley) 143
On the Causes of Idiocy (Howe) 140–1
"On the Education of the Imbecile" (Greenwell) 137
On the Origin of Species by Means of Natural Selection (Darwin) 141
"On the Perils of Pains of Invalidism" 70
ophthalmia neonatorum 81
Oppenheim, Janet 67
oralism. *See* "Pure Oralism"
manualism, contrast 102–6
"Ordered South" (Stevenson) 72, 73, 75
Orford, Ellen 134–5, 144
otherness, discourse 97–8
Our Mutual Friend (Dickens) 25

Out from the Darkness (Hendrickson) 92
"overwork" 68, 70–1
Owen, Richard 36

P
Packard, Elizabeth 162–5, 167
    advocacy 163
"Packard Laws," passage 164–5
Packing, The 67f
Panopticum (Castan) 38
paralysis, divine punishment 45
Parsons, Talcott 65
Pasteur, Louis 64
"pastoral power" (Foucault) 9
Pastrana, Julia 11, 38
Paterson, Kevin 116, 127
Pathological Society of London 39
"Patient's View, The" (Porter) 63
Peel, Robert 161
Peet, Harvey 102
Pemble, John 73
People First 130
"perfect monomania" 162
Perkins School 84
"phonophobia" 120–1
phrenology 3
"picture signs" 105
Pietikainen, Petteri 150, 155
Pinel a la Salpêtrière (Robert-Fleury) 150, 151f 152
Pinel, Philippe 129, 149, 150, 158
"Pity the Blind" 86
Pixérécourt, Guilbert de 133
Place in Thy Memory, A (deKroyft) 91
"Plagues of Egypt, The" (Denton) 124
Plumptre, Charles John 118
Poe, Edgar Allan 149, 161, 162
Poole, Grace (Charlotte Brontë character) 157
Poor Law Amendment Act (1834) 10
Poor Miss Finch (Collins) 90
Poovey, Mary 10, 15
"Porcupine Men" (Ballantyne) 36
Porter, Roy 63
"potter's rot" 6
"preservation of health" 10
"prisoner to the couch" 70
Problem of the Feeble-Minded 147
prosthetics 51–6
    availability 51–2
    hands, spoon attachments 7f
    impact 6
"pseudo 'lunatics'" 165

pseudosciences 3
pseudoscientific theories. *See* visual contact
psychiatric disabilities 11
psychiatry, power (criticism) 167
public health, attention (increase) 64–5
"Pure Oralism" 105
Pyle, Walter L. 36, 38

Q
quacks
    experts, complicity 116–17
    labeling 114
Quetelet, Adolphe 4
Qulip, Daniel (Dickens character) 29

R
race 11–13
"races of mankind," scientific study 25
Rammer, Rueben 124
Ray, Isaac 15
reading by touch 82–4
"recapitulation theory," proposal 142
"regulation human being" 28
Reiss, Benjamin 163
religion 15–17
Religious Tract Society 61
Report made to the Legislature of Massachusetts, on Idiocy (Howe) 139
Report on the Sanitary Conditions of the Labouring Population of Great Britain (Chadwick) 41, 64
repression, childhood wishes 119–20
reproductive heterosexuality, antithesis 17
Researches into the Early History of Mankind (Tyler) 105
"revolt of the freaks." *See* freak(s)
Reynolds, Mary 160
rhotacism 114–15
"rhythmus" 118
Rintoul, Suzanne 44
Robert-Fleury, Tony 150
Robinson, Mary Darby 118, 133
    impairment 45
Rochester (Charlotte Brontë character) 149, 157–8
    blindness, symbolic castration 17
    injuries 90
Rockey, Denyse 115
Rodas, Julia Miele 17, 90
Roose, Robson 68
Rosenhan experiment 165
Rosenthal, Moritz 117–18
Rose, Sarah F. 8

Routh, C.H.F. 68
Rowe, Richard 91
Royal Association in Aid of the Deaf and Dumb (RAADD) 106, 108
Royal College of Surgeons 36
    Hunterian Museum 31
Royal Commission on the Blind, the Deaf and Dumb 80
Royal Commission on the Care and Control of the Feeble-Minded 146–7
Royal Earlswood Asylum 139, 139f, 141–2
Royal Institution for the Deaf and Dumb 100
Royal Orthopaedic Hospital of London, establishment 56–7
rubella 96
Rush, Benjamin 155, 158
Ruskin, John 21, 67
Rymer, James Malcolm 126

S
Saint-Hilaire, Isidore Geoffroy 35, 36
Salem Chapel (Oliphant) 144
Sanative Influence of Climate, The (Clark) 61
San Remo as a Winter Residence (Aspinall) 58
Savage Man. *See* "Wild Boy of Aveyron"
"savages," exhibition 33
scarlet fever 96
    epidemic 65
Schaffer, Talia 17, 55
School for the Deaf 101
School for the Indigent Blind 80, 83
Schools of Medicine, testimonials 38
Schweik, Susan 5
science 33–41
scientific knowledge
    inadequacy, examples 64
    process 40–1
scientific medicine, rise 64
scientific museums
    aims/effects 11
    professionalization 38
scientific rationalism, culture 40–1
Scott, Walter 44, 56
script systems, coexistence 82–3
scrofula 141
sedan chairs, importation 45–6
Séguin, Édouard 130, 135, 140
self-determination, impact 11
self-government, impact 11
"selfish," analysis 16
self, notions (growth) 3
self-representations. *See* blindness

INDEX

Sense of Proportion, A 123f
sensory "deprivation" state 8
"Services of Sacred Songs" 91
Sex in Education (Clarke) 14
sexual "deviants" 2
"shattered nerves," victim 68
Shelley, Mary Wollstonecraft 1, 18
Showalter, Elaine 157
Shuttleworth, George 142
Shuttleworth, Sally 157–8
"Siamese Twins" (Chang/Eng) 31
Sicard, Abbé Roch-Amboise 130
"sick folk" 74
"sick role," adaptation 65
sideshow 33–41
sign language 95
    battle 102–6
    celebration 110–11
    denigration 105
    vicar, usage 107f
signs, deaf-and-dumb language 105
Simpson, Murray 140
smallpox
    contagious disease 81
    epidemic 65
Smallweed, Mr./Grandfather (Dickens character) 46–7
Smiles, Samuel 72
Smith, Charlotte 18
Smith, James McCune 159
Snow, John 64
"so-called afflicted" 80
social body 10–11
social capital, absence 41
societal attitudes. *See* blindness
Société des Observateurs de l'Homme 139
Société des Sourds-Muets de Bourgogne 106
Some Accounts of Cretinism and the Institution for its Cure on the Abendberg (Guggenbühl) 135
Souls of Black Folk, The (Du Bois) 149, 156, 160
Southey, Caroline Bowles 136
Southey, Robert 134
Spanish National Deaf School 101
Sparks, Tabitha 90
special education, development 9
"special" education, influence 8–9
"specialty artistes" 23
speech 113
    cultural expressions 122–6
    defects, cure 117

habits, problems 117
"healthy" speech, production 121
historical developments 115–22
social attitudes 115–22
speech-related disorders 114–15
symptoms, iteration 121
theoretical implications 126–8
Spencer, Herbert 10
"spermatic economy" 68
"spotted boys" 28
Squod, Phil (Dickens character) 46–7
Stallybrass, Peter 4
stammerer, melancholia 119–20
"Stammerer's Complaint, The" (Tupper) 125
stammering 114–15
Stammering and Stuttering (Hunt) 122
Starkowski, Kristin 16
Star of Atteghei, The (Browne) 93
state, "idiocy" (danger) 144–7
Stevenson, Robert Louis 18, 20, 69, 73f
    health essays 72–6
"Stimulation of the Alps, The" (Stevenson) 72, 75
Stoker, Bram 20
Stone, Deborah 10
Story of a Working Man's Blindness, The (Campbell) 92
Story of My Life, The (Bridgman) 84
Strange Case of Dr. Jekyll and Mr. Hyde, The (Stevenson) 18, 20
street-seller, immobility 53
stutterer, melancholia 119–20
Stutterer's Friend, The (Wright) 120
stuttering 114–15
    classification 117
    occurrence, "lack of harmony" (impact) 121
stutter, vocal rhythms (conforming) 113–14
Sussman, Herbert 68
Sutton, John Bland 36
Sweet, Matthew 40–1
Sweet, Ryan 51–2, 54
Swett, William B. 109
Swinnerton, John 89
"symbolic castration" 17
Szasz, Thomas 167

T
Tait, George 101
Take Up Thy Bed and Walk (Keith) 20
Tamplin, R.W. 56
Tankard, Alex 21

Tarra, Guilio 104
Taylor, Charles Bell 81, 84
Taylor, W.C. 14
technology 6–8
"Tell-Tale Heart, The" (Poe) 162
"temporal norms" 116
Ten Days in a Mad-House (Bly) 165
Tennyson, Alfred Lord 67, 83, 91
Thelwall, John 115–16, 118
"This Lime Tree-Bower my Prison" (Coleridge) 50
Thomson, Rosemarie Garland. *See* Garland-Thomson
"Thorn, The" (Wordsworth) 17
Thumb, Field Marshall Tom 31
Tiny Tim (Dickens character)
    cripple, archetype 25
    disability, persistence 16
    hope, scriptural allusion 15
    melodrama 18
"Tiresias" (Tennyson) 91
Tongue, The (Bell) 125
Touchett, Ralph (James character) 57, 58
Traité medico-philosophique sur l'alienation mentale (Pinel) 150
Traitement Moral, Hygiène et Éducation des Idiots (Séguin) 130
Trask, Leonard 61
Travels with a Donkey in the Cevennes (Stevenson) 72
Treatise on Insanity, A (Pinel) 150, 153
Treatise on the Cause and Cure of Hesitation and Speech (McCormac) 117
Tregold, A.F. 147
Treves, Frederick 12, 39–40
"trinitarian" treatment 140
Tripp, Charles B. 26, 27f
Trollope, Anthony 43
Trotwood, Betsy (Dickens character) 143
Tuke, Samuel 149, 153–4, 156
Tupper, Martin Farquhar 125
Twain, Mark 124
Twining, William 135
Tylor, Edward Burnet 105
typhus, epidemic 65

U

"ugly laws" 1 5
    impact 6
"ugly" voices, proliferation 127–8
Une leçon clinique à la Salpêtrière (Brouillet) 150, 151f

United States, census (1840) 159
"universal alphabetics" 119
Unspeakable, The (Rymer) 126
uterine disease, immunity 15

V

Van Evrie, John 12
Van Landeghem, Hippolite 93
Varden, Gabriel 137
venereal disease (disability) 45
Victoria Embankment Gardens (London) 89
Victorian Masculinities (Sussman) 68
Victor ou l'enfant de la forêt (Pixérécourt) 133
Villey, Pierre 89
"visible speech," pursuit 119
vision
    absence, divine compensation 85
    loss 81
    privileging, Western culture (theorization) 84
visual contact, dangers (pseudoscientific theories) 5
"vitality" 2
vocal "choreographies," tensions (critique) 115
vocal "gymnastics"/"exercises" 118
Vocal Physiology, Vocal Culture and Singing (Wheeler) 116
vocal production, exercises 113
Von Krafft-Ebing, Richard 12
Voyage Round the World, A (Holman) 92
Vrettos, Athena 13

W

Wages of Sin, The (Malet) 124
walking 49–51
    themes (Romantic poetry) 49–50
Walsh, T.A. 102
Ward, A.B. 70
"Ward No. 6" (Chekhov) 162, 166
Warne, Emoline Ann 91
Warner, Lucien 15
Warne, Vanessa 54–5
Washington, George 12
Watanna, Onoto (Winnifred Eaton) 89
water cure, benefits 66–7
Wear, Andrew 63
"Wear and Tear in London Life, The" (Roose) 68
Wegg, Silas (Dickens character) 25, 52
Wells, H.G. 20
Wernicke's area, discovery 114–15
What Katy Did (Coolidge) 57

What Will He Do With It? (Bulwer-Lytton) 126
wheelchair
　usage 55
　users, sight 47
"wheel-chair maker" (Dawson) 46
Wheeler, J. Harry 116
White, Allon 4
White, Charlotte 1364
White, Edmund 92
"white negro" 31
"White Race," characterization 12
"wholeness" 2
Wilbor, Elsie M. 116
"Wild Boy of Aveyron" (Savage Man) 8, 130–3, 132f
"Wild Man of the Prairies" 38
Wild Men of Borneo 23
Wilson, James 93
Winter, Alison 71
Wit and Humor of the Age (Twain) 124

Witnessing Insanity (Eigen) 161
Wittmann, Blanche 150
Woman in White, The (Collins) 163
Wonderful Spotted Indian, The 32f
woodwork class, boys (photo) 9f
Word of God, hearing (inability) 97
Wordsworth, William 11, 17, 49, 91, 133–4
Work-School for the Blind, Euston Road 85, 86f
Wright, James 114, 120
Wuthering Heights (Emily Brontë) 162
Wyllie, John 115–16
Wynn's Act. *See* County Asylum Act

Y
Yefimitch, Andrey 166
Yonge, Charlotte Mary 16, 17, 57
York Retreat 152, 154, 156

Z
Zulus, exhibition 30, 33